REPRODUCTIVE STATES

REPRODUCTIVE STATES

GLOBAL PERSPECTIVES ON THE INVENTION AND IMPLEMENTATION OF POPULATION POLICY

EDITED BY
RICKIE SOLINGER

AND

MIE NAKACHI

OXFORD
UNIVERSITY PRESS

OXFORD
UNIVERSITY PRESS

Oxford University Press is a department of the University of Oxford. It furthers the University's objective of excellence in research, scholarship, and education by publishing worldwide.

Oxford New York
Auckland Cape Town Dar es Salaam Hong Kong Karachi
Kuala Lumpur Madrid Melbourne Mexico City Nairobi
New Delhi Shanghai Taipei Toronto

With offices in
Argentina Austria Brazil Chile Czech Republic France Greece
Guatemala Hungary Italy Japan Poland Portugal Singapore
South Korea Switzerland Thailand Turkey Ukraine Vietnam

Published in the United States of America by
Oxford University Press
198 Madison Avenue, New York, NY 10016

Library of Congress Cataloging-in-Publication Data
Reproductive states : global perspectives on the invention and implementation of population policy / edited by Rickie Solinger and Mie Nakachi.
p. ; cm.
Includes bibliographical references and index.
ISBN 978-0-19-931108-8 (paperback : alk. paper) — ISBN 978-0-19-931107-1 (cloth : alk. paper) —
ISBN 978-0-19-939544-6 — ISBN 978-0-19-024562-7
I. Solinger, Rickie, 1947– , editor. II. Nakachi, Mie, editor.
[DNLM: 1. Population Control. 2. Internationality. 3. Public Policy.
4. Reproductive Health Services. HQ 766]
HB883.5
363.9—dc23
2015015602

1 3 5 7 9 8 6 4 2
Printed in the United States of America
on acid-free paper

Contents

List of Contributors

SANJAM AHLUWALIA is associate professor, Department of History and Women's and Gender Studies Program, Northern Arizona University. Her book, *Reproductive Restraints: Birth Control in Colonial India, 1887–1947*, was copublished by Illinois University Press and Permanent Black in 2008. She is currently working on a book manuscript on the history of sexology in the twentieth century, while completing research on the history and politics of contraceptive technologies in postcolonial India.

MARGARETH ARILHA is a researcher in reproductive health and population at the Population Studies Center, the University of Campinas in Brazil. Since 1980 Arilha has worked in the fields of gender, reproductive health, and public policy; she has also served as regional advisor at the United Nations. She is a member of the Board of Citizenship and Reproduction Committee, which works in the Brazilian Center for Analysis and Planning.

SONIA CORRÊA is founder of SOS-Corpo-Instituto Feminista para a Democracia (Brazil) and was the coordinator for sexual and reproductive health rights of Development Alternatives with Women for a New Era (DAWN), a southern hemisphere feminist network (1992–2009). She is the coauthor of *Sexuality, Health and Human Rights*.

MAÍSA FALEIROS DA CUNHA is demographer and researcher at the Population Studies Center (NEPO), State University of Campinas in Brazil. Her work focuses on historical demography, the slave family, regional history, quantitative methods, and serial sources.

OMNIA EL SHAKRY teaches at the University of California, Davis, and is the author of *The Great Social Laboratory: Subjects of Knowledge in Colonial and Postcolonial Egypt*. El Shakry's research interests include gender and sexuality in the modern Middle East, and she is a founding member of the Middle East/South Asia Studies Program at UC Davis.

FIROOZEH KASHANI-SABET teaches at the University of Pennsylvania. She has written a number of books, including *Conceiving Citizens: Women and the Politics of Motherhood in Iran*, which received the 2012 book award from the *Journal of Middle East Women's Studies* for outstanding scholarship in the field of Middle East gender studies.

MIE NAKACHI is research associate of the Slavic-Eurasian Research Center at Hokkaido University in Japan. Her publications focus on twentieth-century women's reproduction in the context of demography, state policies, gender relations, wars, and medicine. She is preparing a monograph, "Replacing the Dead: The Politics of Reproduction and Demography in Soviet Russia."

MIHO OGINO, a leading historian of women and reproductive politics in Japan, is the author of *The Road to "Family Planning": Politics Sorrouding the Reproduction of Modern Japan*. She recently retired from the Faculty of the Graduate School of Global Studies, Doshisha University, Kyoto.

DAKSHA PARMAR is a doctoral student at the Centre of Social Medicine and Community Health, School of Social Sciences, Jawaharlal Nehru University. She is working on a doctoral thesis, "Controlling Births and Limiting Population in Maharashtra: 1920–1980."

ELISHA P. RENNE is professor of Anthropology and Afroamerican and African Studies at the University of Michigan. Renne's research in Nigeria focuses on issues relating to medical anthropology, gender relations, religion, and textiles. She is the author and editor of many books including *Population and Progress in a Yoruba Town*.

RICKIE SOLINGER is an independent scholar and curator. She is the author and editor of ten books about reproductive politics and satellite subjects, including *Reproductive Politics: What Everyone Needs to Know*.

ANNETTE F. TIMM is the author of *The Politics of Fertility in Twentieth-Century Berlin* and teaches at the University of Calgary.

TYRENE WHITE is the author of *China's Longest Campaign: Birth Planning in the People's Republic, 1949–2005*, the editor of several volumes, and has written many articles on rural politics and population policy in China. She teaches Politics at Swarthmore College.

Introduction

RICKIE SOLINGER AND MIE NAKACHI

> A new Manhattan project is needed—not to build another atomic bomb which might destroy the world, but a grand and noble project for knowledge and demographic understanding around the world—a project to defuse the population bomb—so that mankind does not multiply itself into oblivion.
>
> William Draper, 1966[1]

> A precise social analysis requires that we pay attention to the specific conditions of history, culture, and locale that give any act of fertility control its meaning.
>
> Rosalind Petchesky, 1990[2]

The case studies in *Reproductive States* explore when and how many of the world's most populous countries invented and implemented population policies in the twentieth century. The authors of these studies, scholars specializing in the reproductive politics of Brazil, China, Egypt, Germany, India, Iran, Japan, Nigeria, the USSR/Russia, and the United States, consider those policies while at the same time offering reflections on the demographic outcomes of those policies and their legacies. Population policy, whether devised to increase or limit growth, most often centers on national efforts to affect rates of reproduction for the total population or for certain groups. It can also include efforts to encourage or discourage immigration, broadly or narrowly; population movement within the state; incarceration, and other matters having to do with the size, character, and distribution of the population.

The essays in this volume focus on the first element: the official and organized policies that governments have pursued to control reproduction and population since the mid-twentieth century. The core of these policies involves forming bureaucracies and supporting new reproductive technologies to control how many people, and which people, are born within their borders.

Taken together, the essays show that the alarmist post-World War II concept, the "population bomb," cut in several directions: it expressed the potential for global cataclysm at the same time that it suggested the potential for coordinated global activism in several areas including family planning, women's rights, and environmental issues.[3] Demographers and policy experts associated the population crisis with the atomic bomb, representing it as an ultimate threat to human existence and an early raison d'être for the United Nations. State population policies in China, Egypt, Germany, Japan, and other countries drew ideas, strategies, and other resources from each other.

Population politics took center stage, structured in large part by the Cold War, as capitalism and communism offered profoundly different visions and solutions for dealing with the world's poor. Over the course of several decades, the United States, often invoking the possibility of apocalyptic global threats, provided an apparatus for addressing the "population bomb." The threat of a demographic crisis gave rise to an effort to circulate goals, experts, money, project designs, products, and other resources around much of the world. Behind the Iron Curtain, the Soviet Union rejected the concept of the "population bomb," arguing that overpopulation could exist only under capitalism, where unequal distribution of wealth created poverty. Moscow-based social scientists insisted that socialism was poverty's only cure.

Both camps attempted to control population but in very different ways. In India, the United States, and some European countries, policymakers typically targeted the poor and racial minorities. The Soviet Union, in contrast, never fully adopted an antinatalist policy targeting ethnic minorities or the poor; and China, with its brutal one-child policy, targeted all ranks of Han society, including even high-ranking Communist Party cadres. But the policy was not applied to minority peoples.[4]

To a greater extent than policymakers in the United States, however, leaders in socialist countries used their power for oversight of female reproductive capacity. Every aspect of life in these countries was a part of state planning, including housing, medical care, and commodity distribution. All these matters were closely connected with the workplace and the party, and women could not escape from this oversight, particularly in urban areas. Indeed, Soviet citizens were accorded few privacy rights (and few rights in general), a situation that facilitated the state's determination to monitor reproduction. In Romania, for example, regular gynecological checkups were used to detect and preserve pregnancies. In China, the same method was used to detect and terminate pregnancies.[5]

Aside from providing an opportunity to compare Cold War population policies, this volume invites comparative readings along numerous axes and suggests that states with profound cultural, historical, and political differences produced population policies with strikingly common elements. Each state, for instance, made a commitment to what is today referred to as "biopower," the capacity of a government to regulate life, health, and the body as it sees fit. Historian Annette Timm, in her essay on Germany in this volume, describes the familiar duality of the most extreme example: the "Nazi policies toward reproduction and sexuality intertwined elements of coercion and incentive in the effort to instrumentalize private spheres of life in the interests of larger ideological goals." In addition, in the postcolonial era and even in the shadow of the Nazi regime, governments in each of the ten countries here discussed relied on persistent philosophies of demographic difference and domination when they made state policy. For example, each country crafted policies and practices that valued and rewarded the reproductive contributions of certain women or certain *populations* (as opposed to *individuals*) while degrading and constraining reproduction among "inferior" populations. National programs sorted and treated fertile women (and sometimes men) on grounds of class, caste, health, and racial, religious, and ethnic characteristics, in effect reflecting and reproducing nationalistic ideas about the valid and favored characteristics of citizenship. Policymakers crafted strategies for achieving outcomes to these questions: Who should be born? Who deserves membership in our culture and the polity? Which women must be discouraged, in which ways, from reproducing? Which ones should be rewarded for having numerous babies?

In each of these ten countries, the degraded status of women facilitated state interventions rendering the ordinary female body a key political resource: available, malleable, and potent material to deploy in the biopolitical project of shaping the state's size, character, and place in the world. Many states—the United States, Brazil, and France, for example—had been involved in versions of this project long before the twentieth century. The French fear of depopulation in the nineteenth century in the face of German fertility is well documented.[6] But with new technological tools and new social welfare bureaucracies, all states—both those attempting to slow population growth and those attempting to stimulate growth—believed that significant state management of sexuality and fertility was an effective way to solve myriad social, economic, political, environmental, strategic, and other problems facing the nation.

The essayists in this volume show how the population policies of some states, such as the United States, were consistent, even over centuries, while other states—Egypt, for example—radically changed the rationale for their policies. These authors also illustrate the ways that policy language was key to inventing and sustaining relevant policy arenas in each of the countries, justifying policies and naturalizing demographic goals. Language facilitated the eclipse of structural causes of national ills and obviated alternative, less coercive pathways to personal and national well-being. Read together, the essays give us an opportunity to assess whether or not state policies met stated goals. Historian Matthew Connelly judges most national population policies as failures. They failed, he argues, because officials aimed to control the intimate lives of those who did not want to be controlled. The essays variously consider the kinds of resistance that state policies stimulated.[7]

The Global Context

For centuries, nations have been concerned about the size and the composition of their populations. Are there enough adults to meet military and labor needs and to satisfy territorial aspirations? Is there enough food to feed the current population and the next generation? How are birth rates, migration, and immigration shaping national and regional population growth and impacting resources? These and other questions have preoccupied leaders, particularly those who generally hoped for high birth rates, and to this end, many had, by the nineteenth century, criminalized women's access to contraception and abortion. Connelly points out, however, that "the idea of controlling the population of the *world* . . . is a modern phenomenon," a project that emerged when improvements in public health, infant survival rates, and generally declining death rates vastly expanded national growth rates. Indeed, rapid global population growth for more than two hundred years has been chiefly an artifact of increased rates of survival, not out-of-control childbearing.

Population-minded politicians and others in the West often collapsed these developments into one trend, widely defined by the mid-twentieth century as a population "crisis," or even a looming catastrophe: too many people relative to the resources necessary to sustain these numbers. This prediction was tightly tied to the vision of Thomas Robert Malthus, the English political economist and demographer who warned of certain disaster from excessive reproduction, especially among the poor, in the context of diminishing resources. More recent predictions of demographic disaster on similar grounds have been called neo-Malthusian.[8]

The Cold War–era divergence mentioned above regarding population policy has roots in the nineteenth century, when Karl Marx and Friedrich Engels criticized, as a capitalist creation, the Malthusian concept of "overpopulation." Following this critique, socialist states were thereafter firmly anti-Malthusian and anti-neo-Malthusian. Socialist leaders described their system as one in which workers could happily reproduce and raise as many children as they wanted. Despite this pronatalist orientation, the socialist system did not advocate a specific doctrine on abortion and contraception. Policymakers did not approve of policies encouraging or promoting abortion and contraception for antinatalist purposes, although they considered both practices acceptable for the purpose of reducing the burdens of working women and mothers. In practice, policies regarding abortion and contraception were subject to dramatic changes across the USSR, depending on official demographic evaluations at any given time.

Outside the socialist camp, an antinatalist population control movement emerged and flourished between the 1930s and the 1970s, the period that marked the collapse of European empires and the rise of former colonies as independent nations. Some have referred to this international movement as "empire lite." Americans and Europeans in this period sought to target and control *populations* rather than geographical territories.[9] From the 1960s forward, many family-planning activists and policymakers believed that rampant population growth was at the root of most global ills, especially, as an article published in 1958 in *Foreign Affairs* had it, as the "chief cause of the gap in wealth and power between rich and poor nations," and that contraception and sterilization offered solutions to social, economic, and political problems around the world.[10]

Ironically, in the 1960s and 1970s, the era of global liberation and civil rights movements, nongovernmental actors associated with the international population control movement laid out and then implemented (alongside state and United Nations officials) strategies for eclipsing reproductive self-determination. Many of those targeted were former subjects of imperial powers, now "independent." Frequently, activists in this era pointed to India, teetering between achieving democracy and collapsing from overpopulation, as an emblem and a laboratory for testing both brown freedom and US-designed and US-funded methods of population control.[11] (China, the other most populous country, reflected the socialist vision of independence and development. Famously, Mao Zedong insisted, "China's large population is a great asset.")[12]

The first efforts to develop an international movement to stem population growth were led by fervent family-planning activists such as Margaret Sanger and by foundations, family-planning and eugenics organizations, and other nongovernmental entities. By the time that Western governments embarked on international population control efforts in the 1960s, they were committed to biopolitically targeted foreign aid. Incorporating population goals into domestic policy, many countries found ways, as Annette Timm points out, to promote pronatalist and antinatalist polices simultaneously, for example, by proscribing abortion for desirable reproducers while pressing antinatalist policies on those defined as racially and eugenically inferior. These efforts fundamentally expressed a postwar certainty that *planning* for a nation's demographic future was appropriate and would pay off.

As mentioned, much of this work was preceded by and then guided by UN technical assistance in the 1940s and 1950s. Among other projects, the UN promoted national census-taking programs, and between the early 1960s and the early 1970s most of the countries represented in this volume had developed professionalized bureaucracies for collecting data and for crafting, implementing, and assessing population policies.[13] In 1965, for example, Egypt funded its Supreme Council for Family Planning to establish a "complete strategy" for a national program and empowered the council to take all necessary steps to do so.[14] Iran both expanded and centralized its programs at this time; and the US Congress agreed to fund contraception as a feature of the War on Poverty.[15]

While socialist regimes were ideologically opposed to family planning, their leaders still considered that, as an element of a planned economy, demographic development was of vital importance. After World War II, newly established socialist regimes copied the Soviet-style planning apparatus, linking demographic data with economic, political, social, and cultural development. During the same period, Communist China developed institutions to collect and analyze nationwide demographic data for the first time in its history. When this process produced new knowledge about the actual size of the country's population, Chinese leaders reconsidered the socialist vision of population growth and development. As the relationship between the Soviet Union and China deteriorated in the Khrushchev years, Mao felt free to develop a particularly Chinese path to addressing population issues. This led to the creation of a state Family Planning Commission in the mid-1960s.

Technological advances in the second half of the twentieth century also gave states new tools and strategies to address and implement reproductive policies. The invention of the computer enabled states to calculate and analyze the population problem; new public relations and advertising schemes that fed multiple, far-reaching media outlets accessible to increasingly literate populations enabled better communication of demographic goals; and new reproductive technologies provided concrete tools for curbing conception.[16] As David Horn, Matthew Connelly, and others have argued, a modern nation's leadership regarded citizens as possessing "social bodies" available for use in political projects such as increasing or decreasing the population for a number of purposes, most important, to boost economic development.[17]

Another irony permeating state responses to the "population bomb" in the postwar decades is the fact that US and UN experts and others invoked the looming demographic apocalypse most powerfully at a moment when, in many "overpopulated" countries, fertility was already declining—without major state-supported family-planning programs. In Brazil, for example, evidence suggests a growing preference at this time for smaller families. But demographers often focused on raw numbers, which were still rising, even though rates were falling.

Western demographers, politicians, and political theorists disseminated their messages around the world, using "exploding world" language and other metaphors of disaster. The "population bomb" functioned as a horrifying "photo negative" of the Cold War: global extinction, two ways.[18] They revived other Malthusian tropes, pressing for programs that would encourage reproductive "quality," not "quantity. While population growth had generally been considered "natural" and beneficial in many countries before the middle of the twentieth century, now states viewed it as undesirable, if not downright criminal—at least for specific populations. In Egypt, experts identified "irresponsible fecundity," and in Iran, the "natural" libidinal tendencies of the peasants. In the United States, the charge was the same. Senator Ernest Gruening, presiding over congressional hearings on the population crisis, and referring to the African American urban poor who reproduced too often and with poor results, announced a national need to "teach these people . . . something about family responsibility."[19]

Repeatedly, authorities in the United States invoked "crime" to describe the act of having too many babies. In marking reproduction among certain populations as aberrant, many government antifertility policies and programs were defined as *disaster measures* against a disease attacking the body politic, a metaphor that justified "treating" whole infected populations by sterilization, as in India and China.[20]

During the Cold War, Western politicians and demographers inevitably justified domestic and global policy efforts using idioms of conflict and war. Chikako Takeshita shows how the intrauterine device (IUD) was introduced as the most effective "'ammunition' for the war on population." A major architect of global programs exhorted his colleagues to amass enough bullets in this war "so that the troops can defeat the enemy," adding that there was no substitute for victory. Mass sterilization and IUD insertions in many locales clearly amounted to violence against "acceptors," that is, women who underwent the operation or had the device inserted in their bodies. Global experts and national, regional, and local authorities described their campaigns as a "war on [excessive] population and hunger," requiring funding on a "war-footing."[21] Many warned that in the absence of sufficient funding, nations would face "a national security risk" equal to the risk posed by nuclear proliferation. An adequate response required rich countries to come to terms with the potential destructiveness of "relatively poor" people around the world, those who were apt to translate their "envy" into "revolt," chiefly by making alliances with the Soviet Union.[22]

In addition to the rhetoric of conflict, states also framed reproductive policies in terms of economic advancement. Laura Briggs has shown how early population control experts defined their work in Puerto Rico in the decades before the middle of the twentieth century as key to transforming a poor country into a "modern nation."[23] In this and other cases—whether countries were attempting to craft policy for boosting or reducing population growth—the goal was most often expressed as modernization through development. Here development depended on achieving optimal population levels. Timm points out that in both East and West Germany, recovery and prosperity were tied to population management; one used communist principles to justify its programs, the other, capitalist. Miho Ogino shows how in Japan, the private sector followed the government's lead. Corporations, eager for productive workers, promoted healthy wives and happy homes as key conditions for enriching corporate coffers, and were as concerned about population control strategies as the Japanese government. This so-called New Life Style Movement had the participation of twenty-four public and private companies, including Toyota, at first; by 1964, 115 companies participated in intracorporate population planning as an economic development strategy.[24]

Famously, at the twenty-fifth anniversary celebration for the United Nations in San Francisco in 1965, President Johnson argued that the most effective way to respond to excessive global population growth was economistic. Every five dollars spent on contraceptives preserved one hundred dollars for investment. In other words, he counseled, taxpayers in rich countries could take comfort in the fact that underwriting birth control for women in Puerto Rico, India, and other demographically challenged poor countries around the world would ultimately pay dividends at home.[25]

The relationship between contraception and development was compelling enough that even so august a figure as Dr. Alan Guttmacher, a president of Planned Parenthood and a lifelong advocate of family planning, urged colleagues not to worry about the medical and other circumstances of "individual women" when they developed IUD programs abroad. Rather, he advised, "We dare not lose sight of our goals—to apply this method to large populations." Indeed, tying control of female sexuality and fertility to economic concerns posed numerous threats to the safety, health, and individual rights of women around the word. A letter from Guttmacher to the chairman of the contraceptive manufacturing company G. D. Searle praising the IUD illustrates this point: "No contraceptive could be cheaper, and also, once the damn thing is in, the patient cannot change her mind," Guttmacher wrote.[26]

States justified their programs to regulate—reward and punish—the reproductive behavior of their citizens by means of a combination of neo-Malthusian, eugenic, and Cold War threats. And while states gave full focus to population control as the key to national health, they regularly ignored other "problematic" domains. As political economist Betsy Hartmann put it, "Population control . . . substituted for social justice, and much-needed reforms—such as land distribution, employment creation, the provision of mass education and health care, and the emancipation of women [which were] conveniently ignored."[27] Further, population control was consistent with—and fortified—what Brazilian scholar and activist Sonia Corrêa and her coauthors call other popular "modern biopolitical concepts": urban cleansing, family hygiene, the reinforcement of female domesticity, and the elimination of sexual deviance. Population control was also justifiable as a logical extension of a number of older, traditional state policies governing sexual and reproducing bodies such as laws against miscegenation, marriage laws, and laws criminalizing abortion.[28]

Again, adoption of population policies in each country was facilitated by the degraded status of females. The second-class status of women naturalized the "disindividuation of women" inherent in population control efforts, especially those that depended on mass targeting.[29] In 1976 alone, India, supported by the United States and the United Nations, sterilized eight million people, and in 1983, China oversaw twenty million sterilizations of violators of the one-child policy. In the early 1980s the Indonesian government rounded up women for sterilization; Mexico and Vietnam also conducted coercive mass sterilizations, and hospitals and government policies in the United States pursued racially targeted sterilization and contraceptive programs.[30] In these countries and elsewhere, politicians, physicians, and demographers, driven, as discussed, by "war mentality," designed fertility-termination or fertility-enhancement programs that defined women (and sometimes men) as exploitable resources. Many programs also dehumanized women in another sense, drafting them—an army of empty (or full) wombs—to fight the state's demographic battles.[31] These attitudes together provided what Takeshita calls "a lubricant for coercive and semi-coercive procedures administered on women of the global South."[32] Taken together, geopolitical goals, the metaphors that justified their pursuit, the low status of women, and the potential violence embedded in new reproductive technologies all shaped the lives of hundreds of millions of women around the world.

The United Nations, Feminism, and "Global Governance"

A number of essays in this volume place state efforts to increase or decrease national growth rates within the context of emergent feminisms in the postwar decades. Indeed, as feminism became an activist force in various countries and in the population-policy arena, women's groups began to claim that *their* interests came first, before the most dearly held population-control claims of governments: before eugenics, resource scarcity, and even, feminists argued, modernization and economic development.

Responding to this emergent global phenomenon, the UN began its joint focus on the condition of women and population policy in 1949, creating the Commission on the Status of Women. The organization itself has defined the 1950s and 1960s as a period of "preliminary consensus building" on the subjects of population and gender, although others have noted that through the mid-1950s, the UN and its agencies avoided visible leadership in population control matters, believing the arena was too controversial.[33] In 1967 the General Assembly adopted the Declaration on the Elimination of Discrimination against Women, and the following year (the same year Pope Paul VI reaffirmed the Catholic Church's opposition to all artificial contraception), it adopted the Proclamation of Teheran, the first international instrument to associate parents with a right to "space" their children—that is, the right to use contraceptives. Not until almost twenty years later, at the Third World Conference on Women in Nairobi in 1985, did the UN issue a statement recognizing women's "basic right to control their own fertility" as the basis for women's status as full persons.

The UN has sponsored declarations and international meetings—in Mexico City, Rio, Cairo, Beijing, Vienna, and elsewhere—that became venues for feminists to condemn both natalist and antinatalist programs around the world, and to define the relationship between reproductive health and full citizenship for women. The impacts of these meetings have been debated vigorously. Indubitably, they brought feminists from around the globe together; led to the creation of influential organizations, such as Development Alternatives with Women for a New Era (DAWN, 1984); and crystalized key demands regarding matters such as the negative impacts of demographic targets, women's right to access to all forms of contraceptives, the dangers of reproductive technologies, and women's role in defining and delivering reproductive healthcare.[34] The feminists who structured these meetings, and the reports and activism that followed them, were enormously influential in repealing coercive population policies. Feminism's focus on human rights has been key to the rise of the reproductive justice framework that defines the most vibrant activism around reproductive politics today.[35]

This was a hard-won influence. Tragically, even as feminists articulated the possibility of liberation through fertility management, the United Nations, US foundations, and individual population control activists, among other entities, continued to respond to the "population crisis" with programs that depended on political, strategic, nationalist, geopolitical, and theological arguments that went against women's interests. When the UN General

Assembly agreed to help countries develop feasible approaches to population control, and established the UN Fund for Population Activities (UNFPA) in 1967, it treated the population crisis in part "as an opportunity to broaden [its] mandate, 'even to move toward world government.'" The same year, leading population controllers in the United States convinced Congress to begin earmarking significant foreign aid funds for population control, with scant reference to women's interests.[36]

In the meantime, the former imperial powers, together with globally focused organizations such as International Planned Parenthood Federation, mounted what Connelly calls a "worldwide movement," organizing a series of "massive campaigns that swept across East and South Asia, Africa, and the Americas from the 1960s to the 1980s," run by "a transnational network of population experts who took up where empires left off."[37] The UNFPA often spoke for this network, as Corrêa, Arilha, and Faleiros da Cunha show, stressing the urgent need to control fertility in recently decolonized countries.[38] In the same year that the UNFPA was established, the shah of Iran, together with twenty-nine other world leaders, signed a population crisis declaration and delivered it to U Thant, secretary general of the United Nations.[39] The reigning "population consensus" of the era aimed to limit population in order to shrink the number of poor people in the world, reduce the labor supply, and protect the environment.[40]

Consensus adherents did not place women's status or interests at the forefront of their concerns, even as feminist perspectives on population control gained focus and prominence. The strategy of one of the most vociferous and influential proponents of US-engineered population control, General William Draper, is telling in this regard. Draper, the cofounder of the US Population Crisis Committee in 1965 and US delegate to the UN Population Commission from 1969 to 1971, provided leadership by promoting the UN World Conference on Population, held in Budapest in 1974, as a forum for "global governance" of population, first and foremost.[41] Women's interests were nowhere to be found in his program for resolving the crisis.

Meanwhile, as ordinary women around the world gained information and the means to control fertility, the birth rate began to decline worldwide—not, according to Connelly, because of state policies.[42] Similarly, Corrêa, Arilha, and Faleiros da Cunha; Sanjam Ahluwalia; and Omnia El Shakry, authors of this volume's essays on Brazil, India, and Egypt respectively, argue that the declining birth rate reflected the personal and political preferences of women, regardless of state rationales. Miho Ogino's essay on Japan also centers on the ways that women expressed their own interests; Ogino describes feminist-led reproductive politics in Japan in the decades after World War II and beyond.[43]

In contrast, women in the Soviet Union, subject to constantly shifting pronatalist policies, were, on the one hand, under the predictive injunction of August Bebel and Friedrich Engels, who believed, as Mie Nakachi shows in this volume, that "overpopulation under socialism [would be] impossible because liberated women, who engage in economic, political, social, and cultural activities, will themselves want to regulate the number of children." On the other hand, state policies constantly pressed women to have many children so that the Soviet Union could compensate for war dead and other causes of population loss. In this case as in others, women's reproductive capacity became a resource for the state, not a potential vehicle of liberation.[44]

Even where feminist movements opposed these kinds of state policies, their efforts could express racial, class-based, and other forms of degrading biases toward women outside of their own spheres. In Brazil and the United States, feminist reproductive politics often foundered on the politics of race. Generally, white-led feminist organizations did not take issue with the public policy tendency to charge women of color with the responsibility to curb their fertility as a matter of duty while celebrating the new "choices" that white women had achieved. Laura Briggs, in her book *Reproducing Empire*, has argued that white US feminists, mounting a drive to "save" working-class Puerto Rican women from sterilization, overlooked the history of Puerto Rican feminists' support for both birth control and sterilization. And Timm shows that in the 1970s, German feminists used "a discourse against population control in the Third World . . . to make a case for expanded rights of citizenship and social inclusion for German women." Most emergent feminist groups with visibility and funding, interested in linking reproductive choice to women's liberation, had not yet uncoupled their views regarding race, class, and demographic crisis from those of the mainstream population activists.[45] Later, as noted above, often in the context of global meetings, feminists from around the world developed a human rights framework that stimulated more capacious and inclusive analyses of reproductive politics and a more coherent basis for opposing population control programs.

The Global Reach of the United States

As most essayists in the volume note, the influence of the United States was virtually ubiquitous through the 1980s. Starting in the 1950s and continuing, the US government sent out a "new jet set of population experts," to shape and fund policy around the world, transforming the "population problem" from a matter of fearful discussion and intellectual debate into a series of domestic and foreign policy initiatives.[46] In May 1967, contraceptives were officially removed from the list of items that were impermissible for foreign aid expenditures, a policy decision that simultaneously targeted population reduction and also extended US authority and clout.[47] Now the United States was setting national and international agendas, calling for and funding international meetings and sponsoring other population control activities.[48]

Taking a leadership role in population control programs worldwide was, indeed, an opportunity for the United States to strengthen its ties to dozens of countries. American policymakers typically blamed overfecund poor women for the array of problems besetting target nations. Adapting Briggs's perspective here, experts moved in to combat "overpopulation," wielding an explanation and a strategy that "served to mask U.S. capitalist extraction [and other interventions as sources of many national difficulties] and to provide an occasion for further U.S. involvement" around the world.[49] Others have pointed out that the American presence ended up protecting US "access to strategic minerals in the Third World," while stifling "radical dissent." In some cases, the United States exercised raw power, as when, in 1966–67, it withheld food shipments to India because policymakers felt that India wasn't implementing population controls with sufficient vigor. President Johnson remarked at the time to a member of his national security staff, "I'm not going to piss away foreign aid in nations where they refuse to deal with their population problems."[50]

When countries did accept US-funded contraceptive programs, American officials were sometimes able to use—and sometimes abuse—their new influence, to the benefit of American contraceptive manufacturers. One such beneficiary was the A.H. Robbins Corporation, which had fielded numerous lawsuits because its IUD, the Dalkon Shield, had caused damage and death. In order to limit its losses, the company shipped a large portion of its remaining stock in bulk, unsterilized, and with the cooperation of US officials, for use by 440,000 women in forty-two countries.[51]

Writers in this volume also illuminate the various kinds of guidance the US government and American NGOs offered clients and even geopolitical adversaries. For example, we see that Germany's postwar population management strategies were based on American ideas about demography and economic growth; that, at various key points, the evolution of China's policy was shaped by US population control discourses; and that the US Population Council "informed Iran's development of a family planning program."[52] Not insignificantly, the United States frequently defined "success" as well as paid for it.[53]

Deep into the postwar period, through the Helms Amendment (1973) and the Mexico City Policy (1984), the United States used its foreign aid programs to shape reproductive health and population programs around the world. The 1973 policy states that "no foreign assistance funds may be used to pay for the performance of abortion as a method of family planning or to motivate or coerce any person to practice abortions." The Mexico City Policy, in force during Republican administrations and lifted under Democratic presidents, prohibits organizations receiving US family-planning funds from using their own non-US funds to provide information about abortion, to make referrals or to provide legal abortion services, or to advocate for the decriminalization or legalization of abortion. These policies have continued to carry political potency despite the fact that the United States has never funded any foreign aid programs that include abortion services. When the United States operates under the Mexico City Policy, countries around the world—and their poorest citizens—have reduced access to both reproductive healthcare—including family-planning services—and tools for HIV prevention and treatment, including abortion services for HIV-infected pregnant women who wish to terminate their pregnancies.

The US-driven concept, the "population bomb," structured the reproductive lives of millions of women in the postwar era and underwrote a raft of reproductive constraints. Today, the politics of religious fundamentalism, championed by conservative political forces in the United States, structures the reproductive health of millions, denying women access to information and services. The Republican Party's hostility to abortion is so complete that during the administration of George W. Bush any initiatives using the language of "reproductive rights" or "reproductive health" were unfundable due to a presumptive association with abortion.[54] Matthew Connelly has observed that the United States, as "the leader of the free world," was an unlikely "pioneer" inventing and pursing policies to harness its own "people's bodies to serve state interests . . . [using] migration and sterilization to control the composition of population." The United States has continued to be a pioneer and a policy-driver, variously assisting or obstructing the plans of other countries to use population policy to meet ideological and political goals.[55]

The Goals of Biopolitics

As the essays in this volume reveal, population policies have made the female body a key tool for achieving national and international goals of many kinds. Governments have used population policy as an instrument for legitimating their power; as a stimulus for political education; as a focus for responding to national crises; as proof of their respect for government-church relations; and, always, as a driver of economic development and nation-building.

A number of governments, needing to legitimate their claim to power, turned to the issue of population after World War II as promising terrain on which to make this effort. Both China and the Soviet Union inflated their census results in the decade after the war to project an image of political strength, stability, and prosperity.[56] Tyrene White shows how, in later years, population policy in China evolved against a volatile backdrop, as a "pawn in leadership struggles." When fertility control was adopted, Mao demanded—and built the habit for—obedience to his campaigns, in this case, campaigns to meet target numbers of gynecological exams and sterilizations and strict compliance to the policy forbidding pregnancies without state-issued birth permits. When quotas were unmet, punishment was forthcoming. The military government in Brazil in the 1960s, committed to the proposition that a "powerful nation meant a populous nation," and necessarily responsive to the dictates of the Catholic Church, resisted the population-control efforts of international NGOs.

The Soviet Union, responding to decades of catastrophic population depletion, used the West's focus on "overpopulation" and the "population bomb" as an opportunity for political education. Soviet leadership argued that these concepts constituted a political strategy designed to conceal the true cause of misery for people in the West: capitalism. In the Soviet Union, therefore, pregnancy and motherhood became seen as patriotic, proof that socialism stimulated reproduction. Soviet leaders based policies on the premise that births were a sign of "happiness among workers" and provided concrete proof that the communist regime was a success. In the Federal Republic of Germany, pronatalist policies were also important to legitimizing the regime, in part by tying childbearing to the benefits of citizenship.[57]

In states pursuing antinatalist policies, the concept of "overpopulation"—and the development of state policies to respond to the crisis—has also been a key aspect of nation-building. This was the case in postcolonial India, where contraception and sterilization became legitimate and necessary "weapons" in the government's fight to save the nation. Elisha Renne describes how antinatalist policies and programs in Nigeria have strengthened and expanded the bureaucratic state even while undermining state power as the government adopts strategies determined by outsiders.

Along with regime-legitimation, the most important state project associated with modern population control projects has been economic development. Omnia El Shakry shows how, in Egypt, by the mid-1970s, the government tied its emerging identity as a neoliberal, capitalist state to demographic goals such as reducing the population and improving its "quality," while fostering better geographic distribution of the people. These efforts, mounted to stave off the threat of overpopulation, were also designed to yield social and economic improvements, from mechanized agriculture and higher literacy rates, to raising the status of women, and an overall enhanced standard of living.

The Iranian case embodies a significant shift; here the government treated population growth as an economic driver in the 1930s but later associated economic development with population constraints. In the earlier period the government pressed for high birth rates in order to produce a "better national work force . . . and to make Iran more relevant in the global community of nations." But by the mid-1960s, the Iranian government mounted extensive family-planning programs, including multi-media-driven public education campaigns, now aiming to "raise the status of the family" and improve the country's economy.[58]

With some notable exceptions—China and the Soviet Union, in particular—the governments represented here, and many others, felt constrained to develop population policies after World War II that met state goals and were in concert with, or did not offend, religious authorities. In Brazil, the church and the state jointly regulated sex and reproduction; the two institutions shared the goals of populating the country and "fulfilling God's design." In Egypt, notably, President Gamal Abdel Nasser became a proponent of family planning, "using Qur'anic and prophetic recitations and emphasizing the importance of maintaining the nation's health."[59] Later, in the 1980s, religious leaders in Egypt frequently took the position that Islam was compatible with modernity, the achievement of which required family planning in this undeveloped, overpopulated country.

In countries where many looked to the Catholic Church for guidance, Pope Paul VI kept the faithful on tenterhooks in the mid-1960s regarding the church's position on solving the population crisis, a world problem that he acknowledged. The pope's ultimate condemnation of artificial contraception was seemingly at odds with his neo-Malthusian outlook; he publicly lamented tragic spikes in global hunger, which he associated with rapid population growth.[60] In the United States 56 percent of Catholics disagreed with the pope's declaration (*Humanae Vitae*), a development that supported President Johnson's decision to establish a Presidential Commission on Population and Family Planning. Many took Johnson's move as an indication that contraception was no longer as politically sensitive as it had been.[61] But in less than twenty years, Americans had to reassess domestic political sensitivities regarding contraception. During Ronald Reagan's administration, in 1984, the US Agency for International Development provided a grant to the Family of the Americas Foundation, a conservative, anticontraceptive organization—a show of support that has been described as "the beginning of a [recurrent] shift toward faith-based rather than evidence-based policy."[62]

Change over Time—and Consistencies

It is worth underscoring again that the essays in this volume show that as states promulgated population policies, the status of women was rarely a central concern, especially when state officials believed that the country faced a crisis that had to be resolved by population management. This was true even after the World Bank, development agencies, and population groups began to associate their programs with improving the status of women; and even after the Ford Foundation and other organizations affirmed the principle that "improving the 'status of women' was not just a means to some other end." For one thing, within countries and among countries, few policymakers had clarity about what measures could be taken, exactly, to improve the status of women.[63]

These measures were hard to identify or credit, especially in relation to population policy, when, as Connelly points out, policies that promised to improve women's status (while resolving economic and political problems on the national level) could have the opposite effect. Policies sometimes continued to give primacy to the protection of patriarchal power and privileges; in China, India, South Korea, and elsewhere women were pressed to have fewer children but to bear sons. Annette Timm relates how in the Federal Republic of Germany, contraception for women was banned in an effort to increase childbearing at the same time that the government distributed condoms to men, to facilitate their sex lives and enhance worker productivity. Firoozeh Kashani-Sabet argues that the accumulation of new knowledge about procreation benefited male experts and men, generally, who "chipped away at the authority of often seasoned female midwives," draining women of their individual authority about sexuality and reproduction and their capacity to make decisions independently.[64]

In countries where population goals changed radically over time, from pronatalist to antinatalist, or where there was debate about the basis for such policies, we can see, as Kashani-Sabet points out in the case of Iran, what remained consistent was the state's continued desire to impose social control over women's bodies and their reproductive choices. Miho Ogino's description of Japan's changing stance shows how, across policy regimes, officials constructed management of fertility as the solution: the use of contraception during World War II was treated as an unpatriotic act; then after the war, given starvation and lack of housing and jobs, its use was considered crucial to warding off Soviet interference.

Similarly, in Nigeria, as the basis for population control shifted from development to maternal and child health, and back again, the "peripheral position of women in the constitution and implementation of these programs" remained constant, as Elisha Renne explains. In the United States, some population experts argued for a national policy informed by humanitarian impulses—democratic values, peace, and prosperity—while others argued that "containment" was the point—policy as a weapon against starvation, instability, and the appeal of communism. In both discourses, management of female fertility—the use of female fertility to achieve national goals—was key. As Kashani-Sabet argues, population policy has been a key resource for ingraining patriarchy in society, underscoring the status of women as "civic wombs."[65]

Since the 1990s, many countries have reconsidered family-planning policy. In Japan, Korea, Taiwan, and Singapore, the birth rate has declined to below-replacement level, threatening to create high labor costs that will lead to future economic decline and the breakdown of social security systems essential to aging societies. In response, these countries have introduced pronatalist measures to encourage increasingly educated and economically independent women to consider having bigger families. As Tyrene White shows, in China, the one-child policy has come to an end because of similar problems, on a more massive scale. In addition, the sex imbalance among the generation born of the one-child policy has posed various social problems, such as a shortage of brides (thus, too many unmarried sons) and a shortage of children who can take care of aging parents. These post-family-planning states are now trying to support individual women's reproductive decisions in ways they previously have not; for example, by providing more childcare institutions for working mothers or encouraging "working from home" for mothers with young children. It is important to note, however, the primary motivation for the state to support women's reproductive role in these cases is still not women's status. Rather, economic development and social security issues are the central concerns. Thus, if the problem of low fertility is resolved, it is possible that state policy would revert to some form of population control and excise supports for women's reproductive lives.

Policymakers face a relatively new arena of questions today regarding how to regulate rapidly developing reproductive technologies and associated commercial practices in ways that appeal to women and promote their reproductive goals and well-being. On the one hand, reproductive technologies have helped thousands of women to conceive. On the other hand, these technologies are predicated on the commodification of the body, body parts, and babies. Egg and sperm donor systems and surrogacy support reproduction without sex and even without gestation. Many countries prohibit surrogacy, but regardless of the law, those who can pay the price are purchasing the womb-services of others; thus, as Ogino shows, constructing national and global systems in which some people with resources can become parents while others, with fewer resources, merely gestate. In Japan, to overcome difficult legal and emotional aspects of surrogacy, some daughters ask their post-menstrual-age mothers to gestate their own grandchildren. These technological developments challenge traditional definitions of family, of bodily integrity, and of the limits of parental obligations, among other matters. Clearly, contemporary, surrogacy-based solutions do not necessarily represent a liberating force for women. After all, when a poor woman can earn money by selling the use of her womb, or when emotional ties are unreasonably powerful determinants, concepts such as "reproductive dignity," "self-determination," and "choice" lose all clarity. There is no question but that we are lacking global consensus regarding these issues, as people travel worldwide to meet their reproductive goals.

Coercion

The degree to which the population policies of the second half of the twentieth century depended on coercion has been a matter of debate for the last fifty years.

In 2006, Dr. Steven Sinding of the International Planned Parenthood Federation, giving testimony before a group studying obstacles to achieving the Millennium Development Goals set by 189 countries in 2000, expressed frustration with the "mythology" that continued to associate population and coercion and thereby hamper efforts to slow the pace of population growth. He remarked that even though China and India had been guilty of some coercion, it was wrong to tar all national programs with the same brush. According to Sinding, this impulse "created a mindset about the past that was wrong and seriously flawed." Sinding and others have cited the successes of twentieth-century population programs, arguing that "those countries and regions where information and contraceptives were made available saw a moderate to rapid decline in the birth rate, . . . [and] an improvement in the economy, the health of women and their families and the autonomy, education, and status of women. The countries where pregnancies remained unwanted and the birth rate did not fall are now seeing an explosive growth of urban slums, a failure of the state of keep pace with educational demands and, in some cases, the continuing oppression of women."[66]

Despite Sinding's claim that the emphasis on coercion is flawed, the antinatalist programs of many governments have concentrated on the "excessively" fertile bodies of minorities. They have used language, made recommendations, and provided funds for activities that, in sum, suggest coercion. This is especially true if we expand the idea of coercion to include forms of pressure beyond forcible insertion of IUDs and mass sterilization.

Midcentury population control experts advised clients abroad in the 1960s that it was time to "get tough," which meant that simply helping couples embark on "family planning" was an insufficiently directive position. President Johnson was not the only executive willing to use food to press a vigorous commitment to contraception. The World Bank, UNFPA, and other powerful organizations gave money to organizations that did the same. The late sociologist Donald Warwick recounted how in 1973 the director of the USAID's Office of Population threatened to take away support for family-planning organizers in Egypt unless they went house to house, providing contraceptives as broadly as possible.[67] As Sanjam Ahluwalia shows, India became the frightening emblem of pending disaster. Without aggressive population control programs, some demographers argued, any country could face the demographic disasters of that nation. When India implemented draconian population-control measures in 1976, the event expressed "the culmination of a worldwide campaign calling for evermore extreme measures" including setting targets for sterilization, ignoring safety controls, disregarding local health services, and depending on incentives for acceptance and punishments for resistance.[68] As indicated earlier, between the 1960s and the 1980s, demographers and politicians used alarming, often hysterical language to describe the global crisis, justifying extreme action against the bodies of reproducing women (and for a time in India, men).[69] The widespread use of target numbers—for sterilization and IUD insertions, in particular—in India, Pakistan, China, and elsewhere, turned "acceptors" into "measurable, knowable, and therefore controllable biopolitical subjects . . . standardized machine-like bodies . . . [and fundamentally] biologically similar beings."[70]

Forms of coercion have varied across time and nations. Corrêa, Arilha, and Faleiros da Cunha describe how authorities in Brazil viewed miscegenation as a "civilizing agent," justifying "sexual predation." In the United States political rhetoric and public funding targeted poor women, particularly poor women of color for sterilization and use of birth control pills and longer-acting contraceptives, as well as loss of public benefits, because they reproduced "unwanted babies" "irresponsibly."

Pronatalist policies have also employed coercive methods. In various periods from World War II until the present, nearly every country covered in this book has criminalized abortion, putting women, doctors, and other facilitators in danger and sometimes behind bars. Illegal, sometimes dangerous abortions cost many women high fees and even their lives. Selective restrictions on contraception, whether legal or administrative, but often in the name of women's health, have served pronatalist goals. Emphasis on collectivist imperatives at the expense of individual rights under socialism led, in extreme cases, to monitoring and surveillance of menstrual cycles to protect against early termination of pregnancies.[71] In addition, state laws have protected male sexual prerogatives and policies have tied reproduction to access to basic resources (food, housing, childcare), especially to reward multiparous women. Those who assess the efficacy of population control programs have often ignored these coercions and the damage they have caused, especially the ways these programs invariably depend on and institutionalize female subordination.[72]

The contributors to this volume continue the project of cataloging the failures of population control.[73] The refusal to acknowledge and address such failures has been defined by Betsy Hartmann as the inevitable result of "a philosophy of domination, for its architects must necessarily view people of different sex, race, and class as inferior, less human than themselves, or otherwise they could not justify the double standards they employ."[74] Often the logics of population control, the imperatives, and the funds to pursue these ends came from outside entities, such as USAID, and did not sufficiently incorporate the worldview of their targets.[75] In addition, El Shakry shows how, in Egypt, women's choices were often at odds with the goals of state-structured family-planning programs, sometimes because women saw the concept of "autonomous choice as contradictory to their sense of agency and subservience to God." Alhuwalia and Parma find that even when policies were not horribly coercive, Indian authorities could still violate women's interests by eclipsing "matters of desire and pleasure, as well as ideas about privacy and citizenship/individualism, in favor of intimacy as an arena of state policy and power." In China, as White demonstrates, the one-child policy had to be modified because of persistent resistance, particularly in villages. In the United States, many state welfare and antipoverty policies were designed to punish poor women. Evidence indicates that if these individuals had had adequate access to contraception and abortion, they could have pursued their own real interest in birth limitation. And after decades of pursuing pronatalist policies, Russia has one of the fastest-declining birth rates in the world.[76]

The most recently implemented population control program treated in this volume, Nigeria's, had been notably unsuccessful, reproducing and amplifying the mistakes of some of its predecessors. The government has taken direction from "outsiders," ignored how the status of women interacts with questions of reproduction, and disregarded religious concerns and the differences between the interests of rural and urban women. Counterproductive competition for program funds—between government departments and between offices at the federal and state levels—has also hampered meaningful implementation of programs. Elisha Renne argues that Nigerians would benefit from government funding to support improved healthcare, educational and employment opportunities, and initiatives to improve the status of women. With these resources, participation in global population initiatives would make sense, but not otherwise. These unattended issues leave Nigeria today with a "policy that mainly exists on paper." Renne concludes that the only road to reducing fertility is "to change economic and social conditions that make large families desirable," but she writes that under present circumstances, "many Nigerians have their own ideas about appropriate family size," and no reason yet to change these ideas.[77]

As Connelly and others have argued, population control has generally failed because individuals and families did not want the state to control their intimate sexual and reproductive lives. When governments aimed to press technological solutions into women's bodies—mass IUD insertions—women often resisted where they could, notably in Tunisia, Haiti, and various places in Southeast Asia. And when women began to possess key resources in the 1960s, such as literacy, birth rates fell, suggesting that government programs accelerated trends that women themselves had already initiated.[78]

Contemporary Frameworks

Today the arena of population policies remains highly ideological and contentious. Prominent studies continue to predict global collapse, focusing on such core facts as these: an additional million people are added to the earth every four and a half days; natural resources are depleted around the globe; millions of poor women lack contraception.[79]

Michele Goldberg, author of *The Means of Reproduction: Sex, Power, and the Future of the World*, writes about the rise of "declinist literature," a genre that associates the fall of the West with its anemic birth rates, and warns of the rise of discontented, superfertile populations in the Middle East and the global South. The American conservative activist Patrick Buchanan has called this trend "the new apocalypse," brought on, he argues, by the rise of feminism.[80] Lester Brown, a longtime advocate of the need to stabilize and reverse global population growth, has recently associated "high levels of fertility . . . with failing states," naming Yemen, Ethiopia, Somalia, the Democratic Republic of the Congo, and Afghanistan, with Pakistan and Nigeria "in the process of failing," because these countries have been unable to get population growth rates under control.[81] In a related argument, Richard P. Cincotta, Robert Engelman, and Daniele Anastasio have argued that "the risks of civil conflict (deadly violence between governments and nonstate insurgents, or between state factions within territorial boundaries) that are generated by demographic factors may be much more significant than generally recognized." This group counsels policies promoting the moderation of population growth to "encourage greater political stability in weak states," claiming that, "on average the decline in the annual birth rate of five births per 1,000 people corresponds to a decline of about 5% in the likelihood of civil conflict." They identify demographic factors most likely to cause these disorders: a "youth bulge" and rapid growth of urban population, followed by inadequate access to cropland and renewable fresh water.[82]

A number of demographers and others decry the "lost generation," the two decades since the issuance of the Cairo Program of Action, following the 1994 International Conference on Population and Development and its call to substitute the focus on population control with a focus on women's reproductive health.[83] These experts point to a number of reasons why, post-Cairo, population growth receives disastrously reduced levels of attention and funding. Factors include the worldwide shift to a broader reproductive health focus, taking attention off birth control; the fact that the global AIDS epidemic has overwhelmed family-planning budgets, already seriously diminished around the world; the public costs of supporting an aging population; and the fact that aid agendas worldwide have been shaped and constrained by religious and other conservative forces.[84]

In recent years, with evidence pointing toward destructive impacts of global warming, some "climate change" activists have given new life to neo-Malthusian arguments for resuscitating population control. Unlike earlier iterations, these twenty-first-century versions generally put the need for "women's equality" at the center of their strategies. For example, environmentalist Robert Engelman recently proposed a three-step solution to climate-driven disaster, focusing on strategies that would lower the birth rates and improve the lives of poor women in the poorest countries. Engelman advocates elimination of all barriers to women's full legal, civic, and political equality with men; educational opportunities for all, with special attention to girls and women; and full access for women and men to a complete array of reproductive health services.[85] Writing in the *Journal of Public Health*, public health and reproductive health experts Judith Stephenson, Karen Newman, and Susannah Mayhew acknowledge that "linking population dynamics with climate change is a sensitive issue," but with programs that respect and protect human rights, they believe, the benefits are vast. Such programs, they argue, could limit or reverse negative impacts of rapid population growth on "human development, provision of basic services and poverty eradication . . . and [improve] the capacity of poor communities to adapt to climate change."[86]

Jade Sasser, a scholar of environmental activism, population, and reproductive justice, provides a cautionary note, warning about the risks of linking population management and climate management, even when women's interests, social justice, and human rights are foregrounded. She argues that "development paradigms, activist discourse, and new demographic-climate studies represent both an expansion of the range of issues considered under the climate change umbrella, and simultaneously a narrowing of understandings of sexual and reproductive health and rights issues for women" in targeted countries. Basically, she warns of the possibility that gendered solutions to climate issues could replicate and revitalize the old population control paradigm.[87]

Sasser and other reproductive justice theorists and activists stress that, historically, population policy has most often targeted the bodies of the poorest and most vulnerable women, as the essays in this volume also make clear. Population policy has typically obscured women's health and material needs, while focusing blame for environmental degradation, failed states, widespread hunger, and other disasters on those with the fewest resources and the least power. Undeniably, population policies aim to transmit a powerful vision and strategy for global redemption. But the policymakers are too often silent regarding the climate impacts of militarism, environmental racism, industrial pollution, energy policies, and consumption patterns in rich countries, among other structural and institutional causes of global warming. In this case, putting poor women first is a red flag and a red herring.

This is not to say, of course, that the reproductive health interests of the poorest and most resourceless women should be ignored lest they be harmed. We know that millions of women around the world want to limit their fertility and are unable to do so. We also know that foreign aid has accomplished—and continues to accomplish—crucial work. In 2014, aid totaling more than $610 million has provided thirty-one million women and couples with contraceptive services and supplies; aid has prevented seven million unwanted pregnancies, three million abortions, and hundreds of maternal deaths.[88] Furthermore, we know that many women want to have more children, but are not able to do so because of the state family-planning policy or because of insufficient resources. The reproductive justice framework that emerged, in part, from the United Nations conferences on women's status and population policy, and reflects the influence of international feminists on those meetings, insists that to achieve the dignified status of full personhood, girls and women must, first of all, be able to control their reproductive capacity. This means possessing the right and the resources to be a mother as well as the right to contracept and the right to terminate a pregnancy.

This triad of reproductive rights—including the enabling resources—constitutes a profound claim that has never been a feature of any country's population policy, pro- or antinatalist. The question that remains, as the human population moves toward nine billion, is whether demographers, politicians, policymakers, environmentalists, and others can turn away from polices that define the bodies of the poorest women as vehicles for achieving various goals of government and instead integrate the reproductive justice framework into their plans for saving the earth.

Notes

1. Hearings, Population Crisis, US House of Representatives, 89th Congress, 1st sess., Part 2A (Washington, D.C.: U.S. Government Printing Office, 1966), 622.
2. Rosalind P. Petchesky, *Abortion and Woman's Choice* (Boston: Northeastern University Press, 1990), 27.
3. The "population bomb" was an expression popularized by the 1968 book of that name by Stanford professor Paul Ehrlich and his wife, Anne, who was not listed as an author. The book predicted dire and looming consequences for the earth due to overpopulation.
4. On this, see Tyrene White's "China's Population Policy in Historical Context" in this volume.
5. On Romania, see Gail Kligman, *The Politics of Duplicity: Controlling Reproduction in Ceausescu's Romania* (Berkeley: University of California Press, 1998). On China, see White, "China's Population Policy" in this volume.
6. Joshua Cole, *The Power of Large Numbers: Population, Politics, and Gender in Nineteenth-Century France* (Ithaca, N.Y.: Cornell University Press, 2000).
7. Matthew Connelly, *Fatal Misconception: The Struggle to Control World Population* (Cambridge, Mass.: Belknap Press of Harvard University Press, 2008). This is a very helpful volume; we relied on parts of it to prepare this introduction and for editorial tasks generally, throughout.
8. Connelly, *Fatal Misconception*, 5–8.
9. Connelly, *Fatal Misconception*, 251, 378.
10. Kingsley Davis, "The Political Impact of New Population Trends," *Foreign Affairs*, January 1958, 293–301; Connelly, *Fatal Misconception*, 87.

11. Wayne H. Davis, "Overpopulated America," in *The American Population Debate*, ed. Daniel Callahan (New York: Doubleday, 1971), 161–67.
12. White's chapter in this volume.
13. Connelly, *Fatal Misconception*, 142–43.
14. Omnia El Shakry, "Reproducing the Family: Biopolitics in Twentieth-Century Egypt," in this volume.
15. Firoozeh Kashani-Sabet, "Iran's Population Policies: A Historical Debate," in this volume; White, "China's Population Policy"; Rickie Solinger, "Bleeding across Time: First Principles of US Population Policy," in this volume.
16. On the impact of computers on population control strategy, see Jeffrey C. Alexander, "Improving Quality of Life, by Limiting Its Quantity, Is Population Center Goal," *Harvard Crimson*, March 13, 1966.
17. David G. Horn, *Social Bodies: Science, Reproduction, and Italian Modernity* (Princeton, N.J.: Princeton University Press, 1994); Connelly, *Fatal Misconception*, chap. 2.
18. See "The World's Biggest Problem—How Experts See It," *US News and World Report*, October 4, 1965, for typical language about "an exploding world"; Connelly, *Fatal Misconception*, 338; also see Matthew Connelly, "The Cold War in Longue Durée: Global Migration, Public Health, and Population Control," in *The Cambridge History of the Cold War*, ed. Melvyn P. Leffler and Odd Arne Westad, vol. 3 (Cambridge: Cambridge University Press, 2010), 466–88.
19. Sanjam Ahluwalia and Daksha Parmar, "From Gandhi to Gandhi: Contraceptive Technologies and Sexual Politics in Postcolonial India, 1947–1977," in this volume; El Shakry, "Reproducing the Family"; and Solinger, "Bleeding across Time."
20. Solinger, "Bleeding across Time"; Connelly, *Fatal Misconception*, 201.
21. Chikako Takeshita, *The Global Politics of the IUD* (Cambridge, Mass.: MIT Press, 2012), 58; the policy architect quoted is Reimert Ravenholt, head of the USAID population program; Connelly, *Fatal Misconception*, 296.
22. The Draper Report, 1959, quoted in Connelly, *Fatal Misconception*, 186; Davis, "Political Impact," 295.
23. Laura Briggs, *Reproducing Empire: Race, Sex, Science and U.S. Imperialism in Puerto Rico* (Berkeley: University of California Press, 2001), 99.
24. Timm, "Biopolitics, Demographobia, and Individual Freedom: Lessons from Germany's Century of Extremes," in this volume; Miho Ogino, "From Abortion to ART: A History of Conflict between the State and the Women's Reproductive Rights Movement in Post-World War II Japan," in this volume.
25. Quoted in Connelly, *Fatal Misconception*, 213.
26. Takeshita, *Politics of the IUD*, 43.
27. Betsy Hartmann, *Reproductive Rights and Wrongs: The Global Politics of Population Control* (Boston: South End Press, 1995), 37.
28. Sonia Corrêa, Margareth Arilha, and Maísa Faleiros da Cunha, "Reproductive Statecraft: The Case of Brazil," in this volume.

29. Takeshita, *Politics of the IUD*, 43.
30. Connelly, "Cold War," 482; also see Elena R. Gutiérrez, *Fertile Matters: The Politics of Mexican-Origin Women's Reproduction* (Austin: University of Texas Press, 2008).
31. Connelly, *Fatal Misconception*, 79.
32. Takeshita, *Politics of the IUD*, 58.
33. Department of Economic and Social Affairs, Population Division, *Population, Gender, and Development: A Concise Report* (New York: United Nations, 2001), 1–4; see Connelly, *Fatal Misconception*, 151, for example.
34. See Hartmann, *Reproductive Rights and Wrongs*, chaps. 7 and 8; Connelly, *Fatal Misconception*, chap. 9.
35. See, for example, Kimala Price, "What Is Reproductive Justice? How Women of Color Activists Are Redefining the Pro-Choice Paradigm," *Meridians* 10 (2010): 42–65.
36. Connelly, "Cold War," 473–74; Connelly, *Fatal Misconception*, 231–32.
37. Connelly, *Fatal Misconception*, 9.
38. Corrêa, Arilha, and Faleiros da Cunha, "Reproductive Statecraft."
39. Kashani-Sabet, "Iran's Population Policies."
40. Hartmann, *Reproductive Rights and Wrongs*, 131–32.
41. Richard Cincotta, Robert Engelman, and Daniele Anastasion, *The Security Demographic: Population and Civil Conflict after the Cold War* (Washington, D.C.: Population Action International, 2003), frontispiece; Connelly, *Fatal Misconception*, 312–13.
42. Connelly, *Fatal Misconception*, 371–73.
43. Corrêa, Arilha, and Faleiros da Cunha, "Reproductive Statecraft"; Ahluwalia and Parmar, "From Gandhi to Gandhi"; El Shakry, "Reproducing the Family"; Ogino, "From Abortion to ART."
44. Mie Nakachi, "Liberation without Contraception? The Rise of the Abortion Empire and Pronatalism in Socialist/Postsocialist Russia," in this volume.
45. Corrêa, Arilha, and Faleiros da Cunha, "Reproductive Statecraft," Petchesky, *Abortion and Woman's Choice*, 130; Briggs, *Reproducing Empire*, 159; Timm, "Biopolitics."
46. Connelly, *Fatal Misconception*, 234; Kingsley Davis, "Population Policy: Will Current Programs Succeed?" *Science*, November 10, 1967, 730.
47. Phyllis T. Piotrow, *World Population Crisis: The United States Response* (New York: Praeger, 1973), 136; Hearings, Population Crisis, US House of Representatives, 89th Congress, 2nd sess., Part 4, Exhibit 138, June 11, 1966, "Short Summary of AID Activities" (Washington, D.C.: U.S. Government Printing Office, 1966), 876–82. In 1965, the World Health Organization began to include birth control in its official programs; *New York Times*, May 22, 1965, 33.
48. See, for example, "Population Council Report," *Studies in Family Planning* 9 (1966): 1.
49. Briggs, *Reproducing Empire*, 108.

50. Quoted in Robert Komer, *The Right Kind of Revolution: Modernization, Development, and U.S. Foreign Aid from the Cold War to the* Present (Ithaca, N.Y.: Cornell University Press, 2011), 108; Hartmann, *Reproductive Rights and Wrongs*, 111; Connelly, "Cold War," 480.
51. Nicole J. Grant, *The Selling of Contraception: The Dalkon Shield Case, Sexuality, and Women's Autonomy* (Columbus: Ohio State University Press, 1992), 31.
52. Timm, "Biopolitics"; White, "China's Population Policy"; Kashani-Sabet, "Iran's Population Policies."
53. See, for example, John D. Rockefeller III, "The Hidden Crisis," *Look*, February 9, 1965, 77.
54. Under administrations of whichever party, funding to support voluntary family-planning services is insufficient, with dramatic health consequences for women around the world. See Michelle Goldberg, *The Means of Reproduction: Sex, Power, and the Future of the World* (New York: Penguin, 2009), chap. 6; also see the website of CHANGE, the Center for Health and Gender Equity, http://www.genderhealth.org.
55. Connelly, "Cold War," 468.
56. Davis, "Political Impact," 294; Nakachi, "Liberation without Contraception?"
57. White, "China's Population Policy"; Nakachi, "Liberation without Contraception?"; Timm, "Biopolitics"; Corrêa, Arilha, and Faleiros da Cunha, "Reproductive Statecraft."
58. El Shakry, "Reproducing the Family"; Kashani-Sabet, "Iran's Population Policies."
59. Gamal Abdel-Nasser, as quoted in Haifa Shanawany, "Stages in the Development of a Population Control Program," in *Egypt: Population Problems and Prospects*, ed. A. R. Omran (Chapel Hill: Carolina Population Center, University of North Carolina at Chapel Hill, 1973), 207.
60. Corrêa, Arilha, and Faleiros da Cunha, "Reproductive Statecraft"; El Shakry, "Reproducing the Family"; *New York Times*, July 30, 1968; Pope Paul VI, "Populorum Progressio Encyclical of Pope Paul VI, on the Development of Peoples," March 26, 1967.
61. Piotrow, *World Population Crisis*, 159–60.
62. Goldberg, *The Means of Reproduction*, 94.
63. Maureen Larkin, "Global Aspects of Health and Health Policy in Third World Countries," in *Globalization and the Third World*, ed. Ray Kiely and Phil Marfleet (London: Routledge, 1998), 94–113; Connelly, *Fatal Misconception*, 316–17, 332.
64. Connelly, *Fatal Misconception*, 348; Timm, "Biopolitics"; Kashani-Sabet, "Iran's Population Policies."
65. Kashani-Sabet, "Iran's Population Policies"; Ogino, "From Abortion to ART"; Solinger, "Bleeding across Time"; Elisha Renne, "Interpreting Population Policy in Nigeria," in this volume.
66. For an example arguing that population policy cannot be equated with coercion, see Martha Campbell, "Why the Silence on Population?" *Population and*

Environment 28, nos. 4–5 (2007): 237–46; Sinding is quoted in "Return of the Population Growth Factor: Its Impact on the Millennium Development Goals," Report of Hearings by the All Party Parliamentary Group on Population, Development and Reproductive Health, January 2007, 11. The following quotation is from the report's executive summary (3–4). Available at http://bixby.berkeley.edu/wp-content/uploads/2009/01/parliamentary_report__population_growth_factor1.pdf; accessed August 1, 2014.

67. Connelly, *Fatal Misconception*, 246; Donald P. Warwick, *Bitter Pills: Population Policies and Their Implementation in Eight Developing Countries* (New York: Cambridge University Press, 1982), 10.
68. Demographers Garrett Hardin and Kingsley Davis were prominent proponents of the proposition that developed countries could face the fate of India, if they, too, did not respond to excessive population growth. See, for example, Davis's classic, "The Urbanization of Human Population," *Scientific American*, September 1, 1965.
69. Ahluwalia and Parmar, "From Gandhi to Gandhi"; and Connelly, *Fatal Misconception*, 230, 256, 262. Connelly writes that despite the anxieties and the alarming language, "the most rapid population growth could never be proven to have caused any particular crisis or emergency" (256).
70. Takeshita, *Politics of the IUD*, 59–60.
71. Kligman, *The Politics of Duplicity*, 148–205.
72. Corrêa, Arilha, and Faleiros da Cunha, "Reproductive Statecraft"; Solinger, "Bleeding across Time"; Nakachi, "Liberation without Contraception?"; Timm, "Biopolitics."
73. Even Kingsley Davis, deeply concerned about "overpopulation," wrote against "the assumption that [population control programs that permitted voluntary participation] are an effective means of controlling population," in 1967. Davis, "Population Policy," 730–39.
74. Hartmann, *Reproductive Rights and Wrongs*, 309.
75. Terence H. Hull and Valerie J. Hull, "From Family Planning to Reproductive Health Care: A Brief History," in *People, Population, and Policy in Indonesia*, ed. Terence H. Hull (Jakarta: Equinox Publishing [Asia], 2005), for an excellent treatment of these matters in Indonesia.
76. El Shakry, "Reproducing the Family"; Ahluwalia and Parmar, "From Gandhi to Gandhi"; Solinger, "Bleeding across Time"; Nakachi, "Liberation without Contraception?"
77. Renne, "Interpreting Population Policy in Nigeria."
78. Connelly, *Fatal Misconception*, 15, 237–38; Takeshita, *Politics of the IUD*, 68.
79. For a recent example, Alan Weisman, *Countdown: Our Last, Best Hope for a Future on Earth?* (New York: Little, Brown, 2013).
80. Goldberg, *The Means of Reproduction*, 202–3; see, for example, Jonathan V. Last, *What to Expect When No One's Expecting: America's Coming Demographic Disaster* (New York: Encounter Books, 2013).

81. Lester Brown, *Full Planet: Empty Plates* (New York: Norton, 2012), 21.
82. Richard P. Cincotta, Robert Engelman, and Daniele Anastasio, *The Security Demographic: Population and Civil Conflict after the Cold War* (Washington, D.C.: Population Action International, 2003), 12–13.
83. See Hartmann, *Reproductive Rights and Wrongs*, 153–55, for an "assessment of the tepid gains" for women at the Cairo conference.
84. "Return of the Population Growth Factor," 9–11.
85. See, generally, Robert Engelman, *Population, Climate Change, and Women's Lives* (Washington, D.C.: Worldwatch Institute, 2010).
86. Judith Stephenson, Karen Newman, and Susannah Mayhew, "Population Dynamics and Climate Change: What Are the Links?" *Journal of Public Health* 32 (2010): 150–56.
87. Jade S. Sasser, "The Wave of the Future? Youth Advocacy at the Nexus of Population and Climate Change," *Geographical Journal* (2013): 1–9.
88. "Just the Numbers: The Impact of U.S. International Family Planning Assistance," Guttmacher Institute, June 13, 2014; available at http://www.guttmacher.org/media/inthenews/2014/06/13/index.html; accessed August 1, 2014.

1

Biopolitics, Demographobia, and Individual Freedom

Lessons from Germany's Century of Extremes

ANNETTE F. TIMM

Contemplating the history of reproductive health in twentieth-century Germany immediately conjures up the extremes of Nazi racial policy. To awaken fears about the dangers of state involvement in individual reproductive choices, one need only mention forced abortion and sterilization, euthanasia, the criminalization of birth control, and various positive eugenic policies meant to create a master race. But the common invocation of the German example as an ethical test case for policy decisions related to reproduction has involved some obfuscation about the longer twentieth-century trajectory of German health policy. International comparisons generally take it as read that the main lesson to be learned from the German example relates to the crimes associated with extreme antinatalism. Yet for well over a century, racially inflected impulses to curtail the fertility of "out-groups" have coexisted with a persistent political imperative to raise the birth rate of those considered to be valuable German citizens. German antinatalism, in other words, has always been selective. There has never been a time in modern German history when a truly antinatalist ethos—a general program of decreasing the birth rate of the entire nation—has held political sway, making the German case somewhat difficult to compare to the other postwar examples in this volume. If we are to understand the larger lessons for a global history of population policy that arise from twentieth-century population policy, I will argue, we cannot confine ourselves to a study of antinatalism.

The most radical lessons of Nazi antinatalism, it must be said, are fairly easily learned. The racial violence of the twentieth century and the abuses of health officials acting under the banner of eugenics in various Western nations have taught us that a state that forbids certain people from reproducing because of their supposed racial or genetic characteristics risks acting unethically, murderously, or with genocidal intent. Much more complex and fraught is the recognition that antinatalism and pronatalism always coexisted in twentieth-century Germany; both were based upon racialist motivations to create an ethnically homogenous nation-state, and it was only in their combination that the extremes of Nazi racial policy were made socially palatable and politically possible. The simultaneous emphasis on both "quantity" and "quality" in German population politics meant that even during the relatively brief time (a little more than twelve years) when Nazi antinatalism took this logic to an extreme, the majority of the population was still experiencing the social and material rewards of government efforts to increase the birth rate. Indeed, it is only the longer trajectory of positive population politics that provides the context and logic for the Nazi extremes. My emphasis in this chapter will thus be on these "positive" inducements to reproduce and their legacies in the post-World War II period.

The murderous extremes of Nazism did have important effects on our understandings of the ethics of population policy. But this understanding came far slower than is generally assumed. Faced with having most (though not all) antinatalist laws declared void by the Allied occupation powers in 1945, and in the midst of dramatic social welfare efforts to cope with the massive migration of displaced people at the end of the war, German policy makers in the immediate post-World War II period tackled the issue of population control with extreme circumspection. In the years of recovery, however, just as they were trying to decide how to preserve the healthcare benefits of attention to reproductive health while still cleansing it of Nazi ideology, international discussions (in organizations like the UN and the World Health Organization) became focused around what quickly came to be known as the "population bomb" in the Third World.[1] In order to be accepted as equal partners in this discussion about what was now considered a global threat, German policymakers thus found themselves in the curious situation of needing to reinvent the language and strategies of population politics—one of the most ideologically sensitive areas of their recent past—in an international atmosphere of increased attention to issues of population control. While German demographic fears—what I will call demographobia—have been concentrated on concerns about population decline, the core belief in government's responsibility to manage and affect population numbers was shared across the Western world and was not definitively called into question by Nazi abuses. In fact, I will argue that the post-World War II shift in attention to the goal of controlling birth rates in Africa and Asia represented a transfer of substantially unchanged European logics of population management to a different geographic space. This prevented any thoroughgoing questioning of the deeper justifications, ethical implications, or actual effectiveness of efforts to manipulate individuals into changing their reproductive decisions that might have occurred if the focus had remained on Europe in the immediate aftermath of the demographic calamity that was World War II. As Matthew Connelly has convincingly demonstrated, the slow process of retreat from the idea that experts could easily persuade whole populations to change their reproductive behavior would begin much later and would involve a hard-waged, feminist-led campaign for the recognition of individual rights and freedom of choice.[2] So it makes little sense to confine our examination of German population policy to its brief period of antinatalist extremity. Instead, I will focus on the various ways in which positive incentives for the majority of the population, not only in the Nazi period, but throughout the twentieth century, helped to solidify public support for population management within Germany, while making it possible for international supporters of new forms of population management to ignore the German example.

None of the varied population policies implemented in the four post-World War I German regimes to be reviewed here actually had much of an impact on long-term birth rates. Indeed, except in cases of extremely draconian implementation, efforts to transform the aggregate reproductive decisions of entire populations through policy alone have never proven successful.[3] This helps to underline why simplistic allusions to Nazi antinatalism are ethically problematic, since they tend to be premised on the idea of a "successful" totalitarian implementation that actually conflates antinatalism with genocide. Measures that we can recognize as antinatalism in the Third Reich were part of an explicitly racist project not only to prevent certain groups from reproducing but to entirely remove them—more often than not through murder—from the population and are thus more accurately described as genocidal than antinatalist. Indeed, "imposing measures intended to prevent births within [a national, ethnical, racial or religious] group" is listed as one of the five acts that constitute genocide in the UN's 1948 Convention on the Prevention and Punishment of the Crime of Genocide. I would draw a distinction between general antinatalist programs that aim at decreasing the overall birth rate of a nation with the goal of economic advancement, and differential and/or eliminationist antinatalism, which seeks to remove the right or the ability of a given minority within a population to reproduce. With this distinction in place, Nazi antinatalism immediately falls into a category quite separate from policies aimed at decreasing the birth rate in, for instance, China and India and thus carries far less comparative importance in a global study of the effectiveness and effects of population policy. For this reason, along with the impossibility of adequately summarizing policies that can only be understood in the larger context of the Holocaust and the Nazi persecution of Jews and other minorities, I will refer only briefly to antinatalism in the chapter to follow. Without declaring Nazism a mere interlude—the logic of Nazi antinatalism and even genocide was, after all, absolutely intertwined with the logic of population management in general—my focus will be the long continuity of German fears about a declining birth rate.

The Origins of German Demographobia

Soon after the founding of the German nation in 1871, demographers, social hygienists, and politicians began warning of an impending population collapse.[4] Having witnessed the dramatic population decline in late nineteenth-century France,[5] German observers predicted and quickly reacted to the first signs that rapid industrialization was leading citizens to limit family size. Fertility declined by 10 percent in half of the regions of Europe between 1890 and 1920, with the northwest (France) leading the way. Germany hit the 10 percent decline mark by 1888, a decade before Britain, the Netherlands, Scandinavia, and Italy and two decades before Russia.[6] Rather than interpreting declining birth rates as an inevitable consequence of industrialization, as we would, contemporaries read the demographic signs as an obvious indication of moral decline, national weakness, and racial degeneration. Already before the Franco-Prussian War of 1870–71, Prussian medical authorities had polled health officials throughout the country and reached a consensus that moral decline, social ambition, and material greed—not economic distress or the adjustment to industrialization—were the primary causes for the falling birth rate.[7] Although not unique to Germany, the shift in demographic patterns gained particular political valence there, partly because it was feared and anticipated before it happened, partly because processes of industrialization and urbanization were particularly rapid, and partly because medicine as a whole, certain medical subspecialties, and the actual delivery of healthcare were particularly advanced.[8] In 1883, the German Reichstag passed legislation to create the world's first national health insurance program in the form of a sickness insurance plan for workers.[9] This Bismarckian policy greatly expanded the scope of medical involvement in society, heightening the inclination to find scientific/medical weapons to fight social pathologies.[10]

The growing popularity of social Darwinian ideas provided further impetus to state intervention into public health and added a specifically scientific edge to fears of demographic decline. Before World War I, Houston Stewart Chamberlain and Ernst Haeckel published widely read popular accounts of Darwinian thought that emphasized the need for German society to strengthen its racial health if it was to survive in the international struggle.[11] Social Darwinian rhetoric became ubiquitous across a wide political spectrum that included right-wing elitist thinkers like Alfred Plötz and radical socialist feminists like Helene Stöcker. But there was considerable debate about how evolutionary or social Darwinian ideas should actually be translated into health and welfare policy, and there was no consensus about how they should influence the ethical standards of patient care.[12] Within the context of the professionalization and specialization of the medical discipline and the competition for the prestige associated with founding new university chairs or governmental agencies, professors of medicine fought for control over the definitions of what was first known as "medical police," or *Staatsarzneikunde*, and what later came to be called social medicine, public health (*Öffentliche Gesundheitspflege*), and social hygiene.[13] The result was a proliferation of new medical and social scientific specialties, such as social hygiene, social pathology, social medicine, and demography. These various population experts aimed their attentions at the population as a whole, and together they vastly increased the prominence of population management ideas within discussions about reforming state welfare. Experts in these fields pointed out disturbing trends in the overall vitality and health of the German population: not only were birth rates declining, it was said, but chronic social diseases (*Volkskrankheiten*) such as alcoholism, tuberculosis, and venereal disease were threatening the genetic stock of future generations. Given the complex social dynamics of these diseases, the problem was attacked not only from a medical perspective, but also with a view to transforming individual behavior. Calls to reverse what was perceived to be both a physical and a moral degeneration of the German population proliferated in academic journals, party political platforms, and the literature of the growing number of voluntary associations dedicated to social reform of one type or another. The term *Bevölkerungspolitik* described all of these efforts to increase both the quantity and the quality of the population as a whole.

Bevölkerungspolitik in the Weimar Republic

The experience of total war in World War I, the mass destruction and the loss of millions of young lives followed by a humiliating defeat, further fueled arguments that only healthy rates of reproduction could ensure the continued survival of the German nation and a rejuvenation of national strength (*Volkskraft*). One contemporary statistician calculated a total German population loss of thirteen million: two million lost in action; 750,000 civilian deaths in the Allied blockade; 100,000 deaths in the 1918 influenza epidemic; 3.5 million children that were never born; and 6.5 million in population lost to the territorial adjustments of the Versailles Treaty.[14] In this atmosphere, the new medical disciplines that focused on improving the health of entire populations gained particular prominence. Specialties like social hygiene insisted that doctors had to be both socially engaged and economically aware in order to influence the decisions of their patients to support national strength. This rhetoric was full of normative prescription and demands that citizens view their health as an expression of national duty.[15] In summary, nationalist ambitions, concerns about military strength, and social Darwinian understandings of international relations combined with new medical paradigms and welfare strategies to produce an overwhelming consensus that the state had to play a role in influencing individual reproductive decisions. Eugenic thinking permeated the healthcare professions and the thinking of welfare advocates, with an emphasis on a simultaneous improvement of both the quantity and the quality of the population. The conviction that it was necessary to manage the German population in order to ensure the survival of the nation thus permeated public policy discussions; it was not limited to the sphere of reproductive healthcare. However, we miss something if we assume that the key lesson of these developments is that they produced only unwanted incursions into the private decisions of individuals whose reproductive decisions were now somehow guided from above. The results for individuals were much more ambivalent and the political effects of their reactions more far-reaching.

As I and others have argued, the argument that the falling birth rate represented a national tragedy and a threat to Germany's position of international strength was common across the political spectrum.[16] But it is worth pausing to consider what these fears actually produced in terms of healthcare measures. In large cities like Hamburg, Berlin, Düsseldorf, and Cologne, urban health bureaus were established to coordinate an extremely broad spectrum of healthcare provision. Clinics to educate and treat victims of tuberculosis, venereal disease, alcoholism, and psychiatric illness, along with efforts to promote mothers', infants', and children's health became fixtures of the urban landscape. The marriage counseling clinics that opened in large cities across the republic were certainly inspired by eugenic principles that supported an increase in the birth rate and the prevention of genetic illness; but they also provided information about birth control along with psychological, legal, and economic advice that was gratefully accepted by those suffering the lasting effects of the war and interwar poverty on family life.[17] Dramatic efforts were made to reintegrate injured veterans into the workforce through the development of work-appropriate prosthetics and occupational therapy.[18] Much ink has been spilled about the normalizing tendencies of these bureaucracies and the degree to which they presumed public authority to influence private decisions and life-choices, particularly for the working classes. But there can be no doubt that they also provided services that prevented disease, lessened individual suffering, and provided access to information about preventive healthcare. As Greg Eghigian has argued, when services were cut back in the wake of escalating inflation in the mid-1920s, the competition for scarce social and medical resources was fierce. It became "necessary to prove that one's needs were more pressing, one's predicament more dire, one's sacrifice far greater than anyone else's" in order to gain access to needed and desired medical services.[19]

The fact that health and welfare services had come to be perceived as a right of citizenship caused enormous dissatisfaction with the government when access became more competitive, a fact that eventually threatened the legitimacy of the republic. As social insurance and access to medical care became ever more universal, a sense of entitlement—what Claude Lefort has described as an "awareness of rights"—was created. Rights, Lefort argues, do not simply "exist," but are created as "publicly recognized principles" that are only partly embodied in law and are based on actual practice within the space of civil society; these principles are not *entirely* under the control of the state.[20] German citizens conceived of these new services as something they were owed, and rhetoric about the duty to provide the state with children only increased this sense of entitlement. As services in support of higher birth rates became available to more and more Germans, health and welfare policies motivated by nationalistic goals took the political function of providing citizens with a sense of belonging and inclusion.

Nazi Demographobia

This emphasis on providing citizens with social benefits as a means of creating social cohesion did not disappear after the Nazis seized power in 1933. Instead, it became ever more radically intertwined with a racial logic that clearly distinguished between those for whom reproduction was considered desirable and those who were considered genetic threats to the strength of the nation. Soon after coming to power, National Socialist leaders launched an extensive propaganda campaign that used terms like "differential decreases in the birth rate," "quantity versus quality," and "constitution of the genetic makeup of our volk" to argue that the unfit had to be prevented from reproducing in order to forestall racial degeneration.[21] The July 14, 1933, sterilization law (the Law for the Prevention of Hereditarily Diseased Offspring decreed mandatory surgical sterilization of all people with hereditary diseases.[22] Abortion laws, which had been liberalized somewhat in the Weimar Republic, were tightened in May 1933.[23] While those of lesser value (*Minderwertigen*) were often forced into having an abortion, abortions were illegal for those considered to be healthy and genetically valuable.[24] Differential access to abortion based on racial criteria can thus be viewed as a form of coercive pronatalism that coexisted with antinatalist measures forced upon those declared racially and eugenically of lesser value.[25] The emphasis was always on making sure that healthy babies would be born, while little attention was paid to the desires of the mother.[26] Even though Nazi sterilization and abortion laws appear at first blush to have been antinatalist, the ultimate goal was always to increase the number of "desirable" births. In the twisted Darwinian logic of Nazi lawmakers, an ever-increasing number of diseased individuals was overwhelming societal resources and leading to *both* a qualitative and a numerical decline in the German population. The logic was made explicit in the almost simultaneous promulgation of the Law for the Protection of German Blood and German Honor (*Blutschutzgesetz*—blood protection law) and the *Ehegesundheitsgesetz* (marital health law, officially called the Gesetz zum Schutze der Erbgesundheit des deutschen Volkes) in 1935. The former outlawed marriages between Jews and gentiles and classified Jews according to degree of racial mixing, while the latter prohibited marriages between partners likely to produce no or only "undesirable" offspring.[27] While both appear antinatalist, the intent was actually to make sure that "fit" Germans would marry and reproduce only with each other.

For the majority population—those who were targeted with pronatalist policies—the effects of these laws were ambivalent. While certain avenues of reproductive choice were closed off, access to services and healthcare often improved. This too was a continuation of the effects of eugenic thinking that had already had an impact on healthcare in the Weimar period; any increase in services produced a sense of entitlement. The party's own rhetoric about the long-suffering *Volksgemeinschaft* (the national or "people's" community) only increased public expectations of rewards for sacrifices suffered during World War I and its economically disastrous aftermath. Even as Nazi theorists of population management were becoming ever more vocal about the groups who should be excluded from the benefits of citizenship—particularly Jews and other racial minorities—and even as the sterilization law made it clear that "racially pure" Germans could be legally prevented from reproducing for eugenic reasons, the general rhetoric on the subject of measures to protect the population promised German citizens improvements in their access to welfare and care. The balance between pronatalism for the "racially valuable" German citizens and antinatalism for those considered unfit was already made clear in Adolf Hitler's *Mein Kampf*:

> That which today all sides have neglected in this area, the *völkische* state must make up for. It must place race at the center of everyday life. It must guarantee [racial] purity. It must declare the child to be the most valuable product of any volk. It must see to it that only those who are healthy produce children; that only one sin really exists: to bring a child into the world despite one's own illnesses or one's own inferiorities, while there is one highest honor: to forgo it. On the other hand it must also stand as reprehensible to withhold healthy children from the nation.[28]

Racial logic underlay both the exclusion of the "unfit" and the valorization and provision of care and honors for the "fit."

Arthur Gütt, ministerial director of the *Volksgesundheit* (people's health) department of the Reich Ministry of the Interior made the link between Nazi eugenics, racism, and population policy explicit in his various pronouncements on the need to control reproduction. Social policy, Gütt argued, must contain both "eliminationist" (*ausmerzenden*) and "supportive" (*fördenden*) policies so that the inferior (*Minderwertigen*) and weak no longer drained away resources from the important task of fortifying genetically healthy and valuable (*lebenswerten*) Germans.[29] The Nazis were single-minded in their desire to eliminate all types of disability from German society, and they relied on a racialized definition of the volk to justify the separation, segregation, and eventual sterilization or elimination of both unfit Germans (mentally retarded, congenitally diseased, homosexuals, political dissidents) and otherwise genetically healthy non-Germans (Jews, Gypsies, and Slavs).[30] Too much has been written about the consequences of this ideology to even summarize here, and the harshest resulting measures (euthanasia and racial genocide) fall outside the purview of this chapter.[31] For our purposes, it is only necessary to emphasize that Nazi policies toward reproduction and sexuality intertwined elements of coercion and incentive in the effort to instrumentalize private spheres of life in the interests of larger ideological goals. Coercion often went hand in hand with state-legitimizing incentives meant to create compliant and supportive citizens. The combination is clear in Nazi policies toward birth control and extramarital sexual activity.

Very soon after the seizure of power, Nazi health and police authorities shut down the birth control clinics that had proliferated in the Weimar Republic.[32] This fact is generally cited as a key indication of Nazi tendencies toward sexual repression and the control of women's reproductive choices. Yet despite these early measures, birth control practices were widely disseminated in the Third Reich.[33] Contraceptives only came under a comprehensive ban in January 1941, when Heinrich Himmler issued a police ordinance banning their production and distribution.[34] It is particularly significant that Himmler's ban excluded condoms—a rather large loophole. Concerns about venereal disease and the view of many Nazi leaders (particularly Himmler) that male workers and soldiers required sexual outlets to be effective and productive persuaded them that condoms had to remain available to men seeking the services of prostitutes. While women's sexuality was conceived exclusively in terms of the relationship to reproduction, men were expected (even encouraged) to stray, in the interests of improving fighting morale and worker productivity. Nazi leaders like Himmler simply assumed that even family men would be promiscuous. He made sure that there were brothels at the front to service soldiers who might otherwise stray into homosexuality.[35] This seemingly incongruous balance between a ban on birth control on the one hand and various efforts to actually foster extramarital sex on the other represents another lesson of the German case. It makes it clear that we only have one part of the story if we focus exclusively on "family policy," a term that, by often unacknowledged extension, is most often deployed by historians (and other social scientists) to refer to policies directed exclusively toward women.[36] Contrary to some stereotypes, the Third Reich was not a particularly sexually repressive society,[37] since individuals were encouraged to engage in sexual activity outside of marriage as long as it resulted in the birth of more "Aryan" babies or invigorated men for productive work in industry and soldiering.[38]

Himmler believed that male military and sexual prowess were linked: The best soldiers, he insisted—those most likely to require prostitutes for sexual relief on the front or those who had children with more than one woman—would also be the most productive citizens.[39] Soldiers engaged in the invasion of Poland in 1939 were thus released "from otherwise necessary bourgeois [*bürgerlicher*] laws and habits" so that children could be conceived "even outside of marriage with German women and girls of good blood." Bourgeois values were to take a back seat to the "victory of the child" as a necessary corollary to the "victory of the sword."[40] Hitler, though less vocal on the subject, agreed, insisting that "our uprising has nothing to do with bourgeois virtues. We are an uprising born of our nation's strength—the strength of its loins as well, if you like."[41] Only sexual activity that was thought to threaten fighting strength—such as homosexuality—was harshly repressed.[42] Even adultery was openly tolerated—one might even say fostered—in the SS: Lebensborn homes provided discreet and luxurious settings for the pregnant mistresses of SS members.[43]

Other pronatalist rewards were directed at the traditional family but carried a similar combination of incentive and coercion. Beginning in June 1933, recently married couples who met strict racial and health criteria could apply for loans of up to one thousand Reichsmarks to buy goods needed to establish a household. The fact that one quarter of the loan was immediately forgiven upon the birth of each child made the pronatalist intent of the policy clear. The goal was to coax working women back into the home and into motherhood, since eligibility depended upon the wife giving up paid employment.[44] The initial results seemed wildly successful: almost half

(42.6 percent) of all newlyweds had successfully applied for loans by 1937.[45] But by then an economy that was booming in part through massive military spending was quickly reaching full employment, and the requirement for women to give up their job was dropped. The pronatalist intent was thus always intertwined with the goal of economic management. As Michelle Mouton has demonstrated, the actual recipients of marriage loans were also generally acting out of economic self-interest. Few initially thought through the implications of the racial testing that they would have to undergo, which could lead to the discovery of medical conditions and referrals for sterilization, not to mention similar dangers for the extended family. Most saw the loans as a way of achieving the goals that they had already set for their married lives—to furnish a nice home and to fill it with children.[46] Gabrielle Czarnowski has convincingly demonstrated that any small increase in the birth rate brought about by the loans was temporary: It was a product of the fact that couples who had postponed marriage because of the economic crisis of the late 1920s and early 1930s suddenly had the economic means to fulfill their plans.[47]

A similarly positive effect was initially achieved by the practice of rewarding mothers of many children with service crosses and small gifts.[48] Beginning in 1939, crosses were awarded to mothers with four or more children (in bronze for four or five children, silver for six or seven, and gold for eight or more) on Mother's Day—now on August 12, Hitler's mother's birthday. Like the marriage loans, these crosses also awakened a sense of entitlement in the population and were meant to integrate their recipients into the ideological and social structure of the Nazi state. Irmgard Weyrather has argued that the crosses functioned "as a binding agent to the regime and as content of the political religion of National Socialism."[49] Reactions to the medal ceremonies were generally positive. Government informers (SD), who collected data on public opinion about the medals, noted that the most significant complaints arose when mothers considered to be "asocial" (that ill-defined term that could encompass anything from having a child who had stolen something, to obvious social dysfunction, criminality, or mental illness) were granted motherhood service crosses.[50] In general, though, propaganda efforts paid off with large numbers of applications for the crosses. In the first few years of the program, for example, the Berlin district health offices were flooded with applications and begged for extra personnel to process them, particularly once war began in 1939.[51] Wolfgang Benz estimates that at least 4.7 million women had been awarded the motherhood service cross by 1941.[52] Award ceremonies and propaganda made explicit connections between the war effort and the mothers who had provided the Reich with sons and soldiers.

Both marriage loans and motherhood service crosses were essentially pronatalist programs that encouraged individuals to view having service as a rendering of service to the state. They were, however, absolutely intertwined with Nazi racial goals. Only "racially valuable" individuals were eligible to receive these awards, and these apparently "positive" eugenic measure provided public health doctors with a wealth of genetic and social information about prospective marriage candidates that could be used for negative eugenic purposes.[53] Nevertheless, even in the combination of pronatalism and selective antinatalism, the programs attracted considerable voluntary compliance and proved to many citizens that Nazi rhetoric about supporting the family had some substance.[54] The fact that they had little actual effect upon long-term birth rates should not detract from the fact that they were generally perceived by the public as a right of citizenship.

In sum, we must carefully separate the two threads of Nazi population policy—the emphasis on increasing birth rates and the radical exclusions of the racially and genetically "unfit"—while still recognizing their symbiotic interaction and ideological unity. Winfried Süß warns us to beware of assuming that there was something in the logic of social insurance that inevitably led to the racial state—that Nazi health politics simply radicalized the collectivist urge of a universal system to produce a "final solution for the social question" in its exclusionary and ultimately murderous racial hygiene policies. This explanation of the radicalization of health policy in the Third Reich, Süß claims, is too "global" while being historically imprecise. It suggests that what we have thus far understood as somehow truly unique about the Third Reich—the "physical annihilation of the excluded [*Ausgegrenzten*]"—is actually an "inherent element of all capitalistically organized industrial societies." Racism as the driving force of Nazism actually recedes as a causal factor in these arguments,[55] which is a distortion of the reality that I have just described. Ironically, the focus on medical care as virtually exclusively associated with racial policy has underemphasized the degree to which it was also a factor in creating the sense of belonging that made nonmarginalized Germans feel at home in the *Volksgemeinschaft*. Just as some groups were being murderously removed from the national community, the financial and cultural rewards to racial insiders had become a powerful force of social and political integration. As Martin Geyer has argued, "The ideology of the *Volksgemeinschaft*, the basis of which was the concept of the racial equality of all Germans, had a strong egalitarian foundation," which "explains the strong emphasis on setting up an inclusionary system of social welfare."[56] Those most threatened by economic uncertainty were the ones being promised that the crisis could be overcome through a reevaluation of each individual's role and duty in society. This sense of belonging and the memory of the benefits that had been achieved for average citizens had lasting legacies into the postwar period.

From *Bevölkerungspolitik* to Cold War Demographobia

Nazi ideologists relied on a fairly common susceptibility to theories of demographic demise and their ability to create panic in a population. I call these moods "demographobia" because they have inevitably been proven to rest upon wildly exaggerated projections and assessments of the irrationality of individual actors that have far more to do with ideology than with a measured analysis of social and cultural responses. Alarmists who initially make the call for radical state action to bring about demographic change manage to convince a plurality of social and political actors that a turning point has been reached. In the past century of German history, these moments have coincided with periods of economic crisis; they occur at times when there is a cacophony of social commentary about an impending transformation of the social, national, or international balance. As Reinhart Kosselleck famously argued, the concept of crisis in European culture derives from the Hippocratic description of that stage of an illness where a verdict between life and death hangs in the balance—where some kind of irrevocable decision about the path forward needs to be made.[57] In the post-Enlightenment world, Kosselleck argues, the concept of crisis is frequently described in economic terms. We experience social crisis when what we perceive as a natural economic balance, "the equilibrium between supply and demand, between production and consumption, between the circulation of money and the circulation of goods, is disturbed."[58] In Germany, the dire economic crisis of the 1920s and early 1930s, which produced an inflationary catastrophe followed by a severe depression, provided fertile soil for the seeds of demographobia. This interplay between ideological motivations to control individual behavior and the phases of economic crisis that provide these ideologies with legitimacy is critical to understanding the various phases of German population policy in the twentieth century.

At the end of World War II, the entire logic of population management was thrown into crisis on various levels. As after World War I, German defeat was underlined in demographic terms, though this time population losses were accompanied by physical destruction. Michel Hubert has estimated that even leaving aside deaths among German minorities in eastern Europe, the German population that had been within the nation's 1937 border declined by 6 percent as a result of the war. Civilians were affected to a far larger degree than in World War I, with at least two million deaths due to bombing, street fighting, and the effects of expulsion.[59] However, these immediate and dramatic losses, which massively accelerated in the final months of the war,[60] were initially balanced by the crisis of needing to house and feed an influx of close to twelve million ethnic Germans expelled from formerly German or occupied territories in eastern Europe into the now considerably reduced territory of defeated Germany. Including those who fled eastern Germany because of the Soviet occupation, this meant that by 1950, 16 percent of the West German population was made up of people who had voluntarily fled or been forcibly expelled from eastern Europe.[61] This influx of refugees had to look for housing in cities, like Berlin, where approximately 45 percent of the housing stock had been destroyed or made uninhabitable. (In all of Germany, about 25 percent of the housing stock was destroyed and only 40 percent was undamaged.)[62] The early phase of re-evaluation of population policy in the period of Allied occupation was thus dramatically affected by a demographic crisis, and these numbers alone stress that ideological convictions about the need to increase the birth rate were tested by a demographic reality that balanced massive population loss with the problems of integrating a temporary surplus of displaced people.

Nonetheless, German health authorities also quickly recognized that their Allied occupiers had somewhat compatible understandings of the ethics of population management, at least in certain key respects. The transition from Nazism to a post-World War II regime of population control that integrated Germany began with a discussion of laws. Control Council Law No. 1 (Article II) and Military Government Law No. 1 (Article II) made it impossible to apply any German law that discriminated on the basis of race. This automatically repealed the *Blutschutzgesetz*, which restricted interracial marriage. But while twenty-five explicitly Nazi laws were repealed by Allied orders, neither the Marital Health Law nor the Law for the Prevention of

Hereditarily Diseased Offspring (the sterilization law) were stricken from the books. Only parts of the Marital Health Law were affected by the anti-racism clauses of Control Council Law No. 1. Requirements to state one's race, for instance, could no longer be enforced. But it was initially unclear how much of the rest of the law was still in effect. In December 1946, memos circulated within the British Element of the Control Council complaining that the old forms for application to marriage were still in use in registry offices across the British Zone—questions about race were simply being lightly crossed out with pencil.[63] Concerns about the racist nature of Nazi marriage laws did not, however, prompt either the British or the Americans to reject the eugenic provisions of either the Marital Health Law or the 1933 sterilization law.

Discussions between Germans and their occupiers about the future of marital health laws reveal the degree to which eugenic thinking had not yet been fully discredited in the post-World War II period. Neither the British nor the Americans had any objection to withholding marital health certificates (thus preventing marriage) if one member of the engaged couple carried a specified hereditary or infectious disease.[64] German officials, meanwhile, tended to support the idea of premarital health certificates while being far more reluctant to actually prevent marriage in the case of illness.[65] The exact legal standing of the Marital Health Law remained unclear even when, in February 1946, the Control Council announced that a new marriage law (Law No. 16) would come into effect in March. Law No. 16 annulled the general Nazi marriage law of July 6, 1938, but not the Marital Health Law of October 18, 1935.[66] But confusion continued to reign, with the British Military Government admitting the 1935 Marital Health Law was technically still in effect in 1948. The British military government therefore gave the president of the Central Justice Office in the British Zone the task of drafting a new marriage law to overcome these contradictions.[67]

These discussions continued well into the years of the Federal Republic. In meetings with government officials in the Interior Ministry in 1951, various welfare and feminist groups expressed their "grave misgivings" about any laws that would fundamentally endanger the "constitutional right to protection of the freedom of the individual and to bodily integrity." Their insistence that provisions in the proposed Marital Health Law called to mind Nazi ideology, however, initially fell on deaf ears.[68] In the end, however, the efforts of the Health Section to reinstitute a eugenically inspired marital law failed. The Ministry of the Interior called off all further discussion of the law in October 1951 and reiterated its position in November 1952. Although members of the Health Section continued to push for a law into the late 1950s,[69] two counterarguments combined to strike down their efforts: (1) the constitutional argument that a forced exchange of health certificates before marriage was not reconcilable with constitutional rights to individual freedom and bodily integrity; and (2) the practical argument that the money required to set up a system of marital health examinations could not be justified given how unlikely it was that these measures would actually affect individual marriage choices. By this point it had become clear that marital health certificates had virtually no effect on people's decision to marry. Which of these two factors (constitutional arguments or statistical ineffectiveness) had the biggest impact on the demise of antinatalist principles in Germany is difficult to determine. But these discussions make it clear that eugenic thinking endured well into the postwar period and was not substantially diminished under the influence of occupation.

The sterilization law followed a similar trajectory of enduring acceptance and eventual demise. It presented a particular conundrum for Allied occupiers, whose efforts to eradicate all signs of the Nazi dictatorship conflicted with their own less than democratic policies and thinking in this area. Having prompted the forcible sterilization of approximately 350,000 people during the Third Reich, the July 1933 Law for the Prevention of Hereditarily Diseased Offspring was not repealed by the occupation powers after 1945. With the exception of the British, the Allied solution was simply to close down the notorious genetic health courts, making it generally impossible to actually apply the law. The Americans hesitated. Legal and social health experts had nothing against the principles of the law (which resembled laws instituted in several US states) but they suspended it until a public interest in reinstituting these policies could be proven to be consistent with the democratic wishes of the German people.[70] Only the British chose to continue applying a subsection of the law—article 12, section 2, paragraph 1—that called for the reopening of legal proceedings in cases of possible miscarriages of justice. On July 28, 1947, the British Military Government imposed a "Decree on the Resumption of Proceedings in Genetic Health Matters."[71] District courts were to reopen cases already tried by the Nazi genetic health courts. If a decision was overturned, the applicant's legal expenses and the costs of surgery to restore fertility (when medically possible) were carried by the state. All cases in areas where there was no longer a functioning district court were tried in Hamburg. No similar laws were introduced in the other zones or in Berlin, so during the period of direct occupation, victims of the Nazi sterilization law could only seek redress if they resided in the British zone.

The difficulties of these discussions about former Nazi laws reveal the degree to which international discussions about population management were caught in ethical dilemmas. There was considerable consensus between all Western powers that state interventions into marital and reproductive choices were necessary and desirable to promote social cohesion and economic vitality. Nazi abuses could not be entirely ignored. And yet they also did not produce a fundamental rethinking in this immediate post-World War II period. The founders of two separate West German states in 1949 were thus perhaps even less likely to reappraise ideological beliefs in the need to raise the German birth rate than they might have been without the influence of the occupiers. The Soviet-occupied East, of course, followed quite a different trajectory that would be too complex to track in this short chapter. Suffice it to say that in both Germanies, the continued hold of ideologies of population management were intimately tied to specific theories of economic recovery and prosperity—one communist and the other capitalist.

The Federal Republic, Economic Logics, and the "Population Bomb"

Despite the extreme devastation of war and the difficulties of rebuilding in the second half of the 1940s, West Germany soon made a massive economic turnaround. By 1954, people had begun to speak of an "economic miracle"—a *Wirtschaftswunder* initially spurred along by American aid and fueled by the integration into a system of global trade. This reintegration into the international economic system of the West meant that German science and scholarly work was once again open to international influences. By the 1960s at the latest, social policymakers in Germany were profoundly influenced by comparative developments in other Western and non-Western countries. It is no accident, I would argue, that discussions of eugenic marital laws and other traditional measures of *Bevölkerungspolitik* faded away in the Federal Republic at exactly the same time that a worldwide discussion about the dangers of a population explosion in the Third World was beginning to pick up steam.[72] The debates about the continued ethical validity of eugenic laws that I have described above are followed in the very same archival files by reports from the UN on population control measures in countries like India.[73] There is no accompanying reflection about the irony of shifting from debates about *increasing* the population at home to a discussion of *decreasing* it abroad. But this should not be so surprising, since, as I have demonstrated, in the twentieth-century history of population policy in Germany pronatalism and antinatalism always coexisted. What had shifted, mostly as a consequence of American occupation and the dynamics of the Cold War, is a replacement of the militaristic/nationalistic justification for population management with an economic one. Pronatalist population policies in Germany had always had an economic impact upon the less privileged members of society, and had become fiercer during times of economic crisis, such as in the early 1930s. By the late 1950s and early 1960s, however, a particularly American insistence upon economic growth came to dominate. This economic logic could be equally well applied to the "developed" economic structures of West Germany and the "underdeveloped" situation in the Third World. It was no contradiction, in other words, to assume that one economy would need to be managed to increase its birth rate, while others would need to be managed in the opposite direction.

By the 1960s and 1970s, of course, the terms of the debates on population policy had somewhat changed. In my book *The Politics of Fertility in Twentieth-Century Berlin* I note a dramatic disappearance of the word *Bevölkerungspolitik* and its replacement with more innocuous and supposedly less ideologically loaded terms like population science (*Bevölkerungswissenschaft*) in the popular press, academia, and political rhetoric. And yet the motivations for addressing demographic concerns were similar. When West Germans rather suddenly jumped on the bandwagon of population control announced by *The Population Bomb*, the 1968 book by the American biologist Paul Ehrlich and his wife Anne, it was not a complete reversal of tone. Indeed, the very same experts on the very same committees who had just been discussing the possibility of instituting new eugenic and marriage laws to encourage higher birth rates were the ones to form new federal population commissions so that they could serve on international committees discussing the *problem* of high birth rates in the Third World. The transitions here are complex, and have yet to be fully investigated. While the influence of American economic theory shifted attention away from demography and toward technological advancement as the route to German economic prosperity, the links between economic growth and population growth never entirely disappeared.

Alarmism about Third World birth rates did not go unchallenged in the more politically pluralistic atmosphere of 1970s West Germany. Feminists, such as those of Berlin's Brot und Rosen collective, linked Third World population control to what they viewed as a new phase of patriarchal medicalization of women's bodies made possible by the birth control pill.[74] Their rhetoric presented a confused interpretation of the history of population policy that linked it only to the colonization and repression of "others" without addressing the history of positive eugenics and pronatalism. Nonetheless, their arguments highlight how closely tied issues of population control were to the discourse of German citizenship in this period. A discourse against population control in the Third World was deployed to make a case for expanded rights of citizenship and social inclusion for German women.

As in past eras, the revival of population rhetoric was not an exclusively right-wing affair, and it was framed as an issue of domestic prosperity. It was a liberal minister of the interior—Hans-Dietrich Genscher—under a social-democratic chancellor—Willy Brandt—who issued the decree for the 1973 creation of the Bundesinstitut für Bevölkerungswissenschaft—the Federal Institute for Population Research. Today BiB still proclaims its purpose as the exploration of "problems of the declining national birth rate, migration in Europe, and cooperation between the Federal Republic and developing countries on population questions."[75] Mere months after the institute's creation, the Organization of Arab Petroleum Exporting Countries (OAPEC) proclaimed the oil embargo that began a worldwide recession. The new economic crisis coincided with a revival of demographobic rhetoric, this time focused on the dangers of population explosion in poorer nations. The fact that this increased attention occurred at the precise moment when German demographers seemed to have escaped their association with Nazism and were re-establishing their roles as advisors to government is, I think, no accident. Both were efforts to forestall what was viewed as a looming economic crisis. Both the population explosion in the Third World and the effects of the oil crisis threatened to stall economic growth, thus placing the economic prosperity on which West German democracy was based at risk. A deep structure of understanding about crisis and economic cycles was at work here. German discussions about population management from the 1950s on were infused with American ideas about economic growth, and the specific decisions made about population policy coincided with specific economic transitions.

Conclusion

Massive upswings in political rhetoric on population in Germany coincided with the post-World War II crisis, the depression of the late 1920s and early 1930s, and the 1970s oil crisis. In every case economic insecurity reinforced the argument that the birth rate was intimately connected to economic success. Under the Nazis, this economic argument was militarized and racialized, while in the period of the Cold War it was tied to international discussions about economic growth and development. Any critique of biopolitical practice thus requires us to understand the constructed nature of economic logics.[76] Particularly in the second half of the twentieth century, virtually all calls to increase or decrease the birth rate were justified with economic arguments.[77] Yet the primary effects of social, health, and welfare measures put in place to affect the birth rate in Germany have not been to actually change the birth rate in any significant or lasting way but to put services in place that were, more often than not, used by individuals to implement decisions that they had already made about how many children they wanted to have. Some scholars, like Thomas Etzemüller and Christoph Butterwege, have insisted that these various policies have served to preserve the class system by controlling only the decisions of those of lesser financial means.[78] In the postwar period, they point out, this often placed the emphasis on immigrants and preserved a fundamentally racialist discourse by giving it other names. While it is critical to point out that arguments privileging pronatalism over and against immigration by their very nature depend upon understanding the nation as culturally and ethnically homogenous, the long history of population policy in Germany that I have presented calls into question the insistence that these policies are universally regressive in class terms. If we want to understand how such policies were so enduring, and how they were easily assimilated into a postwar international ethos of population management, then we must recognize that pronatalism could also serve the purpose of state legitimation. Health and welfare policies motivated by *Bevölkerungspolitik* in Germany were often received as a valorizing benefit of citizenship by those who took advantage of them. They were not always imposed upon unwilling subjects. Saying this does nothing to diminish our emphasis on the ideological, eugenic, and even racist motivations for these policies. Instead it highlights the reasons they were accepted even after democratic principles were reintroduced in the post-World War II period.

Notes

1. Paul R. Ehrlich [and Anne Ehrlich], *The Population Bomb* (New York: Ballantine, 1968).
2. Matthew Connelly, *Fatal Misconception: The Struggle to Control World Population* (Cambridge Mass.: Belknap Press of Harvard University Press, 2010), esp. 370–84.
3. As Connelly puts it, "It turns out that about 90% of the difference in fertility rates worldwide derived from something very simple and very stubborn: whether women themselves wanted more or fewer children" (*Fatal Misconception*, 373). See also Nico Keilman, "European Demographic Forecasts Have Not Become More Accurate over the Past 25 Years," *Population and Development Review* 34, no. 1 (March 1, 2008): 137–53. Keilman insists, on the basis of a statistical analysis of fourteen countries, that "[demographic] forecasts have not become more accurate since the early 1950s" (145). Meanwhile Lant H. Pritchett, in "Desired Fertility and the Impact of Population Policies," *Population and Development Review* 20, no. 1 (March 1, 1994): 1–55, argues that any arguments demonstrating change in aggregate fertility as a cause of family-planning services are "typically based on analytical errors." Instead, national birth rate variations are the result of national variations in the desire for children in different places and times (2).
4. One could actually begin even earlier, with the concerns about population decline voiced in the 1760s and 1770s by Johann Peter Süssmilch, King Frederick II's chaplain and now often hailed as the father of German demography. See Maria Sophia Quine, *Population Politics in Twentieth-Century Europe* (New York: Routledge, 1996), 52–88.
5. For overviews, see Quine, *Population Politics*, and Karen Offen, "Depopulation, Nationalism, and Feminism in Fin-de-Siècle France," *American Historical Review* 89, no. 3 (1984): 648–76.
6. John R. Gillis, Louise Tilly, and David Levine, "Introduction: The Quiet Revolution," in *The European Experience of Declining Fertility, 1850–1970: The Quiet Revolution* (Cambridge, Mass.: Blackwell, 1992), 1. See also John Knodel, *The Decline of Fertility in Germany, 1871–1939* (Princeton, N.J.: Princeton University Press, 1974) and Simon Szreter, Robert A. Nye, and Frans van Poppel, "Introduction: Fertility and Contraception during the Demographic Transition: Qualitative and Quantitative Approaches," *Journal of Interdisciplinary History* 34, no. 2 (2003): 141–54.
7. Paul Weindling, *Health, Race and German Politics between National Unification and Nazism, 1870–1945* (Cambridge: Cambridge University Press, 1989), 263 and 270–80.
8. Many of the most important public health innovations (such as Robert Koch's discovery of the tuberculosis bacillus in 1882 and his proof of the contagious nature of cholera in 1884) had been achieved in Germany, and by the late nineteenth century the prestige of doctors and medical researchers was immense. For an example of how this prestige affected internal city politics and decisions

about public health projects, see Richard Evans, *Death in Hamburg: Society and Politics in the Cholera Years, 1830–1910* (New York: Oxford University Press, 1987).

9. Accident insurance followed in 1884, invalid and old-age insurance in 1911 (by which time 67 percent of the population was covered by one form or the other). Each branch of the three types of insurance was separately administered through regionally organized employee/employer boards. In 1927, unemployment insurance was also available. For more precise statistics, see Greg A. Eghigian, "Bureaucracy and Affliction: The World of German Social Insurance and the Birth of the Social State, 1884–1929," Ph.D. diss., University of Chicago, 1993, 7–9.
10. Donald W. Light, "State, Profession, and Political Values," in *Political Values and Health Care: The German Experience*, ed. Donald W. Light and Alexander Schuller (Cambridge, Mass.: MIT Press, 1986), 3.
11. For a wonderful summary of how social Darwinism has been employed by historians, see Richard J. Evans, "In Search of German Social Darwinism: The History and Historiography of a Concept," in *Medicine and Modernity: Public Health and Medical Care in Nineteenth- and Twentieth-Century Germany*, ed. Manfred Berg and Geoffrey Cocks (Washington D.C.: German Historical Institute; Cambridge: Cambridge University Press, 1997), 55–80.
12. See Evans, *Death in Hamburg*.
13. On medical professionalization in Germany, see Charles E. McClelland, *The German Experience of Professionalization: Modern Learned Professions and Their Organizations from the Early Nineteenth Century to the Hitler Era* (Cambridge: Cambridge University Press, 1991); McClelland, "Modern German Doctors: A Failure of Professionalization?" in Berg and Cocks, *Medicine and Modernity*, 81–98; Claudia Huerkamp, *Der Aufstieg der Ärzte im 19. Jahrhundert: Vom gelehrten Stand zum professionellen Experten—Das Beispiel Preußens* (Göttingen: Vandenhoeck & Ruprecht, 1985); Huerkamp, "Ärzte und Professionalisierung in Deutschland: Überlegungen zum Wandel des Artzberufs im 19. Jahrhundert," *Geschichte und Gesellschaft* 3 (1980): 349–82; Michael Hubenstorf, "Von der 'freien Arztwahl' zur Reichsärzteordnung—Ärztliche Standespolitik zwischen Liberalismus und Nationalsozialismus," in *Medizin im "Dritten Reich,"* ed. Johanna Bleker and Norbert Jachertz, 2nd ed. (Cologne: Deutscher Ärzte-Verlag, 1993), 43–53; Michael Kater, "Professionalization and Socialization of Physicians in Wilhelmine and Weimar Germany," *Journal of Contemporary History* 20 (1986): 677–701; and Reinhard Spree, "The Impact of the Professionalization of Physicians on Social Change in Germany during the Late 19th and Early 20th Centuries," *Historical Social Research* 15 (1980): 24–39.
14. Quine, *Population Politics*, 17–18; Cornelia Usborne, *The Politics of the Body in Weimar Germany: Women's Reproductive Rights and Duties* (London: Macmillan, 1992), 31.
15. For detailed accounts of the history of eugenics in Germany, see Peter Weingart, Jürgen Kroll, and Kurt Bayertz, *Rasse, Blut und Gene: Geschichte der Eugenik*

und Rassenhygiene in Deutschland (Frankfurt am Main: Suhrkamp, 1988); Klaus Scherer, *Asozial im Dritten Reich: Die Vergessenen Verfolgten* (Münster: Votum Verlag, 1990); Monika Daum and Hans-Ulrich Deppe, *Zwangssterilisation in Frankfurt am Main, 1933–1945* (Frankfurt am Main: Campus, 1991); Jürgen Reyer, *Alte Eugenick und Wohlfahrtspflege: Entwertung und Funktionalisierung der Fürsorge vom Ende des 19. Jahrhunderts bis zur Gegenwart* (Freiberg im Breisgau: Lambertus, 1991).

16. Annette F. Timm, *The Politics of Fertility in Twentieth-Century Berlin* (New York: Cambridge University Press, 2010); Atina Grossmann, *Reforming Sex: The German Movement for Birth Control and Abortion Reform, 1920–1950* (Oxford: Oxford University Press, 1995); Weindling, *Health, Race*; and Michael Schwartz, *Sozialitistische Eugenik: Eugenische Sozialtechnologien in Debatten und Politik der deutschen Sozialdemokratie, 1890–1933* (Bonn: J.H.W. Dietz Nachfolger, 1995).
17. Timm, *The Politics of Fertility*.
18. Michael Geyer, "Ein Vorbot des Wohlfahrtstaates: Die Kriegsopferversorgung in Frankreich, Deutschland und Großbritannien nach dem Ersten Weltkrieg," *Geschichte und Gesellschaft* 9 (1983): 230–77; and Deborah Cohen, *The War Come Home: Disabled Veterans in Britain and Germany, 1914–1939* (Berkeley: University of California Press, 2001).
19. Greg A. Eghigian, *Making Security Social: Disability, Insurance, and the Birth of the Social Entitlement State in Germany* (Ann Arbor: University of Michigan Press, 2000), 227.
20. Claude Lefort, *The Political Forms of Modern Society: Bureaucracy, Democracy, Totalitarianism* (Cambridge: Polity, 1986), 23 and 261.
21. Cited in Gisela Bock, *Zwangssterilisation im Nationalsozialismus: Studien zur Rassenpolitik und Frauenpolitik* (Opladen: Westdeutscher Verlag, 1986), 90.
22. For an official text and explanation of the law, see Arthur Gütt, *Gesetz zur Verhütung erbkranken Nachwuchses vom 14. Juli 1933, mit Auszug aus dem Gesetz gegen gefährliche Gewohnheitsverbrecher und über Massregeln der Sicherung und Besserung vom 24. Nov. 1933* (Munich: J. F. Lehmann, 1934).
23. Paragraphs 219 and 220, which had been eliminated from the penal code in Weimar-era reforms, were reintroduced, once again prohibiting education about abortion or abortifacients.
24. A woman who procured or induced an abortion for herself or the practitioners of abortion were subject to between one-day and five-year detentions, or up to fifteen years if money had changed hands. See Lisa Pine, *Nazi Family Policy, 1933–1945* (New York: Berg, 1997), 20.
25. See Gabriele Czarnowski, *Das kontrollierte Paar: Ehe- und Sexualpolitik im Nationalsozialismus* (Weinheim: Deutsche Studien Verlag, 1991), 15; and Atina Grossman, "The Debate That Will Not End: The Politics of Abortion in Germany from Weimar to National Socialism and the Postwar Period," in Berg and Cocks, *Medicine and Modernity*, 195–96.

26. That Nazi medical authorities envisioned abortion primarily as a eugenic measure was further emphasized in the Reichsärztekammer's 1936 "Guidelines for Interruption of Pregnancy and Sterilization on Health Grounds," which narrowed the possibilities for therapeutic abortions (i.e., abortions made necessary by threats to the woman's health) to only very severe cases. Grossmann, "Debate That Will Not End," 196.
27. The law also only applied to German citizens, or in cases of a German man marrying a foreign woman. If a German woman married a foreign man, their future children were not considered Germans and the woman lost her citizenship. Additional decrees to the marital health law stipulated that health certificates (*Ehetauglichkeitszeugnisse*), which had been certified by newly created counseling centers for genetic and racial health (*Beratungsstellen für Erbgesundheit und Rassenpflege*), had to be exchanged before marriage.
28. My translation of a quote from *Mein Kampf*, cited in "Grundthemen der weltanschaulichen Schulung: Bevölkerungspolitik des Dritten Reiches und ihre Träger" n.d., an internal educational pamphlet for health administrators, Bundesarchiv Berlin (hereafter BAB), NS 22/521.
29. He uses these terms in "Grundthemen der weltanschaulichen Schulung," 8.
30. See Bock, *Zwangssterilisation im Nationalsozialismus*. It is now becoming commonplace to think of euthanasia as the first stage of the Holocaust. See Michael Burleigh, *Death and Deliverance: "Euthanasia" in Germany c. 1900–1945* (Cambridge: Cambridge University Press, 1994); and especially Henry Friedlander, *The Origins of Nazi Genocide: From Euthanasia to the Final Solution* (Chapel Hill: University of North Carolina Press, 1995).
31. Leaving aside works that specifically set out to describe and explain the Holocaust, the most oft-cited general accounts of Nazi racial hygiene and eugenics are Weindling, *Health, Race*; Michael Burleigh and Wolfgang Wippermann, *The Racial State: Germany, 1933–1945* (New York: Cambridge University Press, 1991); Robert N. Proctor, *Racial Hygiene: Medicine under the Nazis* (Cambridge, Mass.: Harvard University Press, 1988); and Peter Weingart, Jürgen Kroll, and Kurt Bayertz, *Rasse, Blut und Gene: Geschichte der Eugenik und Rassenhygiene in Deutschland* (Frankfurt am Main: Suhrkamp, 1988).
32. Grossmann, *Reforming Sex*, 136–49; and Gabriele Czarnowski, "Frauen—Staat—Medizin: Aspekte der Körperpolitik im Nationalsozialismus," *Beiträge zur Feministischen Theorie und Praxis* 8 (1985): 84–85. Authorities initially relied on anticommunist legislation to shut down the clinics, since many were run by the KPD or by communist doctors. See Pine, *Nazi Family Policy*, 19.
33. Historians have not yet achieved consensus on the availability of birth control in the Third Reich. This is perhaps a problem of definition. The fact that condoms were excluded from laws outlawing birth control in the Third Reich meant that they were officially classified as prophylactics (against venereal disease), despite the fact that they could also be used for birth control. Historians (not to mention their historical sources) have not always been specific enough about what

they mean when they write about birth control. When, for instance, Robert G. Waite, argues that that even teenagers were "well acquainted with contraceptives" in the early 1940s and that teenage girls in Lüneburg were using birth control regularly, he does not say what kind of devices or practices they were actually using (see Robert G. Waite, "Teenage Sexuality in Nazi Germany," *Journal of the History of Sexuality* 8, no. 3 [1998]: 434–76). It is necessary, in other words, to distinguish between prophylactic birth control (condoms), nonprophylactic birth control (which can include, of course, various forms of continence and "natural" methods), and nonprophylactic contraceptive devices.

34. Discussions about making birth control illegal, supported by Adolf Hitler, began much earlier. See the minutes of meeting of the Sachverständigen Beirat für Bevölkerungs und Rassenpolitik, August 3, 1933, in BAB R43 II/720a, Bl. 120ff.

35. The brothel system was institutionalized in February 1936, when the Supreme Command of the Wehrmacht declared the construction of military brothels "an urgent necessity" and insisted that health authorities should restrain themselves in arresting prostitutes who might be used for this purpose. See Christa Paul, *Zwangsprostitution: Staatlich Errichtete Bordelle im Nationalsozialismus, Reihe Deutsche Vergangenheit* (Berlin: Edition Hentrich, 1995), 12, and "Niederschrift der Sitzung des Wohlfahrtsausschusses des Deutschen Gemeindetages zum Thema 'Bewahrungsgesetz,'" February 27, 1936, cited in Detlev J. K. Peukert, *Grenzen der Sozialdisziplinierung. Aufstieg und Krise der deutschen Jugendfürsorge von 1878 bis 1932* (Cologne: Bund-Verlag, 1986), 281.

36. See, for example, Pine, *Nazi Family Policy*; Irmgard Weyrather, *Muttertag und Mutterkreuz: Der Kult um die "deutsche Mutter" im Nationalsozialismus* (Frankfurt am Main: Fischer Taschenbuch Verlag, 1993); and Czarnowski, *Das kontrollierte Paar*. For a counterargument that exposes the ideological and historically inaccurate nature of the claim, commonly made by Germany's New Leftists in the 1960s and 1970s, "that it was sexual repression that engendered the Nazi capacity for cruelty and mass murder," see Dagmar Herzog, "'Pleasure, Sex and Politics Belong Together': Post-Holocaust Memory and the Sexual Revolution in West Germany," *Critical Inquiry* 24, no. 2 (1998): 393–444, esp. 397.

37. This has been well documented in Dagmar Herzog, *Sex after Fascism: Memory and Morality in Twentieth-Century Germany* (Princeton, N.J.: Princeton University Press, 2005).

38. I explore this subject in more detail in Annette F. Timm, "Sex with a Purpose: Prostitution, Venereal Disease and Militarized Masculinity in the Third Reich," *Journal of the History of Sexuality* 11, nos. 1–2 (2002): 223–55.

39. See his famous October 1939 speech, in which he called upon all racially "valuable" and patriotic Germans to produce children, even if they were illegitimate, to feed the nation's need for soldiers. This was a very controversial stance, even within the party. See George L. Mosse, *Nationalism and Sexuality: Middle-Class Morality and Sexual Norms in Modern Europe* (New York: H. Fertig, 1985), 166–67. The impact of the speech on actual practice has

been vastly overblown, particularly by those who have used it to make the inaccurate claim that Himmler's *Lebensborn* maternity homes were "breeding farms" where SS soldiers impregnated fertile Aryan women. The most authorative book on the *Lebensborn* is Georg Lilienthal, *Der "Lebensborn e. V.": Ein Instrument nationalsozialistischer Rassenpolitik* (Stuttgart: Fischer 1985). Actual practice in *Lebensborn* homes must be distinguished from the fantasies of some Nazi leaders (particularly Himmler) about policies to be introduced in the future. See Hans Peter Bleuel, *Sex and Society in Nazi Germany*, ed. Heinrich Fraenkel, trans. J. Maxwell Brownjohn (Philadelphia: Dorset Press, 1973), 169.

40. "SS-Befehl für die gesamte SS und Polizei," October 28, 1939, in BAB NS19/3973.
41. Quoted in Hans Peter Bleuel, *Sex and Society in Nazi Germany* (New York: Dorset Press, 1996), 3.
42. For brief overviews of the persecution of homosexuality in the Third Reich, see Geoffrey Giles, "The Denial of Homosexuality: Same-Sex Incidents in Himmler's SS and Police," *Journal of the History of Sexuality* 11, nos 1–2 (2002): 256–90; Geoffrey Giles, "'The Most Unkindest Cut of All': Castration, Homosexuality, and Nazi Justice," *Journal of Contemporary History* 27, no. 1 (1992): 41–61; and Erwin J. Haeberle, "Swastika, Pink Triangle, and Yellow Star: The Destruction of Sexology and the Persecution of Homosexuals in Nazi Germany," in *Hidden from History: Reclaiming the Gay and Lesbian Past*, ed. Martin Duberman, Martha Vicinus, and George Chauncey Jr. (New York: New American Library, 1989).
43. SS officers were compelled under a 1936 order to become supporting members of Lebensborn e.V., an organization dedicated to helping racially valuable families with many children and unwed mothers about to give birth to racially valuable children. An excerpt from this order is reprinted in BAB NS19/3973, Bl. 9–10. Married men in SS units were often given short leaves to visit with their wives in hotels near the front, in the hopes that they would conceive a child. For an example of Himmler's orders to this effect, see BAB NS19/2769 and BAB NS19/3594.
44. For an extended examination, see Czarnowski, *Das kontrollierte Paar.*
45. Cited from *Statistisches Jahrbuch* 58 (1940): 52, in Michelle Mouton, *From Nurturing the Nation to Purifying the Volk: Weimar and Nazi Family Policy, 1918–1945* (Washington, D.C.: German Historical Institute; New York: Cambridge University Press, 2007), 57.
46. At least 20 percent of applications were rejected, mostly for health but also for political reasons. See Mouton, *Nurturing the Nation*, 56–61.
47. Czarnowski, *Das kontrollierte Paar*, 104 and 112.
48. See especially, Weyrather, *Muttertag und Mutterkreuz*.
49. Weyrather, *Muttertag und Mutterkreuz*, 151. For a copy of the official policy, see "Das Ehrenkreuz der Deutschen Mutter," *AGfV Mitteilungen* no. 2 (January 16, 1939): 1–2.

50. Weyrather, *Muttertag und Mutterkreuz*, 147.
51. See, for example, the letter from the district of Treptow to the Oberbürgermeister, May 6, 1939, in Landesarchiv Berlin, Rep. 12, Acc. 1641, Nr. 247. In October 1939, the Reich Ministry of the Interior issued a directive to all regions to immediately clear up the backlog of applications, and make every effort to ensure that at least all those women over fifty years of age had their crosses in hand before Christmas. Letter describing RMI memo from Oberbürgermeister Berlin, October 30, 1939, in Landesarchiv Berlin.
52. Wolfgang Benz, *Die 101 wichtigsten Fragen—Das Dritte Reich* (Nördlingen: C.H. Beck, 2008), 24.
53. Czarnowski, *Das kontrollierte Paar*, 109.
54. Robert Moeller, *Protecting Motherhood: Women and Family in the Politics of Postwar Germany* (Berkeley: University of California Press, 1993), 17.
55. Winfried Süß, *Der "Volkskörper" im Krieg: Gesundheitspolitik, Gesundheitsverhältnisse und Krankenmord im nationalsozialistischen Deutschland, 1939–1945* (Munich: R. Oldenbourg Verlag, 2003), 25–26.
56. Martin H. Geyer, "Social Rights and Citizenship during World War II," in *Two Cultures of Rights: The Quest for Inclusion and Participation in Modern America and Germany*, ed. Manfred Berg and Martin H. Geyer (New York: Cambridge University Press, 2006), 146.
57. Reinhart Koselleck, "Some Questions Concerning the Conceptual History of 'Crisis,'" in *Culture and Crisis: The Case of Germany and Sweden*, ed. Nina Witoszek and Lars Trägårdh (New York: Berghahn Books, 2002), 13.
58. Koselleck, "Some Questions," 18.
59. Michel Hubert cites 5.3 to 6.9 million military casualties. The variation is partly a matter of deciding which soldiers to count, since citizenship and ethnic belonging were not easily distinguished during this period. See Michel Hubert, *Deutschland im Wandel: Geschichte der deutschen Bevölkerung seit 1815* (Stuttgart: Franz Steiner Verlag, 1998), 272.
60. Rüdiger Overmans, "Die Toten des Zweiten Weltkrieges in Deutschland: Bilanz der Forschung unter besonderer Berücksichtigung der Wehrmacht und Vertreibungsverluste," in *Der Zweite Weltkrieg. Analysen, Grundzüge, Forschungsbilanz*, ed. Wolfgang Michalk (Munich: Piper 1989), 862–63.
61. Robert G. Moeller, *War Stories: The Search for a Usable Past in the Federal Republic of Germany* (Berkeley: University of California Press, 2001), 3. Moeller relies on a comprehensive survey of the scholarly literature on the expellees to dispel some of the exaggerated claims about German deaths. See his footnotes on pp. 201–2.
62. Jeffry M. Diefendorf, *In the Wake of War: The Reconstruction of German Cities after World War II* (New York: Oxford University Press, 1993), 125–26.
63. Control Commission for Germany (British Element), B.A.O.R. to Legal Division, December 6, 1945 in Public Record Office (hereafter PRO) FO 1060/917.
64. Foreign Office (German Section)—Legal Division, memo of July 9, 1945, in PRO FO 1060/1004. On American thinking, see "Marriage of CCG Civilian

Personnel to Ex-enemy Nationals," December 20, 1946, PRO FO 1049/619. The Americans insisted upon blood tests to rule out syphilis. This decision was first discussed by the Directorate of Internal Affairs and Communications in the Allied Control Authority. See "Prohibition of Marriage of Persons suffering from Venereal Disease," October 26, 1946, PRO FO 1050/737. American soldiers had to wait to apply for a marriage permit until between three and six months prior to their return to the United States. See Petra Goedde, "From Villains to Victims: Fraternization and the Feminization of Germany, 1945–1947," *Diplomatic History* 23, no. 1 (1999): 1–20, esp. 11.

65. See Oberpräsident Nord Rhine Province to British Military Government, July 24, 1945, in PRO FO 1013/1937; and Hans-Ulrich Sons, *Gesundheitspolitik während der Besatzungszeit: Das öffentliche Gesundheitswesen in Nordrhein-Westfalen, 1945–1949* (Wuppertal: Peter Hammer Verlag, 1983), 46.
66. British Military Government officials also translated *Eheunbedenklichkeitsbescheinigungen* as "certificates of no impediment."
67. Sons, *Gesundheitspolitik*, 46; and Präsident des Zentral-Justizamts für die Britische Zone (Baerns) to various health and welfare administrations in the British zone, March 31, 1948, in Bundesarchiv Koblenz (hereafter BAK) B142/4115.
68. See the minutes of a meeting (in Trier) of the "Arbeitskreis I der AG der Innenministerien der Länder" to discuss the new proposals for a marriage counseling law, April 4, 1951, and "Entwurf eines Eheberatungsgesetzes . . . Besprechung am 25. und 26.7.1951," in BAK B142/4115.
69. See the exchange of letters on the subject between Hans Harmsen and members of the Health Section (O. Buurmann and Dr. Habernoll) from October 1956 to May 1957, in BAK B142/4115.
70. The American position was defended by the chief of the Legal Division, Office of Military Government, Charles Fahy, in a series of meetings on the subject between July and November 1945. NARA/260/OMGUS 17/53—1/4, 1. B 1. R. See also comments from Reg. Rat Kloesel (Württemberg-Baden) and Dr. Meyer's review of developments in Berlin in "Niederschrift über die Sitzung des Ausschusses für Fragen betreffend Ausstellung von Eheunbedenklichkeitsbescheinigungen der Arbeitsgemeinschaft der für das Gesundheitswesen zuständigen Minister der Länder," January 12, 1950, in BAK B142/4115.
71. Verordnungsblatt für die britische Zone 1947, S. 110. Copy in BAK B142/4115.
72. An example of postpill German Malthusianism can be found in Gerd von Wahlert, *30 Milliarden Menschen? Weltbevölkerung und Pille* (Stuttgart: Kr euz-Verlag, 1970).
73. See, for example, the folder entitled "Ehegesundheitswesen im Auslande," March 1954–March 1963, in BAK B142/4115. The "population explosion" scare took off with a vengeance with the publication of Ehrlich's *The Population Bomb*.
74. They pointed to evidence that fears of population growth in the Third World and among poor populations in the United States had motivated funding for

research into the pill. See Barbara Sichtermann, "Die Frauenbewegung und die Pille," in *Die Pille: Von der Lust und von der Liebe*, ed. Gisela Staupe and Lisa Vieth (Berlin: Rowohlt, 1996), 55–66.

75. Bundesinstitut für Bevölkerungsforschung, http://www.bib-demographie.de (accessed May 15, 2010).

76. See the useful discussions in Ulrich Bröckling, "Human Economy, Human Capital: A Critique of Biopolitical Economy," in *Governmentality: Current Issues and Future Challenges*, ed. Ulrich Bröckling, Susanne Krasmann, and Thomas Lemke (New York: Routledge, 2010), 247–68; and Urs Stäheli, "Decentering the Economy: Governmentality Studies and Beyond?" in Bröckling, Krasmann, and Lemke, *Governmentality*, esp. 270–72. Both authors rely upon Foucault's concept of governmentality to make the case that economic structures require more attention from historians and theorists of culture. Stäheli argues that social theorists have tended to treat the economy as a quarantined place where entry might result in "becom[ing] infected by the virus of essentialism" (270).

77. Susan Greenhalgh, "The Social Construction of Population Science: An Intellectual, Institutional, and Political History of Twentieth-Century Demography," *Comparative Studies in Society and History* 38, no. 1 (1996): 25–66.

78. See Thomas Etzemüller, "Die Angst vor dem Abstieg—Malthus, Burgdörfer, Sarrazin: Eine Ahnenreihe mit Immer derselben Botschaft," in *Der Mythos vom Niedergang der Intelligenz: Von Galton zu Sarrazin: Die Denkmuster und Denkfehler der Eugenik*, ed. Michael Haller and Martin Niggeschmidt (Wiesbaden: Springer, 2012), 158; and Christoph Butterwegge, "Sterben 'Die Deutschen' Aus? Demografiediskurs und Bevölkerungspolitik als Einfallstore eine Biologisierung des Sozialen," *Schulheft* 124 (2006): 45–46.

2

Bleeding across Time

First Principles of US Population Policy

RICKIE SOLINGER

First Principles

Histories of domestic population policy in the United States usually begin in the mid-twentieth century, around 1962. At that point, scientific and technological developments, together with political and financial resistance to welfare provision, stimulated city, state, and federal governments to fund programs dispensing contraceptive information and materials to poor women living with their husbands. But, in fact, population policy in North American began in the prenational period when colonial leaders, animated by concerns about labor needs and about preserving white racial purity and white supremacy, developed what I am calling "first principles," leading to laws and policies for addressing those concerns, thereby shaping a new racialized nation-state.

Throughout this period and continuing, what we have come to refer to as "reproductive politics"—"Who has power over matters of sex, pregnancy, and the consequences?"—has rarely, over time, incorporated the interests of women. Rather, reproductive politics has been a crucial aspect of policies and laws devised to solve certain large social, economic, political, and moral problems facing the North American colonies and then the United States. Solutions pressed women variously, according to their race and class, to reproduce or not, in order to solve these problems—demonstrating that for more than three centuries, sexual intimacy and its outcomes have provided a crucial realm for state regulation and control.

Population policy, animated by these "first principles," has continuously functioned as a key engine for defining and reproducing racial difference; for legalizing and perpetuating the body as real property; and for structuring women's conditioned and variable access to full citizenship.[1]

During the eighteenth century, the men who made and enforced laws governing sexual relations were legislating in an era of complex interracial contact and very limited knowledge about separating sex and pregnancy. Legislators crafted laws to regulate sexual intimacy for a society in which some people were the property of other people, and in which matters of race and property, labor requirements, and population growth interacted as reproductive matters, stimulating the emergence and evolution of population policies for a new country.

The early laws show what all laws show: lawmakers' worries about what ordinary people will do if their behavior is not regulated; that is, these early laws let us glimpse what people were actually doing in an unregulated state. The first colonial laws forbidding marriage between white women and African men, for example, suggest that at the time these laws were enacted, white women were forming intimate relations including marriage, with Africans, even with enslaved African men. If these everyday relations had been rare or nonexistent, laws like these would have been unnecessary.

Early laws governing sex and pregnancy show that founding fathers and the leaders of subsequent generations believed that regulated reproduction was crucial to building and keeping the United States a "white country." Laws ensured that whites alone were citizens and property owners and that enslaved Africans were—both as labor and as property—the producers but not the owners of wealth. Laws, along with military victories, ensured that Native populations were "removed" from properties that whites could use to consolidate their holdings and their territorial supremacy. All these laws depended on defining and policing race by regulating reproductive practices and thereby racializing the nation.

Controlling reproduction was a key strategy for enforcing the distinction between races; for establishing the legal meanings of racial difference; for defining the special degradations of nonwhite women; and for facilitating white supremacy, generally. The reproductive capacity of enslaved and Native women was the resource whites relied on to produce an enslaved labor force, to produce and transmit property and wealth across generations, to consolidate white control over land in North America, and to produce a class of human beings who, in their ineligibility for citizenship, underwrote the exclusivity and value of white citizenship.

The process of constructing a system of chattel slavery took more than 150 years on the North American continent, over which time legislators steadily alienated black men from citizenship rights of many kinds. Yet the serial decisions—the formal and informal regulations—to treat black women as breeders constituted their ultimate degradation and provided the foundations of the slavery system. The first of these laws, enacted in the Virginia Colony in 1662, was An Act Defining the Status of Mulatto Bastards. Turning English common law on its head, the law adapted an old practice to meet the labor and other needs of an underpopulated land: if the father was enslaved and the mother was enslaved, the child would be born enslaved. If the father was a free man and the mother was enslaved, the child would be born enslaved, not free as common law would decree. Clearly, after 1662 the fertility of the enslaved woman became the basis for the increase of human property. Just as clearly, the new law encouraged white men, now excused from punishment for sexual exploitation of their human property, to seek power, pleasure, property, and profit by impregnating enslaved women.[2]

These laws also clarified, hardened, and policed racial boundaries. They (and laws against interracial marriage) set the pattern for colonial and then state legislatures for nearly two hundred years—and beyond—laying the foundation for an enduring reproductive politics that sexualized race and racialized sex.

Children born under these laws embodied the enslaved mother's sexual degradation and also her degradation as human property, reproducing a commodity, not a person, at the will of the owner. Her womb became a manufactory, a site of value only if it churned out product. Reproduction under enslavement depended on denying enslaved women a cluster of racialized reproductive privileges, including the right to choose one's sexual and procreative partner; the right to give birth to a child, not a commodity; the right to value as a person, not as an engine of reproduction; the right to marry and thus to have a so-called legitimate child; the right to form, sustain, and protect one's family; the right to be the mother of one's child.[3]

In the early national period, as major resources were devoted both to expanding slavery and killing Native people, no racial distinction was more crucial than the one accorded to the white married mother. This figure embodied an exclusionary racialized ideal. She was instructed to engage in marital sexual relations in order to give birth to white citizens for a white republic. Above all, white mothers were proscriptively paragons of white purity, the necessary opposite of the degraded and enslaved brood mare.[4]

The racialization of reproductive politics was complicated by questions regarding the sex and reproductive activities of poor white women, especially those unprotected by husbands and fathers. Like black women, their wombs produced the future laboring class, mostly in the free labor North, generating wealth for white property and business owners. Poor domestics and women who bore children without marrying were now the only white women still prosecuted for crimes such as infanticide and fornication. (The sexual and reproductive behavior and misbehavior of patriarchally protected white women could now be treated as a private, family matter, another privilege of race and class.) Poor white women whose sexual and reproductive behavior blurred the distinctions between slaves and free women could be mortified (whipped) in public, a mark and a definition of race and racial degradation. Poor white women could be chaste or unchaste. As servants and other low employees, they were likely to be viewed as "unchaste," their class status opening them to sexual exploitation and marking them as sexually degraded, like slaves.[5]

Ultimately, prescriptive literature, public humiliation, and racial ideologies were not enough to maintain the chastity of Liberty's Daughters. In the first half of the nineteenth century, powerful religious, medical, and legal authorities asserted that white chastity depended on legally enforcing the strictest relationship between sex and reproduction through the criminalization of abortion and contraception. Evangelical Protestant authorities of the period proclaiming sacred motherhood; newly minted physicians expressing concern about safety; social commentators speaking as champions of the future citizens of the republic: all these magisterial voices and others invoked abortion and contraception as a crime against chastity, against the most defining attribute of white womanhood in this slaveholding country.[6]

Contraception and abortion were emblems of unchaste and unfaithful women because they suggested the impossibility of knowing whether one's child was legitimate or illegitimate—a condition that would, intolerably, make white children the same as enslaved children. In the emancipation era, white male religious authorities organized strenuously to force their vision of *the race* onto the bodies of white women. Doctors and legislators ensured that no matter the outcome of the Civil War, the future of slavery, or the demographic viability of the Indian, laws over women's bodies would make sure that white women would remain chaste and thus remain white.

I am arguing here that among the first principles of reproductive politics—a key arena for forging nation—were these:

- Dominion over women's reproductive bodies was crucial to solving basic labor and power relations on the North American continent and then in the United States.
- The maintenance and extension of racial slavery required racialized laws and policies governing women's sexual and reproductive lives.
- Likewise and reciprocally, the construction and maintenance of white supremacy depended on the same.
- Maintaining stratified and conditional citizenship for women (in comparison to less conditioned white, male citizenship) was equally dependent on these laws and policies.

At the end of the narrative above, I mention that nineteenth-century laws and policies outlawing contraception and abortion, understood as key to enforcing white chastity, provided a powerful opportunity for religious authorities to claim a stake in secular policy formation; and reciprocally, these church-based initiatives laid down a pattern for politicians and policymakers to incorporate religious accommodation into secular law and policy.

As North American colonial authorities and then the US government deployed these "first principles," they were typically unconcerned with women's lives, their bodies, their needs, their decision-making capacities, their rights, and their human dignity. Rather they defined reproduction as key to solving social problems—labor needs, immigration, the so-called population bomb of the mid-twentieth century, poverty, racial discrimination, crime. Solutions flowed from the conviction that social, economic, political, and moral problems besetting the United States could be solved best if laws and policies and public opinion pressed women to reproduce or not in ways that were consistent with a particular version of the country's real needs.

This brief overview of "first principles" of US population policy demonstrates the government's long-standing interest in setting and managing demographic goals. It also provides context for considering government activities in the early 1960s—in the midst of intense concerns about threats to American society associated with the "population explosion," the civil rights movement, and the reach of Soviet power—when politicians and policymakers placed the just-released birth control pill and other technological developments at the heart of innovative population policies while relying on old principles.

Postwar Global Management

The US government moved to include population policies and politics in its global management portfolio after World War II. And after years of uneven movement toward this goal, the United Nations took the first steps in building a case for an international response to the postwar world "population crisis," releasing major documents in 1953 and then in 1958 that drew attention to the growing gap between the birth rate and the death rate, globally, showing how new antibiotics, the use of DDT, and other public health developments were extending the lives of millions in underdeveloped countries.[7] In 1962, the UN General Assembly concluded its first debate on population with a resolution calling for intensified international cooperation to develop effective solutions to this world crisis.[8] The following year, underscoring the leadership of the UN, the first Asian population conference, in New Delhi, appealed to all UN agencies "to provide technological assistance on request for research and action" to limit excess population growth.[9] And in September 1965, the UN World Population Conference convened in Belgrade, where 835 demographers, statisticians, physicians, urban planners, and other population experts from eighty-eight countries met for two weeks and presented more than five hundred papers, most of which argued in one way or another that the choice facing the world was "population control or disaster."[10]

At the UN and then in the United States, the nature of policy debates about global (and domestic) demographics—chiefly, whose reproductive capacity should be honored (implicitly) and whose constrained (explicitly), and how—gyrated in the 1950s and early 1960s between "humanitarian" discourses and "containment" discourses. The former maintained that fertility control facilitated self-governance, democratic values, peace, and prosperity. The latter argued that population control was a key Cold War weapon against starvation, poverty, and other forms of instability that, if not checked, would strengthen the appeal of communism around the world.

But before the United States, itself, would become an official advocate of population control, its political leaders had to overcome their reluctance to speak publicly about this matter.[11] Within one week in 1959, both President Dwight Eisenhower, in his last year in office, and the presidential hopeful, John Kennedy, explicitly excluded a role for the US government as a supplier of birth control assistance to "foreign nations." Both were worried about offending Catholics, both the church and voters, and also about associating themselves with matters of sex. Eisenhower, who had taken quiet steps to promote population control in poor countries and who would later publicly support these programs, famously said now, "I cannot imagine anything more emphatically a subject that is not a proper political or governmental activity or function or responsibility." And Kennedy declared that it was "not in the national interest" for the United States to promote this activity overseas, characterizing such work in anticolonialist terms, as "a mean paternalism" and "a great psychological mistake for us to appear to advocate limitation of the black or brown or yellow peoples whose population is increasing no faster than in the United States."[12] Just four years later, reflecting one of those shockingly quick public opinion flip-flops common in the United States, President Lyndon Johnson signed the first legislation to provide foreign aid funds for birth control.[13] Now the United States had both feet in: population control quickly occupied the heart of US-sponsored development programs overseas. These projects frequently used a containment discourse, justifying modification of female fertility in the name of anticommunism.[14]

US funding for population projects became an increasingly urgent foreign-policy priority in the mid-1960s as a world food shortage—a "genuine Malthusian crisis"—took shape, the result of meteorological events and agriculture "backwardness," in addition to population surges and declining death rates. President Johnson, citing "the growing scarcity in world resources" committed US ingenuity and cash to what became Food for Freedom, a program recognizing "for the first time, as a matter of United States policy, the world population explosion's relationship to the world food crisis." Food for Freedom aimed to solve hunger problems that might otherwise "fan agitation for revolution in areas not now Communist." Even more gravely, a top US military figure linked famine and overpopulation to World War III, warning that "if man is not able to control population growth when people are starving, uneducated, and without housing, they will eventually explode.... They can be manipulated by any despot with a promise of something better. ... Unless we solve that prime problem of population, there will be war." By the late 1960s, the Agency for International Development (USAID) became key in this domain, developing contracts with universities and other research groups, conducting policy meetings, and translating the results into "feasible projects" for disseminating birth control programs, globally.[15]

Defining the Terms

At home, feasible projects had been funded and managed so far only by nongovernmental entities, chiefly foundations and privately funded birth control organizations.[16] But now in the 1960s, with the US government beginning to invest massively in programs abroad, a number of politicians and policymakers began to press for federally funded domestic programs as well. For one thing, some key participants challenged government officials to explain how they could justify telling other countries what to do about their population problem when so "little was being done on a Federal level in this country."[17] John D. Rockefeller III, the most influential and munificent private supporter of global population programs, remarked that overpopulation wasn't "somebody else's problem" any more, or just for "people in far-off countries." Rockefeller cited numerous negative impacts of population increase in the United States, but, pointing toward the imminent emergence of a broadly embraced environmental argument for birth control, and referencing his family's special contribution, he particularly lamented a future when too large a population would necessitate "rigid rationing of the use of national parks."[18]

But in the mid-1960s in the midst of the civil rights movement, the most powerful and prevalent argument for federal funding to support domestic population control was a ghetto-containment position, one that I've argued elsewhere was deployed in part as a backlash position against the human rights claims of African Americans and the efficacy of civil rights legislation.[19] Proponents of the containment position cited the especially high birth rates of Negroes who "reproduced beyond the capacity of the economy to handle," naming escalating welfare costs, overcrowded urban schools, urban crime, and other ills linked to the impacts of the Great Migration. Zoologist Marston Bates worried about "prostitution, alcoholism, drug addiction, and violence" in the ghetto, remarking on this urban construct's resemblance to "the behavioral sink of rats, except that [the ghetto] continues to reproduce."[20] A New York reporter lamenting the lack of congruence between the "revolutionary research in birth control methods" taking place in that city in the 1960s and the complete lack of access to contraception among ghetto women noted that "mothers [there] still live in as dark ignorance as the peasants of a remote Pakistani village." Another commentator regretted that Negroes in Georgia reproduced more rampantly than women in India. The US government feared Soviet interest in both nations and preferred to emphasize America, itself, as invulnerable, featuring images of modern, self-governing individuals and communities, not pockets of "dark ignorance."[21]

But by the early 1960s, many social scientists and policymakers spoke frequently about the problems of the dark ignorance in the ghetto, with its rampant sexuality, overpopulation, and poverty. Before this time, some argued, population growth had been widely treated as "a natural phenomenon, more like hurricanes than like a crime." Now a number of sociologists and others subscribed to a "demographic orthodoxy," the conviction that rapid population growth, like criminal activity, harmed social well-being. Experts and authorities had an obligation to control it, they said.[22]

One medical expert of many who defined contraception as a panacea for social ills wrote, "Until the production of unwanted babies by incompetent and irresponsible parents is checked, welfare babies [will continue to] grow up in slums and under such conditions that they can seldom escape becoming delinquents or public charges."[23] Other commentators expressed faith that birth control would create a "more bearable environment" for the poor themselves. But all population controllers imagined a straightforward strategy: the poor must be made to understand that they could end their own poverty the same way they created it, through fertility.[24]

The focus was, however, seldom on quality of life for the poor themselves. Lawyer and chief administrator of the Tennessee Valley Authority and the Atomic Energy Commission, David Lilienthal, appropriating a new specialty, wrote a long piece for the *New York Times Magazine* in the mid-1960s foreseeing the impact of overpopulation in the United States. He described "a nightmare," the strangulation of basic systems—education, water, air quality, and power.[25] Secretary of the Interior Morris K. Udall foresaw extensive labor unrest, crime, and mental illness. And Senator Ernest Gruening (D-Ark.), one of the country's chief champions of population control, joined those who associated the threat of overpopulation with the threat posed by our totalitarian enemies, warning that too many Americans would lead to a loss "of freedoms, privileges, and good life we enjoy today."[26]

Typically in the 1960s during the height of the civil rights movement, demographers and journalists as well as politicians and policymakers pointed out that "nonwhites" and poor people had higher birth rates than other groups and blamed the nation's "acute problems" on this fact.[27] One biologist compared the "'turfs' of urban gangs" to "territories of wild animals," exclaiming with general hopelessness that "we must do something." Hugh

Moore, an American businessman and key funder of the movement to curb overpopulation, committed his resources to an unforgettable series of racist subway ads in New York, asking, "Have you been mugged today?" Moore linked urban crowding to crime to African American males as a tactic to make his population project "real."[28]

Even more socially noxious than the mugger was the mugger's baby-self, the "unwanted infant," a trope used in ways that connoted both rubbish and a future juvenile delinquent. Unwanted children were individuals who "should have never been born, for the simple reason that there was no one to take decent care of them. They are," wrote anthropologist Ashley Montagu, "a disaster." Senator Milliard Tydings (D-Md.) defined the social consequences of the unwanted child, a future juvenile delinquent: "When there comes into the world a child who is not wanted and who is not planned for, serious trouble and social unrest are invited."[29] In a country focused with anxiety and hope on the black freedom struggle, African American fertility—the engine of the slavery regime and southern wealth for centuries—was now a national scourge.[30] Moreover, according to Philip M. Hauser, an administrator of the US census, a leading scholar of urban studies and demography, and a president of the American Sociological Association, the high fertility rates of African Americans "gravely exacerbated" racial tensions in the United States and constituted a more serious impediment to equal rights than other forces, such as white racism.[31]

In the population control literature of the time, the "unwanted child" was the offspring of "irresponsible reproduction."[32] To the extent that commentators imagined the mother of this child, she was typically described as engaging in a "hit-and-run sex life," ignoring contraceptive possibilities and incapable of caring for the child who was destined, in any case, to become a public charge, perspectives that led to the emergence of the iconic "welfare queen" a few years later.[33] (An early adopter, James R. Dumpson, the first African American welfare commissioner in the United States when he took over the New York City department in 1959, told a *New York Daily News* reporter the next year that "ladies have babies by assorted gentlemen so as to keep the relief checks growing fatter each year.")[34]

Together, the twinned tropes "unwanted child" and "irresponsible woman" structured policy initiatives premised on restrictive parenting and coercive contraception. According to many public health officials, the IUD, newly available, promised the best solution for the poor and the "low intelligence group," better than the pill because it required "no thought or action on the part of the patient."[35] Summing up a prominent strain of population-control activism in the 1960s, Garrett Hardin, an influential antigrowth ecologist who promoted abortion and sometimes even famine and war as antidotes to what he described as disastrous rates of population growth, observed, "If parenthood is a right, population control is impossible. If parenthood is only a privilege . . . then there is hope for mankind."[36]

On the ground, in the clinic, population policy sometimes materialized—in a cultural moment that saw the psychologizing of everything—as a psychological fitness test for both contraceptive use and motherhood. A Planned Parenthood official described a state health department plan that called for staffing family-planning clinics with "fourteen psychiatrists, social workers, psychologists, and genetic counselors, but only five obstetricians." The official asked incredulously, "Is it contemplated, as a matter of public policy that each impoverished woman must undergo a psychiatric, social, and genetic work-up before she is examined and issued a prescription for pills?"[37]

Some policymakers, sensing that the Catholic Church was less adamantly opposed to contraception in the early 1960s than earlier, now defined "the culture of poverty" as the most virulent challenge to population control. They decried a way of life in which women were mired in serial pregnancies while their sexual partners insisted that manliness required unprotected intercourse and that robust reproduction was the only way to fight "genocide."[38] But, in fact, close studies of these matters in major cities around the country showed that poor women and men did not want more children than their middle-class counterparts. Poor women reported that they had children beyond the number they desired because they didn't know how not to get pregnant. Scholars, welfare administrators, public health physicians, and others who looked directly into this matter reported that poor women were absolutely eager for birth control. A North Carolina welfare official said that when his office sent "homemakers" out into the community, knocking on doors, asking the woman of the house if she wanted to "learn something about this subject," no one "ever had one door slammed in [her] face." In Chicago, the number of patients, most of them poor, who sought birth control at Planned Parenthood clinics doubled in the first nine months of 1962.[39]

A report from Detroit a few years later, after the rebellion of the summer of 1967, showed a stunning commitment among the poor to contraception. Dr. Gary London, a physician attached to the Office of Economic Opportunity, reported, "We have a family planning program, funded by OEO, which is situated in the heart of the riot area. On the block where that building is situated, all the buildings on the block were burned and gutted [during the urban rebellion in July 1967], except for two. When the smoke cleared there, they found two unburned buildings. One was the Negro church . . . the other was the family planning center."[40]

Also in the mid-1960s, the Amalgamated Laundry Workers, representing many African American women and in part responding to these workers' demands, launched a free birth control program through its health center.[41] Even the South Christian Leadership Council, belying the common wisdom that African American men were uniformly opposed to birth control for religious, political, and masculinist reasons, issued a publication at this time, "To Make Family Planning Available to the Southern Negro though Education, Motivation, and Implementation of Available Services."[42]

Urelia Bowen, a deeply respected African American social worker in Philadelphia, commented on the dilemma facing African American women who wanted to plan their pregnancies in the mid-1960s—and on the political context that shaped their intimate lives. "It is too bad . . . the thrust for world population control should have come at the height of the civil rights struggle," she said, and that Negro women are "the targets." She pointed out that these women, like others, "don't want children they can't take care of, but we are afraid to trust you when your offered help has so often turned out to be exploitation. Negroes are never going to accept birth control . . . from the hands of white people," she concluded, so the only solution was for people in the community to be trained in family planning themselves.[43]

These activists and ordinary people challenged the harsh, ascendant orthodoxies that identified population control and privileged parenthood as the antidote to poverty and our damaged democracy. Another challenger was Michael Harrington, although his challenge was implicit. Harrington's book, *The Other America: Poverty in the United States* (1962) was a broadly influential assessment of the forces harming the lives of millions in the United States. Most notably, this slim volume shaped the thinking of Presidents John Kennedy and Lyndon Johnson, as well as the designers of specific Great Society programs.[44] They were drawn to Harrington's thesis that all the foundational structures of society in the United States—economic, political, cultural, psychological—were both racist and indifferent to the needs of the old and other vulnerable people. The poor could only achieve well-being, and the United States could only achieve moral high ground, he argued, when new policies and programs repaired basic structures.[45]

In the early months of the mass phase of the civil rights movement, Harrington's jeremiad exhorted Americans to face the shame of widespread privation. The point here is that he cited segregation as a cause of poverty. He cited the invisibility of the poor, bad welfare policies with inadequate and poorly distributed benefits, deindustrialization, unemployment, mental illness, and racism—but not overpopulation.

Harrington's comprehensive thesis was bolstered from a number of directions. Mollie Orshansky, a government economist and inventor of the Orshansky Poverty Threshold, a system of assessing the relationship between household income and poverty, cited "disadvantage in the hiring hall" and discrimination, generally, as proof that "something more than family planning is involved."[46] Prominent sociologist Herbert Gans agreed, suggesting that if academics and activists, politicians, and policymakers truly wanted to eliminate poverty, they should study the economy, society, and the "cultural patterns" of the *affluent* that "combine to keep people in poverty," rather than focusing endlessly on the "supposed sexual overactivity and irresponsibility of the lower classes" and on whether or not the poor could be convinced to use birth control.[47] The analyses of Harrington, Orshansky, Gans, and others did exert influence at the highest level of government but did not derail the appeal of population control as a focus for strategic planning. The enduring strength of the population control perspective, even during the most receptive period for human rights claims, is a key to understanding the short life of liberal reform in this era. It is also key to understanding the resurgence of conservative social policy that followed the diminishment of Great Society programs.

The "Contraception-Adoption Explosion"

Lyndon B. Johnson assumed the presidency in 1963 facing an array of political and policy matters that engaged population policy, as it was defined at the time. He took early policy positions on poverty, juvenile delinquency, urban decay, and crime; the citizenship status of African Americans; government relations with the Catholic Church; the status of women, including how to define the government's role in supervising access to contraception (a policy area that increasingly involved discussions about what to do regarding the high incidence of illegal abortion); threats to environmental quality and basic services including housing, water, air, and food; and welfare provision and taxes. Johnson was also dealing from the first with questions about the nature of US leadership in the world population crisis, and with the relationship between overpopulation in developing countries and opportunities of communist governments to extend their global power. In the case of each of these policy areas, population policy generally, and birth control specifically, were implicated, even while parts of the polity still grappled with matters of religion, morality, and the legality of distribution and sale of contraceptive materials.[48]

At the same time, a growing number of government entities, foundations, academics, new academic centers, and NGOs were endorsing and supporting efforts to make contraception a key component of public health provision in the United States.[49] In fact, even without a huge financial commitment from the federal government, the United States was on the threshold of a "contraception-adoption explosion."[50] What amounted to a broad-based "population lobby" now pressed Johnson to make a public commitment to fighting overpopulation and committing government resources to birth control programs, which he eventually did—with one sentence—in his 1965 State of the Union address. He said, "I will seek new ways to use our knowledge to help deal with the explosion in world population and the growing scarcity of world resources."[51] Later the same year, at the twentieth-year anniversary celebration of the United Nations in San Francisco, President Johnson explicitly included the United States in what he now defined not as a moral, religious, legal, or feminist matter, but as an economistic project for all: "Let us in all our lands—including this land—face forthrightly the multiplying problems of our multiplying populations. . . . Let us act on the fact that less than five dollars invested in population control is worth one hundred dollars in economic growth."[52] At the same time, LBJ, the first American president to speak positively about birth control, linked the project to the structures and aims of his War on Poverty, indicating his belief that a technological solution—the IUD, the birth control pill—could play a role—or could be a tactic—in ameliorating the many social ills he had been called on to address.[53]

Johnson made his public statements in 1965, the same year that the Supreme Court, with *Griswold v. Connecticut*, responded to the "contraception-adoption explosion" and finally removed all state barriers to the distribution and sale of contraceptives. These events together with a huge public demand for contraception also stimulated a rash of legislation. Ten bills concerning access to birth control were introduced in Congress in that year, and soon thereafter, Congress inserted—some might say "hid"—funding for family planning in Social Security legislation—a significant "first" and a signal that the government embraced the premise that contraceptive use meant fewer babies, which, in turn, meant less poverty.[54]

President Johnson recognized that he would have to deal carefully with Catholic bishops regarding these policy developments. According to policy historian Donald Critchlow, "The administration consciously decided to pursue a strategy that downplayed public fanfare for an incremental approach to family planning," even while Johnson, himself, kept close contact with a number of Catholic bishops.[55] The tactic seemed to work. By the late 1960s, when Department of Health, Education, and Welfare (HEW) funding for family planning was almost seven times what it had been in 1965, the bishops tacitly agreed to stand aside and accept government policies as long as they were not coercive and as long as they included a "natural" option, often referred to by Catholic spokespersons as a "choice."[56] Now family planning had the support of former presidents, of President Johnson, congressional majorities, eleven state legislatures, and, according to a number of polls, the majority of Catholics in the United States.[57] With approval expressed in so many quarters, and for so many different reasons, family planning was no longer a "fringe" cause in the United States.[58]

The last stage in the process of birth control's transition from secret to fringe to mainstream policy issue is especially well documented because of the extensive US Senate hearings on the "population crisis," 1965–67, and the full, published records of these hearings. Called and conducted by Alaska Democrat senator Ernest Gruening, the hearings brought together politicians, academics, journalists, religious leaders, local and state family-planning program designers and providers, ordinary citizens, and others, to speak about the importance of contraception in the modern world and the need for government structures to combat overpopulation.

Testifiers generally focused on one of the following arguments for robust government involvement: (1) the need to rebalance population growth and economic growth, as well as the birth rate and the death rate, before a resource catastrophe occurred; (2) the need to attend to quality-of-life issues before total environmental degradation ensued; (3) the need to relieve population pressure as a strategy to protect democracy and capitalism and to prevent the hungry masses from turning to communism; (4) the need to protect the United States from committing "race suicide"; (5) the need to provide poor women with access to the same contraceptive options as middle-class women already had. A few testifiers took the contrarian position that population growth was still good for the country because each additional American was a producer and a consumer adding to the country's technological and economic expansion.[59]

Throughout the many sessions, over several years, politicians spoke movingly about their vast relief that the "climate of opinion had changed" and that contraception was no longer unmentionable in the halls of Congress. Representative John Conyers (D-Mich.) expressed his satisfaction that the time had passed when "foreign governments had an easier time obtaining Federal assistance for their birth control programs than [do] our own States and cities."[60] Katherine B. Oettinger, longtime chief of the Children's Bureau in the Department of Health, Education, and Welfare (and later, deputy assistant secretary for family planning and population), asked, "Who of us would have dreamed that the propelling forces of the last few years could have so nearly erased the strictures surrounding the right of individuals to plan their families?" She also reported on the explosion of public family-planning programs in states between 1964 and 1967, noting how "encouraged" she was "that declines in birth rates are registered in areas of the lowest educational attainment—the highest incidence of poverty—the highest rates of illegitimacy—the largest number of children per family." And physicians came to testify in celebration of the "upsurge of interest," informing Congress about the medical schools and the schools of public health, nursing, and social work that were adding contraception to their curricula.[61]

The hearing records provide information about US media treatment of contraception in the early and mid-1960s, highlighting, for example, that in 1963 newspaper stories about birth control rose 55 percent over the previous year, to 11,699 articles.[62] But everywhere in the 1960s, birth control was on public display, from television's *CBS Reports*, to advertisements in the New York subways that urged riders to attend the World's Fair and learn about our population crisis and what to do about it, to casual disclosers that Arthur Godfrey and other celebrities had "confessed" their sterilizations in public, making the practice more acceptable.[63] *Look*, *Good Housekeeping*, and most other mass circulation periodicals, reaching millions of Americans, began to regularly publish articles addressing such topics as "Can We End the Battle over Birth Control?"[64]

Newsweeklies regularly reported on birth control clinics ("new ones open every week") and the economics of contraception versus welfare.[65] And major newspapers published Gallup poll numbers tracking public opinion regarding the population crisis and attitudes toward and use of birth control. In 1965, for example, the *Washington Post* reported that 78 percent of Catholics and 81 percent of all Americans favored the dissemination of information about contraception.[66] In the same year, Gallup found that most Americans thought that the population crisis was a "more serious problem" facing the country than crime, racial discrimination, international communism, or the threat of nuclear war. Only the need to aid "backward nations"—a related matter—was assessed as "more serious."[67] President Johnson, Congress, and the Supreme Court largely followed and did not lead public opinion regarding the acceptability and efficacy of contraception. The federal government did, however, carve out a leading role in making birth control available to poor women.[68]

Population Control versus Human Rights

Insofar as the federal government had a population policy by the mid-1960s—and there were prominent observers who denied that such a thing existed—the Johnson administration did not take pains to define its policy intentions precisely. At various times President Johnson and others in his administration claimed support for contraception in the name of national security, public health, the integrity of the family, reduction of welfare costs, the freedom to choose, and individual conscience.[69] But its most visible programs clearly associated family planning with the War on Poverty and defined contraception as "the most effective anti-poverty program" available and as "a crucial part of community efforts to reduce poverty and dependency." In 1965, the Department of the Interior became the first federal agency to offer direct birth control information and materials; the department's target population was Native American females on reservations and other poor, indigenous women. The next year, the OEO funded fifty-five programs around the country for indigent, married women.[70]

Federal funders created partnerships with state commissions, local social service agencies, nonprofit organizations, and courts, all of which intensified the government's commitment to use contraception to target the "dependency" problem of poor women. State and local organizations often defined their commitment to contraception in terms similar to those used by the Illinois Commission on Birth Control, which supported "birth prevention" and urged the Illinois Department of Public Aid to protect the state's coffers by dispensing birth control materials. The commission stressed that even though these activities facilitated the separation of sex and pregnancy, the commission did not judge them to be at odds with the department's opposition to promiscuity, fornication, and immorality.[71]

In the same vein, a prominent public health officer in Kentucky explained that "tubal ligation" amounted to "preventative welfare," and a study of court-ordered sterilization in the mid-1960s found new support for this option "among [authorities] seeking to reduce the welfare rolls."[72] Judges, as well as the general public, cited frequent federal policy pronouncements associating contraception with the end of dependency—and also repeated prominently circulated "quotations" of poor women to make sense of federal and state population policy during the civil rights era. For example, in trying to explain the sharp increases in welfare expenditures in New York, Philadelphia, and other cities in the mid-1960s, a commentator wrote that the best way to understand policy exigencies was to attend to the answer of the unwed mother when she was asked by a judge, after she had freely admitted that each of her eight children had a different father, to name her real boyfriend. "My real boyfriend, she allegedly replied, 'is the welfare department.'"[73] Ultimately in the second half of the 1960s, under federal guidance, most states moved to tie eligibility for family-planning programs to economic vulnerability and receipt of public assistance.[74]

In this context, policy discussions and public opinion regarding contraception for the poor did not easily incorporate the concept of "rights." In fact, at the height of the civil rights movement, the period between the 1963 March on Washington and the assassination of Dr. Martin Luther King Jr. in 1968, policymakers named "television scenes of large impoverished families" as "the best advertisement" for contraception for the poor. These images stimulated the largely white viewers to "see" a racialized view of "the undeserving poor" and to affirm attitudes about the "duty" of women in this group to use birth control. By late 1965, responding both to what their constituents wanted and to the widely accepted notion that poor women had the "duty" to use birth control, the OEO began to finance medical personnel, clinics, and contraceptive materials for poor women, targeting inner-city neighborhoods.[75] Two years later, convinced that "permissive" welfare policies were underwriting too much sex and too many births among poor women, Congress "quietly," and with bipartisan support, passed legislation mandating that 6 percent of its total HEW appropriation be earmarked for family-planning programs based in welfare departments and allowed the federal government for the first time to give grants to voluntary agencies such as Planned Parenthood. Government policy now squarely focused on contraception as a tool for "breaking the cycle of poverty" and added programs to reverse the rising rates of out-of-wedlock pregnancy among poor teenagers.[76]

Despite new structures and new funding, prominent advocates of contraception, population control, and the development of robust, effective public policy still lamented the uneven state of services in the United States and counseled government authorities to "learn from developing nations [how] to equalize family planning opportunities for all citizens."[77] Organizations as different as the American Public Welfare Association and the National Academy of Sciences spoke out now about contraception as a basic and fundamental "human right." The chairman of the board of the New York Life Insurance Company asked, "Would anyone today think of withholding polio shots" because a family could not afford medical care? Since no one would countenance such a thing as that, then why, the executive asked, should lack of income prevent access to another medical necessity, contraception?[78] Others pointed out that when public policy served the birth control needs of the poor, it was only "providing them with the same right that our better educated and more affluent population now has access to as a matter of course."[79] This language briefly allied contraception with the equal rights claims of the civil rights movement.

A close reading of public policy statements in this period, however, shows a rapid transition from references to contraception as a "human rights" issue to language defining contraception as an individual "choice." Senator Gruening, well versed in all the arguments favoring birth control at the time, noted that government policies and programs were most frequently justified in terms of "freedom-of-information, civil libertarian, personal-freedom-of-choice arguments."[80] These terms were compatible not with the human rights or equal rights thrusts of the civil rights movement, but with its calls for equal opportunity and individual responsibility.

Wilbur J. Cohen, a longtime architect of social welfare programs and President Johnson's undersecretary of HEW in 1965, linked the formation of an "intelligent choice" about birth control to the fulfillment of the promises of citizenship in a democracy.[81] And Cohen's boss, John Gardner, the secretary of HEW, defined "freedom of choice" as a path for allowing all persons to "choose in accordance with the dictates of their consciences."[82] In the spring of 1966, President Johnson regularly spoke about "the freedom to choose" and, forging new policy, decreed that the government would now provide contraceptive services to any woman who chose to use birth control, the unmarried as well as the married. "Choosing" contraception thus assigned the achievement of lofty policy goals to fertile women and their "choices" about fertility. Diminishing discrimination, reducing the size of government, leveling class differences, and fostering personal responsibility: all of these noble goals were now the responsibility of poor women.[83]

Indeed, the idea of "choice" as the necessary basis of human dignity was frequently at the center of numerous policy goals of the era, including key conservative goals such as enabling and ennobling postwar consumerism ("free market" choice); sanctioning resistance to government coercion, in this case, to school integration ("school choice"); and as the rallying cry of the Catholic Church's demand for public accommodation of the church's opposition to birth control ("free choice").[84]

When commentators and politicians spoke about the power of "choice" in this era, they often imagined *themselves* as choice-makers, picking among policy options, presenting predetermined "choices" to "these people" who "we need to teach . . . something about family responsibility." Their rhetoric also reflected a strong commitment to the idea that constraining the fertility of poor women was a public good, essentially a strategy for refreshing and reinvigorating our democratic society.[85]

Frequently, it was hard to detect women's interests in the matter at all. State commissions on birth control rarely included women.[86] When the national educational television channel, NET, broadcast a series on the important issues of the day to one hundred affiliated stations in 1965, the episode on birth control explored many reasons to support birth control; no "women's issues" were among these.[87] The "illegitimacy" crisis was foregrounded in the policy arena not because it revealed the problems that young, unmarried, and resourceless women faced because of their gender, race, and class. Rather, "illegitimate" pregnancy was defined as the cause of the welfare-dependency disaster and a signal of the breakdown of the American family.[88] Liberal champions of birth control for the poor argued that if employers opened more jobs to women, birth rates would go down, casting antidiscrimination as an instrumental—economic and demographic—not a feminist, goal.[89] Garrett Hardin proposed that population control "must be exerted through females," by which he meant the sterilization of poor women. Nodding condescendingly toward feminism in 1970, he apologized in advance for his analysis, which "the Women's Liberation Movement may not like."[90]

As political scientist Rosalind Petchesky has pointed out, population control enthusiasts hoped to impose contraception on poor women without threatening any prevailing family, sexual, or gender-related norms. Or, one must add, any racial norms.[91] Ultimately, proponents of population control policy relied most heavily on racialized tropes, the "unwanted child" and "irresponsible parent," and on hysterical language (for example, "the screaming need" to depress population growth), tropes that became key to mobilizing resistance against goals of the civil rights movement and to building the antiwelfare movement of the next several generations.[92] A critical mass of resisters in legislatures and elsewhere championed the idea that the sexual and reproductive irresponsibility of African Americans and other poor women of color was the engine driving America's decline; birth control was more ameliorative than voting, in this view.

The Church in the Public Square

In the early 1960s, choice and constraint were at war with each other in the Catholic Church too, with consequences for population policy in the United States. Here I will look at three aspects of this relationship between the Catholic Church and the contraception issue in the 1960s. First I consider the context in which American Catholics reported in the 1960s that they were making up their own minds about the ethics of contraception and about whether to constrain their own fertility, no matter what the church decreed. Second, I will look at the ways that the Catholic Church used contraception, inimical to the church's teachings, to claim a considerable stake for the church in public policy formation. And, finally, I consider how Congress, as well as state and local legislatures, responded to the church's claim, incorporating a religious accommodation in legislation and policy dealing with contraception, even while the political culture was moving toward legalization for women of all ages and marital statuses, and at the same time that evangelical movements were gathering adherents and influence.[93]

In 1959, the United States Conference of Catholic Bishops, rejecting the procontraception direction of public policy, issued this fiat: "Catholics will not support any public assistance, either at home or abroad, to promote artificial birth prevention."[94] Soon thereafter, with Vatican II, a reflection of Pope John XXIII's interest in shaping church doctrine and principles relevant to the modern world, doors appeared to be opening that had until then seemed "forever shut." The church's new emphasis on marriage as a "love relationship," among other developments, suggested that previous dicta about conception and contraception were "less frozen" than before and that church leaders had begun debating these matters with "amazing frankness."[95]

Ordinary American Catholics took heed and took license. By 1964 over half admitted they managed their fertility artificially.[96] In the spring of that year, Pope Paul VI acknowledged that the church was subjecting contraception "to study, as wide and profound as possible." In the meantime, observers reported that an "uncertain silence" prevailed in Rome.[97]

In the States, however, no such silence prevailed. Throughout the early 1960s, prominent American Catholics spoke out, making a variety of arguments supporting contraception, including claims based on tolerance and pluralism, democratic values, cost-benefit analysis, and management of the population explosion. Mass media magazines featured essays such as "Let's Take Birth Control out of Politics" in which a Catholic cleric promoted the idea of an ecumenical solution—"a sound public policy" suitable for Catholics, Protestants, and Jews.[98] In the *National Review*, Garry Wills's "Catholics and Population" expressed a Catholic's view that the rights of majorities and minorities must both be protected and begged his coreligionists not to "inflict their code on others."[99] A Chicago businessman and chairman of the Illinois Public Aid Commission testified before Congress as a Catholic and as a man who understood "the ruinous cost" of ignoring the economic benefits of birth control. He said, "It is not at all out of order to count . . . [the] dollars involved."[100] Catholic sociologist Paul Mundy also spoke in Congress, praising the current willingness of Catholic moralists to take "the facts of demographics" into consideration when they weighed the church's commitment to unimpeded fertility against "the magnitude of the [demographic] problems ahead."[101]

Other prominent American Catholics were concerned that widespread use of birth control was a dangerous challenge to the prestige—the infallibility—of the church and suggested a more modern and progressive view of the source of institutional authority.[102] Cardinal Cushing of Boston, for example, linked the intelligence of the average, committed Catholic with independent thinking and tolerance regarding contraception, a claim that brought editorial praise from *Life* as an expression in concert with a less authoritarian church and "an enlarged area of personal responsibility and choice."[103] Indeed, others argued that a number of recent events—the election of a Catholic president, Vatican II, the population explosion, and the pill—together encouraged American Catholics to "make their own individual choices on matters of public policy and private morality over the years to come."[104]

Two books by Catholics authors—Dr. John Rock's *The Time Has Come: A Catholic Doctor's Proposals to End the Battle over Birth Control* (1963) and Notre Dame law professor John T. Noonan Jr.'s *Contraception* (1965)—were widely read, reviewed, and prominently labeled "breakthrough" and "intellectual watershed" events, respectively.[105] Rock pointed out that the pill, newly marketed, was simply a more precisely targeted variant of the church-approved "rhythm method" and no more unnatural than restricting sex to "safe" periods. Noonan's book had such a dramatic impact in part because the author laid out scores of "substantial shifts" in the church's approach to contraception over two thousand years. Noonan also argued that Catholic opposition to birth control in this country was often less a matter of theological doctrine than one of politics and ethnic enmity.[106]

As Catholics all over the world debated the future of the church's position on contraception—many expecting that the church would soon find contraception a "licit" practice—the pope asked American bishops for a period of silence. But again, Americans were not silent. The winter 1965 issue of *Theological Studies*, the Jesuit journal, included a plea that Catholics be permitted to use oral contraceptives.[107] And a representative to the Family Life Bureau of the National Catholic Welfare Conference (the precursor of today's United States Conference of Catholic Bishops), Monsigneur John Knott, worried publicly about the fact that American Catholics were rebelling against church authority by resisting marital advice from priests. He also objected strongly to government policies that pressed poor people, a naturally disorganized population, he felt, to use contraception successfully.[108]

Typically, Catholic clerics greeted the various public policy initiatives with deep ambivalence, finding some parts "in accord with the Church's teachings and other parts not." Judging from prominently published opinion pieces, many took the position that public funding of contraception—a practice inimical to church teaching—could be tolerable, if policies guaranteed a lack of coercion and preserved individual moral choice.[109] Also, a key group of Catholic authorities who generally opposed contraception aligned themselves with the concept of "responsible parenthood," despite the racial and ethnic overtones associated with this prevailing policy goal. These developments reflected the fact that by 1965, or even slightly earlier, the "population lobby" had built a scientific and religious coalition that normalized public discussion of the population crisis, contraception, and public policy. The coalition was committed to the task of both accommodating and co-opting the concerns of American Catholics.[110] A solid majority of American Catholics themselves came to "believe that the Church [would] eventually approve of some method of birth control such as the use of pills."[111]

At the highest levels of the church, however, there were calls for federal government neutrality in the United States; for the church to remain consistent in its opposition to contraception; and for maintaining the prevailing "contraception mentality."[112] Catholics leaders promoted a negative stand on contraception as a crucial "bulwark against abortion"; liberal Catholics were painfully aware that advocates of contraception were often advocates of legal abortion. One observed, "Every time Alan Guttmacher [a physician and a leading voice in the movement for legalization of abortion] opens his mouth, we shudder."[113]

Citing the church's position on contraception in 1965 as causing "anguish of many souls," Pope Paul VI appointed an advisory committee to study the matter.[114] As Rome brought together fifty-seven persons from twenty countries "to give [the church] guidance without ambiguity," the pope addressed the United Nations, declaring his own position: All countries must strive "to multiply bread so that it suffices for the tables of mankind . . . and not rather favor an artificial control of birth, which would . . . diminish the number of guests at the banquet of life.[115] By 1966 the committee was "in turmoil," and members were quoted expressing their impatience and frustration. One asserted, "The Church is in chaos" over its position on contraception.[116]

Ultimately, in mid-1968 the pope issued *Humanae Vitae*, the culmination of his four-year consideration of birth control that amounted to "an unequivocal No." The faithful would continue to be restricted to sexual abstinence and the rhythm method, even while the document elevated conjugal love for its own sake to equal status with procreation, a development that created, for some, hope for more changes to come.[117]

The US government was not constrained by the silence, the internal chaos, or the ultimate "no" coming from Rome. After the Supreme Court's *Griswold v. Connecticut* ruling overturned all state laws limiting access to contraception, the federal government was increasingly willing to extend its population-control activities deep into the arenas of public health and welfare policy. At the same time, there is no question but that women's liberation organizations and other feminist groups supplied massive support for legalization of both contraception and abortion, for sexual and gender equality, and for the idea that managing one's fertility is not incompatible with being a Catholic. Mainstream feminist activism insisted that "family planning" and "population control" politics give way to a politics of "reproductive rights" and then a politics of "choice."

Mainstream feminist work proceeded, however, across an historical period—the late 1960s through the 1990s—and in a dominant political context that was anti-welfare provision, anti-immigration, and in permanent backlash mode against the gains of the civil rights movement. The chief spokespersons for these positions increasingly drew on evangelical and Catholic religiosity to oppose women's reproductive rights as well as the other human rights advances of the 1960s and 1970s.

The severe contraction of welfare provision, along with welfare innovations such as "family caps," the promulgation of Hyde Amendment (which explicitly renewed religious accommodation in the arena of reproductive policy), sterilization practice in some hospitals, and court-mandated contraception in this period demonstrated a continuation of racialized population policy in the United States. When solid, ongoing mainstream feminist opposition to assaults on the reproductive dignity of poor women did not emerge, the possibilities of a unified women's movement for reproductive safety and dignity for all women was weakened.

Since the 1960s, at the point when women gained technological "choices" about fertility, politicians and policymakers have cast poor women, particularly poor women of color who have "too many" children as bad choice-makers, endangering the economics, the environment, the "original culture" of America. Backlash politics in the 1970s and 1980s against the gains of the civil rights movement often focused on—and aimed to constrain—the reproductive lives of African American, Puerto Rican, and Mexican American women, using public housing and childcare policies, welfare exclusions, and even sterilization and incarceration. Welfare reform legislation in the mid-1990s was built on the proposition that single pregnancy and motherhood are the chief causes of poverty and criminality in the United States. Politicians and others interested in "reforming" welfare belittled other explanations such as low wages, scarce and expensive housing, lack of medical insurance, and daycare programs.

The alleged reproductive behavior of bad choice-makers has been used in recent years to justify revitalizing population-control policy in the United States. Since the mid-1990s, twenty-four states have implemented a child exclusion or family cap rule in their welfare programs; most exclude all cash benefits for a newborn. Today fifteen states maintain these exclusions that try to function as a form of population control, limiting the number of children born to families receiving public aid. The nine states that repealed a family cap law looked at projected fiscal impacts of lifetime costs associated with being raised in poverty, as well as data showing that family caps increase child poverty and do not lower birth rates of poor women, most of whom already have low birth rates.[118]

Critics have called the impulse to enact and sustain these kinds of legislative punishments "explicitly racially linked," because they define certain children as valueless and expensive; and they define certain mothers as reproductively irresponsible, engaged in "gaming the system," essentially prostitutes, having sex (and children) for cash. These characterizations and the public policies and judicial decisions that institutionalize them are based on the modern equivalents of "first principles." They resonate with the conditions of those who mothered under slavery, women who were denied the right to have a so-called legitimate child; the right to form, sustain, and protect their families; the right to be the mother of their own children. As these first principles continue to animate reproductive politics in the United States, proponents find themselves facing the emergent energy of the reproductive justice movement that makes plain the ways that matters of fertility are embedded within multiple struggles for social justice.

Notes

1 The first section of this chapter draws from chapter 1 of my book *Pregnancy and Power: A Short History of Reproductive Politics in America* (New York: New York University Press, 2005).

2 Carol Berkin and Leslie Horowitz, *Women's Voices, Women's Lives: Documents in Early American History* (Boston: Northeastern University Press, 1998), 13; Paul Finkelman, "Crimes of Love, Misdemeanors of Passion: The Regulation of Race and Sex in the Colonial South," in *The Devil's Lane: Sex and Race in the Early South*, ed. Catherine Clinton and Michele Gillespie (New York: Oxford University Press, 1977), 128.

3. See Kathleen Brown, *Good Wives, Nasty Wenches, and Anxious Patriarchs* (Chapel Hill: University of North Carolina Press, 1996); Brenda Stevenson, "Distress and Discord in Virginia Slave Families, 1930–1860," in *In Joy and Sorrow: Women, Family, and Marriage in the Victorian South*, ed. Carol Bleser (New York: Oxford University Press, 1992), 46; Marie Jenkins Schwartz, *Born in Bondage: Growing*

Up Enslaved in the Antebellum South (Cambridge, Mass.: Harvard University Press, 1992).

4. Linda K. Kerber, *Women of the Republic: Intellect and Ideology in Revolutionary America* (Chapel Hill: University of North Carolina Press, 1980); Mary Beth Norton, *Liberty's Daughters: The Revolutionary Experience of American Women, 1750–1800* (Ithaca, N.Y.: Cornell University Press, 1980); and Ruth H. Block, "American Feminine Ideals in Transition: The Rise of the Moral Mother, 1785–1815," *Feminist Studies* 4 (1978): 101–26.
5. Cornelia Hughes Dayton, *Women before the Bar: Gender, Law, and Society in Connecticut, 1639–1789* (Chapel Hill: University of North Carolina Press, 1995).
6. See, for example, Catherine Clinton, "Wallowing in a Swamp of Sin: Parson Weems, Sex, and Murder in Early South Carolina," in Clinton and Gillespie, *Devil's Lane*; Catherine Beecher, "Treatise on Domestic Economy," excerpted in *Root of Bitterness: Documents on the Social History of American Women*, ed. Nancy Cott, Jeanne Boydston, Anne Braude, Lori D. Ginzberg, and Molly Ladd-Taylor, 2nd ed. (Boston: Northeastern University Press, 1996), 132–37; Nancy Cott, "Passionlessness: An Interpretation of Victorian Sexual Identity, 1790–1850," *Signs* 4 (1978): 219–36; Cornelia Hughes Dayton, "Taking the Trade: Abortion and Gender Relations in an Eighteenth Century New England Village," *William and Mary Quarterly* 48 (1991): 19–49.
7. *Determinants and Consequences of Population Trends* (New York: United Nations, 1953); *The Future Growth of World Population*, Population Studies No. 28 (New York: United Nations Department of Social and Economic Affairs, 1958).
8. "UN as Center of Population Focus," *New York Times*, December 18, 1962.
9. Phyllis T. Piotrow, *World Population Crisis: The United States Response* (New York: Praeger, 1973), 82.
10. Population Crisis: Hearings on Foreign Expenditures of the Committee on Government Operations United States Senate, 89th Congress, lst sess., Part 3B, 1931–67 (Washington, D.C.: U.S. Government Printing Office, 1966).
11. See Donald T. Critchlow, *Intended Consequences: Birth Control, Abortion, and the Federal Government in Modern America* (New York: Oxford University Press, 1999), chap. 1 for a discussion of the prefederal, largely foundation-driven, efforts to control world population, before the mid-1960s.
12. Quoted in Critchlow, *Intended Consequences*, 44; *New York Times*, November 28, 1959, 1. Eisenhower publicly announced his new opinions in "Let's Be Honest with Ourselves," *Saturday Evening Post*, October 26, 1963, 27.
13. Foreign Assistance Act of 1963 (Public Law 88-205).
14. Linda Gordon, *Woman's Body, Woman's Right: Birth Control in America* (New York: Penguin, 1976), 346; Laura Briggs, *Reproducing Empire: Race, Sex, Science, and U.S. Imperialism in Puerto Rico* (Berkeley: University of California Press, 2002), 140. Regarding the connection between population control and American Cold War anticommunism, see William Draper's definition of population control as "decreasing opportunities for communist political and

economic domination in developing nations," quoted in Critchlow, *Intended Consequences,* 43; and Hugh Moore's letter to John D. Rockefeller III: "We are not primarily interested in the sociological or humanitarian aspects of birth control. We are interested in the use which the Communists make of hungry people in their drive to conquer the earth." Quoted in Crichlow, 9. Both Draper and Moore were private citizens and engines behind the involvement of American foundations in birth control programs overseas. Both were extremely well connected and highly influential in this domain throughout the 1950s and much of the 1960s.

15. Piotrow, *World Population Crisis*, 112–13; *New York Times*, January 5, 1965, 16; William Paddock and Paul Paddock, "Today Hungry Nations, Tomorrow Starving Nations," in *The American Population Debate*, ed. Daniel Callahan (New York: Doubleday, 1971), 110–32; US Congress, House of Representatives, Committee on Agriculture, The Food for Freedom Act of 1966, Report No. 1558, 89th Congress, 2nd sess. (Washington, D.C., 1966), 4; "The World's Biggest Problem," *U.S. News and World Report*, October 4, 1965; US Congress, Senate, Subcommittee on Foreign Aid Expenditures of the Committee on Government Operations, Population Crisis, 89th Congress, 1st sess., Part 2, 382; Piotrow, *World Population Crisis*, 83–84; also see Piotrow, Parts II, III, and IV regarding the history of the role assumed by the Agency for International Development (USAID) in creating and disseminating population control programs in this era.
16. Matthew Connelly, *Fatal Conception: The Struggle to Control World Population* (Cambridge, Mass.: Belknap Press of Harvard University Press, 2008), 179–80.
17. "William M. Blair, Udall Offers Aid on Birth Control, First Direct U.S. Help to go to Reservation Indians and Other Wards of Interior," *New York Times*, June 20, 1965.
18. John D. Rockefeller III, "The Hidden Crisis," *Look*, February 9, 1965, 75–80.
19. Rickie Solinger, *Wake Up Little Susie: Single Pregnancy and Race before* Roe v. Wade (New York: Routledge, 1992, 2000), chap. 7.
20. Marston Bates, "Crowded People," in Callahan, *The American Population Debate*, 81.
21. Testimony of Edwin Bayley, Population Crisis, 89th Congress, 1st sess., Part 3B, 1981; Testimony of Dr. Robert Nelson, Population Crisis, 89th Congress, 1st sess., Part 2B, 1074; Testimony of Marion Sanders, Population Crisis, 89th Congress, 1st sess., 1980.
22. Patrick Ball and John Wilmoth, "Population in the Popular Press, 1946–1987: Toward a Theory of Social Problems," Center for Research on Social Organization, Working Paper Series No. 404, May 1991, 4.
23. H. Curtis Wood Jr., MD, "Unplanned Children: Whose Burden? Whose Care?" *Medical Opinion and Review*, March 1966, 28–35.
24. Population Crisis, Hearings, 89th Congress, 1st sess., Part 3B, 1179; Larry Bumpass and Charles F. Westoff, "The 'Perfect Contraceptive' Population: Extent

and Implications of Unwanted Fertility in the U.S.," *Science*, September 18, 1970, 1179.

25. David E. Lilienthal, "300,000,000 Americans Would Be Wrong," *New York Times Magazine*, January 9, 1966; also see John B. Calhoun, "Population Density and Social Pathology," in *The Urban Condition: People and Policy in the Metropolis*, ed. Leonard J. Duhl (New York: Basic Books, 1963), 33–43.
26. Morris K. Udall, "Spaceship Earth—Standing Room Only," in Callahan, *The American Population Debate*, 84–95; Ernest Gruening, Population Crisis, Hearings, 89th Congress, 1st sess., Appendix 4, 2244.
27. Robert Cook, ed., "New Patterns in U.S. Fertility," *Population Bulletin*, Population Reference Bureau, September 1964; Philip M. Hauser, *Population Perspectives* (New Brunswick, N.J.: Rutgers University Press, 1960), 158.
28. Bates, "Crowded People," 82; "Crime: Rising Tide, Its Upsurge Stirs a Quest for Causes and Cures," *Newsweek*, August 16, 1965, 21; see Critchlow, *Intended Consequences*, 151.
29. Ashley Montagu, Population Crisis, Hearings, 89th Congress, 1st sess., Part 3A, 1365 and Appendix 4, 2267, 45; also see statement regarding "presumably unwanted children [as]. . . a frequent ingredient in the cycle of poverty," of New York representative James Sheuer, Part I, 419.
30. Rowland Evans and Robert Novak, "Birth De-control," cited in Critchlow, *Intended Consequences*, 75.
31. Philip M. Hauser, Population Crisis, 89th Congress, 2nd sess., Part 1, 109.
32. Rockefeller, "The Hidden Crisis," 80; Hauser, *Population Perspectives*, 171.
33. Jack Shepherd, "Birth Control and the Poor: A Solution—Mecklenburg County, N.C. Challenges the Belief That Birth Control Is for the Rich and Not the Poor," *Look*, April 7, 1964, 63–67; Critchlow, *Intended Consequences*, 124; Dorothy Roberts, *Killing the Black Body: Race, Reproduction, and the Meaning of Liberty* (New York: Pantheon, 1997), 149.
34. Douglas Martin, "James R. Dumpson, a Defender of the Poor, Dies at 103," *New York Times*, November 8, 2012.
35. "Minutes of Advisory Committee on Family Planning," Georgia Department of Public Health, Population Crisis, Hearings, 89th Congress, 1st sess., Appendix 4, 2054.
36. Garrett Hardin, "Parenthood: Right or Privilege," *Science*, July 31, 1970, 427.
37. Frederick S. Jaffe, Population Crisis, 90th Congress, 1st sess., Part 1, 199.
38. See, for example, Frederick S. Jaffe, Population Crisis, Hearings, 89th Congress, 1st sess., Part 1, 199–200.
39. Director, Department of Public Welfare, Mecklenburg County, NC, Population Crisis, Hearings, 89th Congress, 1st sess., Part 3B, 1773; *The Growth of U.S. Population: Analysis of the Problems and Recommendations for Research, Training and Service*, Committee on Population, National Academy of Sciences-National Research Council, Washington, D.C., Publication 1279, 1965; Lois Wille, "The

Tug of War on Birth Control: What It's About," *Chicago Daily News*, September 13–18, 1966, Parts 1, 2, 3, 4.

40. Dr. Gary London, Health Division, Office of Economic Opportunity, Population Crisis, Hearings, 90th Congress, 1st sess., Part 1, 98.
41. *Washington Post*, January 15, 1963, A-5.
42. Critchlow, *Intended Consequences*, 49.
43. Hannah Lees, "The Negro Response to Birth Control," *The Reporter*, May 19, 1966, 46–48; Uvelia Bowen obituary, *Richmond Times-Dispatch*, May 28, 2010.
44. Michael Harrington, *The Other America: Poverty in the United States* (New York: Macmillan, 1962); Maurice Isserman, *The Other American: The Life of Michael Harrington* (New York: Public Affairs, 2001); Maurice Isserman, "Michael Harrington: Warrior on Poverty," *New York Times*, op-ed, June 19, 2009.
45. Harrington, *The Other America*, 71.
46. Mollie Orshansky, "Measuring Poverty," *National Conference on Social Work, 1965* (New York: Columbia University Press, 1965), 218–19; Ben J. Wattenberg with Richard M. Scammon, "Our Population: The Statistics Explosion," *The Reporter*, March 25, 1965, 40–41.
47. Herbert Gans, "Poverty and Culture: Some Basic Questions about Methods of Studying Life Styles of the Poor," prepared for the International Seminar on Poverty, University of Essex, April 1967, quoted by Frederick S. Jaffe, "Family Planning and Public Policy: Is the 'Culture of Poverty' the New Cop-Out?" Population Crisis, Hearings, 90th Congress, 1st sess., Part 1, Attachment B, 195–98; also see Joseph P. Martin, MD, chairman of the board of a birth control clinic in Cleveland, Ohio, Population Crisis, Hearings, 89th Congress, 2nd sess., 165–73.
48. Piotrow, *World Population Crisis*, 232–33; Callahan, *American Population Debate*, xi–xiii.
49. These included the State Department, USAID, the United Nations, the National Institutes of Health, the National Institute of Child Health and Human Development, the World Health Organization, the Senate Foreign Relations Committee, the House Judiciary Committee Subcommittee on Immigration and Population; the National Academy of Sciences Committee on Science and Public Policy, the Georgetown Center for Population Studies, the Harvard School of Public Health Population Institute, and the Ford and Rockefeller Foundations, which had been involved with the population issue for several decades. The American Public Health Association adopted a policy supporting birth control as key to the health programs of federal, state, and local government agencies in 1965. The American Assembly of Columbia University held forums on the population issue around the country in the early 1960s in conjunction with organizations such as the New England Assembly on the Population Dilemma, the Minnesota-Dakotas Assembly, the Southwestern Assembly, the Middle-America Assembly on the Population Dilemma, and others.

50. Donald J. Bogue, *The End of the Population Explosion* (Garden City, N.Y.: Doubleday, 1971), 53.
51. Quoted in Critchlow, *Intended Consequences*, 70–71.
52. "Address in San Francisco," June 25, 1965, *Public Papers of the Presidents of the United States: Lyndon B. Johnson*, 1965, book 2 (Washington, D.C.: U.S. Government Printing Office, 1966), 705.
53. Critchlow, *Intended Consequences*, 84; Piotrow, *World Population Crisis*, 227–28.
54. "Federal Stand on Population Control May Be Nearing," Congressional Fact Sheet on Birth Control, June 11, 1965 (Washington, D.C.: Congressional Quarterly); Critchlow, *Intended Consequences*, 50–51.
55. Donald Critchlow, "Birth Control, Population Control, and Family Planning: An Overview," in *The Politics of Abortion and Birth Control in Historical Perspective*, ed. Donald Critchlow (University Park: Pennsylvania University Press, 1996), 11; also see Piotrow, *World Population Crisis*, 160.
56. Critchlow, *Intended Consequences*, 83.
57. George Gallup, "The Gallup Poll—81% for Dissemination of Birth Control Data," *Washington Post*, January 6, 1965.
58. General William H. Draper Jr., "Americans Take Action in 1965," Population Crisis, 89th Congress, 1st sess., Part 2A, 617; R. Dowse and J. Peel, "The Politics of Birth Control," *Political Studies* 13 (1965): 179–97.
59. Ball and Wilmoth, "Population in the Popular Press," 6.
60. Congressional Record, February 8, 1966, 2438–39; Population Crisis, 89th Congress, lst sess., Appendix 4, 2138.
61. Population Crisis, 90th Congress, 1st sess., Part 1, 50–58; Population Crisis, 89th Congress, 2nd sess., Part 4, 811–15.
62. Population Crisis, 1st sess., Part 3A, 1315; also see Piotrow, *World Population Crisis*, "Periodical Coverage of Birth Control 1915–1969"; "*New York Times* Coverage of Birth Control and Population 1959–1970"; and "Changes in Attitudes and Practice in the 1960s, Attitudes of Catholics toward Making Birth Control Information Available," 21, 22, 26.
63. "Abortion and the Law," an hour-long documentary dealing with the moral, legal, and medical issues associated with the rising incidence of abortion in the United States, on *CBS Reports*, April 5, 1965; quoted in Rockefeller, "The Hidden Crisis," 75; Hardin, "Parenthood," 427.
64. See, for example, John Rock, "Can We End the Battle over Birth Control?" *Good Housekeeping*, July 1961; Father John O'Brien, "Let's Take Birth Control out of Politics," *Look*, October 10, 1961; see Piotrow, *World Population Crisis*, 71.
65. See, for example, *U.S. News and World Report*, May 22, 1965, 65–66.
66. Gallup, "81% for Dissemination."
67. Poll sponsored by the Population Council and reprinted in Population Crisis, 90th Congress, 1st sess., Part 1, 28.
68. See Charles F. Westoff, Robert G. Potter Jr., Philip C. Sagi, and Elliot G. Michler, *Family Growth in Metropolitan America* (Princeton, N.J.: Princeton University

Press, 1961) and Charles F. Westoff, Robert G. Potter Jr., and Philip C. Sagi, *The Third Child* (Princeton, N.J.: Princeton University Press, 1963).

69. Oscar Harkavy, Frederick J. Jaffe, and Samuel M. Wishik, "Family Planning and Public Policy: Who Is Misleading Whom?" in Callahan, *The American Population Debate*, 327–28; Ben Wattenberg, "The Nonsense Explosion," in Callahan, 107.
70. John Gardner, secretary of HEW, quoted in Critchlow, *Intended Consequences*, 77; William M. Blair, "Udall Offers Aid on Birth Control: First Direct U.S. Help to Go to Reservation Indians and Other Wards of Interior," *New York Times*, June 20, 1965.
71. "Report of the Illinois Commission on Birth Control, Resolutions," reprinted in Population Crisis, 89th Congress, 1st sess., Appendix 4, 2060.
72. "Report of the Illinois Commission," 2080; E. Z. Ferster, "Eliminating the Unfit—Is Sterilization the Answer," *Ohio State Law Journal* 27 (1966) 519–633.
73. Wood, "Unplanned Children."
74. Population Crisis, 89th Congress, 1st sess., Appendix 4, 2032.
75. Piotrow, *World Population Crisis*, 91; also see Martin Gilens, *Why Americans Hate Welfare: Race, Media, and the Politics of Anti-Poverty Policy* (Chicago: University of Chicago Press, 1999).
76. Critchlow, *Intended Consequences*, 75–79.
77. Critchlow, *Intended Consequences*, 86.
78. Population Crisis, 89th Congress, 1st sess., Part 3B, 1790 and Appendix 4, 2336.
79. Population Crisis, 89th Congress, 1st sess., Series 2, Part 1, 151.
80. See Piotrow, *World Population Crisis*, 107, quoting Gruening.
81. Wilbur Cohen, June 8, 1965, Population Crisis, Hearings, 89th Congress, 2nd sess., Part 5A, 1196–97.
82. John W. Gardner, "Memorandum to Heads of Operating Agencies," January 1966, reproduced in Hearings on S. 1676, Part 5, 783.
83. See Lyndon B. Johnson, "Health Message to Congress," March 1, 1966; Nan Robertson, "Unwed to Receive Birth Control Aid," *New York Times*, April 1, 1966.
84. See generally, Rickie Solinger, *Beggars and Choosers: How the Politics of Choice Shapes Adoption, Abortion, and Welfare in the United States* (New York: Hill and Wang, 2001).
85. See, for example, Population Crisis, Hearings, 89th Congress, 2nd sess., Part 2B, 1072.
86. See, for example, Population Crisis, 89th Congress, 1st sess., Appendix, Part 4, 2058.
87. *Regional Report: Birth Control*, NET Report, broadcast September 29, 1965; transcript printed in Population Crisis, Hearings, 89th Congress, 1st sess., Part 3B, 1974–86.
88. The growing number of illegitimate pregnancies and births at the time was a particularly important factor in building support for public funding of birth

control. See Population Crisis, Hearings, 89th Congress, 2nd sess., Part 3, 634; Critchlow, *Intended Consequences*, 82.

89. See Albert P. Blaustein, "Considering What Kinds of Laws Would Depress Procreation While Not Violating Great Society Norms," Population Crisis, Hearings, 89th Congress, 2nd sess., Part 2, 468.
90. Hardin, "Parenthood." In "Population Policy: Will Current Programs Succeed," Hardin argued that all the current arguments for population policy were insufficient. He believed that the only successful strategies would require "changes in the structure of the family, in the position of women, and in sexual mores." *Science*, November 10, 1967, 730–39.
91. Rosalind Pollack Petchesky, *Abortion and Woman's Choice: The State, Sexuality, and Reproductive Freedom* (Boston: Northeastern University Press, 1990), 132.
92. Joseph P. Martin, MD, Cleveland, Ohio, Population Crisis, Hearings, 89th Congress, 2nd sess., Part 3, 704.
93. See Leslie Woodcock Tentler for an orientation to this subject. *Catholics and Contraception: An American History* (Ithaca, N.Y.: Cornell University Press, 2004).
94. "Population Planning," reprint of the 1959 statement of the American bishops, November 26, 1959, in *Commonweal*, January 22, 1965. A report on the bishops' statement was provided by the *New York Times* on November 26, 1959, 43. Phyllis Piotrow clarifies the church's previous attempts to align policy with exigency, showing how Pope Pius's encyclical *Casti Connubii*, issued on December 31, 1930, both "denounced contraception and [hinted at a natural method to avoid pregnancy] . . . a doctrinal escape route that soon became a well-traveled highway." Later, in 1951, Pius XII endorsed the "rhythm system" and "specifically expressed hope that science could develop a more secure basis for its use." *World Population Crisis*, 11, 51.
95. See Paul Mundy, "Some Moral and Ethical Aspects of Population Control," reprinted in Population Crisis, Hearings, 89th Congress, 1st sess., Part 3A, 1538–39; John Cogley, "The Catholic Church Reconsiders Birth Control," *New York Times Magazine*, June 20, 1965; Steven M. Spender, "The Birth Control Revolution," *Saturday Evening Post*, January 15, 1966, 21ff.
96. Robert E. Hall, MD, "The Church and the Pill," *Nation*, October 5, 1964, 191–93.
97. Piotrow, *World Population Crisis*, 108.
98. O'Brien, "Let's Take Birth Control," 67.
99. Garry Wills, "Catholics and Population," *National Review*, July 27, 1965.
100. Arnold Harold Maremont, President, Maremont Corp., Chicago, congressional testimony, Population Crisis, Hearings, 89th Congress, 2nd sess., Part 3, 692.
101. Mundy, "Moral and Ethical Aspects," 1539.
102. See, for example, Lois R. Chevalier, "The Secret Drama behind the Pope's Momentous Decision on Birth Control," *Ladies Home Journal*, March 1966, 79ff.
103. Cushing is quoted in Cogley, "Catholic Church Reconsiders"; *Life* editorialized, "Cushing speaks with a peculiarly American voice, but his remarkable statement is in accord with the trend of Pope John's Aggorniamento toward less

authoritarianism and an enlarged area of personal responsibility and choice." "Population Explosion and Anti-Babyism," *Life*, April 23, 1965, 6.

104. John A. Schnittker, "The Catholic as Citizen," congressional testimony, Population Crisis, Hearing, 89th Congress, 2nd sess., Part 5B, 1545–48.
105. John Rock, *The Time Has Come: A Catholic Doctor's Proposals to End the Battle over Birth Control* (New York: Knopf, 1963); John T. Noonan Jr., *Contraception* (Cambridge, Mass.: Harvard University Press, 1965); Thomas K. Burch, "Landmark Work on Contraception," book review, *Harper's*, August 1965, 113; a review of John Rock's book was featured in *Time*, and Rock was on the cover of *Newsweek*. His book was endorsed by Cardinal Cushing in the *New York Times Book Review*, April 20, 1965, 6.
106. Burch, "Landmark Work on Contraception," 113; Schnittker, "The Catholic as Citizen," 1548.
107. Joseph Roddy, "Catholic Revolution: Will It Bring a New Church Policy on Birth Control? Can the Bishops Cut Down the Pope's Supremacy?" *Look*, February 9, 1965, 22–27.
108. Monsigneur John Knott, quoted in Critchlow, *Intended Consequences*, 128.
109. Rev. Dexter L. Hanley SJ Div., Institute of Law, Human Rights and Social Values, Georgetown University Law Center, gathered fifty cosigners to endorse his position that the church could support use of public funds for family planning and birth control "so long as human life and person rights are safe-guarded and no coercion or pressure is exerted against individual moral choice." Reprinted in Population Crisis, Hearings, 89th Congress, 1st sess., Appendix 4, 2193; "Priest Raps State Policy on Family Policy," *Morning Record of Meriden, CT*, February 13, 1967.
110. Piotrow, *World Population Crisis*, 72; *Regional Report: Birth Control*, in Population Crisis, Hearings, 89th Congress, 1st sess., Part 3-B, Exhibit 237, 1974.
111. "Catholics See Approval of Birth Control," *Washington Post*, August 20, 1965. The article reports on a recently released Gallup poll that found that more than six of ten Catholics "believe that the Church will eventually approve of some method of birth control such as the use of pills." Fifty-five percent of respondents believed the church would express approval within five years; 26 percent predicted approval by 1975.
112. The archbishop of Washington, D.C., delivered a sermon at St. Matthew's Cathedral in late August 1965 calling for federal government neutrality on matters involving birth control, at least until "word was received from the Holy Father in Rome." Quoted in Population Crisis, Hearings, 89th Congress, 1st sess., Part 3A, 1313; Chevalier, "The Secret Drama," provides the voice of a typical church conservative: "If the Church could have misled the faithful on so grave a matter [as birth control], with such grave consequences and for so long a period, what value or reliability could be attached to any of her moral teachings?" Another added, "If anyone thinks the Church is going to stand up and

say the hell with *Casti Connubii*, he's crazy." Also see Cogley, "Catholic Church Reconsiders."

113. Chevalier, "The Secret Drama."
114. Quoted in Cogley, "Catholic Church Reconsiders"; Robert McClory, *Turning Point: The Inside Story of the Papal Birth Control Commission, and How* Humanae Vitae *Changed the Life of Patty Crowley and the Future of the Church* (New York: Crossroads, 1997).
115. Chevalier, "The Secret Drama"; the pope is quoted in Steven M. Spencer, "The Birth Control Revolution," *Saturday Evening Post*, January 15, 1966, 21ff.
116. Chevalier, "The Secret Drama."
117. Piotrow, *Global Population Crisis*, 159–60; *New York Times*, July 30, 1968, 1, 30.
118. Elena R. Gutiérrez, "Bringing Families Out of 'Cap'tivity: The Need to Repeal the CALWORKS Maximum Family Grant Rule," Issue Brief, Center on Reproductive Rights and Justice, Berkeley Law, April 2013.

3

From Abortion to ART

A History of Conflict between the State and the Women's Reproductive Rights Movement in Japan after World War II

MIHO OGINO

In the long "postwar" period from the end of World War II to the present, Japan's reproductive policy has undergone several changes according to its population circumstances. In the early years, Japanese women welcomed the state's initiative in legalization of abortion and introduction of family planning. But when the state tried in the 1970s and 1980s to curtail women's right to abortion, women activists rallied for reproductive freedom. The Eugenic Protection Law, enacted in 1948, legalized both abortion and eugenic sterilization. This law remained the focus of conflicts between the state, the women's reproductive rights movement, and the disability rights movement well into the late 1990s. As a consequence of the bitter historical experiences related to the EPL, many Japanese feminists are critical of the recent development regarding assisted reproductive technologies and legitimization of their use in the name of "woman's right to self-determination" or "woman's right to choose."

Abortion under the Eugenic Protection Law

In 1945, Japan was defeated in World War II and was placed under occupation of the Allied Powers, actually the United States, until the restoration of sovereignty in 1952. During the war, under the slogan of "Bear and multiply," the Japanese government encouraged women to get married young and bear five children to fulfill the "national mission of motherhood." Any attempt to access birth control or abortion was forbidden and considered an unpatriotic deed. With the end of the war, however, Japan quickly faced a serious problem of overpopulation. While the national territory of Japan was drastically reduced by the loss of overseas colonies including Korea and Manchuria, large numbers of people returned from abroad as demobilized soldiers or repatriated citizens to the devastated land, and the postwar baby boom ensued. Amid starvation and lack of dwellings and work, many resorted to illegal abortion and child abandonment. In this context, there was such a great demand for abortion that not only obstetrician-gynecologists but also surgeons, dentists, ex-corpsmen, and even veterinarians performed illegal abortions under what many have claimed were filthy and dangerous conditions.

The GHQ/SCAP (General Headquarters / Supreme Command of Allied Powers), headed by General Douglas MacArthur, paid close attention to the population issue from the onset of occupation. Personnel feared that the new population density would cause food shortages and other difficulties and might lead to antagonism and rioting against occupying forces, giving the Soviet Union a pretext to interfere in the occupation administration. Some of the American consultants to SCAP, especially Warren Thompson, a demographer, strongly recommended that SCAP adopt an explicit birth control program to reduce the birth rate and help the economic recovery of Japan. MacArthur preferred to take a stance of "protective neutralism," stating that decisions about birth control should rest entirely with Japanese and not with the occupation administration. But some senior officers, including Crawford Sams, chief of SCAP's Public Health and Welfare Section, disagreed and tried to pressure the Japanese government to take effective measures to curb population increase.[1] The Japanese government, however, was unenthusiastic about introducing birth control in the early stages of occupation. In this state of national emergency the Eugenic Protection Law was enacted in 1948.

In Japan, induced abortion was criminalized by the Penal Code in 1880, and this Anti-Abortion Law (Datai-zai) persists even today. Under the new Eugenic Protection Law (Yusei hogo-ho), however, induced abortion was justified when the continuation of the pregnancy or childbirth would be physically detrimental to the health of the mother, and also for eugenic reasons or rape, or because the pregnant woman or her spouse had leprosy. In the next year, economic reasons were added as another legitimate ground for abortion. A further amendment in 1952 made the previously required investigation of each abortion applicant by a local screening committee unnecessary. Now the consent of the woman's husband and the attending obstetrician-gynecologist were the only prerequisites for the operation. The penal code that banned abortion was never repealed, but since the interpretation of what constitutes "economic reasons" tended to be very broad and loose, prosecution under the Anti-Abortion Law became extremely rare. Thus, unlike women in many other countries who had to fight a long battle for their right to safe and legal abortions, the government granted Japanese women de facto abortion-on-request as a means of fertility control.

Under the new law, the number of induced abortions reported by ob-gyns doubled between 1949 and 1950 and rose sharply thereafter to the peak of more than 1.17 million cases in 1955. It is highly probable that the actual number of abortions was far greater than the reported cases because ob-gyns in private practice tended to underreport the number of operations to escape taxation. In concert with the skyrocketing of abortion cases, the birth rate dropped quickly from 34.3 per thousand in 1947 to 28.1 in 1950 and 17.2 in 1957.[2] That is, the birth rate was reduced by half within a decade. Undoubtedly, such a great success in suppressing fertility (and its role in subsequent economic reconstruction) would have been impossible, or at least much retarded, without the liberalization of abortion, a policy change that became a quick fix for alleviating the burden of a rapidly growing population.

In addition to the pressing need for population control in the postdefeat confusion, such a prompt and smooth "popularization" of abortion might be explained by the lack of strong opposition from Japanese religious groups. Even though the two major religions, Shinto and Buddhism, do not approve of the act of abortion, they scarcely voiced opposition openly and fiercely at the time, as the Catholic Church and some Protestant denominations in Western countries, including United States, have done. Both Shinto and Buddhism, and accordingly many laypeople in Japan, consider abortion as a kind of "necessary evil" that we human beings cannot help committing sometimes in our lives.

Development of the Family-Planning Movement

In contrast with prompt postwar legalization of abortion and ready acceptance of it at the popular level, the decision to introduce contraception and family planning at the government level lagged behind, although both birth control activists from the prewar era and the media vocally expressed concern about the population problem and the need for birth control. On the American side, not SCAP itself, but groups such as the Rockefeller Foundation and the Pathfinder Fund, which was founded by Clarence Gamble, an out-and-out eugenicist and birth control activist, showed strong interest in the population problem in Japan and East Asia. These groups exerted influence upon Japanese activists and bureaucrats who were interested in the population issue; they provided financial support for research and introduced family planning in Japan.

Yoshio Koya, the head of the National Institute of Public Health (Kokuritsu Koshueisei-in), was one of the protégés of these American patrons. Even though he had played a key role in the formulation of pronatalist population policies during wartime, he turned into a proponent of family planning after Japan's defeat, claiming that reducing the birth rate was necessary for the recovery of the Japanese economy. But being a staunch supporter of eugenics, he was afraid that if only people of the educated middle class and above practiced contraception, and lower-class citizens did not, this would eventually lead to "reverse selection," that is, degeneration of the overall quality of the population. During a tour of public health programs in the United States in 1950, Yoshio Koya was impressed that public health nurses in Mississippi cleverly conveyed general education about personal health and family planning while working with African American clients.[3] After Koya returned to Japan, he conducted experimental family-planning education programs from 1950 to 1953. First he targeted three villages in Yamanashi and Kanagawa Prefectures, then households of coal miners in Tohoku area, and finally households of welfare recipients in Tokyo, proving, he argued, that even citizens of lower and poor strata were able to implement contraception satisfactorily if they were given contraceptive methods and motivation to suit their respective conditions by means of systematic and thorough guidance.[4]

Because of Koya's success, together with a growing fear of health hazards associated with abortions, cabinet members decided in 1951 to support contraception over abortion and to begin training public health nurses and midwives as contraception counselors.

In the private sector, the Kawasaki Plant of the Nippon Kokan, a big steel company, created its own population control strategy at this time. In 1952 the company began to engage in family-planning guidance, targeting the families of its employees as a part of its labor management strategy, instructing employees in the benefits of raising fewer children in a planned manner through their practice of contraception. The result would be healthier wives and happier homes; and the husbands would be able to devote themselves to their work free from care. This would result in a reduction in accidents during work time, and for the company an alleviation of such financial burdens as medical expenses and family allowances.

The guidance activity was conducted under the instruction of the Population Association of Japan (Zaidan Hojin Jinko Mondai Kenkyukai), a semiofficial body in close relation to the National Institute of Population Problems (Kokuritsu Jinko-mondai Kenkyujo). The employees' wives living in company housing were divided into groups of five, with one housewife appointed as a facilitator. Contraception instructors hired by the company carried out group guidance sessions with each group, followed by detailed one-to-one guidance by means of individual visits. When the instructors made the rounds of women's houses, they sold contraceptive items such as condoms and spermicides at cost.[5]

The Nippon Kokan trial worked well, leading to a rapid reduction in the number of both births and abortions and in the number of workers' injuries during production work, all of which resulted in economic benefits for the company. Seeing this success, a growing number of other big corporations launched similar programs, now dubbed the "New Lifestyle Movement." By September 1956, twenty-four large public and private corporations, including Toyota Automobiles and Japan National Railways, had adopted the program, and twenty-five additional corporations were making preparations to offer their employees these services. It is estimated that a total of 115 corporate bodies had joined the movement by 1964 and the number of employees targeted amounted to 1.7 million.[6]

The New Lifestyle Movement offered employees' wives family-planning instruction and also various educational activities including instruction in management of the family budget, cooking, knitting, sewing, flower arrangement, childcare, and domestic hygiene as well as field trips, according to the housewives' requests. Housewives believed that all of these activities would make their lives happier, as well as more efficient and comfortable. The wives of corporate employees were thus mobilized and situated as the shadow workforce of corporate society: they contributed to workplace productivity through their efforts at rational household management. The typical family in postwar Japan, consisting of a "salary man" husband, a stay-at-home wife, and, on average, two children who would be educated to become the next generation of worker/housewife, was the product of the family-planning movement that the government and large firms jointly implemented. Supported by postwar economic growth, this type of family model spread throughout Japanese society as the ideal way of family life for "the new age."

Even in rural villages, where it was more difficult to carry out such systemic and large-scale family-planning guidance, authorities mobilized midwives and public health nurses who committed themselves earnestly to this new mission of disseminating fertility control to village housewives and their husbands. In agricultural villages, having a large number of children was gradually becoming less advantageous than before because of rapid changes to the industrial structure and the possibility that farmland would be subdivided among offspring because of the amendment to the inheritance law enacted in 1948. Consequently, although a little later than in urban areas, the move toward bearing fewer children gained popularity even in local areas, and the percentage of couples practicing contraception steadily increased from the late 1950s into the 1970s. Moreover, with the diffusion of contraception, the reported number of abortions gradually declined.

Condoms versus the Pill

In spite of the expansion of women's use of contraceptives, abortion remained an important strategy for fertility control. One of the peculiar characteristics of the Japanese fertility control pattern was that the great majority of women who had abortions were neither teenagers nor unmarried, as in many other countries, but were married women.[7] This high marital abortion rate was related to another peculiarity of Japanese contraceptive pattern: that is, long and widespread popularity of condoms.

According to the *Mainichi-shimbun* family-planning surveys, conducted biannually by this major newspaper from 1950 to 2000, condoms have always been the principal contraceptive method, supported by as many as 70 to 80 percent of the respondents.[8] For many Japanese, in fact, contraception is almost synonymous with condoms. The rhythm method or periodic abstinence, and coitus interruptus (withdrawal) follow the condom in popularity, at much lower levels respectively. Many couples use these methods in combination: that is, they calculate "dangerous days" of the female cycle and use condoms only on those days, a less than reliable method resulting in frequent unwanted pregnancies, as well as abortion as a backup solution. Other barrier methods such as the diaphragm are barely known in Japan, and only a small percentage of contraceptors use either IUDs or sterilization. The oral contraceptive pill was not officially approved in Japan until 1999. This is a contraceptive pattern remarkably different from other developed countries, where there is a higher degree of variation of methods and also where hormone contraceptives are more popular.

Why are condoms so popular in Japan? No doubt condoms are both simple to use and safe, causing no side effects and preventing sexually transmitted diseases including HIV/AIDS. They are sufficiently effective if they are used correctly and consistently and can be purchased easily. The quality of condoms is excellent in Japan. But there are additional reasons. In the Japanese family-planning movement, both family-planning organizations and contraceptive counselors have actively promoted the use of condoms because, in addition to the product's convenience, the profit from condom sales has constituted a major source of their income. When the pill was first released in the US market in 1960, family-planning advocates in Japan strongly opposed its introduction in Japan. The pill, they claimed, was so easy to use that it would undermine the use of condoms, a practice then successfully taking root in Japanese society. Furthermore, champions of conservative social traditions, including a number of politicians, opposed the pill, fearful it would promote "sexual immorality," especially among unmarried women. And doctors were unenthusiastic about the distribution of the pill because they were making profits by providing abortions. So the Ministry of Health decided to withhold official approval of the pill as a contraceptive method, initially, officials said, because of the fear of side effects, and later in the late 1980s and 1990s on the pretext that the liberalization of the pill would lead to the spread of HIV/AIDS, which was, in fact, not a major event in Japan.

There is one more important reason for the delay in the pill's official approval: Japanese women, especially feminists flourishing in the women's liberation movement in the 1970s, were very skeptical of the pill. Although there was a small group of women called Chu-pi-ren (abbreviation for a long name meaning Women's Liberation Union Opposing the Anti-Abortion Law and Demanding Liberalization of the Pill) that campaigned flamboyantly for a few years for the official approval of the pill and total abolition of the abortion law, they were rather exceptional among the Japanese women's liberationists.

For example, Yoko Akiyama, one of the early liberationists, reported in a feminist magazine in 1971 that, after having taken the pill experimentally for two months, she and her friends had concluded that, because of the subtle side effects they experienced, "we neither want to take it any longer nor recommend it to other women. The pill is *in no way a good thing*."[9] Also, members of Lib Shinjuku Center, a commune of women in Tokyo, wrote: "If a woman takes the pill because she cannot ask her man to use a condom, she is not taking the pill but is taken by it."[10] In addition to the fear of side effects and inequality of responsibility between a man and a woman, the "unnaturalness" of artificially controlling the natural rhythm of a woman's body by taking synthetic hormones for a long period of time was often cited as yet another reason for its disapproval.

Even in the late 1980s, women who were preparing to start a women's health clinic in Osaka published a book entitled *The Pill: We Don't Choose It*. The authors argue that the pill would not liberate women or improve women's conditions because it places the entire burden and responsibility for contraception on women alone. The pill is a method more liberating for men than for women, they argue. They explain that efficacy and side effects are merely some of the conditions to evaluate in deciding which contraceptive method to use. What is most important is communication between a man and a woman and the sharing of responsibility by a couple. Thus, they maintain that the condom, used in combination with the rhythm method, is the better method, from this viewpoint.

The authors cautioned, "In order not to fail with this method (i.e., condom with rhythm), women must learn about the structure and function of their bodies, know their own sexual reactions, master the correct usage of each method, and build good relations with their partners so that they can use it correctly. At first sight it seems to be a roundabout way, but to live means to keep on making such efforts."[11]

Thus, the pill was generally greeted with suspicion in Japanese feminist circles. It was perceived as a symbol of medical and patriarchal control of women's bodies rather than a mark of women's liberation and sexual autonomy. It was only in the mid-1990s that many feminist activists came to agree that women should have the right to choose contraceptive methods based on enough information about both the merits and demerits of each method and that the unavailability of low-dose pills widely used in other countries is an infringement of Japanese women's reproductive rights. The voices demanding prompt official approval of the pill gained momentum, and finally in 1999, following the very rapid approval of Viagra for men, the pill was officially approved as a contraceptive. However, more than a decade after the approval, the number of pill users in Japan still remains very small, 3.4 percent in 2011, while condom users amount to 85.5 percent.[12] Meanwhile, the reported number of abortions has been decreasing continuously and declined to 202,106 cases in 2011.[13] That is approximately 18 percent of the peak number recorded in 1955.

The Antiabortion Campaigns and the Collision of Women's Rights and Disability Rights

In Japan, the right to having a legal abortion was not won through women's struggle; rather, the state, for its own political reasons, granted women this right. Therefore, the abortion "right" can be modified or withdrawn by the state, as circumstances change. Since the mid-1970s, both the number of births and the birth rate have been declining constantly. At the same time, robust economic growth has made Japan into one of the richest countries in the world, and the low birth rate among Japanese women has come to be regarded as detrimental to both further development of the economy and the future stability of social security. Under such circumstances, political attempts occurred to eliminate the "economic reasons clause" from the Eugenic Protection Law, first in the early 1970s and again a decade later. Since more than 99 percent of abortions in Japan have been decriminalized by this economic reasons clause, its elimination actually means placing a ban on abortion on demand.

In campaigns in both the 1970s and 1980s, a new religious body, Seicho no ie (Home of Life) played the central role in cooperation with some conservative members of the ruling Liberal Democratic Party. Seicho no ie is an eclectic religion founded in 1930 and consisting of elements borrowed from Shinto, Buddhism, and Christianity. Adherents worship the Japanese emperor and imperial household. Members of the political arm of Seicho no ie and other conservatives claimed that since Japan had become sufficiently affluent, there was no need to permit "murders" of innocent fetuses for economic reasons. They submitted a revised bill of EPL to the Diet in 1972. In addition to the deletion of the economic reasons clause, the bill proposed to allow abortion if the fetus was suspected of having a serious physical or mental defect; it also exhorted Japanese women to give birth to their first children at a suitable age. While aimed at increasing fertility rates, the bill simultaneously advocated that the birth of eugenically "undesirable" children should be prevented.

Two different groups immediately took action to oppose the bill. One was composed of the activists of the nascent women's liberation movement. For these advocates, the campaign to defeat the attempt to revise the EPL and defend the right to abortion became the first important opportunity for articulation of "women's autonomy" and "women's right to control their own bodies." A famous slogan, "It is I, a woman, who decides to bear or not to bear," was coined for their antirevision campaign. The other group opposing the bill was composed of people with disabilities, mainly cerebral palsy (CP), belonging to a group named Aoi shiba no kai (Green Grass Group).

In addition to legalization of abortion, the EPL had another face. As is implied by its name, it was a descendant of the National Eugenic Law (Kokumin yusei-ho) enacted in 1940 during World War II. This former law was patterned after the 1933 German Law for the Prevention of Hereditarily Diseased Offspring, the so-called sterilization law of the Nazi regime. It mandated the sterilization of people with "inferior" heredity while banning abortion except for eugenic reasons. The postwar EPL inherited its eugenic character and even strengthened it by stipulating the compulsory sterilization of people with physical or mental hereditary diseases. Furthermore, in spite of the fact that Hansen's disease (leprosy) was already known to be nonhereditary, patients with Hansen's disease or their spouses also became targets of eugenic sterilization and abortion under this new law. Under the EPL, during the period from 1948 to 1996, more than eighteen thousand operations of compulsory or semicompulsory sterilization were approved and carried out.[14] Institutionalized patients with Hansen's disease were not allowed to marry among themselves unless they consented to sterilization; if female patients became pregnant, they were compelled to have an abortion. Furthermore, although there was no such stipulation in the law, in some institutions, women having normal uteri were forced to undergo clandestine hysterectomies if they had physical or mental diseases. The purpose of the operation was to terminate their menstrual cycle and reduce the burden of caring for them.

Aoi shiba was originally an organization for promoting mutual friendship among people with cerebral palsy. In 1970, however, when the case of a mother in Yokohama who killed her young child with CP excited much sympathy for the mother and gave rise to a petition movement demanding a lenient punishment, members of Aoi shiba were shocked and started a very radical movement to claim their right to live. Regarding the revision proposal of the EPL, they felt that the new provision allowing abortion of "defective" fetuses would further justify discrimination against people with disabilities by legitimizing eugenic criteria for life and thus violating their fundamental right to live. They argued that social tolerance for killing a disabled fetus is synonymous with saying to those living with disabilities, "You are not supposed to exist in this world. You should not have been born." They protested in a very defiant and militant manner to attract public attention to their cause, and became the pioneers of the disability rights movement in Japan.[15]

At the same time, activists of Aoi shiba questioned the fundamental validity of abortion sanctioned by the EPL and criticized the claim that abortion was a woman's right to choose, saying that this was nothing but "healthy people's egoism" and that women were taking part in sustaining discrimination against the disabled because of their "internalized eugenic thought." Thus, two socially marginalized groups, women and people with disabilities, were placed in awkward confrontation in connection with the EPL.

Women advocating reproductive freedom were both disturbed and moved by the harsh criticism leveled by disabled people. While they fully believed in the vital importance and necessity of legal abortion for women's lives, they realized at the same time that their claim of the right to abortion under the present state of the law, which was eugenic and discriminatory, could easily be exploited and appropriated for the purpose of promoting the elimination of the disabled. Mitsu Tanaka, one of the well-known figures of the Japanese women's liberation movement, expressed this particular dilemma with which Japanese feminists were confronted at that time in the following way:

> Women's liberationists in Europe and America claim the freedom of and right to abortion because they primarily seek liberation from religious moral systems such as that of Catholicism. In Japan, however, induced abortion has been legalized since 1948, though not in a quite satisfactory manner. We Japanese women have not been forbidden abortion by religious morals but have resorted to abortions because we think we should not give birth, and in doing so have contributed to increasing the benefit of corporations. We cannot and dare not say so readily that abortion is our right. . . . If we do not perceive our pain in conducting forced infanticide and keep resorting to abortions for the reason that there is no way to escape from such a society, we will inevitably be caught up in the stink of this efficiency-oriented, dog-eat-dog world that attaches higher value to production of automobiles than to children's lives.[16]

In spite of their strained relationship, the two groups, feminists and people with disabilities, formed a tentative joint struggle for the purpose of defeating the revision forces, and they succeeded in preventing the proposed revision of the EPL.

In the early 1980s, Seicho no ie and its political agents resumed their campaign for the revision of the EPL. This time, they carefully avoided mention of "fetal disability" in order not to provoke disability activists and focused exclusively on the economic reasons clause, asserting that abortion on demand is violating the "sanctity of life." They held assemblies "to protect the lives of fetuses," funded TV advertisements, published books such as *Is a Fetus Not a Human Being?*[17] and launched a nationwide petition campaign that aimed to collect ten million signatures. It was rumored that there was a close contact between Seicho no ie and the Moral Majority and the pro-life movement in the United States and that Masakuni Murakami, Seicho no ie's political representative in the Diet, learned some of these campaign techniques from the American counterparts.

This time, not only women's liberation activists but also women belonging to more traditional women's organizations, various citizens' groups, trade unions, and even some female politicians of the Liberal Democratic Party, the ruling conservative party that submitted the revision bill, rose to offer wide opposition to the proposed revision. There was a strong sense of crisis among these people in the context of a political atmosphere that was rapidly leaning to the right. One woman of the older generation, the head of the Japan Federation of Women's Organizations (Nihon Fujin Dantai Rengokai), expressed her deep distrust and wariness of the revisionist "pro-lifers":

> Those people who are the core members of the revision movement of the EPL are known on the other side as zealous promoters of the expansion of military capacity and revision of the current constitution. Asserting "sanctity of life" on one hand and demanding military buildup on the other hand, they remind us of those who impelled Japanese people into the war promulgating "Bear and multiply."[18]

Because of such concerted efforts by the antirevisionists, the second attempt at revision failed, and the disappointed and angry head of Seicho no ie decided to withdraw from political activities. At the end of 1989, however, the Health and Welfare Ministry announced its intention to shorten the period for legal abortion from twenty-three weeks to twenty-one weeks of pregnancy. The reason given was that advances in perinatal medicine had recently allowed a premature baby born at twenty-three weeks to survive for more than six months. Although reducing the legal period by two weeks would not immediately threaten women's vested rights to legal abortion, there were fears that teenage girls, an increasing percentage of abortion applicants, and most apt to hesitate and postpone applying for abortion to the last minute, would be affected by this alteration. In spite of the protest and demands from the women's health activists, feminist ob-gyns, and various women's groups that such an important issue must be discussed fully in the Diet and that opinions of women should be consulted before making any decision, the alteration was rushed into law by means of a notification issued by the vice minister of Health and Welfare in March 1990, and it went into effect on January 1, 1991. This was a case in which the women's movement, defending women's interests, lost to the state.

During the 1994 Cairo International Conference on Population and Development, the problematic character of the EPL was brought to international attention by Yuho Asaka, a disabled woman and a peer-counseling activist. At a public hearing on the ways that population policy enacted violence against women, she reported that in Japan the EPL, or rather the eugenic idea embodied in it, had been used by doctors to prevent disabled people from having children, and sometimes led to unnecessary hysterectomies. As a result of both the international stir caused by Asaka's report and the long-standing pressure from the domestic disability rights movement, the government finally decided to revise the EPL in 1996, eliminating all the clauses pertaining to people with disabilities and hereditary diseases and changing its name to the Maternal Body Protection Law (Botai hogo-ho).

Following the revision, disability rights activists organized a group in 1997 that demanded the Ministry of Health and Welfare apologize to and compensate those forced to undergo sterilizations and hysterectomies under the EPL. As a result of fact-finding surveys, some disabled women and ex-patients with Hansen's disease spoke publicly about their experiences under the EPL. Patients with Hansen's disease who had been segregated for long periods of time and who had been forced to undergo sterilization and abortion brought legal actions against the state for discriminatory treatment and won a victory in 2001. As regards people with disabilities, however, the Ministry of Health and Welfare declined to make any apologies or compensation, claiming that eugenic sterilization was legal when these operations were carried out.

Problematizing the Low Birth Rate

In June 1990, major Japanese newspapers sensationally reported that the total fertility rate of Japanese women dropped to 1.57 in 1989. Although it had been known that Japan's fertility rate had been gradually declining since the mid-1970s, this news caused such a furor anew among political and economic circles and the media that a new phrase, "1.57 shock," was coined and became a vogue word of the year. Experts observed that falling birth rates were mainly the result of better educational opportunities for women and an increase in the number of women entering the workforce, both of which led women to marry later and to bear fewer children. After the collapse of Japan's economic bubble in the mid-1990s, the number of young people, both men and women who could not get a full-time, economically stable job increased, with a concomitant rise in the rates of late marriages and the unmarried population. Since the norm of childbearing within lawful marriage is very powerful in Japan, the increase in later marriage and in the unmarried population almost directly leads to a decline in fertility rate.

Throughout the 1990s and into the new century, the ominous prospects of a rapidly aging society, labor shortages, and decline in the Japanese economy have been emphasized repeatedly by political and economic leaders and the media. And Japanese women have found themselves bombarded by both explicit and implicit calls to have more children to save the future of the nation. In 2003, the government enacted a new law named the Basic Law of Measures to Counteract the Declining Birth Rate (Shoshika-shakai taisaku kihon-ho), which listed such measures as the improvement of employment and childcare services, provision of local support in childrearing, and reduction of childcare costs. This effort has failed to produce any substantial effects so far. The birth rate hit a new record low of 1.26 in 2005, and even though there has been a slight increase in recent years, the birth rates in 2011 and 2012 were still only 1.39 and 1.41, respectively.[19] Irritated by this status quo, some politicians criticized the "selfishness" of women who refused to bear children. For example, in 2007, Hakuo Yanagisawa, the head of the Ministry of Health, Labor and Welfare (changed from the former Ministry of Health and Welfare in 2001), called women "childbearing machines" and beseeched them to try hard to produce more children.

Against such pronatalist campaigns, feminists and activists, ordinary housewives and working women, and even many men have repeatedly raised their voices in anger and protest. When Minister Yanagisawa's remark was reported by the media, indignant letters of many women and some men poured into the newspapers. They asserted that the decline in the birth rate was an inevitable result of and the price to be paid for post-World War II Japanese society, which consistently placed a priority on efficiency and economic development, forcing long and hard working hours on men, leaving the burdens of raising "good quality" children and domestic labor entirely to women, thus making combining career and childrearing extremely difficult for both women and men. Through such recurrent controversies, it has become clear that today, many people believe that it is individuals, especially women, themselves, and not the state, that should have the ultimate control over reproductive decision-making. A twenty-nine-year-old woman working at a part-time job sent the following letter exemplifying this position to the *Yomiuri* newspaper in 1990:

> It is miserable for a grown-up woman to live without economic independence. So I decided that one child was enough for me. I don't want to spoil the life of either my child or myself. . . . Why should women bear children for the aged and the state? Never, for anything! If they think they need more children, let them use the military budget or something for that. But it's a mistake to reproach women for the decline of the birth rate. I want to say to the state, "Stop exploiting women forever! We won't be duped anymore!" and live my life free from regret.[20]

Feminist Attitude to Prenatal Diagnosis

In addition to the low birth rates, another reproductive phenomenon that has attracted much attention in recent decades is the rising age of women bearing children. This is the result of the increase in later marriages and in the number of women who postpone childbearing into their late thirties and forties because of career and other reasons. While the total number of births is declining, both the number of children born to women in their late thirties and older and the number of infertile women seeking help using new reproductive technologies to get pregnant are increasing. These developments have led to debates regarding whether or to what extent various new methods of prenatal diagnosis should be employed to examine the conditions of fetuses, given what research has revealed about fetal anomalies and advanced maternal age.

Generally speaking, Japanese feminists have not been enthusiastic about utilizing new reproductive technologies for either fertility treatment or prenatal diagnosis, and some are explicitly critical of them. The backdrop for the cautious attitudes of Japanese feminists is the historical experiences of women regarding abortion and the EPL. As a representative case, we can look at the activities and ideas of a women's group in Tokyo named SOSHIREN. Its name is an abbreviation of the original name, which means " '82 Coalition to Prevent the Revision of the EPL for Worse."

SOSHIREN was formed in 1982 by women participating in the second campaign to prevent elimination of the economic reasons clause from the EPL, and since then this group has led the women's health movement in Japan. Some of its members had also participated in the antirevision movement in the 1970s as women's liberation activists were deeply concerned about the eugenic character of the EPL and the potential conflict of interest between women and people with disability. Furthermore, one of the core members of SOSHIREN, Tomoko Yonezu, is herself a woman with a postpolio physical disability. Accordingly, members of this group were fully aware of the problematic peculiarity of the EPL, which combined legalization of abortion and discrimination against the disabled in one law.

After the proposed revision of the EPL was successfully stopped in 1983, women of SOSHIREN decided to continue their activity with the objective of abolishing both EPL and the Anti-Abortion Law in the penal code. They kept in touch with disability rights groups, especially those focused on women with disabilities, continuing discussion with them and participating in various campaigns to end discrimination against the disabled. In this way, women of SOSHIREN have developed a close relationship with the disability rights movement. During this time, SOSHIREN tackled not only abortion and EPL-related issues but also such new issues as population policy in developing countries, assisted reproductive technologies, and prenatal diagnosis.

As mentioned above, as a result of the decades-long concerted efforts of women and people with disabilities, the eugenic clauses were finally eliminated from the EPL, and the name of the law was changed in 1996. This was a long-awaited victory for the disability rights movement; however, since the objectives of SOSHIREN to abolish the Anti-Abortion Law and enact a new reproductive law based on the idea of women's self-determination were not realized, the group decided to continue its activity to protest the state's control of women's bodies and defend women's right to self-determination in reproductive matters.

Prenatal screening is used differently in Japan than in other developed countries. For example, ultrasonography is routinely used during normal pregnancy, and many women welcome it as an opportunity "to meet" their babies before birth, but other prenatal diagnostic techniques such as amniocentesis, chorionic villus sampling (CVS), alpha feto protein (AFP) testing, and triple-marker test (maternal serum screening) are not used so frequently. The number of triple-marker tests conducted in the United States is about 167 times that in Japan, and the frequency of amniocentesis in Germany is more than ten times that in Japan.[21] In Japan, amniocentesis is conducted selectively only when the pregnant woman is relatively old or some form of fetal abnormality is suspected. Preimplantation diagnosis (PID) of embryos created by IVF (in vitro fertilization) is tightly restricted, used only for the detection of a limited number of serious genetic diseases. To be sure, there are medical professionals and corporate executives who advocate further utilization of these screening technologies in Japanese society; however, because of past experiences with the problematic EPL and fierce criticism by disability rights activists, whenever introduction of a new screening method is proposed, there has been considerable hesitation in and ambivalence toward publicly and widely promoting prenatal screening even among medical professionals.

Certainly, prenatal diagnostic technologies are important tools for managing pregnancy and ensuring fetal health and welfare. At the same time, however, these tools are designed to detect fetal defects or abnormalities, and once a defect, such as Down syndrome, is found or suspected in the fetus, many women freely—or under some kind of pressure—choose to have an abortion. In fact, with the steady spread of prenatal diagnostic technologies, experts estimate that at least six thousand abortions were conducted in Japan in the five years from 2005 to 2009 because of fetal abnormalities, twice as many as the number from 1995 to 1999.[22] People with disabilities who oppose prenatal screening identify themselves with the rejected fetus and claim that prenatal screening is nothing but a new form of eugenic selection of life. Some parents of children with Down syndrome also protest against routinization of prenatal screening, claiming that bringing up children with Down syndrome is not the unhappy experience that many people imagine but is, instead, a very precious experience.[23]

The World Health Organization (WHO) states that the application of prenatal screening and subsequent abortion cannot be called "new eugenics" when women are not coerced to have tests and when the woman's right to choose whether or not to keep the pregnancy is guaranteed.[24] However, women of SOSHIREN have a different opinion. They argue that just as women's right to abortion was conveniently used by the state to control the quantity of population in the postwar era, with prenatal screening, the individual woman's "choice" is used to voluntarily control the quality of the human being to be born. Tomoko Yonezu asserts:

> Abortion after prenatal screening is conducted, not because pregnancy itself is unwanted, but in expectation of having a baby. It is a deed to decide whether to welcome that child or not, depending on existence or nonexistence of defects. I think that a fetus is neither an independent life nor a part of [a] woman's body. It is not the same as a person after birth but has a potentiality to become one. Just as discrimination against a living human being because of her or his attributes is wrong, so is discrimination against a fetus. . . . Notwithstanding the fact that it is society's unkindness to people with disabilities that makes their lives difficult, proponents of prenatal diagnosis pretend there is no such liability and try to induce women to select their children, designating such selection a woman's "right" to be practiced at her own responsibility. That is exactly a new trend of eugenics and is nothing but an infringement of women's reproductive rights.[25]

Does this opposition to prenatal testing and subsequent abortion contradict SOSHIREN's support for abortion rights? Women of SOSHIREN do not think so. In their definition, "women's reproductive rights" means the right to choose whether or not to become a parent, and access to both safe and effective contraception and safe and legal abortion is an essential prerequisite for the realization of this right. But to select children depending on their sex or on the existence or nonexistence of defects should not be included in "women's reproductive rights."[26] That is, members of this group think that an abortion conducted because a woman is not prepared to become a mother is different in nature and in meaning from an abortion chosen after prenatal testing that reveals a specific characteristic of the fetus that the woman considers unfavorable. This is the position they have arrived at through continuous and sometimes tension-ridden conversations with disability rights activists.

However, the women of SOSHIREN disagree with the claim of some disability rights activists that selective abortion should be formally banned by law since such a ban would deprive women of a chance to choose based on their free will. Yonezu maintains that, for the purpose of preventing the normalization of prenatal screening and selective abortion, women require better information and support so that they have the resources to bear and rear a child with a disability. Meanwhile, Yonezu and her colleagues believe that the development and application of technologies for preselection such as preimplantation diagnosis should be placed under strict and careful control. "If there exist conditions under which one can bring up a child with [a] disability in a manner not entirely different from that of an ordinary child, then we will be able to choose not to choose our children," says Yonezu.[27]

In the spring of 2013, after much debate, clinical trials of a new testing method, NIPT (Non-invasive Prenatal Genetic Testing), started in several selected hospitals in Japan. NIPT is a method widely used in the United States that analyzes a fetus's DNA using maternal blood to examine probabilities of three types of chromosomal abnormalities, including Down syndrome. Since NIPT is a noninvasive method that does not place much of a burden on the maternal body, it is anticipated that the demand for it will increase in the future, especially among so-called high-risk pregnant women in their late thirties and forties.

Feminist Attitude to ART

Since the birth of the first IVF child in Japan in 1983, fertility treatment has rapidly grown as a lucrative medical industry. In Japanese society, such ideas as "A marriage is not perfect without a child" or "It is a couple's duty to produce a successor to the family" still prevail to a considerable degree. In such a society, there are numerous infertile couples, especially women, who desperately hope to have their own children at any cost and are willing to go through any suffering for that goal. The increase in the number of women who want to get pregnant at older ages when their fertility is declining is another important factor behind the flourishing fertility treatment business.[28]

However, in Japan the conditions under which ART (assisted reproductive technology) is accessible are relatively restricted in comparison with other countries, especially the United States. Historically, clinical application of DI (donor insemination) started soon after World War II in Keio University Hospital when there were no rules concerning reproductive technologies, and it has been continued rather clandestinely, becoming a kind of extralegal fait accompli. However, only legally married couples may apply for this method. Married couples can also seek hormone treatment, AIH (artificial insemination by husband), and IVF depending on their diagnosis, but they cannot arrange for surrogacy or egg or embryo donation. Although Japan has not yet legislated any formal laws governing clinical application of new reproductive technologies, in practice, assisted reproduction via either surrogacy or egg or embryo donation is prohibited by the professional guidelines of the Japan Association of Obstetrician-Gynecologists (Nihon Sanka Fujinka Gakkai), and all doctors are expected to comply with this rule. Furthermore, unmarried people and gay/lesbian couples are basically excluded from access to these technologies because doctors usually consider them unfit to be parents, and sperm-banking or egg donation industries are almost nonexistent in Japan.

Under such conditions, many Japanese couples who can afford it have traveled to the United States, where in some states they can purchase various reproductive services unavailable in Japan such as egg donation or surrogacy. In recent years, destinations have included Korea, Thailand, and India, which is actively promoting the surrogacy business for foreigners. However, when these couples succeed and return to Japan, almost all of them register their children as biological offspring, trying to hide the fact of surrogacy or egg donation, because in Japan resorting to various artificial methods of assisted reproduction is generally regarded as "unnatural" or as "going too far."

But there are exceptional cases in which consumers of these methods speak publicly, justifying their choices. For example, Aki Mukai, a television personality, publicized the fact that because she had uterine cancer, she had had a hysterectomy, losing her uterus and her first pregnancy. Mukai described in detail—in books and even in a TV special—how, using her own eggs, fertilized with her husband's sperm, implanted in the uterus of a surrogate in the United States, she and her husband became the parents of twin boys.[29] But Mukai and her husband had to pay a high price for publicizing the contract surrogacy: the twin's birth certificates indicating Mukai and her husband as parents were not accepted by the Japanese public office since Mukai was apparently not the birth mother of the twins. They complained to the court, but in 2007 the Supreme Court ruled that, although Mukai is the genetic mother of the twins, she could not be admitted as their lawful mother because, according to Japanese law, the mother is the woman who bears a child—in this case, the American surrogate. Mukai had to settle this problem by adopting the twins.

Mukai's case triggered debates among Japanese people over whether surrogate birth should be admitted as a legitimate means of fertility treatment. It seems that public opinion was divided. People sympathetic to Mukai, especially some doctors and infertile women, claimed that it is a part of women's reproductive rights to use surrogacy and other technologies to become a parent and that the law will have to change in accordance with technological advances and opportunities. Those who were critical of Mukai's choice said it was too egoistical to buy another woman's body in order to satisfy her own desire, as well as audacious to knowingly defy Japanese law, which does not allow surrogacy. Amid such turmoil, the Science Council of Japan (Nihon Gakujutsu Kaigi), the academy of distinguished scholars and researchers, submitted a report in 2008 advising the government to formally prohibit surrogate pregnancy by law.[30]

In opposition to this trend, Dr. Yahiro Netsu, who is one of the most vocal proponents of surrogate birth in Japan, spoke publicly in 2009 about the fact that he had provided services in twenty-one cases of surrogate birth in his hospital in Nagano Prefecture and that fifteen children have been born successfully from thirteen surrogate mothers as of 2009. In these cases, the surrogates were either sisters, sisters-in-law, or mothers of the infertile women, and surrogate birth by an infertile woman's own mother accounted for eleven out of the twenty-one cases.[31] It is Dr. Netsu's firm opinion that the commercial surrogacy contract, popular in the United States, is not fit for Japanese society and that surrogate birth by a woman's own mother is the most favorable form of surrogacy because in such a case, it is a deed of unconditional love and self-sacrifice without any exchange of money and because there is little fear of trouble arising among family members. Affronted by Netsu's disregard of the professional guidelines, the Japan Association of Obstetrician-Gynecologists responded by expelling him from membership. However, since this does not lead to revocation of his medical license, the medical practice of Dr. Netsu has not been much affected.

In 2010, Seiko Noda, a popular female politician of the Liberal Democratic Party who had repeatedly proclaimed her earnest desire to be a mother, created a sensation by announcing publicly that she, at age forty-nine, became pregnant through egg donation in the United States. After she turned fifty, she gave birth to her son prematurely in January 2011, but lost her uterus due to a serious postpartum hemorrhage. Despite the fact that Dr. Netsu and some other clinics are known to have dared to use donated eggs in some of their treatments, disregarding the professional guidelines of the Japan Association of Obstetrician-Gynecologists, Noda had to resort to an American agency because in Japan she was considered beyond biological childbearing age and could not find a cooperative doctor. Again, there was much debate in the media and among ordinary people about her choice.

On the other hand, it is interesting that the state appears to be unenthusiastic in enacting a law concerning the extent and eligibility of clinical application of ART. In spite of the fact that the necessity of establishing an official rule has been recognized for a long period of time, that several recommendations have been made by the official advisory council and academic organizations, and that Seiko Noda has repeatedly asserted that Japan should legalize egg donation and surrogacy as an ordinary means of fertility treatment, many Diet members, most of them men, seem to be uninterested in or hesitant about taking up such a controversial and divisive issue. Accordingly, the prospects for early enactment of any law on ART in Japan look dim at the present time.

While many women are sympathetic to Mukai and Noda and praise Dr. Netsu's challenge, opinions are divided even among infertile women. For example, members of the Friends of Finrrage (Finreji no kai), a network for infertile women, together with other feminist groups such as SOSHIREN, are definitely opposed to surrogacy and assisted reproductive technologies. They argue that the reasons women seek treatment for infertility, notwithstanding its high costs and risks, stem from the deep-rooted and internalized social pressure and gender ideology, which insist that "women should bear children" or "a family is not perfect without a child." They allege that surrogate birth is nothing but an exploitation and instrumentalization of woman's reproductive capacity by medical professionals and patriarchal society. The mother who assumes the role of a surrogate for her infertile daughter is urged to do so by tacit pressure from Japanese society that mothers should always assume responsibility and sacrifice themselves for their children.[32]

To be sure, it is not that Japanese feminists are unsympathetic to the plight of infertile people. Some are infertile themselves and know the sufferings and hardship of the infertile very well; but they are deeply critical of the trend to legitimize the rampant use of ART under the pretext that "women themselves want it" or "it is the woman's right to self-determination for her body." That is, they express deep concern about applying the term "woman's right to self-determination" in the context of ART.

Historically, the "woman's right to self-determination" in feminist discourse is a concept originally signifying a woman's "right to choose nonreproduction," particularly in regard to birth control and abortion. Feminists have argued thus: since the phenomena of pregnancy and delivery occur only in the bodies of one sex, women, and since the social foundations of these phenomena—love, sexuality, and marriage—are often regulated within the unequal power relationships between the two sexes and between women and social, political, and religious powers of society, for fairness's sake women should have the opportunity to choose whether or not they want to become pregnant or to continue a pregnancy or not in accordance with their individual will and situation. Thus, the original intent of the right to self-determination or women's right to choose is to reject the control over women's bodies in a patriarchal society that treats women's bodies as procreative equipment. It is, so to speak, a term claimed for resistance's sake.

However, especially in the United States, it seems that the meaning of the right to self-determination has shifted, discarding the original element of resistance against manipulation of the body. It has come to mean, "I own my body; it's my property, so I can decide freely what to do with it." Furthermore, in the course of proliferation of reproductive technologies and the expansion of the reproductive industry, the concept has come to mean specifically, "I have the right to have a child using whatever method available," or "I have the freedom to sell my eggs or to 'rent' my uterus and become a surrogate." Still, there is debate about these matters in the United States, too, and upon unsettled terrain.

Many Japanese feminists are deeply concerned about the idea that a woman's body and her reproductive capacity can be commodified simply if the woman herself chooses or agrees to do so, and that the whole process of procreation can be divided into parts and manipulated at will into such discrete procedures as harvesting excellent eggs from a young and beautiful woman, and after in vitro insemination, placing the fertilized egg in a different woman's uterus so that she can cultivate a fetus for nine months and bear the child to give it to yet another woman. The concern is that the whole process of reproduction is now being treated more and more as merely another kind of commercial production process, and that such a view of procreation is infiltrating American states and other countries that sanction a variety of reproductive businesses and also infecting other areas of the world, including Japan.

It is not that these Japanese feminists, like the women of SOSHIREN, are simply glorifying or essentializing women's reproductive capacity or women's experience of pregnancy. Through their historical experiences related to abortion under the EPL and their tension-ridden relationship with the disability rights movement, they have become very sensitive and alert to the possibility of exploitation of women's bodies by the state, medical power, and the market. And I believe such feelings of apprehension and cautiousness are not limited to Japanese feminists alone. For example, there are some American feminists, with or without disabilities, who have courageously raised their voices to question the meaning or primacy of the "right to choose" and the "right to self-determination" in the context of new reproductive technologies.[33] In the face of the rapidly changing landscape of human procreation, it is time that women of different countries with different historical experiences join in discussions, referring not only to the language of rights or the language of the market economy but also to a new and different kind of feminist language that can better understand and express women's experience of reproduction.

Notes

1. Deborah Oakley, "American-Japanese Interaction in the Development of Population Policy in Japan, 1945–52," *Population and Development Review* 4, no. 4 (1978): 617–43.
2. Mainichi Shimbunsha Jinko Mondai Chosa-kai, ed., *Kiroku nihon no jinko: Shosan eno kiseki* (Japanese Population: The Way to a Low Birth Rate) (Tokyo: Mainichi Shimbunsha, 1990), 345.
3. Yoshio Koya, *Rogakkyu no techo kara* (From the Notebook of an Old Scholar) (Tokyo: Nippon Kazoku-keikaku kyokai, 1970), 126.
4. Yoshio Koya, *Pioneering in Family Planning: A Collection of Papers on the Family Planning Programs and Research Conducted in Japan* (New York: Population Council, 1963).
5. Miho Ogino, *Kazoku-keikaku eno michi: Kindai nihon no seishoku wo meguru seiji* (The Road to Family Planning: Reproductive Politics in Modern Japan) (Tokyo: Iwanami-shoten, 2008), chap. 6.
6. Hisao Aoki, "Family Planning Programs in Industrial Companies," in *Basic Readings on Population and Family Planning in Japan*, ed. M. Muramatsu and T. Katagiri (Tokyo: JOICFP, 1985), 83.
7. Teruko Inoue and Yumiko Ehara, eds., *Josei no deta bukku* (Data Book of Women), 3rd ed. (Tokyo: Yuhikaku, 1999), 62.
8. Mainichi-shimbun-sha Jinko-mondai chosa-kai, ed., *Nippon no jinko: Sengo 50nen no kiseki* (Population of Japan: Trajectory of Fifty Years after the War) (Tokyo: Mainichi-shimbun-sha, 2000).
9. Yoko Akiyama, *Ribu shishi noto* (A Private History of Women's Liberation) (Tokyo: Inpakuto-shuppankai, 1993), 263.
10. Mitsu Tanaka, Soko Mitamura, and Tomoko Yonezu, "Nomasetai hito no piru kara nomitai hito no piru e" (From 'the pill taken for somebody else' to 'the pill taken on my own'), *Lib News: Kono michi hitosuji* 5 (October 10, 1973): 5.

11. Onna no tame no kurinikku junbikai, *Piru: Watashitachi wa erabanai* (The Pill: We Don't Choose It) (Osaka: Onna no tame no kurinikku junbikai, 1987), 128–29.
12. Dai 6-kai danjo no seikatsu to ishiki ni kansuru chousa-kekka (Results of the Sixth Research on Men and Women's Lives and Consciousness), http://www.koshu-eisei.net/upfile_free/20130118kitamura.pdf (accessed August 18, 2013).
13. Dai 6-kai danjo no seikatsu to ishiki ni kansuru chousa-kekka.
14. Yoko Matsubara, "Botai-hogo-ho no rekishiteki haikei" (Historical Background of the Maternal Body Protection Law), in *Botai-hogo-ho to watashitachi* (The Maternal Body Protection Law and Us), ed. Yukiko Saito (Tokyo: Akashi-shoten, 2002), 43.
15. See, for example, Koichi Yokozuka, *Haha yo! Korosuna* (Mom! Don't Kill) (Tokyo: Seikatsu-shoin, 2007).
16. Mitsu Tanaka, "Matamata yusei-hogo-ho kaiaku nanoda!" (Revision for the worse of the EPL), *Lib News* 3 (June 10, 1973): 3–4.
17. Nihon Kyobun-sha, ed., *Taiji wa ningen de nainoka* (Is a Fetus Not a Human Being?) (Tokyo: Nihon kyobun-sha, 1982).
18. Fuki Kushida, "Watashi mo hantai desu" (I am against it, too), *Ima naze yusei-hogo-ho kaiaku ka?* (Why Do They Want the Revision for Worse of the EPL Now?), ed. Fujin Kyodo Horitsu Jimusho (Tokyo: Rodo Kyoiku senta, 1983), 12–13.
19. *Nippon Keizai Shimbun*, June 5, 2013.
20. *Yomiuri Shimbun*, July 3, 1990.
21. Kodo Sato, *Shusseizen shindan* (Prenatal Diagnosis) (Tokyo: Yuhikaku, 1999), 52.
22. *Asahi Shimbun*, April 5, 2012.
23. Akiko Ono, *Kodomo wo erabanai-koto wo erabu* (To Choose Not to Choose a Child) (Osaka: Medika-shuppan, 2003).
24. D. C. Wertz, J. C. Fletcher, and K. Berg, *Guidelines on Ethical Issues in Medical Genetics and the Provision of Genetic Services* (Geneva: World Health Organization, 1995).
25. Tomoko Yonezu, "Shogaisha to josei" (People with Disabilities and Women), *SOSHIREN News* 204 (October 22, 2002): 17–18.
26. "Watashitachi no iken" (Our Opinion), *SOSHIREN News* 171 (October 12, 1999): 5.
27. Yonezu, "Shogaisha to josei," 21.
28. In 2011, the average age of women giving their first birth reached 30.1, the highest on record. *Asahi Shimbun*, June 6, 2012.
29. Aki Mukai, *16-shu: Anata to ita shiawasena jikan* (16 Weeks: Happy Days I Spent with You) (Tokyo: Fusosha, 2001); Aki Mukai, *Puropozu: Watashitachi no kodomo wo unde-kudasai* (A Proposal: Please Bear Our Child for Us) (Tokyo: Magazine House, 2002); Aki Mukai, *Aitakatta: Dairi-haha shussan toiu sentaku* (Here You Are at Last! Our Choice of Surrogate Birth) (Tokyo: Gento-sha, 2004).

30. Nihon Gakujutsu Kaigi, *Seishoku hojo iryo no arikata kento iinkai, Dairi kaitai wo chushin tosuru seishoku hojo iryo no kadai* (Problems of Assisted Reproductive Medicine Centering on Surrogate Pregnancy) (Tokyo: Nihon Gakujutsu Kaigi, 2008).
31. Seiko Noda and Yahiro Netsu, *Kono kuni de umu to iukoto* (Bearing a Child in This Country) (Tokyo: Popura-sha, 2011), 153.
32. In addition to various issues of *SOSHIREN News*, see, for example, Azumi Tsuge, *Seishoku gijutsu: Funin chiryo to saisei iryo wa shakai ni nani wo motarasuka* (Reproductive Technologies: What Will Fertility Treatment and Regenerative Medicine Bring to Society?) (Tokyo: Misuzu-shobo, 2012).
33. See, for instance, Ruth Hubbard, "Eugenics, Reproductive Technologies, and 'Choice,'" *GeneWatch* 14, no. 1 (2001): 3–4; Judith Levine, "What Human Genetic Modification Means for Women," *World Watch*, July–August 2002, 26–29; and Marsha Saxton, "Disability Rights and Selective Abortion," in *Abortion Wars: A Half Century of Struggle, 1950–2000*, ed. Rickie Solinger (Berkeley: University of California Press, 1998).

4

From Gandhi to Gandhi

Contraceptive Technologies and Sexual Politics in Postcolonial India, 1947–1977

SANJAM AHLUWALIA AND DAKSHA PARMAR

> Twenty five years ago controversies raged over the question: Was India overpopulated or not? Some years later, the controversy shifted to the question of whether birth control was good or bad? Today, the issue is not whether India wants birth control or not, but what methods would be most acceptable to people in different strata of life and, what is perhaps even more important, how best to disseminate knowledge of it among the people in the villages.
>
> —S. Chandrasekhar, 1955[1]

This 1955 epigraph maps a deceptively simple linear narrative about the history of the population question and birth control from the colonial to the postcolonial period in India. Its sentiment is consistent with Nehru's proclamation in 1947 that the nation awoke to life and freedom at the stroke of the midnight hour.[2] The truth is, however, that public discourses on "overpopulation" and contraceptive technologies, key aspects of nation-building in postcolonial India, did not mark a clear and clean break from messy political articulations of these issues in the colonial period. Long after independence, lingering intellectual and political legacies of neo-Malthusianism and eugenics continued to shape official contraceptive initiatives for managing reproductive bodies of Muslims, lower castes, urban working poor, and rural peasantry. Even as disciplinary productive power of state and nonstate actors came to reside at the site of subaltern reproductive bodies, only fleeting moments of consensus emerged on the adoption of specific contraceptive technologies from the colonial into the postcolonial period. This chapter narrates a cautious feminist tale, one that recognizes that while reproductive subjects, the Indian state, and nonstate actors need not have necessarily been locked in an irreconcilable conflict over the use of birth control, historically, subaltern subjects and state and nonstate actors brought competing agendas to bear upon the adoption and deployment of contraceptive technologies.

From the 1920s onward public debates on India's demographic shifts and their impact on the British colony proliferated. Indian middle-class men, Western advocates, Indian feminists, medical experts, and the colonial state all appeared to agree that unchecked population growth was an impediment to India's progress, development, and modernity.[3] When Mahatma Gandhi refused to valorize "modernity" and "progress," he presented a dissenting voice, calling to shift the terms of the debate from a focus on statistics to a rejection of unfair distribution of resources.[4] But even as colonial elites (Western and Indian) generated a dense discourse around population growth and the importance of birth control, they failed to endorse a method of contraception for mass adoption. Gandhi's position was internally less fractured, focusing on the unequal distribution of resources and rejecting neo-Malthusian claims that population growth threatened national resources. In addition, Gandhi was deeply suspicious of mechanical and chemical contraceptive technologies. He lent his reluctant support to the rhythm or safe-period method for managing fecundity within monogamous heterosexual matrimony.

The history of contraception is a particularly productive site for recovering the sociocultural investments in human body and sexuality in twentieth-century India. From the 1920s onward elites identified birth control as an effective techno-scientific tool for governing subaltern reproductive bodies and simultaneously for enabling sexual expressions divorced from procreation within bourgeois matrimony. Rejecting Gandhianism for the most part, these elites marked lower castes, working poor, and Muslims as hypersexual and hyperfecund, and hence a drain on national resources. They heralded contraceptive technologies as effective in rationalizing reproduction among these groups for the sake of national well-being. Besides the promise of social engineering, Indian bourgeois advocates such as A. P. Pillay, N. S. Phadke, and Kamaladevi Chattopadhyaya highlighted the advantages of birth control for women. Even as these advocates supported the use of contraception, there was no consensus among them on the "ideal" form of birth control for mass adoption. Pillay was one of the leading Indian sexologists of the twentieth century. Trained as a biomedical doctor, he wrote extensively on issues of sexuality and reproduction. Pillay listed the pros and cons of different contraceptive techniques in his book *Birth Control Simplified*,[5] supporting use of the diaphragm pessary and cervical caps, but arguing against the use of intracervical and intrauterine devices, which he regarded as harmful and in need of condemnation.[6] In his book *Sex Problem in India*, Phadke advocated for the use of Dutch Cap or Mensinga Pessary as opposed to Pro-Race Cap.[7] Kamaladevi Chattopadhyaya, one of the leading Indian feminists of the twentieth century, supported the use of contraceptives, but she did not advocate any specific method of birth control. Gandhi, along with other conservative nationalists, lamented the use of birth control as a corrupt Western influence on Indian women that would disconnect sex from reproduction.[8] Debates on birth control at this time showed how sexuality was a dense transfer point of power, where politics of gender, class, caste, race, and community intersected in overlapping and complex ways primarily to reaffirm structures of domination.

The British colonial state in India generated encyclopedic information on Indian demography. Beginning with the census of 1871, the state was deeply invested in counting its colonial subjects and placing them into rigid categories of caste and community.[9] Decennial census reports furnished statistical ammunition to defend arguments about the country's impending demographic catastrophe. Experts consider the 1931 census report as a watermark within the history of the debate on India's "overpopulation."[10] The Famine Committee report and the Bhore committee report[11] took off from the narrative set in place in the 1931 census. Colonial state committees throughout the 1930s and early 1940s cautiously lent their support to birth control as a means for addressing India's population problem, even while arguing that public opinion in India was not ready to accept birth control.[12] While there is little evidence of strong public opposition to birth control within the official archives, the colonial state's unwillingness to invest in public health initiatives must have hindered wider dissemination of contraceptive knowledge and access in the preindependence period. The postcolonial Indian state inherited the terms of the debate on overpopulation and birth control from the colonial period, and newly elected representatives of the nation, in ways similar to their colonial predecessors, questioned public willingness to support state-led contraceptive initiatives.

Just as internal fractures marked colonial state politics on demography, development, and contraceptive use, competing perspectives pulled the postcolonial state in contradictory directions and rendered its initial attempts to promote birth control quite tentative. India became the first state to formally adopt family planning as part of its public health initiative, when it set up a Ministry of Health and Family Planning in 1951.[13] The inauguration of India's family-planning program was faced with the contradiction of reconciling neo-Malthusian and eugenic principles with Gandhian abstinence, a project that would create a globally unique birth control experiment. Given pressures, particularly from transnational institutions such as the Ford Foundation and the Population Council, which favored widespread imposition of birth control on the poor, the state was hard pressed to challenge Malthusian and eugenic ideals from the late 1950s into the 1970s. In the later years of the republic, beginning in approximately the late 1950s and early 1960s, the state abandoned Gandhian ideals of abstinence, experimenting instead with aggressive interventionist projects, promoting specific contraceptive technologies for mass adoption.

State-sponsored initiatives for population control recognized contraceptive technology as a convenient tool for institutionalizing a Malthusian project aimed at lowering overall national fertility rates, while simultaneously pursuing eugenic goals of narrowing the fertility rates along axes of class, caste, community, and spatial divides between India's rural and urban populations. In advancing various contraceptive options, the Indian state and other entities did not seek to uniformly redesign the functioning of Indian reproductive bodies across the board. Initiatives for promoting contraceptive usage were undergirded with elitist constructs of subaltern subjectivities, specifically as these related to reproductive sexuality. Here we recount how the emancipatory possibilities of modern contraception were compromised when policymakers eclipsed matters of desire and pleasure, as well as ideas about privacy and citizenship/individualism, in favor of intimacy as an arena of state policy and power.

Once contraception was identified as a tool for realizing national demographic goals, policymakers focused on discovering an "ideal" method—one that was simple, safe, reliable, and cheap. State and nonstate entities such as the Family Planning Association of India experimented with different technologies, trying to find a method that the masses would be likely to adopt. At the same time, policymakers vacillated between advancing a single-method mass approach and a cafeteria approach, allowing citizens to make informed choices on their own among a number of options. This uncertainty reflected policymakers' conviction that different users would have different capabilities. Some citizens, based on class, caste, community, and gender identity, were understood as less capable than others of embodying responsible fecundity. Experts typically represented subaltern groups as irrational subjects incapable of making informed contraceptive decisions who could not be entrusted with regular and precise execution of birth control techniques. Thus the state created top-down interventions to significantly redesign the sexual lives of these groups through contraceptive technologies, even imposing irreversible technologies based on a one-time contraceptive procedure. Middle-class women, on the other hand, were recognized as responsible procreative citizens entitled to exercise a choice in their adoption of a birth control method.

While the essentially elitist nature of the birth control project in postindependence India marks clear continuities with a history going back to the late nineteenth century, the actions and discussions of the post-1947 era also make evident the presence of new pressures, not the least of which were the pressures of a functioning democracy and the transformations in the nature of Indian and global politics from the era of Mahatma Gandhi and Jawaharlal Nehru to the reign of Indira Gandhi. The history of promoting a modern reproductive consciousness in postcolonial India appears to be deeply fissured and internally conflicted, especially when viewed through the prism of birth control. This chapter will focus on three forms of birth control techniques and procedures adopted in postcolonial India—the rhythm method, the loop or IUD, and mass sterilization campaigns that culminated with draconian measures during the period of the National Emergency between June 1975 and March 1977. In each instance, we will look at the tangled relationship between the technique/method and reproductive bodies, within the framework of social stratification based on class, caste, community, and gender. The National Emergency from 1975 to 1977 marks a significant watershed in the history of birth control in postcolonial India. While there may be some continuities with an elitist and demographically driven agenda on the part of the state after 1977, the excesses of the Emergency ensured that the state could not function in the same manner after that date as it did before. Even as this chapter traces the history of three contraceptive technologies from (Mahatma) Gandhi to (Sanjay) Gandhi, it also alludes to how this historical legacy continues to shape contemporary contraceptive perceptions and practices, particularly as it pertains to sterilization.

The rhythm method was advocated in the heady days of early independence. Despite Nehru's own commitments to a modern, technocratic future, Gandhi's legacy was still visible and significant in the upper echelons of Indian politics.[14] Nehru's desire to maintain a consensus often overrode his own agendas, and we see this reflected in a number of his political decisions. For one thing, he included some of his staunchest opponents in his cabinet, including, for instance, right-wing opponents such as Shyama Prasad Mukherjee, who would go on to found the Jana Sangh, the precursor to today's Hindu Nationalist Bharatiya Janata Party, and left-wing opponents such as Dr. B. R. Ambedkar. That Nehru would appoint a staunch Gandhian such as Rajkumari Amrit Kaur as his first health minister is consistent with his efforts to build consensus. Through its early experiments in the rhythm method, the Indian state sought to suture Gandhian abstinence with modernist sensibilities about conjugal sexuality.

The Indian state adopted the intrauterine device (IUD) as a form of birth control in the early 1960s, possibly toward the very end of Nehru's tenure as prime minister. Lal Bahadur Shastri took over from Nehru in 1964, and the state's focus on IUDs at that time was part of a larger technocratic turn that also saw the Indian state (and global actors such as the Ford Foundation) making huge investments in many other kinds of technologies such as agrarian technologies that resulted in the Green Revolution.[15] The introduction of IUDs parallel these other innovations in many ways, not the least because they were supported by powerful Western advocates, in this case, the Population Council and Ford Foundation. Nor should one forget the changing domestic political contexts and compulsions of this time. The narrow victory of the Indian National Congress in the 1967 elections clearly demonstrated that voters were more than willing to challenge a leadership that did not deliver on its electoral promises. In line with this political energy, Indian citizens were not willing to unquestionably accept the options for reproductive control that their leaders offered in the 1960s.

The sterilization campaigns of the 1970s occurred in the context of new kinds of international and domestic pressures. Domestic food shortages meant greater dependence on foreign food aid in the early years of Indira Gandhi's tenure in office.[16] This aid came tied to various demands made on the state, including the adoption of stricter birth control measures. Domestic political compulsions and her own political proclivities led Indira Gandhi to adopt a strong populist persona, undermining the influence of many leaders in her own party. When populism failed to deliver what it promised, in 1974 the Indian electorate threatened to turn against the woman whom they had deified as a goddess incarnate in 1971.[17] Indira's response was the declaration of a National Emergency, the two-year period that also saw the emergence of her son, Sanjay, as the de facto supremo of Indian politics.[18]

Abacus and *Malas*: The Indian State and Its Adherence to Gandhian Abstinence through Experiments with the Rhythm Method or "Safe Period"

In the 1950s Gandhian ideals of sexual abstinence had a continuing hold on Indian consciousness, a possible explanation for the state's adoption of the rhythm method as the first national birth control the program in the world. After all, rhythm was the only method that Gandhi reluctantly agreed to support during his debates on birth control with Margaret Sanger in the 1930s.[19] In addition, the first union health minister, Rajkumari Amrit Kaur, as a Gandhian and a Catholic, was only willing to support rhythm, the recently church-approved method. To augment the imprimatur of Gandhi, Amrit Kaur sought the help of a Western consultant through the World Health Organization (WHO) to operationalize this aspect of Gandhian legacy.

WHO assigned Dr. Abraham Stone, the medical director of the Margaret Sanger Research Bureau in New York, as the consultant to the Indian government in 1951. Through WHO, Stone was advised to concern himself with the rhythm method of birth control, since "the Indian government is definitely for the moment unwilling to consider any other type of family planning in India."[20] While Stone had studied the rhythm method in New York, he sought suggestions from his Indian colleagues on how best to help women, particularly urban working-class and rural women, keep track of their fertility cycles. One colleague suggested using beads strung together as a necklace or *mala*.[21] Different colored beads could be used to mark "safe" and "unsafe" days for intercourse. The physician or health worker would help string the necklaces for women on the basis of their individual cycles, instructing them to move the beads daily in one direction. Another colleague suggested that women could use an abacus to keep count of "baby" and "nonbaby" days.[22]

The rhythm method imposed a new "scientific" understanding about bodies on ordinary people, requiring women to meticulously track their fertile and less fertile days. Women encountered many practical difficulties as they tried to use the abacus or the *mala*. How could they determine the color of the beads at night? Planners tried to address this difficulty through designing a *mala* with different colored beads, and different shaped beads—red round beads indicated fertile days and square green beads infertile and safe days for coitus. But then women realized that one bead had to be pushed each day, but what if they lost track of which way to push the bead. Stone's team designed a necklace with a safety catch to allow the beads through only in a clockwise direction.

Even as Stone and his Indian colleagues addressed technical glitches in the design of the colored *malas*, they did not account for cultural barriers that further hindered the success of their experiment. These difficulties had to do with the fact that the target population of users did not possess the kind of "scientific" orientation required for successful implementation. According to reports, some women and men believed that merely wearing the *malas* would ensure contraceptive protection. Some believed all they were required to do was to move the beads daily to ensure safety from conception. Some women were hesitant to wear the *malas*, which they understood to violate their privacy by marking their menstrual cycle in public. Given that in some communities menstruating women were considered to be in a ritually impure state, some women felt they could not handle the beads themselves, and in some instances they asked a neighbor to mark the days of their cycle by moving the beads. Given that the beads were associated with menstruation, the *mala* itself was considered unclean, so some women left them in the cowshed instead of bringing them into the house.[23] According to a family-planning worker, there was general distrust of the bead system as a form of contraceptive.

> But these ignorant poor souls could not understand the idea of the beads. They would ask, Do we not avoid pregnancy by just pushing the beads? Are they enchanted? Or, Are you gods to stop giving children by such simple method? If you were so powerful, why not you give children for those who do not have any and who are praying to God every moment to bless them with children?[24]

Despite these problems, the Indian health minister, Stone, and others such as C. P. Blacker of the British Eugenic Society and S. Chandrasekhar, an Indian demographer and minister for health and family planning in 1967, all considered the rhythm method a culturally appropriate form of birth control for India because of preexisting cultural practices of abstinence inscribed within Indian traditions of marital coitus as well as Gandhian legacy. While conducting two pilot studies on the rhythm method in India, one in Lodi Colony, an urban setting in New Delhi, and another in Ramanagaram, a rural community in Mysore, Stone and his team also collected data on "Conditions of Sex Union." The findings pointed out the various intrafamily cultural dynamics that determined sex life within matrimony in India. Joint/multi-generational family structures in India practiced spatial segregation of sexes. Within these familial settings, the study reported, married couples did not solely make coital decisions. Instead, elders in the family determined when the couple was allowed to have coitus. Religious practices also prohibited coitus on certain days. Social beliefs associated with menstruation, pregnancy, and lactation imposed further abstinence on certain times. This preexisting cultural acceptance of sexual abstinence within matrimony in India, Stone and his team believed, could be particularly conducive for the successful adoption of the rhythm method, as it would merely require a slight shift in temporal and biological sensibilities within marital coitus. Couples, therefore, only needed to be educated about the correlations between female *ritu* / fertile period, coitus, and conception.[25]

Even as the rhythm method was espoused as a culturally acceptable form of contraception for Indians, birth control advocates expressed doubts about the ability of subaltern groups to manage their fertility in accordance with the menstrual cycle of women. According to Chandrasekhar, "The illiteracy and ignorance of our women is a formidable obstacle. We cannot entrust mothers with a contraceptive and some printed instructions. Our mothers, like conservative and illiterate mothers in other parts of the world, are notoriously ignorant of the structures and function of their reproductive systems."[26] In a similar vein, R. D. Karve, an early pioneer of birth control in India, voiced his objection to the adoption of the rhythm method, asking, "Is the rhythm method so simple that it can be easily grasped by idiots, whether literate or illiterate? It is certainly nothing of the kind. To apply it properly, observations have to be taken for at least six months in order to decide which days are safe for any particular woman, assuming that there are any such. Are illiterate persons capable of taking these observations themselves and decid[ing] which days they have to abstain? Even Dr. Stone does not think so . . . In my opinion, it is utterly stupid."[27]

Karve, Pillay, Dhanvanti Rama Rao, and members of the All India Women's Conference (AIWC), a leading national women's organization, strongly disapproved of the health minister's initiative to invite Dr. Stone to promote what they considered an unsuitable contraceptive technique. AIWC members suggested that the monies be given to their organization to carry out more relevant research on the topic. Karve, Pillay, and Rama Rao, all early Indian pioneers in the field of birth control, were miffed with the state for ignoring their work. Pillay used his *International Journal of Sexology* (*IJS*) to publicly register his objections to Dr. Stone and the health minister's pilot study. According to him, anthropologists would be intrigued with the health minister's assumptions that the rhythm method was in some ways consonant with the spirit and tradition of India![28] In another comment on the rhythm method in *IJS*, Pillay editorialized, "The enormous waste of public funds on a fad like the rhythm method will not be tolerated in any other country but India."[29] Rama Rao in a letter to Margaret Sanger also expressed her disagreement with Dr. Stone's pilot studies in India, writing:

> Dr. Stone stayed with me. We had very interesting conversations, and I took the opportunity to express doubts about the Rhythm System, especially for India, with her large illiterate population. I also told him that a number of us felt that he would be undermining the work we had been doing, for there was an impression spreading that a well known expert like him was propagating the Safe period theory in preference to contraceptives.[30]

India's experiment in the rhythm method attracted global attention. In her letter to *Eugenics Review*, Marie Stopes, a leading British birth control advocate, commented negatively on Dr. Stone's pilot projects as a "disaster for India!"[31] Questioning the effectiveness of rhythm, she asked, "Why should India thus be used as a helpless guinea pig? It is cruel as well as foolish to try to persuade Indian women to use a method which is so difficult to learn and manage, so unsuited to their personal needs, which has physiological and psychological harmful reactions even when successful, and which is so unsafe."[32] In addition, Blacker remarked on the importance of the study for generating information that might be useful in Catholic countries, where there was strong opposition to mechanical or chemical contraceptives. In the absence of the Catholic Church sponsoring an inquiry into the rhythm method, India's pilot study, Blacker argued, could prove to be useful for other global locations.

What explains the widespread support for pilot projects to study the efficacy of the rhythm method in the early years of the Indian republic? To begin with, it appears that the public discourse merged economic needs and competing philosophical traditions, in ways that identified the rhythm method as an attractive and viable birth control technique. While being "free," the rhythm method was additionally understood as being culturally aligned with marital coitus practices among Indians. The advocates of the rhythm method therefore argued that it did not impose a sexually alien regime within the Indian conjugal context. However, even when rhythm was understood as culturally appropriate for Indians, experts balked at promoting its mass adoption. Reasons for its lukewarm reception lie as much in the nature of the Indian state in the early 1950s as in the limits of rhythm itself. While population control was recognized as a state concern, neither Nehru nor Amrit Kaur were willing to compromise on social democratic and secular principles. Through the pilot projects, the state focused on generating information and consensus among its citizens, instead of imposing top-down reproductive decisions. Moreover, Gandhian ideals continued to have a hold on state imagination in the early years of the newly independent nation, and rhythm was understood to be aligned with Gandhi's advocacy of sexual abstinence.

The fate of the rhythm method was structured by the state's lack of vigorous support and also by the experts' doubts. Rhythm required careful and continuous vigilance on the part of women in tracking their menstrual cycles. Its contraceptive success was rooted in communication among couples, necessitating men's sexual cooperation. Its continuous adoption as a contraceptive could not be determined outside of the conjugal unit. All of these characteristics tempered its attractiveness for mass adoption among advocates of birth control, some of whom flatly doubted the ability of subaltern groups to rationally manage their sexual and reproductive lives. But according to one commentator, even if the rhythm method is understood as a failed experiment within the Indian context, it demonstrated a "greater demand than was expected for information on family planning: that is to say that the *principle* of family planning was found to be widely acceptable."[33] The Indian state met the demonstrated demand for birth control through Gandhian advocacy of rhythm, marking this as an idiosyncratically fractured episode within the larger history of contraceptives in postcolonial India.

Loop or IUD: War on the Womb

A national canvas is an inadequate frame for narrating the history of the introduction of the Lippes Loop or IUD in India in the early 1960s because the US-based Ford Foundation and Population Council were deeply implicated in bringing the IUD to India. Sheldon Segal, the Population Council researcher sponsored by Ford, personally helped to smuggle the first Lippes Loop IUDs into India disguised as Christmas ornaments.[34] Douglas Ensminger, the head of Ford in India, was frustrated with the Indian health minister, Sushila Nayyar, who was reluctant to support the introduction of the IUD. Nayyar, also a Gandhian like her predecessor, Amrit Kaur, doubted the loop's safety and appropriateness for India. Ensminger accused Nayyar of earmarking monies for her own projects; according to him, "Her every move was directed toward diverting budgeted funds from family planning activities to build up the public health infrastructure." Ensminger's criticism captures the focus of global politics and discourse on population in the 1960s. Reproductive health and rights were not part of the vocabulary and worldview of the population control lobby in the 1960s.[35] Only after an assurance of support from the Ford Foundation in 1965 did the Indian Council of Medical Research approve the adoption of IUDs within the national family-planning program. Even as the Indian state was reluctant to promote the plastic IUD or Lippes Loop, global nonstate actors such as the Ford Foundation and the Population Council pushed for its adoption as a mass-based contraceptive technology. The Population Council, funded by the Ford Foundation, promoted IUDs because they were regarded as "cheap, convenient and safe, requiring a minimum of both personal and professional attention."[36] IUDs were also preferable since they placed less responsibility on users than did the rhythm method, which relied on individuals to manage their sexual practices. The Population Council also provided grants and technical assistance for manufacturing Lippes Loops in India and other "developing" countries, such as Pakistan, Egypt, Taiwan, Hong Kong, and Turkey.[37]

Despite its initial reluctance to promote IUDs in India, the state zealously promoted this method from 1965 onward. "Loop squads" were created, and cash incentives were provided to both acceptors and doctors to ensure that between 1965 and 1967 the targeted numbers of IUDs were inserted. Because of its low cost and reversibility, IUD use boomed within a very short time. The state set targets that were time-bound for recruiting acceptors, and in the first two years, close to two million Indian women were fitted with an IUD.[38] According to Mohan Rao, "The intrauterine contraceptive device (IUCD) was hailed as the magic bullet to defuse the population bomb."[39]

Amid the fervor to promote this contraceptive technology, neither the state nor the nonstate actors explored the challenges of its mass adoption in a country such as India, with its weak healthcare infrastructure. In the initial enthusiasm to promote IUDs as a panacea for India's population problem, women were indiscriminately fitted with any size IUD.[40] Clinics were not always well stocked, and staff did not always evince consideration for women's well-being, especially when the focus was on targets of time-bound insertions. One observer reported that clinics typically "lacked even soap to keep hands and instruments sterile. . . . [W]orkers . . . would wipe bloody IUD inserters on their saris or with a cloth after each procedure, then reuse the inserter on other patients, spreading disease."[41] In some instances, the IUDs were inserted in a camp setting where the necessary prescreening left much to be desired. In a Bombay camp only 4 percent of women were rejected for IUDs based on their medical condition. According to Kumudini Dandekar, a demographer at the Gokhale Institute of Politics and Economics in Poona, this figure in the Indian instance was suspect, given that other countries had a rejection rate of over 20 percent for IUD acceptors, based on medical contraindications. Since Indian women were unlikely to have fewer gynecological problems than women in other parts of the world, Dandekar argued that the criteria being employed in the camps was either overly liberal or defective. According to Dandekar, eligibility for the loop was held up for "acute and chronic pelvic infection, cervical erosion, fibroids, dysfunctional uterine bleeding, vaginitis, cervical polyp, fibrosis of cervical canal, suspected malignancy and pregnancy."[42] These conditions were likely to have been common among Indian women, given their general lack of access to medical facilities. However, because of lax screening in camp settings, they were not spotted.

In the early years of its introduction in India, the number of acceptors for IUDs among rural women was impressive. Despite elite assumptions about rural women's irresponsible and indifferent attitudes toward managing their fecund bodies, rural adopters of the loop were highly motivated; after all, they were "willing to travel long distances withstanding the absence of transport facilities." Women adopted the loop in some instances despite their husband's objection or without even discussing it with their husband and other relatives.[43] Many women persevered using the loop despite adverse medical consequences such as excessive bleeding and cramping. The fact was people in poor and rural communities were very interested in both the rhythm method and IUDs. In the end, however, success was not sustained because the authorities persisted in uncritically and overenthusiastically promoting the idea that one device fit all; this orientation and its harmful consequences became the main cause for the IUD program's rapid decline after 1967.

In fact, by 1972, India as a whole almost backed out of the program. According to Dandekar, India's IUD experience was not a positive one, compared to the experience of South Korea or Taiwan. In India, the state, population experts, and providers focused on targets instead of on the well-being of women. Realizing this focus, Indian women became widely and rapidly disenchanted with IUDs. After 1967 the numbers of IUD adopters fell sharply. Many women had their loops removed and counseled their friends and relatives to do the same. David Mandelbaum, an anthropologist, recounts an example from Sherupur, a village in the state of Uttar Pradesh (UP), where "exaggerated stories regarding bleeding connected with the IUCD arouse untold fears,"[44] becoming a common subject of village gossip. The bleeding caused panic, and a rage to remove the "bloody" device spread among women adopters, their families, and communities. Physicians involved with the IUD program also recounted some of the "atrocity stories" circulating among village women. In some instances the physicians conceded deficiencies in techniques and general sloppiness, usually the result of pressure, they claimed, to meet target quotas.[45]

Women adopters also cited cultural conflicts associated with the use of IUDs: "Among Muslims, the urine drops which sometimes remain with the thread of the IUD can 'pollute' a woman's body and hence she can't offer prayer till she has taken bath."[46] Prolonged bleeding, spotting, and other menstruation changes caused many Hindu women domestic inconveniences, as menstruating women were seen as being in a ritually impure state and hence barred from participating in household chores and celebrations. While IUDs were advertised as a "free" contraceptive, and the acceptor was given a small cash incentive, episodes of prolonged and heavy bleeding meant women had to invest more time in making homemade sanitary napkins or spend more money to purchase store-bought brands, regarded mostly as an expensive "luxury" consumer item even within Indian middle- and lower-middle-class households.

The loop was typically adopted as a form of contraceptive among younger couples seeking to space their children. But in the hands of the state and organizations such as the Population Council and Ford Foundation, IUDs were enthusiastically embraced as a "weapon" in India's war on population. But this war on the womb crumbled when many rural and poor women claimed an independent relationship to their own fecund bodies and refused to comply with elite biopolitics that linked the adoption of a techno-scientific contraception to national governance and well-being. Many rural and poor working-class women forged an independent relationship to their fecund bodies, challenging elite efforts to bring their subaltern bodies within the ambit of governance. A UN representative to India was perspicacious in acknowledging personal rather than nationalistic impulses directing women's use of birth control, commenting insightfully that "no woman ever had an IUD inserted for the sake of the Gross National Product."[47] In fact, one could even argue that both the symbol and the reality of the menstruating female thwarted the elite biopolitical project of governing reproductive bodies through techno-scientific designs.

Observers reported that women received six rupees to have an IUD inserted and then paid a *dai* (midwife) one rupee to have it removed.[48] The *Mukherjee Committee Report* on the performance and supervision of IUD insertions in India did not give much weight to claims of "malpractice," that is, that women had the loop removed and reinserted in order to get the incentive monies, preferring simply to focus on the number of IUD adopters. For the members of this committee, it was unthinkable that "many women will submit themselves repeatedly to the examination and insertion of IUCD to make this small amount of money."[49] Program managers from Uttar Pradesh, Tamil Nadu, and Kerala, argued against raising incentive monies for IUD acceptors. What the Mukherjee report disregarded these managers accepted as a valid reason for maintaining meager incentives for IUD acceptors. According to these regional program managers, if the money for accepting IUDs was increased then acceptors (women) would remove an existing IUD and return for repeated insertions.[50] Historian Dorothy Roberts recounts how the incentive program for IUD insertions led to the emergence of an "IUD Factory" within Pakistan, "where doctors, motivators, and women collaborated to have IUDs repeatedly inserted, removed, and reinserted for multiple bonuses."[51] Even as some Indian state representatives favored pursuing an incentive-based program to promote the use of birth control, the cash incentive program underwriting the introduction of IUDs in countries such as India (and Pakistan) had the potential of abusing women's bodies for meager profits, particularly in moments of financial troubles associated with droughts and famines.[52]

The gap between the interest of the contraceptors and those of the Indian state widened further with the increasing complications that women suffered from the mass insertion of IUDs in the early years of its introduction. Had women been carefully screened and provided adequate information regarding what to expect, the story of the loop in India might have been different.

Empowering women by enabling them to have greater control over their reproductive bodies, though, was not the underlying purpose of introducing and promoting the IUD in India. Instead, IUDs were identified as affording a modern technological solution to India's population problem. Given the predominantly utilitarian understanding of the elite population control lobby, the IUD campaign in India acquired a "character of a mass drive to sell a new brand of toothpaste.... [O]bjections and doubts were swept aside and a virtual mass hysteria was built up."[53] Given the side effects and inconveniences, it is not surprising that the dropout rate for IUDs reached 80 percent in India in the 1970s.[54]

Democracy between the *Danda* and the Free Radio: The Indian State and Adoption of Sterilization

According to Kamala Mankekar the first *nasbandi* (vasectomy) in India was performed in Pillay's Bombay clinic in 1931.[55] As early as 1948 a recommendation in the National Planning Commission's subcommittee called for birth control on eugenic grounds, recommending "sterilization of persons suffering from transmissible diseases of serious nature, such as insanity or epilepsy."[56] Despite early calls for sterilization of target groups, only in 1959 was this method favored within the state's "cafeteria approach."[57]

In 1958, the state made its first effort to promote sterilization, beginning in Madras city, where physicians were given a cash award of twenty-five rupees to perform vasectomies on the poor. Later, the Madras government offered rewards to "canvassers" and to those undergoing the operation themselves. Government employees were given leave with pay for a weekend as well as a cash grant for voluntarily undergoing sterilization. The program was further extended in 1959, increasing the incentive for sterilization to thirty rupees to the recipient. State representatives argued that the money was a compensation for wages lost through absence from work and for transport costs. The central government recognized the program for its success and pushed various agencies to support sterilization as a form of voluntary birth control method. In September 1961 the Central Council of Health recommended the intensification of the program. The number of sterilizations from 1950s to 1974 steadily rose, making male sterilization one of the most popular options available through primary health centers across the country.[58]

Starting in 1970, the government set up vasectomy camps as a way to extend the reach of sterilization as both a contraceptive method and a tool to stabilize population growth. The first camp was set up in the Ernakulam district of Kerala state, where, in 1970, at a month-long mass session 150,005 vasectomies were performed. Encouraged by this success, a second camp was organized in the same city in July 1971. At the second camp 62,913 vasectomies and 505 tubectomies were performed. State officials argued that these numbers demonstrated "that large masses of people can be motivated to accept sterilization in a short span of time by an organized and concentrated effort. They provide a spectacular example of a family planning program transcending the traditional health and family planning network to become a total community effort."[59]

State government transported men and their families to the camp site, which was set up as a festive *mela* (fair). They provided careful screening before the operation and distributed cash incentives of forty-five rupees along with gifts of saris and plastic buckets worth fifty-five rupees. Authorities also provided a free meal and provided free entertainment and transportation back home for the acceptors and their families. Postoperative care was also available for the acceptors.

Organizers of camps argued that these community spaces provided significant psychological benefits to the acceptors, invalidating commonly held fears associated with vasectomy. Indeed, the mass camps marked a new and important intervention in promoting a male-centric contraceptive. As a state initiative, mass vasectomies sought to significantly alter masculine performitivity, especially as it related to male sexual and reproductive bodies within matrimony. Organizing these mass vasectomy camps in the style of village *melas* was an effort on the part of the state to gain legitimacy by using a familiar setting to accomplish a deeply unfamiliar act: shifting the traditional gendered use of contraceptives from women onto men. A community-based modality would ally masculine anxieties associated with loss of manly selfhood due to vasectomy. The camps by attending to and reinforcing the contours and content of masculinity provided a new and modern space for enactment of collective masculinity in service of the nation. S. Krishnakumar, the district collector of Ernakulam, Kerala state, argued:

> This group participation provided [a] psychological sense of security and support to each individual, allayed his fears, and reinforced his conviction. It took the focus off what, to the individual if he were alone, would loom large as a serious surgical interference with his reproductive physiology. The presence of

friends and acquaintances reinforced the individual's sense that what he was doing was socially acceptable.[60]

The state of Gujarat carried out a two-month mass vasectomy camp between November 15, and January 15, 1971. The camp was originally planned for a month, but was extended because of "spontaneous public response and continued sustained general demand for vasectomies."[61] The Gujarat camps set a world record in male sterilizations through a total of 221,933 vasectomies being performed in the two months, and in sheer numbers Gujarat camps outdid the camps in Kerala. In the Gujarat camps there were no provisions for tubectomies or IUDs. Once again, the state staged a prominent gendered shift in contraceptive targets. But even when the state constructed men as principal acceptors, not all men were equally targeted. In Gurajat 65 percent of the acceptors were illiterate; 77 percent were employed in agriculture, and all acceptors were clustered at the low end of income groups.[62] Thakor and Patel summarized the camps as possessing "well defined objectives; advance planning; efficient organization and management; education and motivation; mass publicity; higher incentives; active participation of government, semi-government, and voluntary organizations; and support of top officials."[63] Yet the authors ignored the working of class, caste, community, and gender politics in their assessment, presenting instead a sanitized narrative of state machinery and its success in reassigning normative masculinity in the service of the nation.

In her work Susan Davis reports that the sterilization camps were immensely popular in the early years of their introduction in India, for a number of reasons. The high motivation among officials organizing these camps helped generate local interest, and men received much higher cash incentives and more goods, usually worth one hundred rupees, far more than women received for accepting IUDs. Mass media and advertisement were an important component in ensuring high numbers of operations in these camps. Motivators visited individuals at home, plus the festival atmosphere at the camps made them attractive spaces for people in urban and rural areas. Contrary to common belief, sterilization had been a popular form of contraception before the National Emergency declared by Indira Gandhi in 1975, in part because the IUDs had acquired a bad reputation following the complications they caused and the rumors about harm that circulated among users.

Despite the initial success of the mass sterilization camps, especially if success is measured in terms of numbers of sterilizations performed between

1971 and 1973, the program soon encountered obstacles. Motivators liked the camp approach, but the primary health centers (PHCs) and family-planning centers did not because these entities could not compete with the incentives, cash or goods, that the camps offered. Center personnel actively opposed the camps for this reason and because they disapproved of the fact that the intense focus on sterilizations in the camps eclipsed other forms of contraception offered through the center. Most important, public health experts complained that the logistical issues of postoperative care and proper screening were compromised in the camps. In light of criticism and limitations of the mass camp approach, state governments decided to experiment with minicamps in 1973–74. In a report to Parliament, the Ministry of Health and Family Planning stated:

> While the number of vasectomy operations did touch a record level, it has been felt that in a larger perspective, such camps might become counterproductive. It was, therefore, decided not to continue this strategy on a regular basis but to make optimum utilization of available resources to strengthen the normal program, even at the risk of a decrease in number of acceptors in the short term.[64]

Sterilization acquired a particularly disagreeable reputation during the internal National Emergency between June 1975 and March 1977. During this period the central government, working through different states and union territories, coerced many men to seek out sterilization. After the announcement of the national elections on January 18, 1977, sterilizations virtually stopped.

Under Sanjay Gandhi's five-point program in 1976,[65] family planning emerged as a priority.[66] He and his cronies in Delhi established coercive sterilization campaigns with huge quotas, and overenthusiastic state leaders competed to raise these quotas with the intent to curry favor with Sanjay Gandhi. International agencies such as the Washington-based Population Reference Bureau also influenced Sanjay Gandhi's attitudes toward population control. While poverty eradication, development, and "modernizing" were the ostensible justifications Sanjay Gandhi used for promoting family planning during the emergency, it was also his personality that allowed him to push through antidemocratic measures to achieve his goals. According to historian Matthew Connelly:

> A man with no formal title who answered to no one—not even his mother—was just the kind of person to lead a population control campaign. It suited both Sanjay's politics and his temperament. He was an outspoken anticommunist,

favored foreign investment, and cultivated contact with the Americans (much to his mother's embarrassment).[67]

In their enthusiasm to embrace Sanjay Gandhi's directives on population control, different states introduced various draconian measures to meet their target. For instance, in Bihar food rations were withheld from a couple with more than three children; in Uttar Pradesh teachers were required to undergo vasectomies or lose their jobs; in Maharashtra a compulsory sterilization bill was successfully introduced into the State Legislative Assembly but did not become law, as the president of India withheld his signature, perhaps merely because the timing was not propitious.[68] After Indira Gandhi had declared elections in January 1977, there was some effort by the Congress Party to distance itself from the forced sterilization campaigns, arguing that the abuses were a result of "over-enthusiastic supporters of compulsory sterilization within the bureaucracy."[69] Even though the Maharashtra bill never became the law, it is significant to note that this bill called for the male partner and not the female to be sterilized after 180 days of the birth of their third child. Exceptions were allowed if all three children were of the same sex or if the youngest child was older than five, a provision likely relevant[70] only in instances where the family did not have a male child. Even though the bill failed, its intent was to advance, through state power, the dominant cultural preference for male children, even as it challenged cultural preferences for larger families.

In most states local civil servants, such as police officers, railway ticket collectors, and managers of fair-price/ration shops, demanded that eligible male members of every family undergo vasectomies, or else the men were threatened with arrest or loss of services. In order to advance its biopolitical project of securing "rational" fecund citizen bodies, the state tapped into all existing political, economic, and sociocultural apparatuses. One scholar has observed,

> The issue of licenses for guns, shops, cane crushers and vehicles, grant of loans of various kinds, registration of land, issue of ration cards, exemption from payment of school fees or land revenue, supply of canal water, exercise of powers on shopkeepers, any form of registration, appointments, transfers, bail applications, facilities relating to court cases—all were linked with the procurement of cases of sterilization.[71]

While the initial mass camp sterilization programs relied on material incentives, during the Emergency, the sterilization campaign turned extremely coercive, using threats and disincentives associated with loss of services. The "gift" of a free radio has come to stand in for the sterilization campaigns in many popular narratives associated with the Emergency period.[72] Indeed, a free radio was offered as an incentive to poor people, but in some instances the acceptors waited for a long time to receive their "prize," only to be disappointed and cheated out of a good faith deal they had entered into with the state. In a short story "The Free Radio," Salman Rushdie provides a moving illustration of the duplicitous state scheme. The protagonist Ramani, a poor rickshaw driver, defends and rationalizes his "choice" of sterilization saying:

> It is not so bad. . . . It does not stop love making or anything. . . . It stops babies only and my woman did not want children anymore, so now all is hundred per cent OK. Also it is in national interest. . . . And soon the free radio will arrive. . . . It is how the Government says thank you. It will be excellent to have.[73]

Ramani embraces his contraceptive responsibility, linking his performance of unfertile masculinity simultaneously to conjugal obligation and to responsible citizenry. After his vasectomy, he patiently waits for his free radio, which never arrives. When he reenters the caravan (many traveling clinics were used in rural areas to perform vasectomies) to claim his rightful reward, he is beaten up and sent out bleeding, without a transistor radio. This act of deceit captured in fiction was played out in numerous rural and urban settings as part of the forced sterilization initiative during the Emergency. In some instances, the high pressure on various levels of state employees to meet their target and acquire more "acceptors" created a new variety of a middle man—*dalal*, or commission agent. The *dalal* worked to bail out officers in distress, procuring for them vasectomy cases at a price. The *dalal* carried out "business" with or without the collusion of the PHC staff, getting false or noneligible cases by underpaying the acceptor. Rural and urban poor men were lucky if they received 25 of the 105 rupees typically earmarked for acceptors; the remaining was divided up between the PHC staff and the *dalal*.[74]

Some other excesses reported during the course of the forced sterilization program included predawn raids carried out on villages. Villagers would hide in the fields for days, and return only after a specific number of sterilizations (a number satisfying the village quota) had been performed. These raids, sometimes even carried out on public buses, constituted strategies for procuring acceptors in Rajasthan, Haryana, Uttar Pradesh, Punjab, and Madhya Pradesh.[75] Moreover, the sterilization program caused civilian deaths and casualties, though the number of dead remains uncertain. In one instance, police fired on Muslims in the Old Delhi area of Turkman Gate, claiming the disorder was due to the local resentment against slum clearing, whereas the residents claimed it was a result of the new family-planning policy of the state.[76] A "mini-Jallianwallah Bagh" incident occurred in Muzaffarnagar district of UP, where police opened fire on crowds protesting against forced sterilization of men whom the police had randomly rounded up and driven to sterilization camps.[77] In addition to fatalities associated with these encounters with police, records show 1,774 deaths during the Emergency that were associated with botched sterilizations. The total number of sterilizations conducted during the twelve months after April 1975 reached a staggering 8.26 million. For historian Patrick Clibbens, the figure is higher: "Almost 11 million people were coercively sterilized in two years," though he is referring to the twenty-one-month period of Emergency from June 25, 1975, to March 21, 1977.[78] According to some other scholars, the total number of sterilizations was higher than those performed over the previous five years in India and was also more than the number of procedures done in any other country in the world up to that time.[79]

In spite of the rising popular protests against sterilization, there was some support for Sanjay Gandhi's family-planning program. According to demographer Ashish Bose, Sanjay's supporters commented on "how bold he is! He is getting Muslims thrown out of unauthorized settlements. He is getting Muslims sterilized. Only he can solve India's population problem. The country needs danda (rod), not democracy."[80] Many in their enthusiasm to achieve the targeted number of sterilizations were callous about complications or fatalities. For instance Dr. D. N. Pai, director of family planning in Bombay, is reported to have said without irony:

> If some excesses appear, don't blame me. You must consider it something like a war. There could be a certain amount of misfiring out of enthusiasm. There has been pressure to show results.[81]

The sterilization program during the Emergency stands out as a unique and unparalleled state initiative in engineering national demographic shifts from above. What also stands out in this instance of state intervention is the rare focus on placing the contraceptive burden on men. This was a singular moment in the contraceptive history of India, when men's bodies were targeted as reproductive bodies.[82] According to journalist Vinod Mehta, "Sterilization, no doubt, was *the* birth control panacea for India."[83] Of all the possible reasons for the focus on men, one must begin with the limited medical infrastructure during the Emergency. Under these conditions, sterilizing women in large numbers would not have been medically feasible. Mehta provides a succinct account of the medical rationale that guided state preference for male sterilization. He points out that "the surgery involved was minor: it lasted no more than three minutes, could be performed on local anaesthesia, needed no hospitalization, and in the words of Dr. Pai, a devoted and tireless apostle of sterilization, without a drop of blood."[84] The Emergency's quota-driven mass approach to sterilization also favored men. Moreover, in targeting men, the state was directly focusing on the sexual decision-makers within Indian patriarchal households, thereby obviating complicated negotiations with other stakeholders within a multigenerational family unit, particularly elders in the family.

This gender shift in contraceptive use requires further analysis. Even as birth control was extolled—as empowering women—many birth control advocates questioned women's ability to use this technology correctly. Subaltern women in particular were repeatedly represented as intellectually incapable of following contraceptive instruction. It would appear then that when the state shifted to the male target, it was taking an opportunity to optimize success. With vasectomies men were not obliged to or responsible for regularly monitoring their sexual and reproductive behavior. Notably, the Emergency vasectomies did not simplistically target all men, but deliberately marked men along class, caste, and community affiliations. The reproductive bodies of working-class, agricultural laborers, lower-caste, and Muslim men were specifically marked as undisciplined and hyperfecund, and as such ideal for vasectomies.

The vasectomy policy led to a major political fallout for the ruling Congress Party in the elections of 1977. The Congress Party lost the elections, and the anger around *nasbandhi* (sterilization) was one of the major contributing factors that accounted for its electoral losses. Even if one agrees that reproduction is not central to men's identities in the same way that it is for women, the state-orchestrated mass sterilization campaigns during the Emergency were popularly understood as placing excessive burdens on masculine sexualities and men's overall health.[85] According to Mehta some of the pervasive myths associated with vasectomy that circulated in the public realm during the Emergency related to loss of male virility. It was feared that men would become impotent and weak and that their wives would turn promiscuous.[86] Historian Veena Talwar Oldenberg described an instance that captures popular anger against state-led sterilization initiatives that focused on yet another understanding of male bodies. In Lucknow, a Muslim cleric explained the impact of *nasbandhi* to his male audience: "This is what a vasectomy does; your own polluting emissions will collect inside and cause you to sicken." Oldenberg adds that the cleric went on to declaim with "considerable conviction; his explanations getting farther and farther from reality, describing how their male genitalia would wither and fall off and they would be eunuchs. The crowd made horrified noises and said that this was against God and religion but they were afraid of what the Government might do to enforce this policy. They cried death to the Congress Party and its leaders: Sanjay Gandhi *murdabad*! Indira Gandhi *murdabad*! Congress party *murdabad*!"[87] Added to these slogans was one that emerged specifically in North India: *Indira hatao, indiri bachao* (get rid of Indira and save your penis), capturing the popular "hatred" against Congress-led male-sterilization initiatives.[88] Further linking the male sterilization initiative of the Emergency to the figure of Indira Gandhi, Raj Thapar, a well-known woman journalist, turned to popular psychology, suggesting that Indira Gandhi was "the woman who wanted to kick all men around for the one failure of her marriage."[89]

Even as Indira Gandhi was awarded the United Nations Population Award in 1983 for promoting a national population control program, family-planning initiatives were adversely impacted through her and her son's ill-conceived, overzealous, and largely antipeople sterilization drive.[90] A signal consequence of the mass sterilization drive during the Emergency, has been the shift to female sterilization today as a favored forms of contraceptive in India.[91] Instead of shared contraceptive responsibilities, women disproportionately shoulder this burden, fostering an almost exclusive "female contraceptive culture."[92] The contemporary contraceptive scenario might have been different had the twenty-one months of National Emergency not impeded India's postcolonial democratic trajectory, leaving in its wake a marred and prejudiced public memory of male sterilizations.

Conclusion

What narrative emerges when we read the history of the postcolonial Indian state through the prism of birth control? Contraceptive technologies did not operate on the fringes of state power. Instead they were significant tools the state selectively deployed to repopulate and regenerate its citizenry along axes of class, caste, community, and gender. Looking at the brief span of three decades, 1947–77, it appears that the newly independent state experimented with two extreme ends of the political spectrum ranging from Gandhian advocacy of self-control through the rhythm method on one end, to a fascist genocidal policy of forced sterilizations of subaltern groups on the other. Even while contraceptive technologies were heralded as intimate symbols of Indian modernity, their use was sought to secure traditional hetero-patriarchal households, where the state authorized and legitimized the preference for sons over daughters.[93]

The history of contraceptive adoption in postcolonial India also highlights the inadequacy of a national framework, given the active involvement of nonstate actors such as the WHO, Population Council, and Ford Foundation, and foreign aid from countries such as the United States. Abraham Stone from New York led the pilot projects on the rhythm method in India; the Population Council and Ford Foundation were central in making the Lippes Loop available in India; President Lyndon Johnson pressured Indira Gandhi to make "a personal commitment to a more forceful population control program."[94] US food aid during Indira Gandhi's leadership was tied to population control. The Ford Foundation and the Population Council speculated about mass involuntary methods with individual reversibility for India.[95] Even as the Indian state, during the Emergency, unleashed a coercive sterilization program, the larger global context that pushed and promoted a singular contraceptive technology cannot be ignored within a historical narrative regarding contraceptive use in postcolonial India.

The history of three contraceptive initiatives discussed in this chapter highlight the ability of techno-scientific interventions to manipulate reproductive bodies, in some instances turning them into sterile entities. Nonetheless, as evident in all three instances, subaltern bodies were not inert entities that state and nonstate actors could willfully manipulate. Technology did not have a free hand in imposing temporary or permanent sterility onto sexual and reproductive bodies. Male and female bodies of contraceptors imposed limits on technological designs of control and manipulation. Colored beads for monitoring women's fertility ended up as jewels on the horns of cows. The effectiveness of IUDs as "fit-them-and forget them"[96] were foiled through women's decisions to seek paltry but meaningful sums through multiple removals and reinsertions. An unprecedented and outrageous number of vasectomies led to the overthrow of the dynastic Congress Party through general elections and mass disenchantment both with family-planning programs and Indira Gandhi. As evident through the discussion in this chapter, birth control is a generative site for recounting how histories of bodies, reproduction, nation, and the world are mutually constituted and reconstituted, in turn animating a complex political web of power along axes of race, class, caste, community, gender, and sexuality.

Acknowledgments

We would like to thank Mohan Rao and Sanjay Joshi for their comments on a draft of this chapter. Rickie Solinger read multiple drafts and provided detailed and thoughtful suggestions for revisions; we thank her for her time and indulgence in getting this chapter ready for publication.

Notes

1. S. Chandrasekhar, "Birth Control in India Today," in *Population and Planned Parenthood in India* (London: George Allen and Unwin, 1955), 83.
2. The reference is to Jawaharlal Nehru's speech to the nation on August 15, 1947. For a full version of this speech, see Brian McArthur, ed., *Penguin Book of Twentieth-Century Speeches* (London: Penguin,Viking, 1992), 234–37.
3. For details on the positions of these various constituents on birth control in colonial India, see Sanjam Ahluwalia, *Reproductive Restraints: Birth Control in India, 1877–1947* (Urbana: University of Illinois Press, 2008).
4. Ahluwalia, "Global Agenda and Local Politics," in *Reproductive Restraints*, 54–85.
5. A. P. Pillay, *Birth Control Simplified* (Bombay: D.B. Taraporevala Sons, n.d.).
6. Pillay, *Birth Control Simplified*, 133–34.
7. N. S. Padhke, *Sex Problem in India* (Bombay: D.B. Taraporevala Sons, 1927), 236. Also see Ahluwalia, "Demographic Rhetoric and Sexual Surveillance," in *Reproductive Restraints*, 46–50.
8. Ahluwalia, *Reproductive Restraints*, 54–85, 110–12.
9. See Bernard Cohn, "The Census, Social Structure and Objectification in South Asia," in *An Anthropologist among the Historians and Other Essays* (New Delhi: Oxford University Press, 1987), 224–54.
10. David Arnold, "Official Attitudes to Population, Birth Control, and Reproductive Health, 1926–1946," in *Reproductive Health in India: History, Politics, Controversies*, ed. Sarah Hodges (Delhi: Orient Longman, 2006).
11. *Famine Inquiry Commission Final Report, 1945* (Delhi: Manager Publications, 1945); *Report of Health Survey and Development Committee* (Delhi: Manager Publications, 1946). This report was popularly referred to as the Bhore Committee report.

For more details on the discussion of birth control in both these reports, refer to Ahluwalia, "A Fractured Discourse," in *Reproductive Restraints*, 133–37.

12. Ahluwalia, *Reproductive Restraints*, 115–18.
13. B. L. Raina, *Planning Family in India: Prevedic Times to Early 1950* (New Delhi: Commonwealth Publishers, 1990).
14. For details, see Ramachandra Guha, "The Conquest of Nature," in *India after Gandhi: The History of the World's Largest Democracy* (London: Picador, 2007), 201–25.
15. For discussion of the Green Revolution in India, see Francine Frankel, *India's Political Economy, 1947–2004: Gradual Revolution* (New Delhi: Oxford University Press, 2005).
16. Guha, "War and Succession," in *India after Gandhi*, 387–415.
17. The reference is to the Indo-Pak war of 1971; for details, see Guha, *India after Gandhi*, 457–66.
18. For details on the Emergency, see Guha, *India after Gandhi*, 493–521. Also see Emma Tarlo, *Unsettling Memories: Narratives of the Emergency in Delhi* (Berkeley: University of California Press, 2003).
19. For details on the debate between Gandhi and Sanger on birth control, see Ahluwalia, *Reproductive Restraints*, 54–84; also see Anna Aryee, "Gandhi and Sanger Debate Birth Control," in Hodges, *Reproductive Health in India*.
20. B. L. Raina, "The Colored Beads," in *Planning Family in India*, 134.
21. *Mala*, Hindi for necklace.
22. Abraham Stone, "Fertility Problems in India," *Fertility and Sterility*, May–June 1953.
23. Many of these instances of cultural barriers to the success of the rhythm method are recorded in Stone, Chandrasekhar, and Raina's essays cited above. Also see Purnima Chattopadhayay-Dutt, "Traditional and Natural Family Planning Methods in India," in *Loops and Roots: The Conflict between Official and Traditional Family Planning in India* (New Delhi: Ashish, 1995), 321.
24. *Final Report on Pilot Studies in Family Planning*, vol. 2, *Appendices* (New Delhi: WHO Regional Office for S. E. Asia, September 1954), 84.
25. Chattopadhayay-Dutt mentions tribal women in the Indian state of Orissa also observing an indigenous rhythm method. These women tied a sickle on their hips as a sign of being in *ritu*, their fertile days, and hence signaling to their men to stay away. For details, see Chattopadhayay-Dutt, *Loops and Roots*, 313–14.
26. S. Chandrasekhar, "Administrative and Human Problems," in *Population and Planned Parenthood*, 72–73.
27. R. D. Karve, "The So-Called Rhythm Method of Birth Control," *Indian Medical Journal*, May 1952, 131–32.
28. A. P. Pillay, "Mechanical Contraceptives, Barrenness and Immorality," *International Journal of Sexology*, May 1953, 246.
29. A. P. Pillay, "The Rhythm Method of Birth Control," *International Journal of Sexology*, November 1953, 97.

30. Mrs. Dhanvanti Rama Rao's Letter to Margaret Sanger, December 11, 1951, Watumull Foundation Records, Rama Rao folder, Sophia Smith Collection and Smith College Archives. I would like to thank Karen Kukil at Smith College for making the papers from this collection available for us.
31. For more details on the work of Marie Stopes, see June Rose, *Marie Stopes and the Sexual Revolution* (London: Faber and Faber, 1992).
32. Marie Stopes letter to the editor of *Eugenics Review*, April 1952, 58–59.
33. C. P. Blacker, "The Rhythm Method: Two Indian Experiments: II," *Eugenics Review*, October 1955, 169.
34. The Lippes Loop had to be smuggled because the devices had not been approved for use in India. Union Health Minister Nayyar gave conditional approval for the loop's use early in 1964, after being personally assured by population controller Alan Guttmacher that the device was safe. The Indian government approved use of the loop in 1965. Kathleen D. McCarthy, "From Government to Grassroots Reform: The Ford Foundation's Population Programs in South Asia, 1959–1981," in *Philanthropy and Cultural Context: Western Philanthropy in South, East, and Southeast Asia in the 20th Century*, ed. Soma Heva and Philo Hove (Lanham, Md.: University Press of America, 1997), 136.
35. For more details on the global population discourse and politics as it evolved over time, see Matthew Connelly, *Fatal Misconception: The Struggle to Control World Population* (Cambridge: Belknap Press of Harvard University Press, 2008); Alison Bashford, *Global Population: History, Geopolitics, and Life on Earth* (New York: Columbia University Press, 2014).
36. Donald T. Critchlow, *Intended Consequences: Birth Control, Abortion, and the Federal Government* (New York: Oxford University Press, 1999), 28.
37. Critchlow, *Intended Consequences*, 28.
38. According to Oscar Harkavy and Krishna Roy, eight hundred thousand women were fitted with IUDs in 1965–66, and that number rose to a million in 1966–67. For details, see Harkavy and Roy, "Emergence of the Indian National Family Planning Program," in *The Global Family Planning Revolution: Three Decades of Population Policies and Programs*, ed. Warren C. Robinson and John A. Ross (Washington, D.C.: World Bank, 2007), 316.
39. Mohan Rao, a professor at the Center of Social Medicine and Community Health, Jawaharlal Nehru University, New Delhi, introduction to *From Population Control to Reproductive Health: Malthusian Arithmetic* (New Delhi: Sage, 2004), 17.
40. S. N. Agarwala, "A Follow-up Study of Intrauterine Contraceptive Devices: An Indian Experience," *Eugenics Quarterly* 15, no. 1 (1968): 41.
41. Matthew Connelly, "Population Control in India: Prologue to the Emergency Period," *Population and Development Review* 32, no. 4 (December 2006): 657.
42. Kumudini Dandekar, Vaijayanti Bhate, Jeroo Coyaji, and Surekha Nikam, "Place of IUD in the Contraception-Kit of India," *Artha-Vijnana* 18, no. 3 (September 1976): 193.

43. Dandekar et al., "Place of IUD," 195.
44. David G. Mandelbaum, "Traditional and Modern Resources for Next Stage," in *Human Fertility in India: Social Components and Policy Perspectives* (Berkeley: University of California Press, 1974), 80.
45. Mandelbaum, "Traditional and Modern Resources," 81.
46. Chattopadhayay-Dutt, *Loops and Roots*, 134.
47. Sir Colville Deverell, who led the UN mission to India to evaluate its family-planning program in 1965, quoted in G. F. Salkend, "Communicating Family Planning in India," *India International Center Quarterly* 8, nos. 3–4 (December 1981): 284.
48. Connelly, "Population Control in India," 658.
49. *Mukherjee Committee Report*, Government of India, Report of the Special Committee Appointed to Review Staffing Pattern and Financial Position under the Family Planning Programme (New Delhi: Government of India Press, 1966), 37.
50. For more details on IUD incentives, see J. K. Satia and Rushikesh M. Maru, "Incentives and Disincentives in the Indian Family Welfare Program," *Studies in Family Planning* 17, no. 3 (May–June 1986): 136–45.
51. Dorothy Roberts, "From Norplant to the Contraceptive Vaccine: The New Frontier of Population Control," in *Killing the Black Body: Race, Reproduction and the Meaning of Liberty* (New York: Vintage Books, 1999), 143.
52. Michael E. Latham, a political scientist, argues that given the three-year drought in India that began in 1966, many Indians came to believe that they had little choice but to accept the incentive monies tied to IUD insertions and also sterilization. For details, see Latham's chapter, "Technocratic Faith: From Birth Control to the Green Revolution," in *The Right Kind of Revolution: Modernization, Development, and US Foreign Policy from the Cold War to the Present* (Ithaca, N.Y.: Cornell University Press, 2011), 108.
53. D. Banerji, "Health Services and Population Policies," *Economic and Political Weekly*, August 1976, 1249.
54. Chattopadhayay-Dutt, *Loops and Roots*, 135.
55. Kamla Mankekar, *Voluntary Effort in Family Planning* (New Delhi: Abhinav Publications, 1974), 17; also cited in Susan D. Evans, "Politics and Administration in India: The Role of Sterilization Program in Indira Gandhi's Emergency Rule," M.A. thesis, Duke University, 1978, 22. Salman Rushdie's short story "The Free Radio" is a fictional account of the vasectomy experiment during the Emergency period. For details, see Salman Rushdie, *East West Stories* (New York: Pantheon, 1994), 19–32.
56. Mohan Rao, citing from the National Planning Committee's Subcommittee on Women's Role in Planned Economy. For more details, see Rao, *From Population Control*, 20.
57. S. Chandrasekhar is credited with espousing this approach, which laid down that "theoretically all the scientifically approved contraceptives are available to

the people in the Government Family Planning clinics, but for mass consumption only four methods are now advocated and made available." These included vasectomy for fathers and tubectomy for mothers, IUD or loop, condom, and pill. S. Chandrasekhar, "15 Million Babies Less This Year," special cover story, *Enlite*, November 30, 1968, 13–14.

58. For figures and details on the expansion of the sterilization program, see Susan D. Evans, "History of the Program," in "Politics and Administration," 22–28.
59. S. Krishnakumar, "Kerala's Pioneering Experiment with Massive Vasectomy Camps," *Studies in Family Planning*, August 1972, 177–85.
60. Krishnakumar, "Kerala's Pioneering Experiment," 181.
61. V. H. Thakor and Vinod M. Patel, "The Gujarat State Massive Vasectomy Campaign," *Studies in Family Planning* 3, no. 8 (August 1972): 186. Dr. Thakor was the director of Health Services, and Mr. Patel was mass education media officer of the Family Planning Project; both were from the Gujarat State.
62. Thakor and Patel, "Massive Vasectomy Campaign," 191.
63. Thakor and Patel, "Massive Vasectomy Campaign," 192.
64. Evans, "Politics and Administration," 42.
65. Family planning was not included in Indira Gandhi's twenty-point program. Sanjay Gandhi was the prime minister's younger son.
66. The other four programs that were part of Sanjay Gandhi's five-point program were tree planting, a ban on dowry, each one teach one, and ousting casteism. Evans, "Politics and Administration," 72.
67. Matthew Connelly, "A System without a Brain," in *Fatal Misconception*, 319.
68. Harkavy and Roy, "Emergence," 311.
69. V. P. Pethe, "Family Planning and the Election Manifestos," *Economic and Political Weekly*, March 1971, 421–23.
70. Lynn Landman, "Indians Repudiate Coercion, Not Family Planning: Will New Government Support Voluntary Program?" *International Family Planning Digest* 3, No. 2 (June 1977): 3.
71. D. Banerji, "Community Response to the Intensified Family Planning Programme," *Economic and Political Weekly*, February 1977, 263; also cited in Evans, "Politics and Administration," 107.
72. The Bollywood film *Nasbandhi* (Hindi word for sterilization) in its song "*Kaya Mil Gaya Sarkar* Emergency *Laga Ke*" (What have you, the government, achieved through imposing Emergency?) captures the popular associations of the government sterilization program with various incentives, including tins of ghee (clarified butter) and radios; see https://www.youtube.com/watch?v=CbHvmMfVY7I.
73. Rushdie, "The Free Radio," in *East West Stories*, 26.
74. Banerji, "Community Response," 265.
75. Banerji, "Community Response," 265.
76. Banerji, "Community Response," 75. For details on the Turkman Gate incident related to the Emergency, also see Nazima Parveen, "Revisiting Turkman Gate:

'Situation under Control,'" *Book Review* 36, no. 1 (January 2012): 51–66; and Tarlo, *Unsettling Memories*.

77. Banerji, "Community Response," 81; Raj Thapar also mentions the incident in Muzaffarnagar and Pipli in her account of the popular resistance that emerged against the state's enforced sterilization program during the Emergency. For details, see Thapar, "Just to Remember," *Seminar* 211 (March 1977): 301–24. This reference is also cited in Evans, "Politics and Administration."
78. Patrick Clibbens, "'The Destiny of This City Is to Be the Spiritual Workshop of the Nation': Clearing Cities and Making Citizens during the Indian Emergency, 1975–1977," *Contemporary South Asia* 22, no. 1 (2014): 51.
79. Harkavy and Roy, "Emergence," 312.
80. Ashish Bose, "The Rise and Fall of Sanjay Gandhi," in *Headcount: Memoirs of a Demographer* (New Delhi: Penguin, Viking, 2010), 27.
81. Evans, "Politics and Administration," 78.
82. The figures for sterilizations are taken from Abhishek Singh, Reuben Ogollah, et al., "Sterilization Regret among Married Women in India: Implications for the Indian National Family Planning Program," *International Perspectives on Sexual and Reproductive Health* 38 (December 2012): 187–95.
83. Vinod Mehta, "Indiri Bachao," in *The Sanjay Story* (Bombay: Jaico, 1978), 114.
84. Mehta, *The Sanjay Story*, 114.
85. Jennifer Denbow presents an argument about the centrality of reproduction in shaping feminine identities. She cites Katherine Franke's idea of "repronormativity," in explaining how "the normative framework encourages reproduction and takes reproductive desire as a given," among women. For details of her argument, see Denbow's essay "Sterilization as Cyborg Performance: Reproductive Freedom and the Regulation of Sterilization," *Frontiers* 35, no. 1 (2014): 107–31.
86. Mehta, *The Sanjay Story*, 115.
87. For details, see Veena Talwar Oldenburg, "A Delicate Touch," *Sepoy*, December 2, 2013, http://www.chapatimystery.com/archives/homistan/a_delicate_touch_by_prof_veena_oldenburg.html.
88. People are fairly familiar with Emergency-related slogans such as "India is Indira, Indira is India," or *woh kehte hai Indira hatao, main kheti hoon garibi hatao* (They say remove Indira, I say remove poverty). However, the link between Indira Gandhi and her government's sterilization program through a slogan is relatively less well remembered within popular discourse in contemporary India. Mehta borrows the slogan for a title of his chapter in the book cited above. There is a brief mention of the slogan in Abijit V. Banerjee and Esther Duflo, *Poor Economics: A Radical Rethinking of the Way to Fight Global Poverty* (New York: PublicAffairs, 2012), 105.
89. Raj Thapar, *All These Years: A Memoir* (New Delhi: Seminar Press, 1991), 429.
90. Connelly, *Fatal Misconception*, 350.
91. Minna Saavala's study in South India identified female sterilization as the more common form of birth control; for details, see her essay "Understanding the Prevalence of Female Sterilization in Rural South India," *Studies in Family*

Planning 30 (December 1999): 288–301. During Ahluwalia's fieldwork in Jaunpur in the late 1990s, female sterilization emerged as one of the more popular forms of birth control women adopted. In Jaunpur this method is colloquially referred to as "operation." According to Matthew C. Gutmann, in Mexico too sterilizations are generically referred to as "la operacion." See Gutmann, "Scoring Men: Vasectomies and the Totemic Illusion of Male Sexuality in Oaxaca," *Culture, Medicine, and Psychiatry* 29 (2005): 86.

92. The phrase is borrowed from Gutmann's essay; for details on how he uses it in his work, see "Scoring Men," 79–80.
93. Urban and rural family welfare centers in Gujarat were asked to update their Eligible Couple Registers; within this it was specifically required that workers list the number of surviving male children. Couples that had at least one son were registered as eligible! Thakor and Patel, "The Gujarat State," 190.
94. Connelly, "Population Control in India," 651–52.
95. Matthew Connelly, "Controlling Passions," *Wilson Quarterly* 32, no. 3 (Summer 2008): 63.
96. Chikako Takeshita, *The Global Biopolitics of the IUD: How Science Constructs Contraceptive Users and Women's Bodies* (Cambridge, Mass.: MIT Press, 2012), 1.

5

Reproducing the Family

Biopolitics in Twentieth-Century Egypt

OMNIA EL SHAKRY

The rapid growth in numbers.
In 100 years from now Egyptians would number 49,600,000.
In 300 years from now they would total 500,000,000.
In 425 years Egyptians would equal the present population of the earth at 2,000,000,000.
In 968 years Egyptians would occupy not only the whole earth but several other planets as well at 973,300,000,000.

—Wendell Cleland (1937)[1]

The "population problem" denotes both the population explosion of other peoples and too low a birth rate of one's own people. During the nineteenth century in France one's own people were French, the others German and British. In Prussia . . . the others were Jewish. Today the others are the Third World. In late-Victorian England, the others were the labouring classes.

—Ian Hacking (1990)[2]

Between 1936 and 1939, the Egyptian Medical Association held a series of forums on birth control and the population problem; the first full-length book on Egypt's population problem was published; the first life tables for Egypt were calculated; a group of university professors organized under the rubric of "The Happy Family Society" to discuss the need for planned families; the first religious edict (*fatwa*) on birth control in the twentieth century was issued by the mufti of Egypt, Shaykh ʿAbd al-Majid Salim; and the Ministry of Social Affairs was created, part of its mandate being the study of the population problem.[3]

The constitution of population both as an object of knowledge requiring observation and management through "numbers, statistics, material phenomena," and as a social problem to be modified for the progress of the human race, I argue, took shape in Egypt in the 1930s.[4] However, the parameters within which the problem of population was discussed during this time period were far broader than that of contemporary discussions, entailing fields of knowledge as varied as medicine, geography, and sociology, in part because of the embryonic nature of specialized fields of expertise such as demography and vital statistics. It is this convergence of overlapping fields of knowledge that took the calculus of life and death, of the fecundity of lands and bodies, into consideration and marked population politics and the scientific reform of society at this time.

Cultural historian of science David Horn has detailed this process for Italy in the 1920s and 1930s, focusing on the formation of reproduction and welfare as objects of social scientific knowledge and new social technologies "intended to confront the 'problem' of declining fertility." Anthropologist Ann Anagnost has explored the notion of China as a nation that is "excessively populous," analyzing how the meaning of the one-child policy in China expanded from a "remedy for under-development" to a "sign of the modern itself." She notes that when the one-child policy was issued in 1978, population was posed not just as a problem, but also as a principal causal factor in China's failure to progress. Both authors treat population as a discursive construction. That is to say, they do not engage with the question of whether China is really overpopulated or Italy really underpopulated. Rather they treat demographic programs and their cultural meanings, neither as effects of objective crises, nor as "mere propaganda," but rather as solutions to a culturally constructed problem.[5] My intentions in this chapter are similar.

This chapter explores twentieth-century biopolitics in Egypt. It traces the origins of population discourse to the 1930s, exploring in depth how population debates revolved around the neo-Malthusian reduction of the birth rate (the problem of quantity), and the improvement of the characteristics of the population (the problem of quality). From the 1930s to the 1960s Egyptian population politics were inextricably linked to the state as the arbiter of social welfare, which was, first and foremost, an interventionist project—whether accomplished through a population policy, a program for land reclamation or social welfare, or the moral education of the demographic masses. By the 1950s and 1960s, a well-formulated population control initiative that included national and religious appeals to family planning was firmly in place, along with the establishment of the Supreme Council for Family Planning. I locate a historical shift, however, in Egyptian population politics during the 1970s, after the economic liberalization policies of Anwar al-Sadat, in which socioeconomic development, rather than social welfare, became the object of state control. Increased demand for family planning was initially linked by the state to the process of socioeconomic development through its population and development program, which focused especially on rural communities. Later, in the mid-1980s and under pressure of international donor agencies, a more direct targeting of family-planning services was deemed necessary.

This chapter, therefore, delineates two distinct biopolitical regimes, including one spanning from the 1930s to the 1960s that was characterized by a more holistic approach to population policy, in which population concerns were embedded within larger social welfare programs that marked the health, wealth, and welfare of the population as their object. After the economic liberalization polices of the 1970s, however, population politics became tethered to socioeconomic development, and the holistic nature of the previous welfare regime was disaggregated into its constituent components. Thus, population control and family planning came to be isolated and pursued with a degree of efficacy previously unknown. Throughout the twentieth century, I argue, Islamic religious discourses were by and large complementary, rather than antithetical, to these modern biopolitical regimes.

Debating Population

Throughout the 1930s and 1940s population was viewed primarily in terms of the problem of the quantity versus the quality of the nation's inhabitants, and configured as a component of social welfare.[6] Population debates thus revolved around two points—both related to the problem of population as a problem of social intervention and engineering. The first issue was the debate over the neo-Malthusian reduction of the birth rate; this concern generated a flurry of empirical, statistical studies on historical demography, and debates as to whether Egypt was in fact overpopulated. The second issue was the improvement of the characteristics of the population either through the encouragement and enhancement of "types" or the elimination of "defectives" through social welfare and eugenics. "Quality" encompassed the social uplift of the mother-child unit (often through maternal welfare programs) and the peasantry (through rural reconstruction projects)—and thus dovetailed with the concerns of rural reformers. What is unique about this time period, however, is the confluence of these two issues. Writers dealt with population as a "total social fact," that is to say, arguments regarding historical demography could not be separated from issues of social welfare.[7] The quantity of the population could not be divorced from its quality.

Prior to the middle of the 1930s population concerns were varied, with colonial figures, such as James Ireland Craig, expressing concerns about overpopulation or population maldistribution as early as 1917; and members of the indigenous intelligentsia, such as Mustafa ʿAmir, noting vast increases in population. But by and large, neither sustained debate nor consensus existed on the state of Egypt's population. Thus, for example, in the late 1920s debates on family law held that Egypt suffered from *underpopulation*, thereby providing a legitimization for polygamy.

After the middle of the 1930s a veritable onslaught of publications, conferences, and debates on population took place both in the mainstream press (in newspapers and journals such as *al-Ahram*, *al-Hilal*, and *al-Muqtataf*), in specialized professional meetings and journals (the Egyptian Medical Association), in the women's press (*al-Nahda al-Nisaʾiyya* and *al-Marʾa al-Misriyya*), and within the religious establishment (*dar al-ifta*). Major establishment figures, including members of parliament and landowners, in keeping with their landowning class interests, argued that the cause of Egypt's poverty was overpopulation and poor public health and housing, rather than the unequal distribution of landed property.[8]

The emergence of population discourse was greatly facilitated by the development of a modern census regime in Egypt under the supervision of James Ireland Craig, who had initiated a statistical regime in which "data was provided which was abstract, quantifiable and transferable."[9] Thus, by 1936, Egypt's population would be thought of *not* as an agglomeration of disparate populations—Upper Egyptian peasants, Bedouin, Nubians, foreigners, but as a homogeneous mass whose quantitative and qualitative characteristics could be observed, analyzed, in effect taken as an object of study—as a total social fact.[10] As such, population became subject to laws and regularities, which needed to be studied to effect the proper transformation of the social and natural world, to align the fecundity of bodies with that of the soil.

A key backdrop for the emergence of population debates in 1930s Egypt was the various international developments in demography, eugenics, and population studies. The convergence of international interest on the question of population in the 1920s and 1930s may be related to several factors—the disintegration of empire, the negative association of eugenics with fascism, European fears of depopulation, and the development and refinement of new forms of geopolitical representation, such as the use of aggregate and comparative statistical measures and the development of historical demography.[11] The interwar period witnessed the proliferation of international birth control movements and conferences, in which birth rates, rather than racial hygiene or eugenic merit, were the main focus of attention. For example, the 1927 World Population Conference held in Geneva under the organization of Margaret Sanger may be taken to mark the beginnings of the construction of population, first, as an international problem, and second, as an object of scientific prediction and management. In the words of one participant, "Production can only be rationalized if one undertakes to rationalize reproduction just as intensively and intelligently."[12] Widely read by the Egyptian intelligentsia, the conference proceedings were critical in the formation of Egyptian debates on population, and in particular regarding the question of the demographic optimum for population.

In contrast to the European colonial concern over depopulation and military expansionism, population debates in the colonial and postcolonial national context were deeply enmeshed in the bourgeois project of nation-building. Throughout the interwar period Egyptian elites mobilized nationalist arguments in debates on population. In 1936 as the Egyptian elite was aspiring to independence from the British, social planners were eager to assert their own controls over the realm of population, a new object of "governance" in the postindependence period. Population was to be rationalized as an object of knowledge and managed in the interest of the people. These concerns were especially salient given the imperialist ambitions of fascist nations like Italy and Germany, which made it apparent that population was a critical component of modern warfare and politics. With Italy on the borders of Cyrenaica and Ethiopia, such concerns were part of the recognition of the importance of numbers—or demographic weight—in the modern era.

Barren Land and Fecund Bodies

The first comprehensive treatment of the population problem of Egypt was Wendell Cleland's 1936 text of the same name.[13] Virtually all studies on Egypt's population problem take Cleland as an entry or reference point, and the enduring impact of Cleland's text on Egyptian population debates should not be underestimated.[14] Henceforth, the neo-Malthusian perspective (in which artificial mechanisms, such as birth control, are proposed to curb population growth so as to regulate the relationship between population and resources) achieved an unparalleled level of dominance in population studies.[15] As late as the middle of the 1960s, Cleland's groundbreaking book was still considered a hallmark of sociological writings on Egypt.[16]

Cleland's study, *The Population Problem in Egypt*, had concluded that based on a comparison between the growth of population and that of cultivatable lands, "the people appear to multiply more rapidly than the acreage."[17] Cleland argued that the density of population and scarcity of arable land and the exceedingly low standard of living and the high rate of unemployment among agricultural laborers were all indicative of overpopulation, the solution to which was an interventionist population policy advocating the use of birth control.[18] According to Cleland, the Malthusian "constant running ahead" of the fertility of man (and, hence, density of population) over that of the soil had led to the deplorably low standard of living and quality of the population.[19] Thus, "If the quality of people is of any importance, then somehow a limitation of numbers must be brought about."[20] For Cleland, the laboring poor and peasantry reproduced "unchecked," as "half-living listless people"—undernourished and debilitated by enervating diseases that "deplete[d] the vitality of the laboring classes," thereby reducing the efficiency of peasant labor.[21]

The issue of the labor efficiency and productivity of the population, particularly the peasantry, was a common concern among those espousing antinatalist positions, and was echoed at the 1937 Conference on Birth Control sponsored by the Egyptian Medical Association.[22] Several speakers, notably, Muhammad ʿAwad Muhammad, a professor of geography at the Faculty of Arts and one of Egypt's first professional geographers, and Mustafa Fahmi, a professor of social science and an official at the Ministry of Education, argued that high birth rates led to lower standards of living and lowered the productive power of the nation.[23] Such arguments had become increasingly common in the second half of the 1930s. The year following the publication of Cleland's book, El-Sayed Azmi, a statistician at the Ministry of Finance, delivered a lecture at the American University in Cairo in which he characterized "rapid and continuous population growth" and population "mal-distribution" as among Egypt's most serious problems, going so far as to suggest the need for embarking on a population policy.[24] Several notable Egyptian public figures and social reformers, such as Mirrit Butrus Ghali (1908–91) and ʿAisha ʿAbd al-Rahman (1913–98), began writing about the problem of rapid population growth in relation to the dearth of agricultural land.[25]

Similarly, in a 1930 text Salama Musa discussed the population problem in Darwinian and Malthusian terms, noting that the more evolved the species, nation, or class, the less fertile its population.[26] High birth rates, Musa claimed, simply led to the general immiseration of the laboring classes, since a smaller laboring population would mean higher wages. ʿAbbas Mustafa ʿAmmar, a young social scientist, was among the first to explicitly call for a national policy on birth control on the basis of such an argument.[27] At the 1937 conference ʿAmmar presented his case for birth control as a philanthropic issue, targeting the rural and urban lower classes as the primary beneficiaries of a birth control program.[28] Evoking in Dickensian-like detail the life of the poor as overburdened with children, he argued that workers and peasants were the most fertile class, and that overpopulation was the root cause of Egypt's poverty.[29]

Thus, the issue of population was discussed in terms of a material relationship between the number and quality of the nation's inhabitants and its national wealth and resources. This often metonymized in the image of a family, which could not sustain itself because it continued to grow although its income was fixed. As Cleland put it, "If capital and income are insufficient for a large national family, and the national family exists in misery, then the next generation should learn its lesson and limit the size of the family, so as to elevate its standards and remove its miseries. Surely a people can be as proud of the quality of its people as its quantity."[30] Cleland, Ghali, Azmi, Musa, and others had posited a fundamental antagonism between the rate of population growth (quantity) and the standards of living of the population (quality), and therefore the productive power of Egypt.[31]

Uplifting Women and Peasants

What solutions existed for such a dire national situation in which population was purportedly outstripping resources? Cleland had proposed a plan for reducing births that included (1) raising the standards of living and hygiene, which would result in decreased fertility[32] (2) promoting birth control clinics (3) and eugenic measures "to restrict propagation of the unfit, limit free social services and raise the age of marriage."[33] To control the peasantry's "natural" libidinal tendencies, Cleland argued, required social intervention, in the form of birth control, as well as moral education and psychological training. Many Egyptians at the Conference on Birth Control agreed. Muhammad ʿAwad Muhammad compared Egypt to China and India, noting favorably the Indian government's efforts to promote artificial birth control.[34] Kamal al-Din Fahmi, a sanitary engineer, presented a triumphalist history of the various birth control movements in Europe and Japan, in order to illustrate the acceptance that birth control had gained over time and place, despite the resistances encountered.[35]

Attempts to improve the standard of living, however, constituted the most successful population policy in the 1930s and 1940s. "Standard of living" encompassed all components involving the population's health and hygienic standards, ideally at a level that would optimize its ability to produce and provide for the needs of the nation. This included the provision of services for the social uplift of women and the peasantry, through maternal welfare programs and rural reconstruction projects.

Beginning in the middle of the 1920s, both private philanthropic organizations and government clinics tried to shape maternal practices and improve child welfare in order to reduce infant mortality.[36] Egyptian mothers were portrayed as ignorant of the principles of cleanliness and hygiene, and so children's dispensaries and maternal-child health clinics sought to instruct mothers "in the methods of cleanliness and the proper feeding and bringing up of their children."[37] In Egypt, as in Europe and the United States, education for working-class mothers addressed this so-called maternal ignorance regarding nutrition, diet, and sanitation through lectures, pamphlets, manuals, female health visitors, women's sanitary associations, and infant consultations.[38] Experts promoted the "scientific" protection of childhood, and Egyptian delegates were sent to attend international conferences.[39]

In addition to a focus on regulating the mother-child unit, experts concerned with the welfare and productivity of the population in the interwar years focused on the Egyptian peasant. According to Azmi, Ghali, Cleland, and others, the most fundamental component in any government population policy would be raising the standard of living of the peasantry. Cleland proposed a vision of structured, hygienic communities of peasants, living in a manner appropriate to the progress and civility of the modern world.

> In the following plan I see an average family of from three to five children with intelligent, literate parents, living healthy lives in solid, clean houses, very simply furnished, which will belong to well ordered, sanitary communities, all members having equal opportunities for plenty of clean water, electric light and power, a well balanced diet with enough protective foods, simple but adequate clothes, steady and sufficient work.[40]

The image of an average family living in ordered and sanitary communities was a powerful one, and one that many of Cleland's ministerial colleagues had been attempting to realize throughout the 1930s and 1940s. Such ideas had been operationalized in governmental programs and policies, such as the experimental village projects undertaken in the Delta between 1939 and 1941 by the Egyptian Association for Social Studies, as well as the model village projects of the Royal Agricultural Society.[41] It must be emphasized that projects such as child-welfare centers and rural reconstruction were essential components of interwar population discourse in Egypt, and thus the concerns of population theorists dovetailed with the concerns of social reformers.

As these discussions make clear, when theorists and social reformers framed reproduction, they rarely included women as agents of their own sexuality and fertility, as anthropologists Rayna Rapp and Faye Ginsburg have so persuasively argued.[42] The case of Egypt has been no different, as women there remained objects of population discourse and targets of intervention, effectively excluded from the public discourse on birth control until the middle of the century. Women's erasure from the discourse of birth control, however, did not go entirely unnoticed. Zahya Marzuq, a member of the Egyptian Association of Social Studies, reprimanded the audience of the 1937 conference on birth control for neglecting women's role in childbearing and childrearing. Marzuq argued that in order for women to provide proper childcare, they had to avoid the perils of early marriage, excessive childbearing, and unwanted children.[43] ʿAbbas ʿAmmar, another conference attendee, addressed the liberation of women directly. Birth planning, he noted, would enable women to coordinate their household and societal duties, enabling them to undertake the necessary reform of Egyptian society.[44] He asked, how could women liberate themselves if childbearing took up all their time? For ʿAmmar, the choice was to be made by women—"the dividing line between her freedom and her enslavement" lay outside the home—in the reformist politics of the day.[45]

Eugenics: *Tahsin al-Nasl*

As noted, the primary conceptualization of the population problem in Egypt at this time was in terms of quality versus quantity.[46] Quality encompassed the general characteristics of the population (age, sex, number of individuals per family, growth rate), their standard of living (which included the level of health, hygiene, and sanitation), and the prevalence of hereditary illnesses, such as mental or physical disabilities. Positive eugenics entailed the propagation of the fit—those who could most contribute to the well-being of the nation; while negative eugenics called for the prevention of mentally or physically "inferior" individuals from reproducing.[47] Population politics during this period was embedded within the larger concern over the health, hygiene, and vitality of the population. The depletion of the social body by the presence of "idle and ill-fed bodies" had to be addressed and remedied through the uplift of the lower classes. Thus, the creation of sound families, the improvement of the characteristics of the population through the encouragement and enhancement of "types," and the uplift of the laboring poor and peasantry through social welfare projects were all crucial to these discussions.[48] The social reform projects discussed in the previous section, which encompassed sanitation, public hygiene, child and maternal welfare, and puericulture, were thus all part of *tahsin al-nasl*.

Negative eugenics was discussed in the Egyptian context, for example, at the 1937 conference, predominantly as the removal, through sterilization, birth control, or confinement, of mental and physical "defectives" from the body politic.[49] For ʿAbd al-Hakim al-Rifaʿi, a professor of political economy at the Faculty of Law, Kamal Fahmi, a sanitary engineer, Ali Bey Fu'ad, director of the Child Welfare Section of the Ministry of Health, and Mustafa Fahmi, a sociologist at the Ministry of Education, the sick or infirm needed to use birth control, and those with sexual diseases, the insane, and the feeble-minded would require sterilization or confinement.[50] Repeatedly, they emphasized the importance of quality (*naw*ʿ), not quantity (ʿ*adad*).[51]

These concerns regarding the removal of mental and physical "defectives" were not simply the social Darwinist musings of a select group. In a series of articles in the popular journals *al-Hilal* and *al-Muqtataf* in the 1930s, authors emphasized eugenic considerations for any population program.[52] For example, ʿAbd al-Wahid al-Wakil, a professor of hygiene at the Medical College and future minister of health, suggested medical examinations for couples before marriage to ensure the health of the couple and the absence of sexually transmitted and hereditary diseases.[53] Similarly, in an article published in the *Journal of the Ministry of Social Affairs* in April 1941, the future Muslim Brother and Islamist Sayyid Qutb proposed the reconsideration of a law in Egypt that called for the medical testing and certification of individuals before marriage by government physicians to ensure the sexual and reproductive health of the couple.[54] The law had been originally proposed to the Senate in March 1928 and was being resubmitted in a modified form in 1941 by the Ministry of Health.[55] This failed attempt to medicalize marriage was one component of state efforts to assert control over the reproductive process. As healthy childbearing became a "national duty," nationalist discourse increasingly took up the women's question, encouraging the mothers of the future to "reproduce less in order to reproduce better."[56]

"Is Egypt Overpopulated?"

Not all Egyptian theorists and reformers accepted neo-Malthusianism in the 1930s and 1940s.[57] For example, writing in 1942, Elie Nassif, a professor at the Royal Faculty of Law in Cairo, composed a critical book-length response to Cleland's proposition that Egypt was suffering from a population problem.[58] Nassif was one of many writers in Egypt at this time who directly criticized the call for birth control. Drawing on the work of Italian statistician Corrado Gini, he emphatically claimed that population doctrines, as well as population itself, had to be historicized.[59] Nassif denied the validity of a universal demographic optimum, that is, a population corresponding to the highest real individual income.[60] Following Gini, he maintained that in certain instances an elevated population density corresponded to economic (and other) advantages. Whereas some races did not require demographic pressure to stimulate a spirit of initiative (e.g., Anglo-Saxons and Scandinavians), he believed that others needed it as a stimulant to progress (Italy and one could add Egypt); for yet others, demographic pressure might have no effect (India and China).[61]

Nassif thus developed a perspective that would account for the historical and cultural determinants of population growth specifically for Egypt. Mobilizing a loosely Spencerian formulation, he sought to explain how the evolution of social structures accounted for Egypt's imputed overpopulation, and how Egypt's population growth was a necessary stimulant to its social, political, and economic development. Of particular concern, he argued, was the fact that the fertility and vitality of the lower classes was continuously outstripping that of the upper classes. Indeed, a crucial component of nationalist thought in the 1930s was the concern for the formation of a *classe dirigente* that would lead Egypt toward an indigenous modernizing nation-state. Social reformers remained concerned that any attempt at inaugurating neo-Malthusian practices would lead the "lower orders" to overwhelm, numerically, the productive and innovative middle classes.

Many opponents of birth control at the 1937 Conference on Birth Control agreed. Thus, Muhammad Hasan and leader of the Muslim Brothers Hasan al-Banna argued that it would be the educated middle classes that would heed the call to birth control, with harmful national consequences.[62] Similarly, ʿAbd al-Majid Nafiʿa, a member of the Chamber of Deputies and a lawyer noted for his fervent economic nationalism, argued that the call for birth control was a "national crime and not a social necessity."[63] Arguing that birth control was antinationalist, and indeed a form of national suicide, Nafiʿa urged the reconsideration of Malthus's population doctrine. Instead, he called for a return to the belief in the strength of population numbers as the vital force of the nation. Population discourse thus entered what historian Roger Owen termed "the ideology of economic nationalism," which associated Egyptian national identity with the consolidation of independent economic interests in industry, agriculture, and finance.[64]

Elie Nassif disagreed with Cleland's analysis that assessed population numbers only in terms of *already* cultivated agricultural land. He saw no reason to assume that an increase in population would be problematic if the increase in the rate of agricultural production continued and innovations in irrigation, draining, and cropping techniques were incorporated.[65] The only "population problem" Nassif acknowledged was the imbalance in the spatial distribution of the nation's inhabitants. Foreshadowing what would effectively become, within a decade, a crucial part of Egypt's population policy, Nassif suggested an internal colonization to obtain an optimal distribution of population.[66] Thus, at the same time that barren lands in the northern Delta were being reclaimed, he suggested, massive transplantations of people—a grandiose plan for interior colonization—could be coordinated, thereby contributing to the social evolution of the nation toward a better social future.

Religious Discourse

Thus far, I have concentrated on scholars whose discussion of the merits and demerits of population control was limited to concerns related to the health, wealth, and well-being of the population and the nation, and yet what of religious discourses? The first fatwa (nonbinding religious edict) issued in the twentieth century on birth control or birth planning was issued in January 1937 by Shaykh ʿAbd al-Majid Salim.[67] It was issued in response to a question regarding the permissibility of child spacing as a safeguard against the inability of the inquirer to raise and care for his children, concerned that he might suffer from ill-health or a nervous breakdown, or that his wife's health might deteriorate due to repeated pregnancies. The fatwa explicitly sanctions the prevention of pregnancy in the circumstances cited in the inquiry, stating, "The husband or wife may with the consent of each other use contraceptive measures to prevent male semen from reaching the woman's uterus." The fatwa continues, "According to later jurists, either the husband or wife may use contraceptives . . . without the consent of the other party," out of fear that "the child born may act evilly because of the corruption of the age." Salim further elaborates on the Islamic position on abortion, noting that "although abortion has not been sanctioned as a rule, it has now been accepted that an exception may be made and abortion be permitted before the child is gifted with a soul, if the present pregnancy endangers the life of the previous child."[68]

Salim's fatwa was argued on both moral and material grounds. It expressed a fear that the newborn child might act evilly (because of general societal religious decline) or be improperly cared for (because of economic, health, or social stresses faced by parents). In this sense, it was consistent with older, premodern edicts, which emphasized fear of the child's moral corruption—whether due to religious decline or improper care—as the predominant motive for birth control.[69] It was within the Islamic discursive tradition, then, that a modern jurist, such as Salim, argued, usually extrapolating by analogy from the justification of coitus interruptus to modern methods of birth control. However, throughout the twentieth century and within the context of the modernizing nation-state, the emphasis would increasingly come to be placed on *rational planning*—planning for a family and for the future in accordance with one's social and economic abilities, and planning for the nation-state in accordance with its resources. In this sense, Salim's fatwa may be considered modern.

Shaykh Salim's fatwa was not, however, taken as axiomatic, and several participants at the 1937 conference on birth control took it upon themselves to discuss the religious aspects of birth control or planning, most notably the supreme guide of the Society of Muslim Brothers, Hasan al-Banna.[70] For al-Banna, Islam was a total system, which encompassed all human affairs, practical and spiritual.[71] According to al-Banna and Issa 'Abduh, his fellow Muslim Brother in attendance at the conference, Islam ordered a continuous state of preparedness and strength for jihad as a religious duty.[72] For al-Banna, the logical corollary was that "Islam commands a multitude of offspring, it incites it and calls for it, and does not ask for control or lessening."[73] 'Abduh posited the encouragement of childbearing as the highest ideal for the Muslim family, arguing that Egyptian family life had become mired in a life of luxury and required a return to simplicity.[74] 'Abduh blamed the un-Islamic state that had neglected the fate of the family, leaving the head of the household to bear the social and economic burdens of the postwar period.[75] Indeed, social welfare projects formed the cornerstone of the Muslim Brotherhood's response to the economic difficulties of the interwar and postwar period, and the foundation of their critique of the secular state.[76] In point of fact, a focus on the family was a discursive thread held in common among all who debated the question of population control regardless of their specific position on birth control.

The Modern Family

At the same time that theorists and others constructed population as a statistical and material phenomenon—an object of knowledge requiring observation and management—nationalists and social reformers were in the process of transforming "the family" from a *metaphor* to an *instrument* of governance. That is to say, there was a shift away from the use of metaphors of homes and families to discuss the state of the Egyptian body politic, toward discursive practices that targeted actual families as objects of social intervention. As practitioners in their various fields, social reformers outlined the problem of population as a problem of social intervention and engineering. Population discourse in twentieth-century Egypt normalized monogamous sexuality within the parameters of modern family life—bourgeois companionate marriage, small family size, and middle-class hygiene—while organizing reproduction within a framework of social reform.[77] This entailed the dual process of assigning women to healthy, modernized, and regulated reproduction and childrearing, while tasking men with the management of birth control, either in their domestic capacity as heads of household, or in their political capacity as social reformers.

Social scientific discourses emerged surrounding the optimization of the species body and its "biological processes: propagation, births and mortality, the level of health, life expectancy and longevity."[78] Such attempts at the "intelligent and constructive production of the human race" *necessarily* relied on a statistical and empirical notion of "population" as a quantifiable essence, but operated, predominantly, through the instrumentalization of the family. The two principal anxieties of this period, the problem of population and the regulation of women and the peasantry, crystallized in the concern for—and the determination to modernize—the family unit. Experts believed that creating the modern family (indeed modern citizens) required the construction of new dispositions (self-governance, self-improvement), new habits of cleanliness and hygiene, and the cultivation of new sensibilities appropriate to the order of the modern world.[79]

Planning the National Family

It is not difficult to imagine the scene in Tahrir Province, the definitive land reclamation project inaugurated under Gamal Abdel Nasser, upon the arrival of a high-profile visitor—such as the Yugoslavian ambassador or the representatives of the newly formed National Assembly, all of whom visited in 1957.[80] Former peasants appeared now as citizens: men dressed in gingham shirts and overalls, and women dressed in white shirts, black skirts, and printed headscarves, looking quite "picturesque" for the cameras. Early morning visitors would no doubt witness the call to attention, the daily salutes and nationalist songs sung in unison. Visitors would also surely note, as scholar Doreen Warriner did during her 1956 visit, that settlers had been subjected to "complete human reconditioning. . . . Every aspect of their lives was disciplined and standardized."[81] Visitors might also have remarked upon the rows of new houses, each identical to the other, "consisting of two rooms, a hall, a kitchen, and a bathroom . . . a front terrace and a backyard," all "carefully planned and built according to health conditions."[82] The village itself, with its spacious and straight roads, and a main square situated in the center (with buildings for village administration, a cooperative center, school, nursery, and clubs for migrants and employees), would have appeared quite unlike any other "typical" Egyptian village in the Delta.[83] An especially astute observer might have also noticed the peculiar absence of any children running around the village—since all were safely ensconced in daycare centers.

Land reclamation projects, such as in Tahrir Province, formed a cornerstone of the Nasserist conception of the population problem. These projects were launched in the 1950s to address the slow rate of expansion of cultivated land area relative to rapid population growth and to facilitate a better population distribution. The totalizing model of social welfare embodied in the Tahrir Province project recalled the multitude of social welfare projects developed in the 1930s in response to the "population problem" that marked women and the peasantry as targets of moral and material improvement. These attempts at the reconstitution of both the Egyptian mother-child unit and the peasantry focused on reconstructing bodies and minds: building and cleaning villages and homes, and producing healthy children, and thus constructing a "new Egyptian."

By the 1950s Egypt's political climate was characterized by a statist ideology of rational planning, scientific research, and social welfare. Even though population growth was considered a far larger problem than in the previous period, population politics under Nasser continued to frame social welfare (and not economic development) as the primary object of state concern. Government efforts focused both on reducing population growth through nascent family-planning efforts and on expanding horizontally to reclaim land. Here I focus on the government sponsored family-planning programs that mobilized ideologies of national and social progress and that emphasized family planning as an integral component of the welfare of the state and its people, a culmination of the discourse on social welfare of the 1930s.

In 1953 the minister of social affairs, Dr. 'Abbas Mustafa 'Ammar, submitted a memorandum to the Permanent Council for Public Services highlighting the gravity of Egypt's population problem and its implications for the health, education, and welfare of the people.[84] The memorandum inaugurated an official state discourse on population and family planning and urged the formation of a National Commission for Population Questions. The memorandum stated, "It is essential for the responsible authorities to take a definite attitude towards the population problem and to play a positive role in alleviating all evil consequences. . . . In our opinion, any reforming and welfare policy which disregards population growth is but a short-sighted policy."[85] The commission's charge was to study population trends in Egypt, the impact of population growth on economic development, and the methods that influence population trends "in such a manner that may advance the welfare of the individual, family and society," and to make recommendations for a national population policy.[86]

The commission's first meeting, held in January 1954, included twelve members, among them ministers of social affairs, public health, and agriculture, as well as economists, demographers, statisticians, and physicians. The tasks of the commission were distributed among demographic, economic, and medical subcommittees that placed heavy emphasis on social planning and scientific research. Significantly, the medical subcommittee was "to help spread sex-education at different levels through audio-visual aids; to inaugurate family planning clinics for the purpose of experimentation with various contraceptives to determine the actual degree of acceptability and effectiveness."[87] These were among the first programs of their kind in the Middle East.

In 1954, during a press conference, Lieutenant Colonel Husayn al-Shafaʿi, a member of the Free Officers who later became a minister of social affairs, was asked his opinion on birth control policies and replied,

> Not only do I approve of birth control, but I also believe that it has become a social necessity. Over-production in population, as well as in other fields, becomes waste. Human waste, which has resulted from unlimited reproduction, has created complex social problems.[88]

Al-Shafaʿi conceptualized population as a component aspect of production, arguing that biological reproduction was outstripping material production. Similarly, in the same year at a speech given at al-Azhar, on the second anniversary of the revolution, President Nasser declared, "Our greatest calamity, a legacy of the past, was continuing to live on limited resources which did not increase. It was similar to a family whose children were continuously increasing, on a constant income that never grew."[89] Nasser's comparison of the state to a family that could not feed itself highlights the paternalist, etatist role of the state, and underscored the idea that population growth was a process related to a set of fixed resources. It followed from this, then, that efforts would concentrate on either territorial expansion in the form of land reclamation or on reducing birth rates.

Scholars have noted that population work in the 1950s was more experimental than operational and was not characterized by an explicit birth control agenda as part of the state's population policy. Indeed, in those years birth control work was done "quietly on the side" by private voluntary organizations run mostly by women.[90] It would not be until 1962, when Egypt's National Charter was officially promulgated, that the state would shift toward a more explicit family-planning agenda.[91] Egypt's 1962 National Charter enshrined the family as "the first cell of society" and demonstrated the importance of "modern scientific planning" and the state's drive toward increased production, with population growth increasingly articulated as a national threat.[92] The Charter articulated this position:

> Population increase constitutes the most dangerous obstacle that faces the Egyptian people in their drive towards raising the standard of production in their country in an effective and efficient way. Attempts at family planning deserve the most sincere efforts supported by modern scientific methods.[93]

The declaration was heralded as a breakthrough regarding the scope of state responsibility for family planning; henceforth limits on the provision of contraceptives would be lifted, mass media efforts would be mobilized, and research efforts aimed at enhancing the public promotion of family planning would be inaugurated.[94]

By 1964 a ministerial committee composed of demographers, sociologists, educators, psychologists, journalists, and theologians was organized to plan and evaluate the dissemination of family-planning information.[95] Social science research on family structure, ideal family size, and reproductive behavior patterns; demographic analysis of census data and vital registration; and biomedical research on contraceptive acceptability all became vital enterprises. In addition, universities vastly expanded training for specialized fields such as demography, statistics, and medical social work, laying the groundwork for the formulation of a population control strategy.[96]

In public speeches at this time, President Nasser explicitly associated population control with the nation's progress:

> The prime minister Zakariah Mohieddin presides over the Birth Control Council. . . . Listen to his plans in the field of social development. . . . We will be unable to provide a decent standard of living to a family that produced many children. There is no need to produce many children at the expense of the mother's health . . . . We know that God provides. God of course said that although he is dependable, we should work. The prophet appealed to our

> rational thinking and told us to stop being fatalistic. . . . If you do not, you are lost and the plan will be equally lost.[97]

Nasser also became more direct in his appeals for the practice of family planning and, according to Haifa Shanawany, "assumed the role of educator, supporting his speeches with Qur'anic and prophetic recitations and emphasizing the importance of maintaining the nation's health."[98]

In 1965 the Supreme Council for Family Planning was founded in order to establish a complete strategy for family planning in the country; to study and coordinate all population affairs, including medical, statistical, social, economic, and all other scientific studies pertaining to family planning; and to develop cooperational links between the various organizations participating in the program's organization.[99] The council was to expand family-planning clinics and services to all parts of the country in order to reduce population growth. The plan became a reality in 1966 with an allocated budget of one million Egyptian pounds.[100] By April 1968 some 2,631 clinics were providing contraceptive services to over 230,000 women.[101] In 1968 a "family-planning week" was sponsored, the first time family-planning efforts received widespread media attention.[102]

Historian Beth Baron has argued that the formation of the Supreme Council for Family Planning signaled a process of "reorganization, centralization, and nationalization."[103] The increased centralization of family-planning efforts eventually led to a top-down approach characterized by a medical and technological, rather than a sociologically or culturally oriented, method. Tracing various attempts to deliver contraception through private voluntary organizations run by women, she notes how community work run through social advocacy eventually gave way to a statist approach in collaboration with large foreign funders: "Egyptian female reformers were sidelined and an opportunity for female-centered family planning was for the moment lost."[104] Yet, at the same time, women's activism had shifted the position of women in this domain. No longer simply objects of population discourse, women were now "reproductive subjects" and active participants in what was being cast as a national struggle for the well-being of society.[105]

Moreover, religious discourses, along with secular state discourses, began to debate family planning and the population problem in terms of the coordination of biological and material production. In 1950 Islamist Khalid Mohammed Khalid, an Azhar graduate, discussed the importance of "planning both the materials and human production of society if a balance between them is to be achieved." Hence he stated,

> There is no hope of improving the standard of living so long as birth-rates are increasing. . . . The problem is complicated by the fact that our society does not realize that it is facing a crisis which may threaten its welfare and progress. . . . This crisis is due to our misconception of religion. Islam permits birth control in the interest of society and for the welfare of the individual.[106]

Religious discourse during the Nasser era shifted in focus toward planning. Within the historical context of state socialism and the modernization of reproduction, family planning fit neatly into the nationalist scheme of planning: planning for a family, planning for the future in accordance with one's socioeconomic capacities and needs, and planning for the nation-state, in accordance with its resources.

Two fatwas issued during this period exemplify the extent to which the issue of family planning was embedded within the social welfare discourse of the time. A fatwa issued by Shaykh Mahmud Shaltut in 1959 dismissed the possibility of an obligatory birth control policy. Rather, he stated that birth control might be allowed under special circumstances for

> women who bear children too quickly in succession, or suffer from contagious diseases, and for the minority whose nerves are weakened and cannot face up to their manifold responsibilities and do not find assistance from their government or the wealthy members of their society that would enable them to shoulder their responsibilities. In such cases, where birth control is individual and specific, it is a remedy designed to avoid well known evils and through which strong and righteous progeny may come into being.[107]

Shaykh Hassan Ma'mun issued a fatwa in 1964, published in the daily newspaper *Akhbar al-Yawm*, along similar lines. Ma'mun began by elaborating upon the original intent of the Islamic call for procreation and multiplication, as being both legitimate and suitable at the time, "as its early followers were few and weak in the midst of a vast majority of aggressive and oppressive people." He continued by stating:

> But now we find that conditions have changed. We find that the density of population in the world threatens seriously to reduce the living standards of mankind to the extent that many men of thought have been prompted to seek family planning in every country, so that the resources may not fall short of ensuring a decent living for its people and to provide public services for them. Islam . . . has never been opposed to what is good to man. . . . I see no objection from the *Shari'ah* point of view of the consideration of family planning

> ... if there is a need for it, and consideration is occasioned by the people's own choice and conviction, without constraint or compulsion.[108]

These fatwas are similar in their emphasis upon the household unit as the level at which the issue of family planning was to be decided, and indeed, in relying upon the Islamic tradition for argumentation, all the fatwas emphasize maternal and familial health and welfare, as well as issues of morality and virtue. What differentiated these fatwas from earlier edicts was the shift in emphasis from familial health to the welfare of the nation-state. Thus, the discussion shifted toward the world's ability to sustain a population that could enjoy a reasonable standard of living, while the emphasis remained upon the general welfare of the people. Family planning, thus postulated, became a concern tied to the viability of the welfare of the nation and its citizens.

What remains clear is that family-planning discourse during the 1950s and 1960s, both religious and secular, was embedded within a social welfare model of governance, wherein family planning was one constituent component of a larger holistic vision for national welfare, addressing psychological, social, and economic issues all at once.

Population and the Discourse of Development

The 1970s, marked by a transition to economic liberalization and an influx of foreign aid, would herald an epochal shift in Egypt's population politics. After the open-door economic policies of Anwar al-Sadat known as *Infitah*, a global shift occurred in which local and international agents (such as the representatives of the state bourgeoisie and capitalist interests in the state apparatus; global multinational corporations with local liaisons; and USAID) actively incorporated Egypt into a neoliberal capitalist regime while dismantling the welfare state. In this environment, socioeconomic development rather than social welfare became the state's primary object of governance. This led to the demonization of "the people," now defined as constituting a population threat to be curbed (or redistributed to uninhabited parts of Egypt) rather than as a national resource to be cultivated.

The principal manifestation of this shift was a new and intense focus on socioeconomic development as a precursor and condition for demographic change. Egypt's official "National Population Policy" was formulated in 1973 and related population growth directly to socioeconomic factors, while its main programmatic expression was the Population Development Program. This phase of population policy (1973–85) emphasized the significance of raising the general standard of living; expanding functional education; upgrading the status of women and increasing their labor force participation; mechanizing agriculture; extending social security; and informing the public of family-planning services, as important factors in, first, spurring economic development and, then, reducing fertility rates.[109]

By 1975 three dimensions of the population problem were emphasized: reducing the growth rate; achieving better geographical distribution of population; and improving the characteristics of the population.[110] The bedrock of these policies was a rural community program, formalized in 1979, that aimed to increase awareness of the population problem, improve knowledge and availability of family planning, and stimulate socioeconomic development.[111] The fundamental premise of these programs was to break the links between low levels of socioeconomic development and high fertility coupled with low rates of labor productivity.[112] Program employees, using "Knowledge-Attitude-Practice" studies, began to track such factors as "cultural attitudes" toward family planning, and, in particular, resistance to family planning.[113] Throughout the 1970s the use of mass communication techniques rapidly expanded and aimed not only at the dissemination of family-planning knowledge, but at the inculcation of small family size norms. For instance, the Ministry of Education introduced population education into the national curriculum in 1974. President Sadat stated, "Probably our failure in solving this [population] problem is due to our over-reliance on the medical aspects alone without making efforts to convince the masses of the value of family planning."[114]

Yet by the early 1980s policymakers, under pressure from international donors such as USAID, began to see the population/development formula as too oblique a means for targeting rapid population growth. Consequently, policies shifted toward family-planning delivery, the National Population Council was founded in 1985, and a new National Population Plan was issued in 1986 and revised in 1992.[115] The 1985 plan emphasized "the rights" of families to decide the appropriate number of children, to obtain information about the means to enable them to achieve this decision, and to migrate internally and externally. The plan also addressed long-standing concerns such as the dissemination of family-planning services, female education and literacy programs, and population redistribution strategies.[116] Overall, the policy shift inaugurated in the mid-1980s highlighted the individual's and family unit's right to reflexively monitor itself; and mass media and educational programs were directed to disseminate new norms of small family size, changes that signaled a new relationship between the individual and the state.[117] As anthropologist Kamran Asdar Ali has argued, this enabled the constitution of new kinds of families imbued with liberal notions of individual rights within the nuclear family.

Two tactics that exemplify the type of shift that occurred in population strategy are the Contraceptive Social Marketing Project (CSM) and the expansion of the Information, Education, and Communication (IEC) program. Social marketing refers to "programs which use commercial marketing techniques, mass media, and existing commercial networks to distribute, promote and sell products, but in which all activities are undertaken with the consumer and larger social objectives in mind."[118] The CSM program aimed to broadly distribute and market contraceptive products throughout rural and urban Egypt. Through these programs, the family-planning user was thus reconceptualized as an individual consumer imbued with liberal choices. The IEC program was established in 1979 in order "to create general awareness of the population problem in Egypt, to develop useful strategies for promoting the benefits of family planning, to give legitimacy to the concept of family planning in Egypt, and to raise the level of family-planning acceptance through dissemination of effective knowledge on contraceptives and sociocultural contraindications."[119] IEC activities were divided between mass media campaigns and face-to-face or interpersonal communication. Initially, IEC focused on general awareness campaigns, but after the mid-1980s, program goals focused on the attitudinal changes necessary for acceptance of family planning.[120] IEC programs focused thematically on emphasizing the health benefits of family planning, as well as its consonance with religious precepts, while dispelling misconceptions and rumors about family planning. Community-based activities targeted individuals in leadership roles, such as religious figures and village leaders and often took the format of community meetings, for example with a local sheikh, medical doctor, and social worker, all presenting information, followed by extensive question-and-answer sessions.[121] Mass media efforts focused on television and radio programming that promoted small family norms or distributed family-planning messages.[122] These ranged from the commissioning of a television serial to short, targeted television advertising spots.[123]

Islamic religious discourse played an essential role in media efforts as well, oftentimes advocating small family size and validating family planning as a religiously valid option. Religious leaders emphasized Islam's compatibility with the goals of modernity—namely, the creation of a healthy and productive citizenry—but differed from earlier religious pronouncements as they explicitly linked family planning with modernization. State-sponsored religious leaders, such as Shaykh Tantawi, a mufti of Egypt, explicitly called for a smaller population:

> Once more we say: Welcome to a good, big, strong, productive population, but not to a weak, poor, and big population that goes astray from the right path and depends on others for its necessities. A smaller population is far better.[124]

Similarly, Gaafar Abdel-Salam of al-Azhar University assessed the legal aspects of family planning at the conference "Bioethics in Human Reproductive Research in the Muslim World" in December 1991, and stated:

> On the one hand we find that family planning is closely linked to human rights such as those concerning the sacrosanctity of the body, the right of the person to marriage and other wide-ranging rights. Family planning is also linked to the rights of society to secure the existence of strong and productive families. . . . The term "family planning" taken up by this conference represents one of the important issues for all societies especially in the developing world as it is used to urge individuals to maintain birth control in such a way as not to harm family members i.e. father, mother, children and family as a whole.[125]

In this same period, al-Azhar, among the oldest religious establishments of learning in Egypt and the Muslim world, launched an International Islamic Center for population studies, with research on population education as one of its main activities. The center aimed to highlight the "relevance of population knowledge in training Islamic theologians and preachers."[126] Likewise, religious leaders such as Jad al-Haq, then grand imam of al-Azhar, noted the need for the wider use of "mass media and other educational channels for showing the advantage of a small family, with easier availability of contraceptives."[127]

In Egypt, orthodox religious discourse attained a remarkable degree of centralization throughout the course of the twentieth century, in part through efforts under Nasser to "control closely the religious institution [of al-Azhar] and to appropriate religion, without making it disappear from the public sphere."[128] In the case of family planning, orthodox Islamic values are disseminated in the form of religious edicts and pronouncements throughout the social body via the mass media (both print media and television), as well as in health and family-planning clinics, and through population education programs in schools and universities.

This is not to suggest that such discourses have been universally accepted or that their hegemony was never contested. Kamran Asdar Ali has noted in his ethnographic research that Islamist discourses, such as those put forth by the Muslim Brotherhood, and even everyday popular discourses, have often critiqued state-sponsored family-planning programs and their orthodox religious spokesmen. Criticism has been leveled on the grounds of geopolitics, domestic politics, and moral reasoning. Critics have noted that family planning expresses a Western desire to reduce the population of Muslims, that state corruption should be blamed for the inequitable distribution of resources, and that widespread contraceptive use will lead to sexual promiscuity.[129] Yet despite these differences of opinion regarding the proper orthodox position of Islam toward family planning, both proponents and opponents of family planning argue precisely on the basis of the religious disciplining of bodily practices as it intersects with the needs of the modernizing nation-state. Thus, for example, all groups involved agree on the importance of modern health and hygiene and on the need for state and nonstate actors to regulate them, a testament to the dominance of biopolitical regimes within both secular and religious understandings of individual welfare and the welfare of the nation.

In sum, the biopolitical regime that marked the 1970s onward tethered population politics to socioeconomic development. In this context, policymakers effectively isolated and targeted population and family planning to a degree previously unknown. New techniques, such as contraceptive social marketing and the state's mass media program, began to specifically target the use and implementation of contraceptive methods. As seen through the trajectory of Egyptian biopolitics the discursive shift that occurred during the 1970s marked the entry into a population regime that worked not by delineating the specificity of health and hygiene practices to mothers, children, and peasants, reconstituting villages by reconstructing them, or reclaiming land and people through resettlement, but rather through the use of media to construct the population problem. In addition, the family unit was continuously monitored through the assessment of total fertility rates, contraceptive prevalence rates, and population densities, in order to meet the operational targets of socioeconomic development. Finally, with the rise of neoliberalism, and the concomitant abdication of the role of the state as guarantor of social welfare, economic inequalities and poverty rates have soared within the neoliberal biopolitical regime.

Conclusion

By all conventional accounts Egypt's population program has been a success, with total fertility rates dropping from 7.1 (1960–65) to 3.9 (1990–92) to 3.1 (2000) to 2.77 (2007).[130] It is tempting to portray this decline in total fertility rates as the triumphant product of an incremental and evolutionary population policy; yet that would belie the crucial distinctions between two fundamental moments of population policy. Such a perspective would also diminish the distinctions between varying ideas about the individual and the collective, as well as various orientations toward social justice and income inequality embedded within each population regime. Indeed, this chapter has delineated two distinct biopolitical regimes. The first, spanning from the 1930s to the 1960s, was characterized by a more holistic approach to population policy in which population concerns were embedded within larger social welfare programs that marked the health, wealth, and welfare of the population as their object. After the economic liberalization polices of the 1970s, however, population politics became tethered to a new objective: socioeconomic development. The holistic nature of the previous welfare regime was disaggregated into its constituent components, and efforts focused on increasing contraceptive prevalence through media efforts and social marketing.

To be sure, within these two biopolitical regimes, the intrusion of the modernizing nation-state into the everyday lives of its citizens has continually expanded throughout the twentieth century. Both state and nonstate actors have been complicit in this process, including nongovernmental organizations and religious institutions and figures. Indeed, religious discourses have often been complementary, rather than antithetical, to biopolitical regimes and their attendant population programs and policies, oftentimes facilitating the instrumentalization of the family by the state.

In thinking about the relationship between gender, reproduction, and demographic mandates in modern Egypt, it is clear that women have functioned as the fulcrum of population policies. While women's voices were marginalized in the 1930s and 1940s, and their efforts to engage population debates took place "quietly on the side," they became more prominently involved in family-planning efforts in postrevolutionary Egypt. Historian Laura Bier and political scientist Mervat Hatem have characterized post-1952 Egypt by state feminism, a process that sought to incorporate women into the public sphere as political subjects, even as it created new classed and gendered hierarchies.[131] As Bier notes, while prerevolutionary discourses viewed women as objects of population policy, in the post-1952 period "Policy planners, public figures, and the press began to talk of gendered national subjects for whom the use of birth control constituted the performance of the duties of citizenship."[132] Indeed, feminists in the 1950s and 1960s often tied family planning to wider emancipatory visions that often focused on the vulnerabilities of rural and urban poor women.[133] And yet women who were engaged in family-planning work should not be viewed as having simply reproduced statist discourses; rather they often simultaneously reaffirmed and subverted population mandates and gendered imperatives.[134] As Beth Baron has outlined, the social and community-based approaches of women involved in family planning in the Nasser era often conflicted with the technocratic and biomedical visions of state agents and international donors.[135] Beyond that, traditional forms of knowledge regarding childbearing and birth control by *dayas* or midwives were often delegitimized throughout this process of encroaching state control over reproduction.[136]

In the neoliberal period, as collective welfare projects were displaced by socioeconomic development and liberal notions of individual choice, family-planning projects were often received in complex and contradictory ways, and the social implementation of the pedagogical project of family planning often confronted its own limitations.[137] As Kamran Ali notes, the social significance of fertility and being fertile in the Egyptian setting meant that decisions regarding fertility control were related to a complex of relations within the household and beyond.[138] In this environment, biomedical conceptions of fertility coexisted with women's own cultural constructions of their bodies, which were not neatly aligned with liberal notions of an autonomous individual and unitary self, but rather linked to a larger social and cosmological world.[139] Women's choices, too, thus did not always align with the goals of family-planning programs. Women not only resisted contraception at times, but also considered autonomous choice as contradictory to their sense of agency and subservience to God.[140]

As Kamran Asdar Ali presciently stated in 2002, "I submit that demographic transition may eventually happen in Egypt. If it does, it will more likely happen as a result of diminishing opportunities for a majority of Egyptians to make a living than as a natural response to better standards of living."[141] Those diminishing opportunities, in addition to the changed nature of relations between rulers and ruled, were the impetus behind Egypt's 2011 revolutionary uprising and its rallying cry of "bread, freedom, and social justice." These are demands that have not been met, it is worth recalling, by the postcolonial state's singular focus on population reduction as the principal vehicle of modernity.

Notes

1. This chapter is based, in large part, on material adapted from: "Barren Land and Fecund Bodies," *International Journal of Middle East Studies* 37, no. 3 (2005) 351–372, and *The Great Social Laboratory: Subjects of Knowledge in Colonial and Postcolonial Egypt* (Stanford: Stanford University Press, 2007), chapters 6–7. It is reproduced with permission. Wendell Cleland, "The Necessity of Restricting Population Growth in Egypt," *al-Majalla al-Tibiyya al-Misriyya* 20, no. 7 (1937): 278–87, quotation, 279.
2. Ian Hacking, *The Taming of Chance* (Cambridge: Cambridge University Press, 1990), 22.
3. See *al-Majalla al-Tibiyya al-Misriyya* 20, no. 7 (1937); Hanna Rizk, "Population Policies in Egypt," in *The Fifth International Conference on Planned Parenthood, Report of the Proceedings 24–29 October 1955, Tokyo, Japan* (London: International Planned Parenthood, 1955), 38; Haifa Shanawany, "Stages in the Development of a Population Control Program," in *Egypt: Population Problems and Prospects*, ed. A. R. Omran (Chapel Hill: Carolina Population Center, University of North Carolina at Chapel Hill, 1973), 193.
4. The quotation is from Mustafa Fahmi, "Hal min al-khiyr li misr fi zurufiha al-haliyya wa fi nitaq hajatuha al-harbiyya in tu'amim fiqrat tahdid al-nasl?!" *al-Majalla al-Tibiyya al-Misriyya* 20, no. 7 (1937): 96–117, quotation, 113.
5. See David Horn, *Social Bodies: Science, Reproduction, and Italian Modernity* (Princeton: Princeton University Press, 1994) and Ann Anagnost, *Narrative, Representation, and Power in Modern China* (Durham: Duke University Press, 1997), 117–37. Works in Middle East studies that have addressed the construction of population include Kamran Asdar Ali, *Planning the Family in Egypt: New Bodies, New Selves* (Austin: University of Texas Press, 2002); Rhoda Ann Kanaaneh, *Birthing the Nation: Strategies of Palestinian Women in Israel* (Berkeley: University of California Press, 2002); and Firoozeh Kashani-Sabet, *Conceiving Citizens: Women and the Politics of Motherhood in Iran* (Oxford: Oxford University Press, 2011). Timothy Mitchell's "The Object of Development," in *Rule of Experts: Egypt, Techno-Politics, Modernity* (Berkeley: University of California Press, 2002), provides a cogent critique of contemporary development discourse and the construction of a population problem in Egypt.
6. See, for example, Dr. Ali Bey Fu'ad, "Tahdid al-nasl," *al-Majalla al-Tibiyya al-Misriyya* 20, no. 7 (1937): 48–56; Dr. 'Abd al-Hakim al-Rifa'i, "Mushkilat al-sukkan

fi misr," *al-Majalla al-Tibiyya al-Misriyya* 20, no. 7 (1937): 135–49; and Fahmi, "Hal min al-khiyr li misr?"

7. I borrow the term "total social fact" from Marcel Mauss, *The Gift: The Form and Reason for Exchange in Archaic Societies* (1925; New York: W. W. Norton, 1990).
8. The most important actors in these debates throughout the nationalist period were Egyptians who wrote in Arabic, with the sole and noteworthy exception of Wendell Cleland, an American.
9. Roger Owen, "The Population Census of 1917 and Its Relationship to Egypt's Three 19th-Century Statistical Regimes," *Journal of Historical Sociology* 9, no. 4 (December 1996): 457–72, quotation 469. At various points in his career Craig served as director of the Computation Office of the Egyptian Survey Department, controller of the Statistical Office and Census Office, controller General of the Census, controller of the Supplies Control Board, and financial secretary of the Ministry of Finance. See J. I. Craig, "The Census of Egypt," *L'Égypte Contemporaine* 8, no. 32 (1917): 209–34; Craig, "The Census of Egypt," *L'Égypte Contemporaine* 17, no. 96 (1926): 434–55; and Craig, "Statistics," *L'Égypte Contemporaine* 26, no. 153–54 (1935): 115–45.
10. My use of the term "homogeneous mass" refers to the process by which population comes to be viewed as a uniform, and national, entity, and resonates with Benedict Anderson's use of Walter Benjamin's concept of "homogeneous, empty time" to refer to the conception of temporality within the modern nation-state. See Benedict Anderson, *Imagined Communities: Reflections on the Origins and Spread of Nationalism* (London: Verso, 1991), 24.
11. See Mark Adams, ed., *The Wellborn Science: Eugenics in Germany, France, Brazil, and Russia* (Oxford: Oxford University Press, 1990); and Mark Mazower, *Dark Continent: Europe's Twentieth Century* (New York: Vintage Books, 1998).
12. Dr. R. Goldscheid, "Discussion," in *Proceedings of the World Population Conference, 29 August—3 September, Geneva*, ed. Margaret Sanger (London: Edward Arnold, 1927), 104–5.
13. Wendell Cleland, *The Population Problem in Egypt* (Lancaster: Science Press, 1936). See also "Egypt's Population Problem," *L'Égypte Contemporaine* 28, no. 167 (1937): 67–87; Cleland, "A Population Plan for Egypt," *L'Égypte Contemporaine* 30, no. 185 (1939): 461–84. Cleland, an American who had lived in Cairo since 1917, was a member of the faculty of the American University in Cairo where he taught psychology. His involvement with prominent ministry officials working on issues such as irrigation, public health, sanitation, and hygiene, impressed upon him Egypt's most serious social issues. Cleland (b. 1888) had served in various posts related to the Middle East before his arrival in Cairo, such as the Syria and Palestine Relief Fund. His book, originally his Ph.D. thesis, was submitted to Columbia University's Department of Sociology, where he earned his doctorate.

14. Cleland's book was favorably reviewed by *al-Muqtataf* and situated as part of a broader set of discussions on population and birth control that had flourished in 1936 and 1937. See "Mushkilat al-sukkan fi misr," *al-Muqtataf*, May 1937, 646–47.
15. It would be grossly erroneous to think of Malthusianism as the product (or "master paradigm") of a bygone era—transformed from theodicy into a secular platitude. Indeed, one can argue that Malthusianism became ever more linked to the idea of the national economy as a self-contained structure. On the modern transformation of the idea of the economy, see Mitchell, "The Character of Calculability," in *Rule of Experts*.
16. Hasan al-Sa'ati, "Tatawwur al-madrasa al-fikriyya li 'ilm al-ijtima' fi misr," *al-Majalla al-Ijtima'iyya al-Qawmiyya / The National Review of Social Sciences*, National Centre for Sociological and Criminological Research (1964): 21–34.
17. Cleland, *Population Problem in Egypt*, 36.
18. Wendell Cleland, "Discussion of Prof. Bentley's Paper: Fertility and Overpopulation in Egypt," *al-Majalla al-Tibiyya al-Misriyya* 20, no. 7 (1937): 296–303.
19. Cleland, "Egypt's Population Problem," 67–68. For a critique of Malthusian thought from a Marxist and neo-Marxist perspective, see Ronald Meek, ed., *Marx and Engels on the Population Bomb: Selections from the Writings of Marx and Engels Dealing with the Theories of Thomas Robert Malthus* (Berkeley: Ramparts Press, 1971). On the postwar use of Malthusian arguments linking poverty to overpopulation, and in turn rationalizing development policies, such as the replacement of peasant agriculture with commercial agriculture, and the wide-scale support of population programs in the Third World and its relation to the Cold War, see Eric Ross, *The Malthus Factor: Population, Poverty and Politics in Capitalist Development* (New York: Zed Books, 1998). There is an extensive literature historicizing and critiquing Thomas Robert Malthus's theory of population, both empirically and theoretically. The literature on Malthus is enormous; two excellent collections, one historical and one contemporary, are *Malthus: Critical Responses*, ed. Geoffrey Gilbert, 4 vols. (New York: Routledge, 1998); and *Thomas Robert Malthus: Critical Assessments*, ed. John Wood Cunningham, 4 vols. (Surry Hills: Croom Helm, 1986).
20. Cleland, *Population Problem in Egypt*, 90.
21. Cleland, "Egypt's Population Problem," 82.
22. The conference proceedings were published in *al-Majalla al-Tibiyya al-Misriyya* 20, no. 7 (1937).
23. Fahmi, "Hal min al-khiyr li misr?" and Dr. Muhammad 'Awad Muhammad, "al-Nawahi al-ijtima'iyya al-khasa bi tanzim al-nasl," *al-Majalla al-Tibiyya al-Misriyya* 20, no. 7 (1937): 57–75. Infant and child mortality, which in 1937 was estimated to account for 65 percent of deaths in Egypt, was also considered a serious loss in productivity. Fahmi, "Hal min al-khiyr li misr?" 110.
24. Hamed El-Sayed Azmi, "The Growth of Population as Related to Some Aspects of Egypt's National Development," *L'Égypte Contemporaine* 28, no. 168 (1937): 267–303.

25. See Mirrit Boutros Ghali, *The Policy of Tomorrow* (1938; Washington D.C.: American Council of Learned Societies, 1953); 'Aisha 'Abd al-Rahman (Bint al-Shati'), *al-Rif al-Misri* (Cairo: al-Matba'a al-rahmaniyya, 1936), a collection of articles printed in *al-Ahram* in 1935.
26. Salama Musa, "Dabt al-tanasul wa man 'al-haml," in *Salama Musa: al-Mu'alafat al-Kamila*, vol. 2, *'Ulum al-ijtima'* (Cairo: Salama Musa lil nashr wa al-tawzi'a, 2002), 217–36.
27. 'Abbas 'Ammar, "al-Nahya al-insaniyya fi mawdu' tanzim al-nasl," *al-Majalla al-Tibiyya al-Misriyya* 20, no. 7 (1937): 187–211.
28. 'Ammar, "al-Nahya al-insaniyya."
29. 'Ammar, "al-Nahya al-insaniyya," 195. At the core of debates on Malthus's theory of population is the question of the origin of poverty, its relationship to progress, and the perfectibility of man and society. See Robert Harry Inglis Palgrave, ed., "Population," in *Palgrave's Dictionary of Political Economy*, 3rd ed., vol. 3 (London: Macmillan, 1927). See also T. Sowell, "Malthus and the Utilitarians," 210–16; D. Harvey, "Population, Resources and the Ideology of Science," 308–35; E. N. Santurri, "Theodicy and Social Policy in Malthus' Thought," 402–18; all in *Thomas Robert Malthus: Critical Assessments*, vol. 1, *The Life of Thomas Robert Malthus and Perspectives on His Thought*.
30. Cleland, *Population Problem in Egypt*, 110.
31. The assumption that standards of living and population growth were inversely related may be traced back to Malthus. For a critique, see Sowell, "Malthus and the Utilitarians."
32. It was in the development of "a psychological attitude, the 'desires,' for fewer and more cultured children, that the peasantry can be made to curb their own growth . . . In more primitive circumstances, such as surround the fellaheen . . . the chief source of recreation is sex, and that raises the birth rate . . . Our aim then would be to do everything possible to sublimate the emotions and attention of the fellaheen while trying to raise their standards." Cleland, "Population Plan for Egypt," 477–78. Such assertions were loosely derived from older nineteenth-century views, such as those of Herbert Spencer, that the fecundity of the civilized races and classes, due to their level of moral and material progress and their preoccupation with matters of the intellect or spirit, was lower than that of the uncivilized.
33. Cleland, "Population Plan for Egypt," 479.
34. Muhammad, "al-Nawahi al-ijtima'iyya," 61.
35. Kamal al-Din Effendi Fahmi, "Tanzim al-nasl fi ba'd al-aqtar—khatina fi misr," *al-Majalla al-Tibiyya al-Misriyya* 20, no. 7 (1937): 118–29.
36. Public governmental organizations (such as the Child Welfare section of the Department of Public Health), as well as private philanthropic initiatives, such as the Lady Cromer Memorial dispensaries, the Society for the Protection of Children, Mabarrat Muhammad Aly (Ouevre Muhammad Aly, Dispensaire pour les femmes et les enfants—Centre de Puericulture et de Pediatrique

Preventive), Mme. Huda Sha'arawi dispensaries, the Egyptian Feminist Union, the Egyptian Child Welfare Association, and the Jama'iyyat ummuhat al-mustaqbal (Société des meres futures) were responsible for the diffusion of health propaganda to mothers and children all over Egypt. See DWQ, *'Abdin, al-Jama'iyyat, al-Jama'iyyat al-Ijtima'iyya, 1899–1952,* Archive Box No. 203; and *'Abdin, al-Jama'iyyat, al-Jama'iyyat al-Ijtima'iyya, 1902–1949,* Archive Box No. 204.

37. Ministry of Finance, *Almanac for the Year 1935* (Cairo: Government Press, 1935), 286.

38. On the history of maternalist processes in Europe and its relation to imperialism, nationalism, and the welfare state, see Gisela Bock and Pat Thane, *Maternity and Gender Policies: Women and the Rise of the European Welfare States, 1880s–1950s* (London: Routledge, 1991); Anna Davin, "Imperialism and Motherhood," *History Workshop* 5 (1978): 9–65; Victoria de Grazia, *How Fascism Ruled Women: Italy, 1922–1945* (Berkeley: University of California Press, 1992), chap. 3; Ute Frevert, "The Civilizing Tendency of Hygiene," in *German Women in the Nineteenth Century: A Social History*, ed. John Fout (New York: Holmes and Meier, 1984), 320–44; Horn, *Social Bodies*; Seth Koven and Sonya Michel, eds. *Mothers of a New World: Maternalist Politics and the Origins of Welfare States* (London: Routledge, 1993). Outside of Europe, see the fascinating study by Nancy Rose Hunt, *A Colonial Lexicon of Birth Ritual, Medicalization, and Mobility in the Congo* (Durham: Duke University Press, 1999); and Asunción Lavrin, *Women, Feminism, and Social Change in Argentina, Chile, and Uruguay, 1890–1940* (Lincoln: University of Nebraska Press, 1995).

39. An official Egyptian delegation was sent to Geneva for the 1925 First General Congress on Child Welfare. At the Congrès Quinzaine Sociale Internationale, held in Paris in 1928, Doctor Sayyid Effendi 'Arif, an administrative inspector, was sent to the Congrès International de la Protection de l'Enfance. See DWQ, *'Abdin, mu'tamarat, 1925–29,* Archive Box No. 59. See also Paul-Valentin, "La Protection de l'enfance: Comment elle devrait être organisée en Egypte," 20eme Congrès International de Bruxelles, *L'Egypte Contemporaine* 14 (April 1923): 371–97; Paul-Valentin, "Une étape nouvelle dans l'organisation scientifique de la protection de l'enfance," *L'Egypte Contemporaine* 14 (January 1923): 10–41.

40. Cleland, "Population Plan for Egypt," 470–71.

41. Mohamed Shalaby, *An Experiment in Rural Reconstruction in Egypt* (Cairo: Egyptian Association for Social Studies, 1950); Ahmed Husayn, "Tajarib islah al-qarya fi misr," *Shu'un Ijtima'iyya* 2, no. 7 (1941): 61–67.

42. Faye Ginsburg and Rayna Rapp, introduction to *Conceiving the New World Order: The Global Politics of Reproduction* (Berkeley: University of California Press, 1995).

43. Zahya Marzuq, "Kilma lil-mara' fi tanzim al-nasl," *al-Majalla al-Tibiyya al-Misriyya* 20 (July 1937): 150–54.

44. 'Ammar, "al-Nahya al-insaniyya."

45. ʿAmmar, "al-Nahya al-insaniyya," 203–4, quotation, 204.
46. Ann Anagnost has discussed the shift from quantity to quality in Chinese population discourse following the 1978 one-child policy. According to her, the Chinese notion of population quality is multivocal and covers a broad range: birth control, childrearing, sanitation, education, technology, law, and eugenics. Although resonating with earlier 1920s eugenics discourse, population discourse in the post-Mao period moved far beyond the concerns of a small elite, to include themes such as blaming national backwardness on poor population quality, the categorization of the rural masses as backward and peripheral by the urban and intellectual elites, and the coupling of "raising the quality of the people" with the building of socialist civilization. Anagnost, *Narrative, Representation and Power*, 118–28. David Horn has discussed the goals of fascist demographic politics: "Rather than purification, the goals . . . were social defense and multiplication, rather than selective breeding and sterilization, its means were improved hygiene, diet and education." Thus, although the emphasis was on quantity in the Italian case, quality mattered at least in preventive terms, a process Horn refers to as "euthenics," by which he means positive eugenics (pronatalist social hygiene). Horn, *Social Bodies*, 60.
47. "Tahsin al-nasl: Itijah ijtimaʿi jadid," *Shu'un Ijtimaʿiyya* 2 (June 1941): 101–3.
48. Broadly, Egyptian ideas on eugenics were only vaguely biological in orientation and were more concerned with social reform, public health, and sanitation. Most of the authors writing on the subject were either members of the medical profession or social reformers. If any particular scientific traditions are to be singled out as exerting the most influence on population writings, it would be neo-Lamarckian and social Darwinian, whereas Mendelian genetics had not yet made serious inroads into discussions of population. The neo-Lamarckian strains are noticeable in discussions surrounding the importance of improving the physical and social environment of the working poor—as well as the general concern for puericulture, hygiene, and sanitation. And although there were those who insisted on sterilization, at least in cases where the genetic basis of disease transmission had been proven beyond a doubt, few argued on Mendelian grounds. Social Darwinism was broached in the few instances where natural selection and elimination were discussed, but its usage was often imprecise. A key figure in debates on biology was Shibli Shumayyil, whose social Darwinism drew from Huxley, Spencer, Haeckel, and Büchner. In fact, Shumayyil had translated Büchner's commentary on Darwin into Arabic. Salama Musa, too, was influential in the transmission of Lamarckian ideas into Arabic. On these figures and on Darwinism in Egypt and Greater Syria in general, see Marwa Elshakry, *Reading Darwin in Arabic, 1860–1950* (Chicago: University of Chicago Press, 2013).
49. There is a vast and rich literature on the development of the eugenics movement, which has gone far in debunking various myths portraying eugenics as solely an Anglo-American phenomenon, as a pseudoscience, as predominantly

Mendelian, and as right wing. See Mark Adams, "Toward a Comparative History of Eugenics," in Adams, *The Wellborn Science*.

50. Dr. Abd al-Hakim al-Rifa'i, "Mushkilat al-sukkan fi misr"; Fu'ad, "Tahdid al-nasl"; Mustafa Fahmi, "Hal min al-khiyr li misr?"; Kamal al-Din Fahmi, "Tanzim al-nasl fi ba'd al-aqtar."
51. "It is to the nation's benefit to have children of healthy build and sound mind rather than a plentiful but disabled and weak minded progeny. . . . Better to live as a progressive nation of small numbers than a populated backward nation." Fu'ad, "Tahdid al-nasl," 49, 51.
52. "Dabt al-tanasul: Haraka ijtima'iyya khatira tu'am al-'alam al-mutamadin al-yawm," *al-Hilal* 33 (June 1925): 938–40; Amir Buqtur, "Ifa al-tanasul wal ighraq fihi: Bahth ijtima'i wa iqtisadi wa sihi," *al-Hilal* 38 (August 1930): 1201–6; "al-shakawi min izdiyad sukkan al-'alam," *al-Hilal* 39 (April 1931): 868–72; "Taqyid al-nasl wal tahakum bi 'adad al-mawalid," *al-Hilal* 39 (July 1931): 1393–96; "Hal nu'amid ila tahdid al-nasl?" *al-Hilal* 40 (December 1931): 234–38; "Taqyid al-nasl am intikhabu," 41 (November 1932): 84–90; "Tahdid al-nasl: Wa atharu al sihiyya wal ijtima'iyya wal dawliyya," *al-Muqtataf* 90 (March 1937): 261–67; Tahdid al-nasl wa mushkilat al-sukkan," *al-Muqtataf* 94 (January 1939): 283–89; "Tahdid al-nasl fil mizan," *al-Muqtataf* 95 (June 1939): 41–45.
53. "Hal nu'amid ila tahdid al-nasl?" 236–37.
54. S.Q., "Sihhat al-nasl: Aham manab'a al-tharwa al-qawmiyya," *Shu'un Ijtima'iyya* 2 (April 1941): 88–93. All indications point to the authorship of Sayyid Qutb, who was a regularly contributing member to the journal. On Sayyid Qutb's writings on social reform, see Alain Roussillon "Trajectoires Reformistes Sayyid Qutb et Sayyid 'Uways: Figures modernes de l'intellectuel en Egypte," *Egypte/Monde Arabe* 6 (1991): 91–139.
55. S.Q., "Sihhat al-nasl," 90. The anonymous article "Tahsin al-nasl," *Shu'un Ijtima'iyya*, also called for the medicalization of marriage licenses. For a rich discussion, see Hanan Kholoussy, "Monitoring and Medicalising Male Sexuality in Semi-Colonial Egypt," *Gender and History* 22, no. 3 (2010): 677–91.
56. Ann Anagnost, "A Surfeit of Bodies: Population and the Rationality of the State in Post-Mao China," in Rapp and Ginsburg, *New World Order*, 22–41, quotation, 31.
57. Elie Nassif, "L'Égypte est-elle surpeuplée?" *L'Égypte Contemporaine* 33, no. 208 (1942): 613–773, quotation in the subhead, 641. An Arabic synopsis of Nassif's article appeared in the same issue, "Hal tashku misr min al-izdiham bi-l sukkan?" 775–91.
58. Nassif, "L'Égypte est-elle surpeuplée?"
59. For Italian statistician Corrado Gini, Malthusian theories of the geometric increase of population were premised on one fundamentally flawed assumption—namely, that "the reproductive powers of populations remain constant throughout their generations." Gini had formulated a theory known as the theory of the cyclical rise and fall of population, whose underlying

postulate was the differential rates of increase of different populations, according to race and class, on the basis of evolutionary biological difference. According to Gini, populations, like societies, individuals, and other organisms, had biological life cycles of birth, evolution, and death. The implications were decidedly anti-neo-Malthusian, since intervals at diverse points in history could represent transitory phases of over- or underpopulation. Corrado Gini, "The Cyclical Rise and Fall of Population," in *Population: Lectures on the Harris Foundation 1929* (Chicago: University of Chicago Press, 1930), 1–140, quotation 4.

60. He referred to proponents of the demographic optimum as "Anglo-Saxon doctrinaires," noting that they excluded the possibility of diverse demographic optima corresponding to the progressive evolution of the social and economic structure of a society and its complexity. These included William Beveridge, Allyn Young, A. M. Carr-Saunders, Edwin Cannan, Hugh Dalton, and Lionel Robbins. For an overview see E. F. Penrose, *Population Theories with Special Reference to Japan* (Stanford: Stanford University Press, 1934), 49–55; Elie Nassif, "L'Égypte est-elle surpeuplée?" 621–38.
61. Corrado Gini, "Some Considerations of the Optimum Density of a Population," in *Proceedings of the World Population Conference, 29 August—3 September, Geneva*, 118–22; Nassif, "L'Égypte est-elle surpeuplée?" 629.
62. Muhammad Hasan, "Mushkilat al-nasl fi misr," *al-Majalla al-Tibiyya al-Misriyya* 20, no. 7 (1937): 183–86; Hasan al-Banna, "Ra'y fi tahdid al-nasl min al-wajha al-islamiyya," *al-Majalla al-Tibiyya al-Misriyya* 20, no. 7 (1937): 217–22.
63. Abd al-Majid Nafi'a, "al-Dawa' ila tahdid al-nasl: Jarima qawmiyya la darura ijtima'iyya," *Shu'un Ijtima'iyya* 2, no .5 (1941): 34–39.
64. Roger Owen, "The Ideology of Economic Nationalism in Its Egyptian Context: 1919–1939," in *Intellectual Life in the Arab East, 1890–1939*, ed. Marwan Buheiry (Beirut: American University in Beirut Press, 1981); Mourad Magdi Wahba, *The Role of the State in the Egyptian Economy: 1945–1981* (Reading: Ithaca Press, 1994); Robert Tignor, *State, Private Enterprise, and Economic Change in Egypt: 1918–1952* (Princeton: Princeton University Press, 1984).
65. Nassif, "L' Égypte est-elle surpeuplée?" 720.
66. Nassif, "L' Égypte est-elle surpeuplée?" 767. Nassif was indeed prescient. A policy of population redistribution through land reclamation and resettlement would later become the cornerstone of the Nasserist population program.
67. Fatwas are issued in response to queries from lay believers. See Hussein Ali Agrama, *Questioning Secularism: Islam, Sovereignty, and the Rule of Law in Modern Egypt* (Chicago: University of Chicago Press, 2012), chap. 5.
68. Shaykh 'Abd al-Majid Salim, *al-Majalla al-Tibiyya al-Misriyya* 20 (July 1937): 55; translated in Abdel Rahim Omran, *Family Planning in the Legacy of Islam* (New York: Routledge, 1992), 250. I have amended the translation from the original text, in Wizarat al-awqaf wa wizarat al-a'lam, *Mawqif al-islam min tanzim al-usra* (Cairo: State Information Service/Information, Education and Communication Center, 1991), 81–82. Note that this is representative of the *Hanafite* school of

jurisprudence. In the Muslim tradition children are reputed to be "gifted with souls" after the first 120 days of gestation.

69. Historically speaking, birth spacing or planning has a long history of debate in the Islamic tradition. The earliest and most comprehensive statement of permissibility on coitus interruptus (*al-'azl*) in Islamic jurisprudence is the medieval text of the *Shafa'i* scholar Imam Abu Hamid Muhammad al-Ghazali (d. 1111). Al-Ghazali deemed coitus interruptus permissible with the following justifications: to avoid fathering children who would become slaves, to preserve the wife's beauty in order to ensure marital bliss, and to avoid economic hardships and "embarrassment" (*haraj*). Abu Hamid Muhammad al-Ghazali, *Ihya' 'ulum al-din* (Cairo: Matba'at al-istiqama, 1965). On the history of birth control in Islamic jurisprudence, see Omran, *Family Planning*, chap. 8; and Basim Musallam, *Sex and Society in Islam: Birth Control before the Nineteenth Century* (Cambridge: Cambridge University Press, 1983).
70. The Muslim Brotherhood was originally founded in Isma'iliyya in 1928 by al-Banna as an alternative associational grouping aimed at encouraging an Islamic revival and introducing Islam into all aspects of everyday life and society. The Society, committed to the ideals of social justice, anti-imperialism, pan-Islamism, and a free Palestine, relocated to Cairo in 1932, where it gained a following that included lower- and middle-class Egyptians (civil servants, urban workers, students, and lawyers), estimated at hundreds of thousands by World War II. Richard P. Mitchell, *The Society of the Muslim Brothers* (Oxford: Oxford University Press, 1993).
71. Al-Banna, "Ra'y fi tahdid al-nasl," 217.
72. Al-Banna, "Ra'y fi tahdid al-nasl," 217, and Issa 'Abduh, "Ra'y fi tahdid al-nasl wa tanzimuhu: Bahth min al-nahyatin al-islamiyya wal iqtisadiyya," *al-Majalla al-Tibiyya al-Misriyya* 20 (July 1937): 155–65.
73. Al-Banna, "Ra'y fi tahdid al-nasl," 218. Al-Banna quotes *ahadith* (sayings of the Prophet) in support of his argument in favor of procreation as the goal of marriage. One recounts a man who approached the Prophet stating that he loved a woman who was of noble birth and rank and wealth but who could not conceive. He then asked the Prophet, "Should I marry her?" The Prophet said no. The man returned two more times. On the third occasion, the Prophet stated: "Marry those that are dear and fertile (*al-wudud al-wulud*) for I shall make a display of you before other nations."
74. Abduh, "Ra'y fi tahdid al-nasl wa tanzimuhu," 157–59.
75. Abduh, "Ra'y fi tahdid al-nasl wa tanzimuhu," 160.
76. Mitchell, *Society of Muslim Brothers*.
77. For a social history of a similar process in Turkey, see Alan Duben and Cem Behar, *Istanbul Households: Marriage, Family and Fertility, 1880–1940* (Cambridge: Cambridge University Press, 1991).
78. As Foucault has taught us so well, power over life is the fundamental site for the deployment of modern power. What is at stake in biopolitics is the optimization

of the strength of the population and its constituent subjects, while simultaneously rendering them more governable. My analysis of population politics is informed largely by the Foucauldian elaboration of governmentality, biopower, and the political investment of the individual body and the body politic. See Michel Foucault's analysis of biopower as found in the *History of Sexuality*, vol. 1, *An Introduction*, trans. Robert Hurley (New York: Vintage Books, 1990); and "Governmentality," in *The Foucault Effect*, ed. Graham Burchell, Colin Gordon, and Peter Miller (Chicago: University of Chicago Press, 1991), 87–104.

79. See Talal Asad, *Formations of the Secular: Christianity, Islam, Modernity* (Stanford: Stanford University Press, 2003), chap. 7.
80. "Al-Safir al-Yugoslavi ya qul: Mudiriyat al-Tahrir min 'azam al-tajarib al-ijtima'iyya fil 'alam," *al-Sahara'* 1, no. 12 (1957): 17; "Ma'al-Nuwwab fi Mudiriyat al-Tahrir," *al-Sahara'* 2, no. 20 (1957). On land reclamation and resettlement, see Wizarat al-istislah al-aradi, al-mu'assassa al-'amma lil istighlal wa al-tanmiya lil aradi al-mustasliha, *Takwin wa tanmiyat al-mujtama'at al-jadida fil aradi al-mustasliha* (Cairo: Ministry of Land Reclamation, 1969); Magdi Hasanayn, *al-Sahara': al-thawra wa al-tharwa—Qissat mudiriyat al-Tahrir* (Cairo: Al-Hay'a al-misriyya al-'amma lil-kitab, 1975).
81. Doreen Warriner, *Agrarian Reform and Community Development in the U.A.R.* (Cairo: Dar al-Ta'wun, 1961), 54.
82. Institute of National Planning (United Arab Republic), *Research Report on Employment Problems in Rural Areas of the United Arab Republic: Report B: Migration in the U.A.R.* (Cairo: Institute of National Planning, 1965), 34.
83. Institute of National Planning, *Research Report*, 34.
84. Abbas Mustafa Ammar, "The Population Situation in Egypt and the Necessity of Planning Population Policy for the Country," in The Egyptian Association for Population Studies, *The Egyptian Association for Population Studies* (Cairo: Imprimerie Misr S.A.E., 1960), 5–17.
85. Ammar, "Population Situation," 13, 15.
86. Ammar, "Population Situation," 15–16.
87. Rizk, "Population Policies in Egypt," 40.
88. Al-Shafa'i, Press Conference (September 14, 1954), as quoted in Rizk, "Population Policies in Egypt," 39–40.
89. Gamal Abdel-Nasser, as quoted in Shanawany, "Stages in the Development," 197.
90. Beth Baron, "The Origins of Family Planning: Aziza Hussein, American Experts, and the Egyptian State," *Journal of Middle East Women's Studies* 4, no. 3 (2008): 31–57, quotation, 36.
91. Baron, "Origins of Family Planning," and Laura Bier, *Revolutionary Womanhood: Feminisms, Modernity, and the State in Nasser's Egypt* (Stanford, Calif.: Stanford University Press, 2011), chap. 4.
92. *Wizarat al-shu'un al-ijtima'iyya, Wizarat al-shu'un al-ijtima'iyya fi khamsa wa 'ishrin 'amm* (Cairo: Information Department, Ministry of Social Affairs, 1964), 49.

93. Quoted in Rizk, "Population Policies in Egypt," 105; Shanawany, "Stages in the Development," 202.
94. Abdel Rahim Omran and Malek el-Nomrossey, "The Family Planning Effort in Egypt: A Descriptive Sketch," in Omran, *Egypt*, 219–53.
95. Shanawany, "Stages in the Development," 205.
96. Shanawany, "Stages in the Development," 204–5. Some of the groundwork for training in statistics had been laid previously. In 1951 a Training Center on Vital Statistics and Health Statistics, sponsored by the United Nations and World Health Organization, was held in Cairo; see "Training Centre on Vital Statistics and Health Statistics for the Eastern Mediterranean," *L'Egypte Contemporaine* 42 (1951): 95–99.
97. Gamal Abdel-Nasser, as quoted in Shanawany, "Stages in the Development," 207.
98. Gamal Abdel-Nasser, as quoted in Shanawany, "Stages in the Development," 207.
99. Omran and el-Nomrossey, "Family Planning Effort," 225–26. The SCFP was a coordinated effort that included ministers of health, education, cultural and national guidance, local government, social affairs, and religious affairs.
100. Warren Robinson and Fatma H. El-Zanaty, *The Demographic Revolution in Modern Egypt* (Oxford: Lexington Books, 2007), 44.
101. Bier, *Revolutionary Womanhood*, 129.
102. Robinson and El-Zanaty, *Demographic Revolution*, 45.
103. Baron, "Origins of Family Planning," 48.
104. Baron, "Origins of Family Planning," 41.
105. Bier, *Revolutionary Womanhood*, 123.
106. Khalid Muhammad Khalid, as quoted in Rizk, "Population Policies in Egypt," 39.
107. Wizarat al-awqaf wa wizarat al-a'lam, "Mawqif al-islam min tanzim al-usra," 143.
108. As quoted in Omran, *Family Planning*, 253–54.
109. Allen C. Kelley, Atef M. Khalifa, and M. Nabil El-Khorazaty, *Population and Development in Rural Egypt* (Durham: Duke University Press, 1982); H. Abdel-Aziz Sayed, "Population Policy in Egypt," Cairo Demographic Center Annual Seminar, 1989); Omran, *Egypt*.
110. Sayed, "Population Policy in Egypt"; Supreme Council for Population and Family Planning, "Itar al-istratijiyya al-qawmiyya lil-sukkan wal-mawad al-bashariyya," Cairo, 1980.
111. H. A. Sayed, "The Demographic Impacts of the Population and Development Program: Some Theoretical and Methodological Considerations," *Dirasat Sukkaniyya: Population Studies* 12, no. 74 (1985): 3–26. The PDP had been initiated on an experimental basis in 1977; by 1978 it was operative in eight hundred villages, by 1979 in fifteen hundred villages, and by 1980 in three thousand villages; see H. Abdel-Aziz, H. A. Sayed, J. Mayone Stycos, and Roger Avery, "The Population and Development Program in Egypt: A Problem in Program Impact Measurement," Cairo Demographic Center Working Paper No. 8, 1984, 1.
112. Kelley, Khalifa, and El-Khorazaty, *Population and Development*, 34–44.

113. Sayed, Stycos, and Avery, "Population and Development Program," 5–6.
114. Anwar al-Sadat, as cited by United Nations Fund for Population Activities, "Arab Republic of Egypt: Background Paper for Population Assistance Needs Assessment Mission," Cairo, 1980, 57.
115. Ali, *Planning the Family*.
116. National Population Council, "National Population Policy," Cairo, 1986; Fatma El-Zanaty, A. A. Hussein, H. A. Sayed, Hassan H. M. Zaky, and Ann A. Way, *Egypt Demographic and Health Survey, 1992* (Cairo: Egypt National Population Council, 1993); Sayed, "Population Policy in Egypt."
117. Ali, *Planning the Family*, 36.
118. J. D. Sherris et al. as cited by Social Planning, Analysis, and Administration Consultants, "Evaluation of Appropriate Mix of Services Offered by Family Planning Outreach Workers," Report Submitted to National Population Council, Cairo, 1991.
119. US Agency for International Development, "State Information Service/ Information, Education, Communication Center Family Planning Project Process Evaluation and Recommendations," Cairo, December 1987.
120. Social Planning, Analysis, and Administration Consultants, "State Information Service/Information Education Communication Center Impact Evaluation Study: Final Report," Cairo, 1988.
121. Ministry of Mass Communications: State Information Service/Information, Education, Communication Center, "Informal Opinion Leaders and Their Credibility in Egyptian Rural Areas," Cairo, 1989; Social Planning, Analysis, and Administration Consultants, "State Information Service/Information Education Communication Center Impact Evaluation Study."
122. Hussein Abdel-Aziz Sayed, Magued I. Osman, Fatma El-Zanaty, and Ann A. Way, *Egypt Demographic and Health Survey, 1988* (Cairo: Egypt National Population Council, 1989); H. Abdel-Aziz Sayed, Fatma H. El-Zanaty, and Anne R. Cross, *Egypt Male Survey, 1991* (Cairo: Cairo Demographic Center, 1992).
123. US Agency for International Development, "Final Evaluation of the Information, Education and Communication Subproject of the Egypt Population/Family Planning II Project," Cairo: September 1993.
124. Shaykh al-Tantawi as cited by Ali, *Planning the Family*, 157.
125. Gaafar Abdel-Salam, "Legal Aspects of Family Planning," in *Proceedings of the First International Conference on Bioethics in Human Reproduction Research in the Muslim World, December 1991* (Cairo: International Islamic Center for Population Studies and Research, al-Azhar University, 1992), 118–36, quotation, 119.
126. Gamal Serour, "Ethical Concerns in the Muslim World and the International Center for Population Studies and Research," in *Proceedings of the First International Conference on Bioethics in Human Reproduction Research in the Muslim World*, 13–16, quotation, 14.
127. Al-Haq, as cited by Omran, *Family Planning*, 10.

128. This is condensing a complex history that I cannot do justice to here. For more on the relationship between al-Azhar and the Egyptian state, as well as on the increased emergence of competing religious visions and authorities, see Malika Zeghal, "Religion and Politics in Egypt: The Ulema of al-Azhar, Radical Islam, and the State (1952–94)," *International Journal of Middle East Studies* 31, no. 3 (1999): 371–99, quotation 373.
129. Ali, *Planning the Family*, 154–60.
130. TFR references the average number of children that would be born to a female if she were to live to the end of her childbearing years and bear children in accordance with current age-specific fertility rates. Total fertility rates for Egypt are taken from El-Zanaty et al., *Egypt Demographic and Health Survey 1992* and UNICEF, as cited by Baron, "Origins of Family Planning," 32. Contraceptive prevalence rates have likewise increased from 24 percent among currently married women in 1980 to 47.1 percent in 1992 to 60.3 percent in 2008. See Robinson and El-Zanaty, *Demographic Revolution*.
131. Bier, *Revolutionary Womanhood*, 2; Mervat Hatem, "The Paradoxes of State Feminism in Egypt," in *Women and Politics Worldwide*, ed. Barbara Nelson and Najwa Chadhury (New Haven: Yale University Press, 1994), 226–42.
132. Bier, *Revolutionary Womanhood*, 135.
133. Bier, *Revolutionary Womanhood*, 136–39.
134. Bier, *Revolutionary Womanhood*, 123.
135. Baron, "The Origins of Family Planning," 41.
136. Bier, *Revolutionary Womanhood*, 142–45; Ali, *Planning the Family*, 85–88.
137. For a discussion of women's experiences with family planning in the Nasser era, see Bier, *Revolutionary Womanhood*, 145–52.
138. Ali, *Planning the Family*, 119.
139. Ali, *Planning the Family*, 99–101. See also Marcia Inhorn, *The Quest for Conception: Gender, Infertility, and Egyptian Medical Traditions* (Philadelphia: University of Pennsylvania Press, 1994).
140. Ali, *Planning the Family*, 118.
141. Ali, *Planning the Family*, 163–64.

6

Iran's Population Policies

A Historical Debate

FIROOZEH KASHANI-SABET

Giving birth is hardly a casual affair. The history of reproduction shows the complexities of maternal politics in Iran. What women and men understood about reproduction shaped their choices about the type of care to seek during childbirth. Although specific rituals related to childbirth differed in form and spirit, and often changed with the times, their existence showed a desire to protect women in labor from some of the unknown dangers of childbirth and to assume control over a mystifying and momentous event in people's lives. The accumulation of knowledge about procreation in Iran altered men's relationships to female bodies. Male figures (hygienists, physicians, and religious leaders) who may have had little actual experience in obstetrics gradually chipped away at the authority of often seasoned female midwives in the birthing process.[1]

Transformations in Iran's culture of childbirth significantly affected gender relations, and the development of modern nursing manifested the authority of modern (male) physicians, as well as the indispensable participation of women in public health management. Women's experiences with conception, pregnancy, and childbirth—as mothers, healthcare professionals, or both—mirrored the broad cultural changes occurring in Iran. In the twentieth century, Iranian physicians slowly made the transition from traditional to modern medicine, although this shift was not devoid of dissent. Despite the infiltration of Western medical thought, entrenched beliefs and superstitions sometimes made it difficult to disseminate new scientific knowledge about reproduction. Even physicians who may not have resorted to talismans to ward off the evil eye had limited access to new approaches to childbirth and maternal care.

Many Persian physicians of the modern era typically drew upon both Islamic and Western medical literature to treat patients.[2] Historically, Islamic notions of conception differed from Western ones, although Greek views of reproduction influenced both schools of thought. Medieval Muslim scholars did not privilege a man's contribution to conception over a women's role, but patriarchy remained ingrained. In fact, relying on the Koran, some medieval Islamic jurists argued that neither the male nor female matter was especially significant. Islamic medical philosophers such as Ibn Sina and Ibn Rushd, however, asserted the dominance of the male sperm in reproduction.[3] These discrepancies suggest that the medieval Islamic world did not have a uniform view of reproduction and female sexuality.[4]

The dearth of medical information about women's internal anatomy meant that female sexuality—and hence human reproduction—remained poorly understood. Information about pregnancy appeared in folkloric literature and was scattered in medical works. In early modern Iran, Safavid physicians built on medieval Islamic medical knowledge to learn about female ailments and reproduction. Although some medical specialization had emerged, male doctors did not typically treat gynecological matters. Rather, midwives treated female conditions, but since most were illiterate, they left no account of their empirical experiences. Few anatomical works focused on the pelvis and other internal parts of the female anatomy, and, as a result, male physicians knew little about women's internal reproductive organs.[5] Medical manuscripts from the Qajar era (1796–1925) typically focused on the etiology and treatment of epidemic diseases such as cholera or smallpox, or they provided general discussions on anatomy and hygiene. One treatise, however, addressed women's diseases specifically, providing explanations and treatment of diseases related to the uterus, including uterine cancer and ovarian irregularities.[6]

In the modern era, as Western medicine rapidly made headway among the elite, Western physicians often spoke of traditional Persian physicians and midwives in derogatory terms. Yet this clash represented more than just a conflict between the East and the West. For similar phenomena had already been observed in other cultures, such as in early modern England, a society that was not influenced by Western colonialism or Islamic belief. Illiterate Muslim women were thus not alone in attaching new meaning to religious concepts related to conception and reproduction. Nor did their unscientific beliefs make them more benighted or ignorant than their Western counterparts, as some modern hygienists contended.[7] What matters here is that both Protestant and Shi'i women, for example, became subjected to similar structures of power intended to circumscribe their individual authority and their independent decision-making in matters of reproduction and sexuality.

The interest in reproduction was tied to a discourse on cleanliness and bodily health. Healthful procreation became appropriated by statist interests and attempts to populate communities with fertile, chaste, and family-oriented subjects. In times of political crisis the need to uphold patriarchy intensified, and control over women and their sexuality reinforced male authority. As Iranians came to understand the process of reproduction better, they strove to regulate maternal care through the expansion of nursing and the regulation of midwifery. These changes became possible as the political climate in Iran emphasized state centralization and the top-down supervision of healthcare. Iranian medical officials hoped to curtail infant mortality through improvements in municipal services and the expansion of clinics.[8] Although male physicians gradually assumed control over the fields of obstetrics and gynecology, they had to acknowledge the salience of involving women in the politics of reproduction.

Population debates emerged in Iran during the nineteenth century as part of a modernist discourse concerned with hygiene and increased oversight of midwives and other healthcare workers. Intellectuals, physicians, and outside observers commented on the high levels of infant and maternal mortality due to frequent outbreaks of epidemic diseases such as plague, cholera, and common childhood diseases. Hygienists also viewed poor sanitation as contributing to the outbreak of contagious illnesses, the prolongation of infirmity, and mortality. At times, male writers and critics targeted the status and education of midwives, healthcare workers who were seen increasingly as exacerbating the country's low population count.

In the nineteenth century Western travelers to Iran and Persian writers commented on the prevalence of infant mortality. In 1843, Reverend Justin Perkins, who opened the American Presbyterian mission in northwestern Iran, observed that a "much larger proportion of children die in infancy in a given population among all classes in Persia, than in America."[9] Perkins noted that while "[b]irths are far more numerous," few children survived to adulthood. While he acknowledged the difficulty in explaining "the cause of such mortality," Perkins speculated that poor hygiene and the early age of marriage were possible contributing factors.[10]

Persian sources reported the mortality of children resulting from epidemics as well. In 1894, the Persian newspaper *Nasiri* confirmed Curzon's conclusions about the fatality of smallpox by acknowledging that "every year many children die or become maimed because of the lack of smallpox vaccinations."[11] Again, in 1898, another source condemned Iran for doing little to combat the threat of smallpox—a "negligence" that had caused numerous preventable deaths. Smallpox not only claimed many lives, it disfigured its survivors, making them, in the words of the prolific scholar Mirza Husayn Khan, Zuka' al-Mulk, "hideous and ugly."[12] Every year smallpox wreaked devastation among children, causing their death or disabling them (*naqis mishavand*).[13] In addition to smallpox, a measles epidemic in Tehran had claimed the lives of many children back in 1896, and the deaths had occurred largely from gangrene, believed to be a side effect of measles.[14] Contagious childhood illnesses that regularly felled Iranian babies included "measles, scarlet fever, whooping cough, mumps, [and] chicken pox," as well as typhoid fever and diphtheria. Unsurprisingly, "the commonest illness of all is smallpox." Though adults also became victims of smallpox, "it is considered a children's illness, because people hardly ever grow up without having had it."[15] By the end of the century, Persian hygienists pondered the outcome of fatal epidemics even as they penned treatises to overhaul public sanitation.

As these indicators show, curbing infectious diseases and prolonging the lives of mothers and children, whose health was particularly compromised in the nineteenth century, made sense both medically and socially. This impetus would have little political significance, however, had it not been co-opted by Iranian modernists and policymakers in the first half of the twentieth century to control the sexuality of women and men in the interests of the nation. For the next fifty years Iranian officials, physicians, intellectuals, and women activists would investigate the high incidence of infant and maternal mortality, offering socially prescriptive measures to counter the possibility of depopulation.[16]

Despite concerns over depopulation in the nineteenth century, Iran did not institute a robust and legally mandated population policy. Little information is available on medical institutions that came into existence at the turn of the century to serve women. In 1908, the newly founded Himmat Hospital in Tehran provided midwifery services, but it likely had limited capacity and popularity. Female patients, moreover, had to be accompanied by a family member who would be willing to care for them.[17] Because the majority of births in Iran still occurred at home with the help of other women, it was imperative to teach them the basic principles of hygiene.

Women's health remained a key to understanding demographic trends, and it literally became a national prerogative to question and supervise women on the tenets of mothering and childrearing. Essential to this project was the need to form a modernist culture that lauded matrimony, domesticity, and motherhood. Popular newspapers as well as school curricula reinforced women's familial responsibilities, even as they invited women to complement their household duties with work outside the home.[18]

In 1916, modern training schools for nurses began operating in Iran under the auspices of Presbyterian missionaries.[19] The mission acknowledged that "the profession is new to this part of the country and our training school is distinctly in the experimental stage."[20] To initiate formal nursing education, the Presbyterian missionaries provided basic guidelines for the first class of nurses in northwestern Iran to include no more than "six candidates at a time." Nursing applicants were required to "give evidence of good moral character, average good health, intelligence and earnestness of purpose."[21] The first six months of training were regarded as "probationary," after which time approved candidates would be admitted to full-time training. The courses of study included physiology, anatomy, practical nursing, and obstetrics.[22] The first class of nurses graduated between 1919 and 1920, and graduation ceremonies, attended by "leading Persian physicians of the city," were held in the men's ward of the Tabriz hospital, which was "emptied and decorated with American and Persian flags for the occasion."[23] By 1919, the American Mission hospital in Tehran had classes for training native nurses,[24] and in 1922, the American Mission hospital in Tabriz reported that "we now have eight native girl nurses in training, four having recently come in after graduating from our Girl's school."[25]

During the interwar years, Iranian health officials, hygienists, and others advocated high birth rates for families, arguing that high birth rates would provide a better workforce for the country, as well as make Iran more relevant in the global community of nations. Health policies focused on reducing infant mortality and maternal deaths, as well as on improving health services and sanitation across the country. In 1925, the League of Patriotic Iranian Women submitted a proposal to the parliament urging Majlis delegates to address the matter of population decline related to contagious diseases and its impact on national priorities. The first article suggested requiring blood tests and other physical examinations for couples before marriage. The second item called for sending students of modest means to Beirut and Egypt in order to instruct them in midwifery. The third point stressed that locally made clothes ought to be used in schools to support indigenous industries.[26] That women took an active role in promoting potential legislation that might serve to improve their health, and to further national ambitions, showed political progress. None of these measures was immediately embraced by the parliament.

Although hygienic conditions for these two populations remained far from ideal—according to Byron Good, a study undertaken by Overseas Consultants in 1949 found infant mortality in Iran to be over 50 percent[27]—still some measure of vital progress had been achieved. In the context of public healthcare, women trained as professional nurses, not just midwives, serving to expand the longevity of infants, mothers, and the infirm. Hospitals built separate women's wards to treat obstetrical cases. Women gained the opportunity to train in the latest techniques of nursing and midwifery and thus prepared the ground for graduating the first class of female physicians. In addition, women paid attention to venereal disease and marital relations, as well as to pregnancy and childrearing. To be sure, the mortality of women and children decreased somewhat in the early Pahlavi years, but the ever-expanding state also intruded further into the lives of citizens as a result of the maternalist discourse.

Iran revamped its healthcare program as a part of several consecutive development plans. During the first development plan, which lasted from 1948 to 1955, new hospitals emerged. An assessment completed midway through the second Seven-Year Plan, which began in 1955, showed a significant increase of government investment in preventive medicine and the treatment of infectious diseases.[28] With the inauguration of the third Five-Year Plan, from 1962 to 1967, the government invested in developing a National Health Services Network, paying more attention to the training of healthcare personnel. To fulfill their military obligations, physicians worked for eighteen months in rural areas. In addition, health services became more specialized during this time, with a demand for a rural midwifery training program.[29]

Assistant nurses, or *behyars*, offered necessary aid to medical professionals and for this purpose received rudimentary health and hygienic training, usually a two-year course of study after completing the ninth grade. *Behyars* often worked in hospitals or health clinics under the direction of more advanced nurses and sometimes served as midwives in rural communities.[30] By 1970 Iran had sixteen nursing schools, three of which operated in Tehran. Of these, only the High Institute of Nursing in Tehran offered a four-year course of study directed toward a bachelor's degree. The others provided a three-year training program in nursing that culminated in a nursing diploma. Except for the newly established schools, the nursing programs graduated approximately 350 nurses per year.[31]

In just over fifty years, the country rapidly multiplied the number of hospitals and clinics to meet the growing public demand for healthcare services. The immunization program succeeded in substantially cutting down on the incidence of diseases such as smallpox and diphtheria, which a century earlier had taken many lives and had contributed to the high rate of infant mortality in Iran.[32] Despite these advances, by 1975 Iran still lacked sufficient nurses in the workforce as compared with other nations, especially in provinces outside the capital.[33]

As Queen Farah Pahlavi went on to mother three other healthy children, including a male "spare," the state ironically took the decision to introduce family planning during the same decade. The emergence of Iran's family-planning policies reflected new public health concerns and efforts to manage the fertility of Iranian women. The founder of the Family Planning Association of Iran, Sattereh Farman Farmaian, observed in her memoirs that "population growth was the most important social problem we faced." According to her, Iranian parents, "made desperate by the arrival of babies they couldn't afford," often felt they had no choice but to abandon their children. Sattereh Farman Farmaian acknowledged the obstacles that lay before her and other family planners in traditional Middle Eastern societies that revered the culture of childbearing. As she noted, "In the Middle East, feelings about the importance of having many children are extremely strong, and it was difficult to convince old-fashioned, traditional Persians like my mother that birth control was not against God's law."[34] Iranians were not the only ones steeped in tradition, however; many religiously inspired movements in the West voiced similar ambivalence toward family-planning policies.[35]

Family planning was not intended to discourage mothering but to manage it. In 1966, the national census determined that Iran's population had increased by approximately 2.5 to 3 percent in a decade.[36] Based in part on this data, Iranian officials introduced population control programs. In 1967, the shah, along with twenty-nine other world leaders, signed a declaration on population that was presented to the UN secretary general, U Thant.[37] That year, Iran introduced programs in support of family planning, which Ayatollah Shariat Madari also endorsed.[38]

Considering the impassioned debates surrounding fears of depopulation during the interwar years, this development may seem surprising. As

Ali Asghar Zahedi, who directed Research and Planning at the Family Planning Division of Tehran, acknowledged, "Prior to 1967, no official steps were taken regarding family planning. On the contrary, the general attitude and the national laws were, essentially, encouraging large families." In fact, "Mothers-of-the-year were selected solely on the basis of the number of children they had raised."[39] In 1966, for example, the mother of the year had given birth to eighteen children.[40]

Like other countries, Iran experienced an about-face in the use of birth control and the evolution of reproductive politics after World War II. The decline of death rates, particularly in developing countries, the increasing independence of women in asserting control over their sexuality, and a belief that multiple pregnancies eventually threatened the health and well-being of mother and child contributed to a reversal of an ideology endorsing family planning.[41] Improved sanitation, physical activity, and attention to personal hygiene had been mantras for Iranian women, and a reduction in childbearing was added as a necessary step in maintaining the health of young women. The initial campaign to keep women's bodies healthy and strong—albeit intended principally to enable women to birth multiple children—contributed to a reduction in maternal deaths by the second half of the twentieth century. What remained consistent was the state's continued desire to impose social control over women's bodies and their reproductive choices. The debate surrounding reproduction demonstrated that, despite the success of Iranian women in gaining the vote, maternalist ideology nonetheless attempted to circumscribe their freedoms in other ways, often by influencing their private, reproductive decision-making and, by extension, their presence in the professional workplace. Although the Population Council, which informed Iranian family planning, urged that "the role of government in promoting family planning should be facilitative and permissive, and in no degree coercive," the absence of an alternative state discourse on the subject sometimes made it difficult for some citizens to embrace other choices, particularly in places where the state exerted undue influence.[42] Just as the state had at one time viewed large families as patriotic, it shifted to a discourse of small families, pinpointing differences in class and education of its citizens.[43]

The state-sponsored family-planning program aimed "to lower the rate of population growth" and "to raise the overall status of the family."[44] In 1967, the Population Council submitted a report to Iran's Ministry of Health highlighting changes in the demographic composition of the country, shifts that had occurred in part because of improvement in public health services. Both economic and social considerations had influenced the changing perspective of an ideal Iranian family size. The report anticipated that "the declining death rate and the likelihood of a higher population growth rate will reduce the pace of increase in per capita income. Thus for both economic and general welfare considerations, in the next decade or two, family planning should be popularized and it should constitute one of our important welfare programmes in the future plans."[45] The Population Council recognized that family-planning would be unsuccessful in areas where infant mortality remained high: "Programs of education and assistance in family planning should therefore concentrate on areas where mortality has fallen. In areas where 50 per cent or fewer children survive to adult ages there is little reason to promote contraception and little chance that it would be accepted."[46] According to Dr. Amir Mansur Sardari, undersecretary of state for family planning, as of September 1968 over two hundred family-planning clinics had been set up in towns and cities throughout Iran.[47] By 1971, rural areas had become targets of Iran's family planning as well.

To promote the program, the Population Council posted a resident advisor to Iran in 1968, and a year later the United Nations assigned a population program officer to Tehran.[48] Although Iran had numerous private and nongovernmental agencies delivering healthcare services, a UN report showed, the "Ministry of Health has been the most important provider of these services."[49] Local health officials disseminated information about population control as well. In November 1967, a seminar on health and family planning was convened in the northeastern province of Khurasan. Dr. Sardari spoke about the hazards of overpopulation, pointing out that economic limitations and social considerations made it difficult to reproduce and nurture families as in the past. Sardari also assured Iranian families that given Iran's "rich natural resources" (*manab 'i tabi 'i-yi ghani*), the purpose of healthcare and family planning principally remained "the well-being of families" (*rifah-i khvanavadah*).[50] Southern Iran held a similar forum two months later. In January 1968, the governor of Khuzistan, along with other government and healthcare professionals, presided at a three-day seminar on family planning. Participants included representatives from the three provinces of Khuzistan, Luristan, and Kahkiluyah.[51] Thirteen two-day conferences were convened between 1967 and 1968, each with an attendance of three hundred. These conferences addressed the topic "Why Iran Needs a Family Planning Program," and instructed participants on the use of contraceptives.[52] By 1971, the program had trained over two thousand physicians, nurses, and midwives, as well as members of the Health and Literacy Corps.

Existing clinics incorporated family-planning services, and the School of Public Health trained students with a focus on family planning. In 1971, Dr. Sardari gauged the success of the program: "One indicator of progress is the response we are getting from the public. The annual number of clinical visits has increased fivefold from 313,000 to one and one-half-million. The number of acceptors of oral contraceptives has risen from 265,000 to one and one-third-million."[53] These statistics did not take account of "commercial sales, which have multiplied 26 times since the start of the family planning program."[54] Nonetheless, assessing birth and fertility rates in Iran gathered from surveys or censuses, Iranian demographer Mehdi Amani concluded that "the birth rate in Iran is high" and that Iran "ranks with those having the highest rates of birth in the world."[55]

Family-planning advocates relied on multiple media to communicate the aims of the program to the Iranian public. For example, at a seminar in Khurasan audiences benefited from lectures as well as films related to healthcare.[56] The media used "radio, television, newspapers, bulletins, films, filmstrips, flannel-graphs, flip charts, pamphlets and posters," but as Nayereh Fotouhi, director of the Women's Corps program observed, "Face-to-face communication still brings the best results."[57] Training of government personnel was conducted in tandem with other efforts directed at educating rural communities about family planning. In particular, postpartum women could become susceptible to family-planning propaganda, since it was believed that "pregnant and newly delivered mothers are in general more receptive than others to accept contraceptive methods for spacing or limitation of their families."[58]

In Iran, as elsewhere, the birth control pill became a popular and accepted form of contraception, though, at times, an ineffective one. In April 1960 the Food and Drug Administration in the United States approved use of the first contraceptive pill, Enovid-10. Once the pills became widely available, the Iranian Ministry of Health authorized importing them to Iran.[59] The availability of the pill, however, did not eliminate the controversies surrounding its use. If anything, women and men raised questions about its safety and efficacy. A cartoon printed in the daily newspaper demonstrates this point. The image shows three pregnant women marching in a row to the delivery room. The picture is accompanied by a sardonic caption that reads: "Users of the birth control pill."[60] The pill's ineffectiveness as a form of birth control for women was evident in its apparent failure to prevent pregnancy. Another cartoon entitled "Quintuplets" depicted an anxious father being greeted by a delivery nurse holding three newborns in her arms. The nurse says: "Come! Hold them so I can bring the other two to you."[61] While this illustration did not specifically target the users of the birth control pill, it hinted at the challenges posed by unfettered fertility for soon-to-be parents. The Iranian public also pondered the safety of the pill. As a relatively new mode of contraception, researchers abroad investigated the effects of hormones on women's long-term health, and the Persian press occasionally discussed the results of such scientific findings. Although one article cautioned that little correlation existed between the pill and cancer in women, nonetheless it acknowledged the difficulty doctors faced in prescribing the pill as a completely safe form of contraception.[62]

Despite persistent social obstacles in their use, the birth control pill and IUD became the preferred methods of contraception for Iranian family planners. The penal code prescribed imprisonment for those assisting in abortions, including mothers.[63] Nonetheless, induced abortion, "one of the oldest" methods of contraception, was still considered "a widely used method of birth control" in 1970s Iran. Abortions were allowed "only on strict medical grounds, to save the life of the woman." However, many medical professionals in Iran believed that "clandestine abortions are frequent," especially in urban areas, though "reliable data on the abortion situation in Iran [are] scarce or nonexistent." Although hospitals provided some statistics, they did not "reflect the true situation in the community as most deliveries and an unknown number of abortions take place outside any institutions."[64] Regarding sterilization, Iranian law did not offer any indications. Sterilization remained "a matter between the doctor and his patient." Apparently, Very "few sterilizations are performed and are mainly tubal ligations."[65] In 1974, a study conducted at the Farah Maternity Hospital in Tehran showed an alarming number of abortions, suggesting that the family-planning program had not effectively prevented unwanted pregnancies.[66] Many of the women seeking abortions were either married teenagers or unmarried school-aged youth.[67] Abortion was legalized in 1977, though valid reasons for the abortion needed to be provided to the physician.[68]

Rural communities depended on midwives for reproductive advice and assistance. In 1971, the United Nations reported that the "proportion of deliveries in Iran conducted by traditional midwives is estimated at about 60 per cent. It is higher in the rural areas and as low or about 10 to 20 per cent in the city of Teheran."[69] The same report indicated that training "traditional midwives in elementary hygiene and in simple obstetric practice, supported by UNICEF, was discontinued some six years ago. The training scheme was regarded as unsuccessful and a decision was made to replace the traditional midwives with trained health personnel."[70] Yet the United Nations committee found that midwives remained central to the birthing process in Iran and recommended not only reviving "the training of traditional birth attendants," but also consideration of "their involvement in family planning programmes."[71] Midwives managed to provide healthcare services—albeit imperfect ones—and to reach out to communities that remained untouched by the state and its modern medical professionals.

Involving midwives in the family-planning program not only made it possible to educate them in accepted medical practices, but also to control their activities through "proper training." Midwives could also contribute to family planning by "reporting pregnancies and births, referring abnormalities for adequate care, promoting and encouraging contraception and becoming distributors of contraceptives such as condoms."[72] In short, the United Nations found that "it seems unlikely that the national family planning programme would reach the majority of the population without the co-operation of traditional birth attendants."[73] This conclusion recognized the trust that rural communities placed in traditional birth attendants. It also highlighted the ways in which the modern health campaign needed the involvement of local communities in areas where the state retained little control over the birthing process. Even if traditional midwives received none of the credit for the reduction of infant and maternal deaths in Iran—and continued to be viewed as in need of basic hygienic knowledge—they were nonetheless regarded as crucial participants in the government's ongoing health campaigns. The development of modern clinics, nursing colleges, and medical schools had not eliminated the role of the traditional midwife in part because of a shortage of trained nurses and midwives and the preference of many rural people for traditional healthcare.[74] The challenges to the implementation of family planning signaled the continued popularity of traditional birthing practices among the rural population.

As the idea of family planning became reality in Iran, the popular press addressed the importance of marriage for the youth. The two subjects went hand in hand and reflected maternalist preoccupations with family and reproductive policy. In fact, the state relied upon the nuclear family to instill a culture that promoted marriage as a necessary social institution defining the interaction of women and men. Lack of financial independence among the youth, however, posed as a disincentive for marriage. As one writer observed, "At the moment, not having a home is the biggest problem faced by a youth in creating a family." Typically, a young worker earned a meager salary and spent much of it on rent. One possibility to alleviate such economic woes was to have government ministries construct housing for its employees. While such suggestions did not always become government policy, these discussions exposed the financial challenges faced by the Iranian youth of the 1960s, economic hardships that affected personal conduct, including the decision to marry.[75]

Although international organizations such as the United Nations became involved in assessing Iran's healthcare and welfare policies, their work rarely focused on the regulation of obstetricians. While medical advances bolstered the public faith in doctors, hospitals, clinics, and other emblems of medical authority—as reflected in the increased involvement of such medical authorities in the healthcare of ordinary Iranian citizens—little public debate existed around the failures, mistakes, and limitations of modern medicine. Iranians would eventually investigate the occasional misuse of modern medicine providing a much-needed corrective to the otherwise laudatory accounts of medical progress.[76]

Persian newspapers rarely reported medical errors, but there were exceptions. In 1967, the daily paper reported that two physicians were arrested on the charge of unpremeditated murder of a woman named Fatima who had given birth at their office. The woman's brother reported that after his sister began experiencing labor pains, he obtained an automobile and took her to the office of the physician, Dr. Isma'ili. After assisting with labor, Dr. Isma'ili then informed the woman's brother that the child had died but that his sister was stable enough to undergo surgery at a private hospital. The woman and her brother awaited the doctor's arrival, and during this interval the patient's condition worsened. When the physician finally arrived, it was not possible to save the woman's life. The inspector's office launched an investigation of the deaths and held the physician Dr. Isma'ili and his wife in custody.[77] Not all incidents of medical malpractice related to childbirth were reported, but it is significant that the state imposed more stringent guidelines and practices to investigate suspicious deaths occurring during labor.

Overall, population politics attracted state attention and investment during the Pahlavi reign. The contradictory practices that become adopted over a fifty-year period speak to the complexities surrounding the management of reproduction in Iran and reflect the changing mores of the country.

When the Islamic Republic was established, it overturned the 1967 Family Protection Law on grounds of Westernism, and initially it was unclear whether contraceptives would be made legally available.[78] The regime encouraged high fertility and adopted a pronatalist stance, partly because of the increased fatalities resulting from the Iran-Iraq War and provided added economic incentives to larger families. In 1986 the national census indicated that the population was increasing more than 3 percent annually. At first officials of the Islamic Republic of Iran lauded the country's considerable population.[79]

After the publication of the 1986 census and the conclusion of the war two years later, the government launched a campaign to control population growth. The Ministry of Health and Medical Education began discussing family-planning options and even invited public debate on the population question in popular daily newspapers.[80] In 1989, a Five-Year Development Plan to control population growth was put forth, which was approved by the parliament.[81] The Ministry of Health and Medical Education also began distributing contraceptives, including pills and condoms, free of charge through its various networks. In 1991, a distinct department for family planning existed, and women health practitioners played an important role in educating rural communities about contraceptive use.[82] By 1999 the nation's supreme leader had passed decrees legalizing contraceptives and sterilization, including vasectomies. The country's only condom factory at the time produced approximately seventy million condoms annually to help with the government's campaign to limit family size among Iranians and to control the nation's swelling population.[83]

At the same time the Islamic Republic has striven to control infant mortality through its healthcare policies. Breastfeeding was stressed in an effort to promote infant health. A study conducted in 1993 recommended that medical education in Iran should place more emphasis on nutrition and especially breastfeeding. The same study further advised that there "is a need for widespread and serious public health education efforts through the mass media (especially radio and television), by religious leaders and clergymen, as well as through textbooks and face-to-face encounters," to promote breastfeeding and to educate mothers about how to maintain their milk supply.[84] In 1999 it was found that the average duration of breastfeeding in Iran, especially in urban centers, was less than the four to six months recommended by the World Health Organization. An experimental study conducted in Shiraz, Iran, concluded that educating lactating mothers about the benefits of exclusive breastfeeding during the first four months after delivery not only increased the rate of breastfeeding mothers but also enhanced the health of their infants.[85]

Nonetheless, infant mortality persisted as a pressing concern in hygiene and population politics. In 1985, the dearth of clean drinking water in some rural communities had been identified as a stumbling block in the government's efforts to improve public health, especially for small children. At that time only 50 percent of Iranian villages had access to clean water. Despite these existing challenges, Ali Reza Marandi, the Iranian health minister in 1985, claimed a significant drop in mortality figures since 1979.[86] Other studies suggest a decline in infant mortality as well. According to demographers Akbar Aghajanian and Amir Mehryar, "Between 1976 and 1991, infant mortality decreased from 112 per thousand live births to 63.2 infant deaths per thousand births. . . . This decline represents a drop of almost 50 per cent in the infant mortality rate." They attributed the decline to increased accessibility to clean sources of water and electricity in rural areas.[87] In 2001, rates of maternal and infant mortality had fallen "to less than ¼ of what rates were 15 years ago."[88] The World Health Organization observed that improved immunizations led to fewer outbreaks of contagious childhood diseases such as diphtheria, pertussis, and tetanus. Less frequent illnesses in childhood also lowered mortality rates in children. In 1980, 31,000 cases of measles had been recorded, while by 2002 the number had dropped to slightly over 9,500.[89]

Like its previous incarnations, the Islamic state was far from rational in executing its maternalist policies. In 1990, for example, President Hashemi Rafsanjani endorsed temporary marriage—the *sigheh*—as a legitimate form of relationship between women and men. Yet Fatemeh Karrubi, who directed the Martyrs' Foundation Hospital Center and whose husband Mehdi Karrubi served as speaker of the parliament, criticized the endorsement of *sigheh*. As Mrs. Karrubi explained, "To establish a permanent foundation for marriage it must be permanent marriage, not a temporary one."[90] The prevalence of *sigheh* might be a deterrent against commitment to a conventional marriage, not to mention a cause in the spread of venereal disease.

To combat newly discovered illnesses, the country recast its campaign against sexually transmitted diseases and drug abuse. In Iran AIDS appeared publicly in 1987, when a child was found to be infected after a blood transfusion. In 1990, the Iranian government reported that eleven Iranians had died of AIDS and that 138 individuals carried the virus thought to trigger AIDS. Indeed, in 1990, the government asserted that the carriers were hemophiliacs who had received blood transfusions infected with the disease prior to 1983.[91] According to news reports, by 1999 there were 203 recorded deaths from AIDS. By 2002 the number of HIV-positive patients in Iran, as well as cases of full AIDS had increased, and many individuals carrying the AIDS virus were identified as male drug users.

The spread of AIDS challenged Iran's Islamic mores and its emphasis on traditional family roles. President Ahmadinejad's infamous denial of homosexuality on his trip to the United States in 2007 only underlined the stigma attached to homosexual behavior in Iran. Just as the Qajar state found it more convenient to attribute the spread of syphilis and gonorrhea to the sharing of opium pipes, the Islamic Republic preferred to explain the spread of AIDS by focusing on the circumscribed population of drug addicts.

Although it was becoming socially imperative to teach the public about the hazards of AIDS, social obstacles compounded the government's efforts to inform citizens and adolescents about modes of contracting the disease. In particular, physicians felt uncomfortable discussing sexuality and the use of condoms. For instance, a brochure apparently distributed to teenagers taught abstinence in the following terms: "The best way to avoid AIDS is to be faithful to moral and family obligations and to avoid loose sexual relations. Trust in God in order to resist satanic temptations."[92] Dr. Mohammad Mehdi, an infectious disease specialist who headed the Iranian Center for Disease Control, admitted then that "we cannot talk about things that are opposed to our culture, opposed to our religious beliefs. Premarital sex is inappropriate and un-Islamic. So we can't say things to teen-agers like, 'Use a condom.'"[93] Nonetheless, Dr. Mehdi, acting on an order from Iran's Supreme Leader, Ayatollah Khamenei, worked to prevent the proliferation of AIDS.

A major step in the government's efforts to acknowledge publicly the spread and threat of AIDS came in 2002, when the National Committee to Fight AIDS recommended that Iranian students receive AIDS awareness information. Although the government's position, in observance of Islamic law, endorsed abstinence until marriage as the best way of avoiding AIDS, it nonetheless planned to inform students about the use of condoms and the possibility of the transmission of AIDS through intercourse.[94] In 2003 the government also decided to start distributing gratis clean syringes to drug users, officially estimated at 140,000, partly in an effort to limit the spread of AIDS.[95]

The Islamic Republic has at times approached veiling, women's health, family relations, and reproduction with little recognition that women actually have "civil liberties" as well as "civic wombs." Women's perspectives on politics and reproduction mattered not only because of their reproductive status, but also because of their rights as citizens. An analysis of Iran's cultural and reproductive policies since 1979 becomes revealing less for the data it includes, than for the dearth of women's voices setting the debate or providing oppositional views. It is this silencing—if not muting—of dissenting opinions that shows the subtle and conspicuous ways in which patriarchy ingrains itself in Iranian society.

Notes

1. This section is adapted from my review article of Mary Fissell's work: "Stepping Out of the Womb," *Journal of Women's History* (Fall 2010): 209–13. Also, Mary Fissell, *Vernacular Bodies: The Politics of Reproduction in Early Modern England* (Oxford: Oxford University Press, 2004).
2. Cyril Elgood, *A Medical History of Persia and the Eastern Caliphate from the Earliest Times until the Year A.D. 1932* (Cambridge: Cambridge University Press, 1951).
3. Leila Ahmed, "Arab Culture and Writing Women's Bodies," in *Women and Islam: Critical Concepts in Sociology*, ed. Haideh Moghissi (New York: Routledge, 2005), 205–8. Also, Basim Musallam, *Sex and Society in Medieval Islam* (Cambridge: Cambridge University Press, 1983). Other important works on women in Islam include the following: Leila Ahmed, *Women and Gender in Islam: Historical Roots of a Modern Debate* (New Haven: Yale University Press, 1993); Nikki Keddie and Lois Beck, eds., *Women in the Muslim World* (Cambridge, Mass.: Harvard University Press, 1980); and Barbara Freyer Stowasser, *Women in the Qur'an, Traditions, and Interpretation* (Oxford: Oxford University Press, 1994).
4. Sherry Sayed Gadelrab, "Discourses on Sex Differences in Medieval Scholarly Islamic Thought," *Journal of the History of Medicine and Allied Sciences* 66 (April 2010): 1–42. Also, Dror Ze'evi, *Producing Desire: Changing Sexual Discourse in the Ottoman Middle East, 1500–1900* (Berkeley: University of California Press, 2006), 16–47.
5. Cyril Elgood, *Safavid Medical Practice; or, The Practice of Medicine, Surgery and Gynaecology in Persia between 150 A.D. and 1750 A.D.* (London: Luzac, 1970), 208–10, 217.
6. "Amraz al-Nisa," Jumada al-Avval 1294 / May 1877. Unpublished manuscript at Astan Quds Razavi, Mashhad, Iran, #805; see chap. 12.
7. F. Kashani-Sabet, "The Politics of Reproduction: Maternalism and Women's Hygiene in Iran, 1896–1941," *International Journal of Middle East Studies* 38 (February 2006): 1–29.

8. For an article encapsulating this idea, see *Ittila 'at*, No. 582, "Sihhat-i 'umumi," September 17, 1928, 2.
9. Justin Perkins, *A Residence of Eight Years in Persia, among the Nestorian Christians* (Andover, Mass.: Allen, Morrill & Wardwell, 1843), 408.
10. Perkins, *Residence*, 408.
11. *Nasiri*, No. 4, 15 Dhul-qa'da 1311 / May 21, 1894, 30.
12. *Tarbiyat*, 2nd year, No. 74, April 10, 1898, 296.
13. *Nasiri*, May 21, 1894, 30.
14. *Tarbiyat*, 2nd year, No. 75, April 11, 1898, 300.
15. Napier Malcolm, *Children of Persia* (New York: Fleming H. Revell, 1911), 84–85.
16. It is important to highlight here that many graduates of colleges in the 1920s and 1930s frequently served in the government. As Reza Arasteh writes, these graduates "filled many key government posts." Reza Arasteh, "The Role of Intellectuals in Administrative and Social Change in Modern Iran," *International Review of Education / Internationale Zeitschrift für Erziehungswissenschaft / Revue Internationale de l'Education* 9, no. 3 (1963): 328.
17. *Sur-i Israfil*, No. 24, 24 Muharram 1326 / February 27, 1908, 6.
18. For more on this idea, see Firoozeh Kashani-Sabet, "Patriotic Womanhood: The Culture of Feminism in Modern Iran, 1900–1941," *British Journal of Middle Eastern Studies*, 32 (May 2005): 29–46.
19. *Cento Conference on Nursing Education, Held in Tehran, Iran, April 14–25 1964* (Ankara, Turkey: Office of United States Economic Coordinator for CENTO Affairs, 1964), 62.
20. Presbyterian Historial Society (PHS), Record Group (hereafter RG) 91, Box 4, Folder 11, received November 23, 1916, "Medical Report," Urumiyah 1916, 2.
21. PHS, RG 91, Box 4, Folder 11, received November 23, 1916, "Medical Report," Urumiyah 1916, 2.
22. PHS, RG 91, Box 4, Folder 11, received November 23, 1916, "Medical Report," Urumiyah 1916, 2.
23. PHS, RG 91, Box 4, Folder 14, "Report of American Hospital, Tabriz, 1919–1920," 2.
24. PHS, "Report of Women's Work in Tabriz, Persia, August 1918 to August 1919."
25. PHS, "Report of the American Mission Hospital at Tabriz, to the Annual Meeting held at Tabriz, Persia, August 1922."
26. *Nisvan-i Vatankhvah-i Iran*, No. 9, July 6, 1925, 2–3.
27. Byron Good, "The Transformation of Health Care in Modern Iranian History," in *Modern Iran: The Dialectics of Continuity and Change*, ed. Michael Bonine and Nikki Keddie (Albany: State University of New York, 1981).
28. Sazman-i Barnamah, *Sanjish-i pishraft va 'amalkard-i barnamah-i 'umrani-yi haft sal-i duvvum-i Iran* (Tehran, 1959), 111–12.
29. Ernest L. Stebbins, "Stebbins Evaluation: Preliminary Report of the Consultant to the U.S. Economic Coordinator for CENTO," *CENTO Conference Series on*

the Teaching of Public Health and Public Health Practice (Ankara: Office of United States Economic Coordinator for CENTO Affairs, 1970), 130–31.

30. G. Saroukhanian, "The Present Situation of Teaching Public Health and Public Health Practice in Iran," *CENTO Conference Series on the Teaching of Public Health and Public Health Practice*, 1970, 85–86.
31. Saroukhanian, "Present Situation of Teaching," 88.
32. Salnamah-i Amar-i Kishvar, Sal-i 1349/1970, 134, and Salnamah-i Amar-i Kishvar, Sal-i 2535 Shahanshahi, 124. Also, H. Mirchamsy, H. Taslimi, and M. Aghdachi, "Résultats des vaccinations collectives," *Acta Medica Iranica* 3, no. 2 (January 1960): 33.
33. Farideh Kiyumehr, "Shakhishayah Bihdasht va Darman," *Shakhishayah ijtima'i-yi Iran 1357*, introduction by Ahmad Ashraf (Tehran, 1978), 162. I thank Prof. Ashraf for pointing out this source to me and for encouraging me to include relevant statistics based on the government's annual reports.
34. Sattareh Farman Farmaian, *Daughter of Persia: A Woman's Journey from Her Father's Harem through the Islamic Revolution* (London: Corgi, 1993), 238.
35. Daniel Callahan, "Contraception and Abortion: American Catholic Responses," *Annals of the American Academy of Political and Social Science* 387, no. 1 (1970): 109–17.
36. Ferydoon Firoozi, "Iranian Censuses 1956 and 1966: A Comparative Analysis," *Middle East Journal* 24, no. 2 (Spring 1970): 221.
37. Charles Prigmore, *Social Work in Iran since the White Revolution* (Tuscaloosa: University of Alabama Press, 1976), 62.
38. Farman Farmaian, *Daughter of Persia*, 259.
39. *CENTO Workshop Series on Clinical and Applied Research in Family Planning*, 1971, 65.
40. *Iran Almanac and Book of Facts* (Tehran: Echo of Iran, 1966), 585.
41. Jan Stepan and Edmund H. Kellogg, "The World's Law on Contraceptives," *American Journal of Comparative Law* 22 (1974): 615.
42. Population Council, "Iran: Report on Population Growth and Family Planning," *Studies in Family Planning* 1, no. 20 (June 1967): 4.
43. For example, a report by the United Nations stated that "there is a high rate of illiteracy especially among women and lack of schools and teachers in rural areas where fertility is high." United Nations, "Population and Family Planning in Iran," prepared for the Government of Iran by a United Nations Interagency Mission (1971), 23.
44. *CENTO Workshop Series on Clinical and Applied Research in Family Planning*, 1971, 43.
45. As cited in the report of the Population Council, "Iran," 3.
46. Population Council, "Iran," 4.
47. A. M. Sardari and R. Keyhan, "The Prospect of Family Planning in Iran," *Demography* 5, no. 2, "Progress and Problems of Fertility Control around the World" (1968): 782.

48. *CENTO Workshop Series on Clinical and Applied Research in Family Planning, 1971*, 74.
49. United Nations, "Population and Family Planning in Iran," 9. One of the nongovernmental agencies providing health services remained the Red Lion and Sun Society. Another was the Institute for the Protection of Mothers and Children.
50. *Ittila 'at*, 4 Azar 1346 / November 25, 1967.
51. *Ittila 'at*, 16 Dey 1346 / January 6, 1968. Dr. Sardari also participated in this seminar.
52. Sardari and Keyhan, "The Prospect of Family Planning," 781.
53. *CENTO Workshop Series on Clinical and Applied Research in Family Planning, 1971*, 44.
54. *CENTO Workshop Series on Clinical and Applied Research in Family Planning, 1971*, 44.
55. *CENTO Workshop Series on Clinical and Applied Research in Family Planning, 1971*, 49–50.
56. *Ittila 'at*, 4 Azar 1346 / November 25, 1967.
57. *CENTO Workshop Series on Clinical and Applied Research in Family Planning, 1971*, 78.
58. United Nations, "Population and Family Planning in Iran," 10.
59. Sardari and Keyhan, "Prospect of Family Planning," 780. For discussion of the pill in the United States, see Cathy Booth Thomas, "May 9, 1960," *Time*, March 31, 2003; "Pregnancy Control," *Time*, April 11, 1960 (accessed online, January 22, 2007). The researcher cited in this article was John Rock, a Roman Catholic "layman" persuaded to pursue his work at the behest of Margaret Sanger, the tireless advocate of birth control in the United States. According to Cathy Booth (cited above), Sanger became a crusader for birth control after watching her mother die at the age of 50 after having endured eighteen pregnancies and eleven children.
60. *Ittila 'at*, 26 Dey 1346 / January 16, 1968.
61. *Ittila 'at*, 6 Azar 1346 / November 28, 1967.
62. *Ittila 'at*, 5 Azar 1346 / November 27, 1967.
63. Jacqueline Rudolph Touba, "Effects of the Islamic Revolution on Women and the Family in Iran: Some Preliminary Observations," in *Women and the Family in Iran*, ed. Ashgar Fathi (Leiden: E. J. Brill, 1985), 140–41.
64. United Nations, "Population and Family Planning in Iran," 15.
65. United Nations, "Population and Family Planning in Iran," 16. In fact, the United Nations recommended that sterilization "be made available more widely to women and men."
66. G. H. Jalali, H. Peyman, and A. Majd, "Study of Abortion at Farah Maternity Hospital, Teheran," *Iranian Journal of Public Health* 2, no. 4 (February 1974): 1–7. Parvin Paidar also refers to this study in her work, *Women and the Political Process in Twentieth-Century Iran* (Cambridge: Cambridge University Press, 1997), 155.

67. Jalali, Peyman, and Majd, "Study of Abortion," 3.
68. Paidar, *Women and the Political Process*, 155.
69. United Nations, "Population and Family Planning in Iran," 18.
70. United Nations, "Population and Family Planning in Iran," 19.
71. United Nations, "Population and Family Planning in Iran," 19.
72. United Nations, "Population and Family Planning in Iran," 19.
73. United Nations, "Population and Family Planning in Iran," 19.
74. United Nations, "Population and Family Planning in Iran," 18: Soodabeh Ghavami, "The Role of the Medical Profession in Family Planning," in *CENTO Conference on Family Planning, Health & Demographic Statistics held in Tehran, Iran, August 12–16, 1973*, 95–96.
75. *Ittila'at*, "Chih konim ta javanan izdivaj konand?" 16 Azar 1346 / December 7, 1967.
76. In 1975, a study on the "use and abuse of antibiotics in Shiraz" supports this point. S. Amidi et al., "Antibiotic Use and Abuse among Physicians in Private Practice in Shiraz," *Medical Care* 13, no. 4 (April 1975): 341–45.
77. *Ittila 'at*, 16 Azar 1346 / December 7, 1967.
78. Homa Hoodfar and Samad Assadpour, "The Politics of Population Policy in the Islamic Republic of Iran," *Studies in Family Planning* 31, no. 1 (2000): 19–34.
79. Farzaneh Roudi, "Iran's Revolutionary Approach to Family Planning," *Population Today* 27, no. 7 (July 1 1999): 4–5; Mohammad Jalal Abbasi; Amir Mehryar; Gavin Jones; Peter McDonald, "Revolution, War and Modernization: Population Policy and Fertility Change in Iran," *Journal of Population Research*, 19, no. 1 (May 2002): 25–46.
80. Hoodfar and Assadpour, "Politics of Population Policy."
81. Abbasi et al., "Revolution, War and Modernization."
82. Akbar Aghajanian and Amir H. Mehryar, "Fertility Transition in the Islamic Republic of Iran: 1976–1996," *Asia-Pacific Population Journal* 14, no. 1 (1999): 21–42.
83. Brian Murphy, "Iran's Birth Control Drive Blessed," Associated Press, October 11, 1999.
84. A. Marandi, H. M. Afzali, and A F. Hossaini, "The Reasons for Early Weaning among Mothers in Teheran," *Bulletin of the World Health Organization* 71, no. 5 (September–October 1993): 561–69.
85. M. D. Froozani, K. Permehzadeh, A. R. Dorosty Motlagh, and B. Golestan, "Effect of Breastfeeding Education on the Feeding Pattern and Health of Infants in Their First 4 Months in the Islamic Republic of Iran," *Bulletin of the World Health Organization* 77, no. 5 (May 1999): 381–90.
86. BBC Monitoring Service: The Middle East; "Iran: Water Supply and Infant Mortality," July 30, 1985.
87. Aghajanian and Mehryar, "Fertility Transition."

88. World Health Organization, "Addressing Chronic Conditions in Primary Health Care," Ministry of Health and Medical Education, Islamic Republic of Iran, 2001, http://www.who.int/chp/knowledge/publications/iccc_ch3.pdf.
89. World Health Organization, "Vaccines, Immunization and Biologicals," http://www.who.int/vaccines/globalsummary/timeseries/TSincidenceByCountry.cfm?country=Iran%20(Islamic%20Republic%20of).
90. Elaine Sciolino, "From the Back Seat in Iran, Murmurs of Unrest," *New York Times*, April 23, 1992. It is curious and not entirely surprising that more than a hundred years after the arrival of the first American visitors to Iran, Sciolino has continued perpetuating the notion of *sigheh* as prostitution or "call-girl business." According to Sciolino, "The world's oldest profession is practiced largely in the form of 'sigheh,' the Islamic practice by which a couple can get married for a few years or months, or, if the rules are stretched, a few hours." *New York Times*, April 23, 1992.
91. "Iran in Brief: Iranian Health Official on Blood Donations," BBC Summary of World Broadcasts, July 28, 1990; "Iran Records More than 200 AIDS-related Deaths," Agence France-Presse, December 1, 1999.
92. "Doctors Urge Moral Behaviour," *APS Diplomat Recorder* 56, no. 6 (April).
93. "Doctors Urge Moral Behaviour," *APS Diplomat Recorder* 56, no. 6 (April 2002).
94. *International Family Planning Perspectives* 28, no. 2 (June 2002): 57, "In Brief: National Committee to Fight AIDS."
95. *Alcoholism and Drug Abuse Weekly* 15, no. 31 (August 18, 2003): 8.

7

Reproductive Statecraft

The Case of Brazil

SONIA CORRÊA, MARGARETH ARILHA, AND MAÍSA FALEIROS DA CUNHA

> "It is heaven": Porto das Galinhas (the Port of Chickens), in Pernambuco. So named because every time a slave ship unloaded its cargo there, a secret password was passed between the region's planters: "The chickens have arrived in the port." The thirty men who were brought by the Creole Nation were taken to a nearby house hidden among tall palm trees, where they were washed and dressed. Sold that same morning for a good price, of which I later learned, they began marching overland toward various farms in the south.[1]

In 2010, some 191 million people lived in Brazil, the fifth largest country of the world in both territorial and demographic terms. The total fertility rate—6.3 children per woman in 1960—decreased to 2.38 in 2000 and then to 1.9 in 2010. Twenty-five percent of the population are under fifteen, 64 percent are aged fifteen to fifty-nine, and 10 percent are older than sixty.[2] This remarkably rapid demographic transition occurred in the absence of stringent fertility control measures and has puzzled not a few demographers. In 1989, the late political scientist Vilmar Faria assessed this sharp fertility decline, explaining that ideas about the ideal family size had changed drastically under the combined effects of certain structural policies implemented by the Brazilian military regime (1964–85): the expansion of the public health network and social security systems, new consumer credit schemes, and enlarged access to new communication technologies, especially television.[3] All of these developments contributed to altered reproductive practices.

Few people today doubt the impact of these structural policies, implemented during a period of steady economic growth. But in order to better grasp the simultaneous rearrangements at work in the realms of gender relations, sexuality, and procreative practices, we must also take into account shifts created by the long re-democratization process that began in the late 1970s and unfolded in the 1980s. This process opened spaces for continuous political mobilization around these gender and health issues and altered patterns of interaction between state institutions and civil society organizations. It involved a wide range of classical political actors—such as unions and popular movements—but also favored the blossoming of unexpected voices and claims, such as those of feminists, gays, lesbians, *travestis*,[4] and sex workers.[5] Another key phenomenon that impacted this process was the coincidental surge of the HIV/AIDS epidemic in the early 1980s and the resulting state policies that it inspired.[6]

The claims and policy proposals in relation to gender equality and sexual and reproductive health and rights and HIV/AIDS that were articulated in the 1980s and 1990s have also intertwined with related transnational flows of discourse that began circulating in Brazil in the mid-1970s in relation to population size and control and women's issues. These discourses intensified under the effects of the series of multilateral debates promoted by the United Nations in the 1990s, which directly addressed these topics.[7] Ironically, over the course of the last ten years, as democracy has become relatively more inclusive and poverty and inequality reduced (if only slightly), regressive policy shifts and threats to recent political and legal achievements in the sexual and reproductive domain have become increasingly grave. This has been particularly the case with regard to the ongoing efforts to make abortion legal and safe in Brazil, but it has also affected the successful and internationally renowned response of the Brazilian state to the HIV/AIDS crisis.[8]

While the Brazilian demographic scenario and the related reproductive policy landscape in 2014 must be understood against this late twentieth-century economic, sociocultural, and political backdrop, we also need to consider the impacts of longer trajectories of statecraft in the fields of population and procreation. It is not analytically sound to propose that colonial norms, nineteenth-century legal frames, or the policies adopted in the early twentieth century have linearly extended into the present and can fully explain key features of contemporary sexual and reproductive politics. Nevertheless, threads and traces can indeed be tracked across distinct conjunctures of Brazilian sexual and reproductive history.

For example, state concerns and related measures in regard to the governance of "unbridled miscegenation," manifested in the heyday of colonization, remained in evidence until the mid-twentieth century. Continuities can also be observed in the legal field, as illustrated by the early eighteenth-century canonical laws regarding marriage that remained on the books until the first days of the Republic in the late nineteenth century, or the 1916 legal definitions of civil marriage the reform of which would only be completed in 2002. Criminal proscriptions with regard to abortion have been enshrined in the three criminal codes (1830, 1890, and 1940) adopted after Brazilian independence in 1822; these have not been substantially altered since: The law enacted in 1940 remains intact today.

This chapter begins by providing a condensed view of some of these genealogical traces. It briefly revisits colonial population trends and norms and conducts a similar exercise with respect to the postindependence period (1822–89) and the first republican era (1889–1930). We then look at the modernizing shifts of the revolution of the 1930s and their aftermath, as these constitute the immediate antecedents of contemporary sexual and reproductive politics in Brazil. Finally, we examine the legal and cultural landscape following re-democratization as this pertains to reproductive policy, mostly through the lens of social struggles that have led to policy changes, regressions, and paradoxes.

These snapshots do not exhaust the examination and interpretation of the complexities implied in these various historical conjunctures. We are aware that each of them could be the object of much more extensive and detailed scrutinizing. Our aim is to fundamentally locate contemporary manifestations of statecraft within this longer cycle. Such an exercise, even if limited and incomplete, can contribute to illuminating the complexities and paradoxes of the present landscape regarding abortion and reproduction policies in Brazil. This strategy allows us to situate claims of human freedom in the realms of sexuality and procreation within a *longue durée* perspective that reveals how deeply rooted the restrictions and strictures of state regulation are and how these disciplinary devices have been and continue to be inextricably intertwined with the dynamics at work in the political-economic formations that encompass cultural constructions, including those embedded in religious doctrines.

Colonial Statecraft: Racial Domination, the Centrality of Marriage, Sexual Hubris, and Miscegenation

In the mid-1800s, the Argentinian diplomat Juan Baptista Alberdi declared that "to govern is to populate."[9] While referring to nineteenth-century Argentina, Alberdi's observation neatly encapsulates the rationale of three centuries of colonial statecraft in other settings such as Brazil, whose territories were originally deemed "empty" by early Spanish and Portuguese conquerors. Historical demographic reconstruction has shown how deeply biased this perception was. In the case of Brazil, for example, demographers estimate that, in the 1500s, the population living in the territory that now corresponds to the nation-state could have been as large as three million people.[10] In 1660, the population in formalized colonial settlements has been estimated at around 184,000 people, primarily composed of indigenous and African slaves, a minority of European colonizers (mostly Portuguese), and persons of mixed race. This population was concentrated in coastal villages in the northeast and southeast, the sole exception being São Paulo de Piratininga, located some seventy miles from the coast.

Colonial domination over the indigenous population was mainly exerted through coercion. Alliances were also quite often established between male colonizers and indigenous chieftains, leading to informal unions between the Portuguese and indigenous women, termed *cunhadismo*.[11] Together with sexual predation upon native women, common to all colonial settings, these alliances inaugurated Brazil's extensive and long-standing practice of miscegenation. Increases in the country's population during the colonial period can be mostly attributed to the African slave trade that escalated after the expansion of the sugar cane economy in the mid-1500s. It is estimated that between the early sixteenth and the nineteenth centuries 3.3 to 6 million enslaved Africans—mostly captured in Angola and the Kingdom of the Congo—were forcibly transplanted to Brazil.[12] Between the sixteenth and nineteenth centuries, the colonial economy shifted from the extraction of tropical products (such as brazilwood) and sugar plantations to gold mining and later coffee export. In 1808, when the Portuguese court, fleeing Napoleon's armies and escorted by the British Royal Navy, arrived in Rio de Janeiro, the colonial population is estimated to have been 2.4 million people.[13]

In Portuguese colonial enterprise the state and the church jointly disciplined sex and reproduction with a view toward territorial occupation and "fulfilling God's design."[14] This strategy translated to the colonies the Council of Trent doctrines focusing on the heterosexual and procreative family as a key to rejuvenating Catholicism and driving back the Reformation.[15] According to both the church and the state, marriage was defined as an indissoluble union aimed at procreation, containing lust, and stimulating mutual aid.[16] The secular and religious normative apparatuses preached the subordination of women to fathers and husbands and the severe punishment of fornication, concubinage, adultery, the rape of virgins, pandering, adultery, male and female sodomy, bestiality, transvestism, the use of masks, and voluptuousness.[17] Restrictions on marriage were based on the rule of "defective blood," which prohibited marriage with non-Catholics: Moors and Jews, including the converted (so-called New Christians) and the many "Others" encountered by the Portuguese during their colonial expansion.[18]

The gender and sexuality landscape of colonial Brazil rapidly became a fertile ground for the application of these norms. The first Jesuits in the colony developed a vision of the local indigenous peoples, mixing innocence with a horror of the natives' (literally) shameless display of nudity and their occasional public engagement in sexual intercourse. Missionaries described indigenous kinship systems and villages as sources and places of fornication, polygamy, and promiscuity. As the transatlantic slave trade escalated, similar tropes were applied to the mores and practices of captive Africans. Shortly thereafter, priests and secular administrators began describing the Portuguese colonizers themselves as easily influenced and "corrupted" by these supposedly powerful webs of nonwhite sexual excesses.[19]

Historians of Brazilian colonial sexuality report in detail how monks and priests made every possible effort to discipline and moralize these "excesses."[20] The indigenous people were married according to church law and slave owners were admonished, without much success, to allow their captives to marry as Christians too. Both secular and religious authorities also openly condemned the extensive concubinage the Portuguese practiced.[21] Periodic visits from the Inquisition and, later on, "disclosures" (known as *devassas*) led by local bishops searched out and punished those who defied the sacrament of marriage, depicting such people as heretics.[22] The demands of the colonial political economy, however, impeded these norms from being universally enforced.

The dominant patriarchal family unit, headed by slave owners, was highly autonomous and resisted interventions by the agents of state or church.[23] The scarcity of white women and the requirements of territorial occupation made it practically impossible for European marriage doctrines and rules of blood to be fully enforced if the overarching objective of populating the territory was to be fulfilled. Consequently, missionaries constantly appealed to the Crown to send white women to the colony, and some were sent (mostly orphans, but also imprisoned prostitutes), inaugurating the first flow of state-sponsored immigration aimed at resolving the problem of interracial sexual intercourse in Brazil.[24] At the same time, colonizers and administrators argued for more flexible rules concerning racially mixed sexual relations, concubinage, and miscegenation.[25]

These rules would, in fact, be adapted, as exemplified by the Brazilian canonical law of 1707, which did not punish concubinage in the case of masters living in union with their female slaves. A more striking example can be found in the Enlightenment-inspired reforms implemented by the Marquis of Pombal, prime minister of Portugal in the mid-eighteenth century.[26] These reforms fully abolished slavery in Portugal and granted freedom to the Brazilian indigenous population, but maintained captive the black slaves whose labor sustained the colonial economy. Pombal did not sever the state's relations with the church, but subordinated the Inquisition to secular power and abolished the burning of heretics and "blood impurity" rules. He also issued a secular ordinance on marriage in order to restrict the practice of endogamy then prevalent among the Portuguese nobility and shifted the governance of the native population to secular authorities.

Pombal also expelled the Jesuits from Brazil by there ending three centuries of this religious order's tutelage over this population. A new law titled the Indigenous Directory shifted the governance of the native population to the secular authorities and stated as its main objectives: to civilize indigenous peoples who still lived as "barbarians," to promote the occupation of the Brazilian hinterland, and to properly defend the new boundaries of the colony. The law not only recognized natives as free men but also banned calling them "niggers"—*negro* in Portuguese—a term that was henceforth to be exclusively applied to African slaves, as well as other forms of discrimination. Most important, the law compelled white colonizers to share a common life with the indigenous population in order to foster public harmony and enhance the civilization, authorizing and encouraging marriages between whites and natives (Articles 89, 90, and 91), making it clear that colonials would not lose their professional status and social privileges if they engaged in mixed marriages with indigenous women.[27]

These reforms were cut short by the death of the Portuguese king, as Pombal was removed and the Directory abolished in 1798 after a few years of sporadic enforcement, often resisted. Pombal's norms and administrative techniques remained relevant in many aspects. First, because they reflected the paradoxes of eighteenth-century liberal governance rationales, combining ideals of freedom and equality with strict control over populations and their reproductive practices, particularly in colonial settings. Even though these norms were secular and differed in many respects from the religious norms they still aimed to discipline sexuality and procreation (through marriage) as privileged loci of social and political administration then being instituted in Europe and its colonies.[28] In other words, the Pombaline reforms were typical biopolitical instruments.[29] Moreover, Pombal's deliberate promotion of selective miscegenation as a civilizing strategy inaugurated a line of policy thinking that would stretch far beyond his time.

One last observation regarding colonial sexual and reproductive norms is that neither state nor canonical law explicitly proscribed abortion, largely because the status of the fetus was unresolved in Catholic theological debates at this time.[30] During the colonial era, undesired or undesirable procreation publicly manifested in newborn children abandoned in churches, convents, and on private doorsteps. In the mid-eighteenth century, a church institution was established—the House of the Foundlings—where anonymous mothers could leave their children to the care of others.[31] Until the late nineteenth century and beyond, the House would be portrayed by moral reformers as providing an institutional incentive to libertine behavior and infidelity.[32]

The Brazilian Liberal Empire: Gender, Race, and Slavery as the Principles of Statecraft

In 1822, when Brazil became an independent constitutional monarchy, 3.9 million people lived within its boundaries, approximately 30 percent (1.1 million) of these being slaves.[33] The juridical architecture of the Brazilian empire strongly reflected its political elites' allegiance to eighteenth-century liberal political ideals, but slavery was not abolished, a decision justified in economic terms, as the slave economy sustained the newly established governing apparatus. The new juridical order also preserved the sharp racial and social hierarchies inherited from the colony, while retaining certain colonial normative definitions.

While all people born in Brazil were granted citizenship on paper, women and slaves were excluded from voting rights, and even for men, an income threshold was established for full suffrage, meaning that many—if not most—free men could not vote.[34] The 1824 constitution also retained Catholicism as the official religion of the empire and, three years later, a National Assembly ordinance reaffirmed the 1707 jurisdiction of the Bahia Archbishopric over marriage.[35] Although a new penal code was approved in 1830, no revised codification of civil law occurred during the whole monarchy (1822–89).

A number of earlier secular and canonical prescriptions concerning sexual and marital transgressions were, however, overruled by the 1830 penal code. In line with the criminal tenets of the French Revolution, the crime of sodomy was abolished, a remarkable development.[36] Modernization did not extend, however, to gender equality in the domains of sexuality and reproduction. The chapter entitled "Crimes against the Safety of the Civil and Domestic State" selectively punished women and single male adulterers, while married men were only penalized if they maintained a concubine.[37]

The most salient illustration of modernized reproductive statecraft included in the 1830 code is the chapter "Crimes against the Security of the Person and Life," which criminalized abortion when performed by third parties either with or without the consent of the pregnant woman (abortion was not subject to any penalty when carried out by women themselves), a definition also inspired by the French laws of 1791 and 1810.[38] The prohibition of abortion reflected both new scientific knowledge of reproduction and the convoluted eighteenth-century ideological constructions aimed at keeping women confined to the private and procreative sphere.[39]

"Reproductive" statecraft was also expressed in the postindependence period by the complex intersection of debates and concerns around the abolition of slavery, nineteenth-century conceptions of racial hierarchies, and the "degrading" effects of miscegenation. In 1831, under British pressures, Brazil approved a law abolishing the slave traffic. This law remained totally ineffective, however, until 1850 when a new law was adopted, which would be consistently enforced. In between the two intervening decades, seven hundred thousand additional captives arrived in Brazil and an abolition movement took shape in the country.[40] After 1850, in the midst of vibrant abolitionism in Europe and elsewhere, it became clear that slavery would sooner or later be abolished, and Brazilian political and economic elites were deeply preoccupied with the potential impacts of abolition.

At the same time, ideologies surrounding the pseudoscientific concept of race began circulating in Brazil. Influential visitors to Brazil included the Comte Gobineau, the author of the *Essay on the Inequality between Human Races* (1855)—who served as French ambassador to the Brazilian court (1869–70)—and the Harvard professor Louis Agassiz (who supported the "scientific" argument of racial polygenism), who visited Brazil in 1865–66.[41] While concerns with race and miscegenation were far from new, the biologically grounded discourses of the nineteenth century added extreme ideas of racial inferiority and the supposedly detrimental effect of race mixing on the ability of nations to become (or remain) civilized. In this context, the long-standing racial mixture of the Brazilian population transformed Brazil into a constant object of scientific inquiry.[42]

The earlier panic regarding slave rebellions—since the early nineteenth century known as *Haitianism*—now overlapped with new fears of the social degradation that would occur through increased levels of miscegenation following abolition. Based upon both old and new ideas regarding the "inferior races" and their supposed propensity to laziness, the argument crystalized among elites that the black population, when freed, would evade work, causing the Brazilian economy to collapse.[43] These fears paved the way for a state-sponsored immigration policy aimed at attracting Europeans to Brazil.[44]

From 1850 onward, São Paulo created plantation-based migrant colonies and after 1870, when it became clear that abolition was finally approaching, these efforts intensified.[45] In this context, immigration policy was crafted and implemented as both a solution for the supposed shortage of labor on the coffee plantations and in other slavery-based economic activities, and as a path toward the gradual "whitening" of the population. "Whitening" was the ideological construct devised by Brazilian thinkers and elites who recrafted the notion of racial inequality in their own terms. As the historian Thomas Skidmore remarks, "whitening" theory was based on the belief that Portuguese blood had cleansing and civilizing qualities (a view of the world already visible in the Pombaline indigenous laws).[46] Utilizing this as their key point, Brazil's racist ideologues reconceived of miscegenation as the preferred path toward civilizing Brazil. According to these beliefs, the greater the number of white people in the population, the easier it would be to erase the negative traces of the "inferior races" in the Brazilian population.

Although agreements between Brazil and Japan from 1908 onward meant that large numbers of Japanese migrants would come to Brazil, the open preference for European immigrants would remain in place during the First Republic and even after its fall in 1930.[47]

In 1872, the first Brazilian national census was undertaken. It counted nearly ten million people within the country's borders, of whom 85 percent were born free and 15 percent were still enslaved.[48] The intensity and scale of miscegenation in the country was reflected in the fact that 62 percent of the population fell into the categories later defined as "brown" or "black."[49] Sixteen years later, when full abolition was finally granted, the slave population was roughly 720,000 people (from fifteen to fifty-nine years old).[50] A year later, the Republic was proclaimed and a new political era dawned that, as noted by the Brazilian sociologist Richard Miskolci in an interview about his book on the first republican period, continued to be haunted by the specters of the past:[51]

> The fear of blacks, after Abolition, came to mean a fear of the people in general, but also gender and sexual anxieties that threatened the project of a nation that was being constructed on the basis of an idealized image of Europe and whose main ideologies were based on a paradigm of whitening and compulsory reproductive heterosexuality.[52]

The Republican Era: Further "Modernizing" Reproductive Statecraft

The transition from empire to republic resulted from the seizure of power by a group of antimonarchist military officers.[53] Republican leaders were radically secular, strongly influenced by the positivist ideas of Auguste Comte and champions of the French and American revolutions. However, these ideals did not exactly translate into new juridical and political realities in Brazil. The republican constitution of 1891 defined, for the first time, a strict separation between church and state, but it failed to include certain guarantees of individual and social rights and kept women and illiterates from voting, as had been previously established by the electoral reforms of 1882.[54]

Several reforms during this period impacted directly on reproductive statecraft, such as a new penal code and the first civil marriage law as well as the emergence of a powerful public health establishment, which gradually evolved from the sanitation and vaccination campaigns implemented by Oswald Cruz in Rio de Janeiro in the early twentieth century.[55] These policy shifts reflected modern biopolitical concepts in regard to urban cleansing, family hygiene, women's role in the household, and sexual deviance. Adjusted to national conditions, these concerns focused on the distortions of the household inherited from colonial times (where racial boundaries were understood to be blurred), the proper education of elite boys (to detach them from this corrupted household environment), and the role of white women as the managers of this privatized, household-based hygienic project.[56]

Nancy Stepan (1994) in her landmark book remarks that British-inspired ideas regarding eugenics began to gain traction in Brazil after 1870, but did not become highly influential for some time. But, French approaches to "improving humanity," based upon Lamarck's theories of environmental and hereditary patterns that constituted the notions of *homiculture* and *puericulture* (or the proper cultivation of human beings) were more rapidly incorporated in early republican public health debates and state discourses.[57] This strand of thought (also described as preventive eugenics) was focused on the negative impacts of women's labor outside of the home and especially upon infant mortality and depopulation. These premises converged with early precepts regarding family hygiene and would have a long-standing effect on Brazilian maternal and child health policies.[58]

Concurrently, lawyers, psychiatrists, and others began to develop diagnostics and interventions aimed at detecting and preventing transgressive social behavior; sexual crimes and deviancy—particularly prostitution—became the main topics of a criminology agenda that targeted the poor.[59] The 1890 reform of the penal code inevitably reflected these trends. Following positivist and criminologist conceptions of "social order," it expanded misdemeanors to include begging, vagrancy, and drunkenness and also the practice of capoeira (a martial art developed by Brazilian slaves). Not surprisingly, it punished voluntarily induced abortions (performed by pregnant women themselves) while at the same time allowing for the reduction of penalties if the abortion was aimed at concealing the woman's "own dishonor." These changes indicate that the influence of the medical profession over procreation and juridical matters had increased since 1830. The 1890 code mirrored the dominant view that the virtues and vices of women spilled over onto their father's and husband's honor.[60]

The premises of the 1890 civil marriage law also embodied a powerful gender bias. Although secular in nature and strongly supported by republican leaders as a sign of liberation from the church's past control over state matters, the new law did not radically differ from the canonical prescriptions that had previously regulated marital unions. The age of marriage was raised for both men and women to twenty-one, and the impediments to marriage were slightly altered. The husband remained defined as the head of the household; he was now obliged by law to provide for his family. The law allowed for divorce and annulment, but the bond between spouses could not be fully severed since divorced people could not remarry.[61]

The classist, conservative, disciplinary, and still highly racialized ideological and political environment of the First Republic became even more restrictive in the mid-1910s when, in the context of the first wave of industrialization in Brazil, a labor strike flared up in São Paulo (1917). European migrants, attracted to the country to whiten and civilize Brazil had also brought with them socialist and anarchist ideas that added to unrest around working conditions and the absence of labor rights. The strike was violently smashed, leaving behind a policy motto that survived well into the late twentieth century: "The social question is a police question."

The strike is also relevant because Renato Kehl, a doctor working in the public health department of São Paulo who had been disseminating Francis Galton's eugenic ideas in Brazil, used the strike to advocate for "racial improvement" in order to contain and control social disruption.[62] In 1918, Kehl created the São Paulo Eugenics Society, which lasted only one year, in collaboration with other respected medical figures such as Vieira de Carvalho, a professor at the São Paulo School of Medicine. The society's members were all heavily involved in the burgeoning, sometimes state-led, hygienist and public health reforms, which were predominantly aligned with the neo-Lamarckian current of preventive eugenics.[63] In 1919 and 1934 Kehl published the *Eugenics Bulletin* and was also the organizer of the First Brazilian Eugenic Congress in 1929. Galton-inspired ideas regarding eugenics were thus interwoven with the theses developed by other highly influential conservative authors who followed other conceptual frames, but also had as their main focus the problem of race and miscegenation in Brazil.[64]

The Brazilian political landscape of the 1920s included the founding of the Communist Party in 1922 and the emergence of fascist groups, inspired by the Italian blackshirts. In 1927, a group of young military social reformers—the Tenentes (Lieutenants)—rebelled against the ruling agrarian elites and their practices of corruption, cronyism, and electoral manipulation. At the same time, public health reform initiatives organized around principles of hygiene and sanitation gained policy muscle. Brazilian advocates of eugenics, who were closely linked with this wider and more prestigious field, also benefited from this development. In 1931, Renato Kehl created the Central Brazilian Commission of Brazilian Eugenics as a platform for influencing the formation of policies in the Vargas era.[65]

The Vargas Era: Reproductive Concerns and Conservative Modernization

The First Republic fell in 1930 under the political upheaval mobilized by the National Alliance for Liberation (Aliança Nacional Libertadora—ANL) led by Getúlio Vargas. The ANL was a coalition of highly heterogeneous political forces, including the new industrial bourgeoisie, sectors of the Tenentes movement, a wide range of social reformers and intellectuals, labor unions, communists, some of the emerging fascist groups, and the social branch of the Catholic Church.[66] Despite their ideological differences, the vast majority of these forces called for strengthening the power of the central state and emphasized their expectation that the new government would play a key role in stimulating economic investment as well as transforming the social structures of Brazilian society.[67]

The new government immediately established an eight-hour workday for laborers in commerce and industry, set equal pay scales for men and women, and defined parameters for child labor. The 1932 electoral reforms secured women's suffrage and the anonymous ballot for persons above eighteen, but maintained the literacy requirement for voting, indicating that not even wide-ranging social mobilization was enough to overcome the elitist premises of the First Republic.

The transformation was not without crisis. In 1932, a separatist rebellion arose in São Paulo and in 1935 came a communist military uprising, both brutally suppressed. In 1937, Vargas closed down Congress and implemented, by decree, a new and extremely authoritarian constitution.[68] Elections were suspended, censorship was imposed, the political police hunted down dissidents, and political power was completely centralized. Many features of Vargas's authoritarian regime, known as the Estado Novo (New State), mirrored the Nazi-fascist regimes in Germany and Italy, as exemplified by the labor laws adopted in 1940, which were directly inspired by Italian legislation and state institutions under Mussolini. A web of connections between Brazil and the regimes of Germany and Italy, which had been evolving for some time intensified and expanded during this period.[69]

Many analysts have interpreted the Vargas era as an example of "conservative modernization."[70] According to the social historian Jose Murilo de Carvalho "[This was] a revolution that started as liberal and anti-oligarchic and which modernized the economy and social rights, but under the effects of tensions between ideologies and interests became an authoritarian regime.... A modernizing authoritarianism."[71] Unquestionably, the Vargas era modernized Brazil, propelling industrialization, internal migration, urbanization, the emergence of both a proletarian social strata, and an expanded urban middle class. The state apparatus was rationalized, and a robust health and education infrastructure was constructed that counted on the ideas and expertise of the above mentioned reformers. Most important, the regime established a solid labor rights framework and the basis of a social security system, which continue to be pillars of state regulation. The sinister side of the Vargas regime and its complex paradoxes, cannot, however, be ignored.

One of these paradoxes was that in spite of the greater influence of the racist ideologies mentioned above, the 1930s witnessed the beginning of a remarkable turn in the Brazilian national debate regarding racial relations. In 1933, Gilberto Freyre's book *Masters and Slaves* was published.[72] While relying on neo-Lamarckian views regarding the overlapping of biology and the environment, the book developed a cultural interpretation of miscegenation, challenging the biological determinism of dominant white-supremacist racial ideologies. Freyre centered his analysis on the dynamics of the "big house" and its intricate and sexualized relations with the slave quarters, jettisoning the biological pessimism of the dominant racial theories of the nineteenth century. Freyre also distanced himself from the idea that "whitening" the population was an effective way to civilize Brazil.[73] Freyre's vision celebrated the intermingling of races and cultures and provided Brazilians with a vision of "racial democracy" that would become dominant in the second half of the twentieth century. His interpretation of "the Brazilian dilemma" rapidly captured the hearts and minds of the country's political elites and became the hegemonic approach to racial relations in Brazil.[74] A systematic critique of what Freyre's positive visions concealed, in terms of acute and persistent racial inequalities, pervasive discriminatory practices and deep patriarchal imprints had to wait until the emergence of a feminist and a broad-based black movement in the late twentieth century.[75]

The relationship between the Brazilian state and the Catholic Church during this period was a key factor in shaping the country's explicit and implicit approaches to population. The church strongly mobilized to influence the outcomes of the 1930 revolution in particular the 1934 constitutional debates.[76] Even though Vargas himself was a nonbeliever (he was deeply influenced by Comtean positivism), the Catholic Church became an indispensable political mediator in the power struggle that followed the revolution.[77]

The conceptions and norms related to gender and reproduction adopted between 1930 and 1945 were inevitably marked by the sharp dissonances and contradictions described above. In 1934, the right to vote and the regulation of women's work had implied the recognition of women as citizens and contributors to the economic modernization of Brazil. During the Vargas era, women's access to education also expanded. On the other hand, however, despite the growing influence of Freyre's theories, the influence of neo-Lamarckian and preventive eugenics was far from extirpated from the field of public health policy. Under the spell of preventive eugenics, the Vargas regime employed strong pronatalist and maternalist ideologies and implemented corresponding health and social policies with the aim of cultivating a large, civilized, and healthy labor force in order to better feed industrialization.[78] It is worth noting that, during this same period, in the United States and Europe, eugenic arguments and policy proposals took the form of curtailing fertility among criminals, the disabled, and so-called inferior races.[79]

Contemporary discourses revolved around the challenge of reducing Brazil's high rates of infant mortality in order to construct a nation of brave and strong citizens. In 1933, a National Conference on the Protection of Infancy was organized to discuss measures aimed at the improvement of children's and mothers' health, and, not surprising, puericulture, or a focus on the hygienic care of children, was at the center of this new movement. At the same time, a social assistance structure emerged organized around the creation of Mothers' Clubs that offered classes on home economics, family hygiene, and family solidarity.[80]

Another domain flagrantly reflecting the dissonances of the Vargas regime was the 1940 penal code reform. With regard to abortion, the 1940 penal code—which remains in full force in 2014—defined the penalty for those who take measures to terminate pregnancy as one to four years of imprisonment. Once again, the conduct of pregnant women who instigated their own abortions was criminalized, punishable by imprisonment from one to three years. Yet, reflecting a further modernized approach to the issue, the 1940 reformers expanded the 1890 definitions concerning the protection of women's "honor," stipulating that there would be no punishment when the abortion followed a rape and that no crime existed when an abortion was necessary to save the mother's life. These revisions indicated a new valuation of motherhood, as previously, maternal death in childbirth was seen as a "natural" sacrifice. A year later, the 1941 Law on Misdemeanors was also adopted, defining as criminal the advertisement of processes, substances, or objects intended to cause abortion, including the advertisement of contraceptive methods. This development reflects the ethos of the time with regard to restricting reproductive autonomy, which is not surprising given the ideology of women as reproducers that prevailed in the period, despite gains in voting and labor rights.[81]

As elsewhere in Latin America, the natalist and maternalist ideologies that guided mother and child health and social policy—as well as legal norms—adopted in the 1930–45 period, would endure. Eventually, they would come to be the most striking feature of modernized reproductive statecraft in Brazil. The mother and child health policy framework, although recast in some aspects, remained uncontested until the 1980s, when the feminist critique of its narrow infant-maternal focus began to gain visibility. In 1997, Ana Maria Canesqui writing about these policies reported that as late as 1965, when a new dictatorship was already installed in Brazil, more than nine hundred Mothers' Clubs (mostly connected to the Catholic Church's social work) were still functioning across the country, collaborating with health authorities in vaccine campaigns and in initiatives that promoted the use of artificial milk.[82] More important, as previously mentioned, 1940 penal code definitions with regard to abortion remain intact today, except for a recent Supreme Court decision regarding the right to abortion in the case of anencephaly.

1960s–1990: The Population Control Era and the Turn toward Rights

After World War II and eight years of Vargas authoritarianism, Brazil began redemocratizing. In Europe and the United States, the tragedy of Nazi policies was fully disclosed, and the connections between demographic and eugenic theorizing created much embarrassment in the nascent field of population studies.[83] The postwar period also witnessed an increase in the scientific respectability of demographics, as the size of a country's population, and its ability to slow the rate of growth, became a core component of economic development assistance, as illustrated by the creation in 1946 of both the Commission on Population and the Division of Population of the recently founded United Nations.[84] This new international emphasis on the size and growth of population led to the establishment of many research centers and nonprofit institutions devoted to the issue in the United States and Europe, and these, in turn, gave birth to the late twentieth-century population control debate. In 1969, when the Fund for Population Activities of the UN was created, a dominant discourse on the urgent need to control the fertility levels in recently decolonized countries of Asia, Africa, and Latin America began to consolidate.[85]

The focus on population growth and control reached Brazil during the military dictatorship.[86] The 1965 coup, openly supported by the United States, in line with the anticommunist ethos of the times, aimed at countervailing progressive reforms then underway in Brazil. The military regime adopted a technocratic approach to state management, focusing on industrial and technological improvements. Another priority of the military regime was the demographic and economic occupation of Brazil's "empty lands," in particular in the Amazon.[87] The dictatorship's economic policy, initially very successful in promoting growth, accentuated inequality and ended up creating the massive external debt of the 1980s. The transition to democracy in Brazil was slow and protracted.[88]

In the 1960s, the rate of population growth was 2.9 percent per year, and Brazil's gross fertility rate was 5.8 children per woman. The country became a target of population control efforts implemented by internationally funded local contraceptive research institutions and family-planning NGOs. This can be exemplified by BEMFAM,[89] the local affiliate of the International Planned Parenthood Federation (IPPF), which began its operations in poor urban neighborhoods and rural areas.[90] Although friendly with the United States, the military regime openly resisted antifertility measures, which is not surprising given how deeply Catholic-influenced natalist views were rooted in Brazilian statecraft. In addition, the military believed that a powerful nation meant a populous nation.[91]

The demographer José Eustáquio Alves reports that in 1967, a Parliamentary Inquiry Commission investigated claims that sterilizations funded by international groups were taking place in Brazil.[92] Also, the regime established an internal migration policy, aimed at the occupation of the Amazon. In 1974, at the first International Conference on Population (sponsored by the United Nations), Brazil fully aligned itself with other developing nations in resisting imposed fertility control measures, declaring "development is the best contraceptive."[93]

Under the surface, however, the military regime's approach to population was more complex. It never prohibited the commercialization of contraceptives (as did other regimes elsewhere in Latin America), and it never openly attacked the family-planning NGOs. A finer reading of the discourse of Brazilian economic planners of the period suggests that many of them, in fact, had made a bet that growth, industrialization, and urbanization would lead to a decline in fertility.[94] This view was consistent with the interpretation elaborated by the political scientist Vilmar Faria that four strategic policies implemented by the military regime—expansion of the health and social security systems, new public credit schemes, and communication policies—were the main factors behind the steep fertility declines experienced by Brazil from the 1970s.[95]

At the micro level of sexual and procreative culture, the shift toward a lower birth rate was decidedly led by women despite their husbands' preferences and the church proscriptions.[96] In the absence of a public policy that offered cheap or free contraceptives in the public health system, women resorted to risky and clandestine abortions or purchased pills sold through market outlets. In the poorest areas, women also accessed services established by family-planning NGOs and, in particular, BEMFAM. In the late 1970s, with the first stirrings of democratization, the government launched a new program aimed at the prevention of risky pregnancies; critics of the regime denounced this effort as the beginning of a fertility control policy.[97]

By the early 1980s, available data showed that poor access to reversible contraception was causing a rapid rise in female sterilizations.[98] Concurrently a vibrant movement supporting democracy in Brazil stimulated public debate about population policies.[99] Located at the intersection between the broader politics of citizenship rights and discussions around health reform proposals, the claims raised by the feminist voices for reproductive autonomy and women's rights were unequivocally fruitful. Since the late 1970s, feminists have worked within a broad-based coalition supporting health reform, spearheaded by professionals and academics but also involving wider and more diverse social movements. In the constitutional reform of 1986–88, this national mobilization established the principles for a universal public health system (SUS).

At the same time, Brazil's emerging feminist movement was widely and openly contesting the long-standing focus on the infant–mother dyad as the center of state policy responses to women's health needs and aspirations.[100] Feminists also attacked the blatant distortions and poor quality of care of private market health outlets and NGO family-planning services, as well as the detrimental effects of illegal abortion and the conditions that led many women to be sterilized.[101] Progressive public servants working at the Ministry of Health responded positively to these critiques and, despite the political constraints of the period, were able to design a new Comprehensive Women's Health Program (PAISM), launched in 1984. The new policy promoted integrated prenatal care, birth and postnatal assistance, cancer prevention, STD care, and adolescent and menopausal care. PAISM also openly discussed the problem of unsafe abortion and included contraceptive assistance and postabortion care in the program's guidelines.[102]

As the women's health policy debate evolved, feminist demands were taken to legislative bodies. As early as 1983, a bill aimed to legalize abortion was presented to and turned down by the House of Representatives' Committee for Constitution and Justice. The constitutional reform (1986–88) widened the space for feminist legal claims. In the new bill of rights, gender equality was enshrined as a basic principle, and Article 226 legitimated the rights of men, women, and couples to family planning, and encoded the state's responsibility for offering contraceptive information and services; it also prohibited any form of demographic control. These principles were later reaffirmed in the Family Planning Law, approved in 1996.[103] Despite strong lobbying by the Catholic Church—which also counted upon the support of the already existing congressional Evangelical caucus—the text of the constitution did not include the premise "the right to life from conception," which was a major breakthrough.[104]

Feminist theorizing and politics in relation to reproductive matters in late twentieth-century Brazil have, therefore, found a path between the Scylla of long-standing state-supported natalism and the Charybdis of fertility control to situate the "problem" within a citizenship and women's human rights frame.[105] This deeply transformed vision was connected with the 1980's global feminist debates on reproductive rights and it would both feed and be enriched, in the course of the 1990s, by the debates that took form in the series of UN-sponsored conferences, in particular the International

Conference on Population and Development (1994) and the Fourth World Conference on Women (1995).[106] One key result in Brazil of this political mobilizing and policy advocacy was that, for the first time since 1940, women were able to gain access through the public health system to abortion in the cases permitted by law. This was achieved initially by a municipal ordinance in São Paulo (1989) and nine years later by a Ministry of Health protocol.[107]

Democratization in late twentieth-century Brazil has also seen diverse Afro-Brazilian movements systematically contesting the persistence of racial inequalities and discrimination concealed under Brazil's dominant discourse of racial democracy, and exposing the long-standing imprints of "whitening" ideologies.[108] These voices have also shaped the constitutional reform process and subsequent policy initiatives and legal reforms.[109] Feminist-led reproductive politics of the last thirty years has, therefore, inevitably intertwined with Brazil's transformed politics of race; as investigations and advocacy have gone forward, controversies and tensions have emerged. In the early 1990s, for example, sharp debates erupted within the women's movement with regard to the racialized differentials in the prevalence of sterilization, then interpreted as a symptom of a deliberate, racially biased policy of population control.[110] This particular controversy would, however, wane as time went by, because data revealed that the factors and racial patterns of sterilization prevalence and women's motivations did not confirm this hypothesis.[111] Recent epidemiological and social research shows, however, that—despite, well-intended policy discourses and guidelines—sharp racial differentials still persist in relation to access to sexual and reproductive care,[112] including in relation to maternal mortality and abortion.[113] Moreover, manifestations of "structural violence"[114] in Brazil remain deeply racialized. This is, for example, illustrated by the distribution of homicides in 2012: 28.2 percent of victims were white, while 71.4 percent were black people.[115] The effects of racism cannot be, therefore, ignored in policy debates concerning racially determined patterns of morbidity and mortality.

Reproductive politics emanating from 1980s feminist critical thinking has challenged the "Governing is to populate" imperative at work since colonial times. Feminists have rejected state policies designed to cope with the Brazilian population's ethnic and racial mix—most of which aimed at compelling women to deliver procreative outcomes approved by the state. Before the twenty-first century and even more clearly in the course of the last decade, the challenges of translating this ambitious politics into transformed statecraft have proved to be daunting.[116]

The Twenty-First Century: *Plus ça change* . . .

The first decade of the twenty-first century will eventually be registered in Brazilian history as a period when the country emerged as a key global player, while the state implemented ambitious infrastructure investments, not seen since the 1970s, and implemented a structural program aimed at consistently reducing poverty levels and dismantling long-standing patterns of inequality. Nevertheless, when seen through the lens of statecraft in the realm of reproduction and sexuality, the picture is decidedly bleaker. The very conceptual frame of Brazil's internationally acclaimed poverty reduction program epitomizes the retrogressive politics shaping this domain.

As in Mexico, in the mid-1990s the Brazilian state began implementing a poverty-reducing income transfer program with women (mothers) as the main beneficiaries.[117] When the program was expanded in 2003, it was renamed the Family Grant (it was previously labeled School Grant). But even before that, as noted by Batthyány and Corrêa (2010),[118] the Brazilian and other similar poverty reduction programs that have mushroomed in Latin America did not include measures to alter the sex-based division of labor and other gender structural biases. Rather, these policies have made instrumental use of long-standing women's socially constructed roles as mothers and caregivers to transform them into poverty managers at the household levels. And when the specific trajectory of policy and legal debates around reproductive policies is examined—particularly in regard to abortion—the revival of conservative ideologies around procreation is even more blatant.[119]

As shown in this article, legal and policy debates regarding the ability of women to interrupt an unwanted pregnancy have always been the thorniest area of reproductive politics, in Brazil and elsewhere. In the late 1990s, the Ministry of Health adopted a protocol to guide access to abortion in the two cases permitted by law.[120] Concurrently, women, couples, and physicians started appealing to the judiciary to grant authorization for abortion in cases of severe fetal abnormality. These ministerial protocol and judicial decisions immediately became the target of antiabortion groups, but by the middle of the next decade the trajectory of struggles around the right to abortion had been more positive than negative. In 2002 when the Workers' Party (PT) won the presidential election, feminist groups were hopeful about further legislative changes, because many of them belonged to the party and the legalization of abortion was enshrined in its program.

These expectations were not unfounded. As the new legislature began (March 2003) a newly elected PT congressman revived and tabled a bill decriminalizing abortion from the early 1990s. These developments prompted the re-energizing and remobilization of the Brazilian feminist movement. That same year the office of secretary for women's policy was created and a national conference was planned to discuss its policy priorities in relation to women rights and gender equality. The conference outcome (July 2004) openly recommended that the 1940 punitive legislation on abortion should be revised. In December, the minister of women's policies announced the creation of a tripartite commission—involving the executive and legislative branches, as well as civil society representatives—to move forward on this recommendation.

The commission functioned from March to August 2004, when it delivered a reform proposal that fully decriminalized abortion until the twelfth week of pregnancy.[121] By then, however, a high-level crisis involving political corruption had erupted, and the overall political climate became entirely unfavorable to the proposed reform. In July 2004, the president, speaking at an event to launch a campaign to raise the self-esteem of Brazilians, said that "Brazilians should not be exclusively concerned with economic problems, but should also devote our attention to the recovery of family and religious values." In the week following the presentation of the bill by the commission, he sent a letter to the National Conference of Bishops to "explain" the corruption crisis in which he also reaffirmed his commitment to "the right to life."[122] The executive branch would retreat from tabling the provision as a policy priority and this became glaringly clear when the draft was presented to the House of Representatives.[123] A few months later a Parliamentarian Grouping for the Right to Life materialized that, since then, has systematically blocked any initiative to reform the 1940 abortion law, presenting at each new legislative session draconian provisions to further restrict access to abortion. In 2010, antiabortion legislators introduced a Statute of the Unborn that, if ever approved, will grant full personhood rights to the fetus if ever approved.[124] The processing of the provision that has been slow until early 2015 is now decidedly sped up.[125]

Not surprisingly, abortion became the central leitmotif of the 2010 presidential elections campaign. Dilma Rousseff, the Workers' Party presidential candidate had, in 2009, publicly declared that abortion should be considered a major public health problem and therefore legalized. By May 2010, she had moved toward a much more careful position, declaring only that "abortion is a matter of public health services." However, this "strategic" retreat did not spare her from pressure and attacks by dogmatic religious leaders, which led her to have a closed conversation with the president of the National Bishops Conference in August 2010. Rousseff's previous support of legal abortion was extensively used by one of her opponents, José Serra, who, ironically enough, had signed, as the then minister of health, the "legal abortion" protocol of 1998.

The results of the first voting led to a second round, when once again abortion continued to be at the center of the electoral debate. Though opinion polls seemed to indicate that abortion was not the most important matter of the day, religious leaders did not let the issue die. Under pressure, candidate Rousseff and President Lula had a closed meeting with the Evangelical leadership in Congress, after which she made public a "letter to the people of God" in which she declared herself to be against abortion and made a commitment not to take any initiative to change existing laws and, if elected, to prioritize policies and programs aimed at the protection of the family.[126] Once she was elected, Dilma Rousseff rapidly and drastically altered the women's reproductive health policy frame crafted in the 1980s. Using the justification of unacceptably high levels of maternal mortality, the post-2010 national policy became once again a narrow maternal health program, now named Stork Network.

Then in late 2011, the presidency issued a special ordinance, MP 577, aiming to register all pregnant women in the country. The Minister of Health justified the norm as a surveillance strategy to control the quality of maternal care. But significantly enough, the text included one paragraph that preconized the protection of the health of the unborn. As strongly asserted by the feminist lawyer Beatriz Galli in 2012, MP 557 openly infringed upon women's constitutional right to privacy and grafted into law a privileged status for the fetus that is not enshrined in the constitution.[127] Under ceaseless feminist pressure, President Rousseff publicly declared that this particular paragraph of the ordinance would be eliminated and a revised text was published. Yet this did not fully resolve the problem because the ordinance was still to be debated by the House and the protection of the unborn could be revived. Strenuous feminist advocacy continued on parliamentarians and the executive until May 2012, when MP 557 was finally archived and the registrations policy was suspended. It should be noted that the political climate with respect to reproductive statecraft has not, since then, substantially changed.

Another episode that gained global visibility while this chapter was being finalized is illustrative of the scale of obstacles impeding the transformation of state actors' views and actions in what regards procreation and women's role. In April 2014, a woman who opted for natural vaginal delivery at home was obligated by a judicial decision, enforced through a police operation, to be subjected to a caesarean section in a hospital. This intervention triggered public manifestations in-country and worldwide and sharply contrasted with the stated objectives of the Stork Network.[128] Dr. Paul Hunt—who was the first United Nations rapporteur on the Rights to Highest Attainable Level of Health—was in Brazil when the episode flared up publicly, and commenting on it, he declared that it implied a flagrant infringement of women's autonomy and could eventually be portrayed as a "veterinarian approach to women's health."[129]

This reactivation of maternalist ideologies and the multiplication of obstacles to sexual and reproductive autonomy clearly derive from forces and factors at work in the immediate political conjuncture, in particular the "return of the religious" in the form of dogmatism that, as elsewhere, now pervades the Brazilian social and political landscape.[130] However, to be more fully understood, this maternalist revivalism must also be placed against the *longue durée* of disciplinary views and norms on procreation and women's role.

Brazilian procreative statecraft has always been imprinted by the norms of the Catholic Church, the political influence of its hierarchy, and related social movements.[131] As Brazil democratized, the country's Catholic Church was deeply transformed under the impacts of the conservative restoration propelled by John Paul II and Benedict XVI. Concurrently, the Brazilian religious landscape was also being altered by the rapid growth of Evangelism in society and also in electoral and parliamentarian politics.[132] All political parties are today deeply affected by these old and new religious dogmatic forces.[133]

Last but not least, these policy shifts that could eventually be portrayed as the "return of the repressed" must also be situated in relation to academic and policy debates regarding the new Brazilian demographic landscape. Since the 1990s one key theme infusing Brazilian population-related debates has been the "demographic bonus," proportionated by the 1970s onward transition, the decline in population, sometimes viewed as a window of opportunity for the state to implement a human development agenda.[134] More recently, however, the potentially negative impacts of fertility decline and aging on health, social security, and economic growth itself are rapidly gaining visibility and legitimacy.

The demographer Ana Amélia Camarano (2013), for example, in a recent article on Brazil's fertility decline advocates for the right to reproduce as the key to the continuity of the human species and calls for state policies to include incentives to raise fertility rates, further reduce infant mortality, and curtail current levels of male mortality (from both violent and external causes).[135] Although the author concurrently emphasizes that the right to abortion and death with dignity should also be part of a revised Brazilian population policy agenda, in the troubled and shifting political and policy scenario described above in which the dynamics are highly determined by the political economy of moral and religious conservatism, this expert open call for incentives to higher fertility has been quickly en easily captured and distorted in the interests of renewed control of women's bodies and roles so as to fulfill the objectives and desires of others. At a public hearing on abortion reform held at the Brazilian Senate on August 6, 2015, a female political scientist speaking on behalf of anti-abortion groups argued that as abortion lowers fertility it negatively affects social security financing, therefore replicating the views deployed in recent demographic debates.

Though domestic politics mainly determine regressions, the emergence of Brazil as global player is also a factor. Its new status has required an image of respectability, that is, shedding the tropes of Brazil as the land of sexual excesses. On the other hand, these dynamics are not easily captured from outside because Brazilian diplomatic positioning with respect to sexual and reproductive rights has remained steadily progressive.[136] In recent years, however, diplomatic positions have been negatively affected both by the country's emergence and by the internal political climate.[137] Nevertheless, Brazil has continued to reaffirm its progressive stances regarding these issues, as illustrated by the August 2013 First Latin American Conference on Population and Development, in Montevideo and the final negotiations of the United Nations agenda for the Post 2015 Sustainable Development Goals in July, 2015.[138] If this seems like a glaring contradiction, it is not the only contradiction in the complex assemblage that constitutes contemporary Brazilian sexual and reproductive statecraft.

Notes

1. José Eduardo Agualusa, *Nação Crioula: A Correspondência Secreta de Fradique Mendes* (Rio de Janeiro: Cryphus, 2001), 91.
2. Instituto Brasileiro de Geografia e Estatística, *Censo Demográfico 2000* (Rio de Janeiro, 2000); Instituto Brasileiro de Geografia e Estatística, *Censo Demográfico 2010* (Rio de Janeiro, 2010).
3. Joseph E. Potter, Carl P. Schmertmann, and Suzana M. Cavenaghi, "Fertility and Development: Evidence from Brazil," *Demography* 39, no. 4 (2002): 739–61.
4. Translator's note: This is an emic category employed in Brazil to designate biologically born males who adopt, more or less continuously, a female gender performance and who often engage in body sculpting practices without, necessarily, desiring to be understood as women or to have gender reassignment surgery.
5. Rafael De la Dehesa, *Queering the Public Sphere in Mexico and Brazil: Sexual Rights Movements in Emerging Democracies* (Durham: Duke University Press, 2010); Adrianna Vianna and Sérgio Carrara, "Sexual Politics in Brazil: A Case Study," in *Sex Politics: Reports from the Front Line*, ed. Richard Parker, Rosalind Petchesky, and Robert Sember (Rio de Janeiro: Sexuality Policy Watch, 2007).
6. Richard Parker et al., "AIDS Prevention and Gay Community Mobilization in Brazil," *Development* 2 (2000): 49–53; Richard Parker, *Bodies, Pleasures, and Passions: Sexual Culture in Contemporary Brazil*, 2nd ed. (Nashville: Vanderbilt University Press, 2009).
7. This cycle started before 1991, with the Children's Summit (1989), but clearly intensified afterward to encompass the Rio Environmental Summit (1992), the International Human Rights Conference of Vienna (1993), the International Conference on Population and Development (Cairo, 1994), the Fourth World Conference on Women (Beijing, 1995), the International Conference on Racism, Racial Discrimination, Xenophobia, and Related Forms of Intolerance (Durban, 2001), and a General Assembly Special Session on HIV/AIDS. Sonia Corrêa and Maria Betânia Ávila, "Direitos Sexuais e Reprodutivos: Pauta Global e Percursos Brasileiros," in *Sexo & Vida: Panorama da Saúde Reprodutiva no Brasil*, ed. Elza Berquó (Campinas: Editora da Unicamp, 2003).
8. Sonia Corrêa, "Brazil: Abortion at the Frontline," *Sexuality Policy Watch Newsletter 8* (2010), available at http://www.sxpolitics.org/wp-content/uploads/2010/10/brazil_-abortion-at-front-line.pdf; Mario Pecheny and Rafael de la Dehesa, "Sexuality and Politics in Latin America: An Outline for Discussion," in *Sexuality and Politics: Regional Dialogues from the Global South*, Rio de Janeiro, Sexuality Policy Watch, 2014, http://www.sxpolitics.org/sexuality-and-politics/pdfs/volume1/4.pdf.
9. Jennifer M. Piscopo, "Female Leadership and Sexual Health Policy in Argentina," *Latin American Research Review* 49, no. 1 (2014): 104–27.
10. Maria Stella Ferreira Levy, "O Papel da Migração Internacional na Evolução da População Brasileira (1872 a 1972)," *Revista de Saúde Pública* 8, Supl. (1974):

49–90; Massimo Livi Bacci, "500 Anos de Demografia Brasileira: Uma Resenha," *Revista Brasileira de Estudos de População* 19, no. 1 (2002): 141–59.

11. In trading or making peace with the colonizers, indigenous groups often offered women to Portuguese men who would then become members of their kinship systems. The colonizers accepted these rules because they were to their advantage and also because they came from a culture in which "marriage" similarly meant alliances between male heads of lineages or households. Juracilda Veiga, "Aproximações entre a Etnologia e os Estudos de Demografia Histórica," in *Povos Indígenas: Mobilidade Espacial*, ed. Marta Maria do Amaral Azevedo and Rosana Baeninger (Campinas: Nepo/Unicamp, 2013).
12. Mariana P. Cândido, "South Atlantic Exchanges: The Role of Brazilian-Born Agents in Benguela, 1650–1850," *Luso-Brazilian Review* 50, no. 1 (2013): 53–82; Luiz Flipe Alencastro, *O Trato dos Viventes: Formação do Brasil no Atlântico Sul* (São Paulo: Companhia das Letras, 2000); Ana Silvia Scott, *Os Portugueses* (São Paulo: Contexto, 2010). The famous Jesuit preacher Antônio Vieira affirmed at the end of the seventeenth century that "he who says sugar says Brazil and he who says Brazil says Angola" (Stuart Schwartz, "A População Escrava na Bahia," in *Brasil: História Econômica e Demográfica*, ed. Iraci Nero da Costa [São Paulo: IPE/USP, 1986], 38).
13. Maria Luiza Marcilio, "Crescimento Populacional da População Brasileira até 1872," in *XXV Reunião Anual da SBPC* (São Paulo: SBPC, 1973), 12.
14. Scott, *Os Portugueses*, 99; Ronaldo Vainfas, *Trópico dos Pecados: Moral, Sexualidade e Inquisição no Brasil Colonial* (Rio de Janeiro: Campus, 1989), 320.
15. Vainfas correctly emphasizes that the Protestant Reformation and the Catholic Counter-Reformation must be understood in light of the concomitant concentration of state power in the hands of absolutist monarchies and their consequent greater control over subject populations. See *Trópico dos Pecados*, 41–141.
16. Helen Ulhôa Pimentel, "A Ambiguidade da Moral Colonial: Casamento, Sexualidade, Normas e Transgressões," *Universitas FACE (substituída pela Universitas Humanas)* 4, nos. 1–2 (2008): 29–63; Vainfas, *Trópico dos Pecados*, 192–290. In Brazil, the first locally defined religious regulation of marriage, enshrined in the 1707 First Constitutions of the Archbishopric of Bahia, would remain intact until the transition to a republican regime in the late nineteenth century.
17. The Philippine codification of Portuguese law substituted the Manueline Ordinances, whose effects were not relevant in the colony. It was adopted during a period when the Spanish Crown ruled Portugal. One important modification the Philippine Code made in relation to previous codes was the transference of punishment of violations of canonical law to secular authorities.
18. Pimentel, "A Ambiguidade da Moral Colonial Casamento; Silvia Hunold Lara, *Ordenações Filipinas*—LIVRO 5 (São Paulo: Companhia das Letras, 1999).
19. Ronaldo Vainfas, *Trópico dos Pecados*, 499–566.

20. Ronaldo Vainfas, *Trópico dos Pecados*, 499–566; Laura de Mello Souza, *O Diabo e a Terra de Santa Cruz* (São Paulo: Companhia das Letras, 1989); Luiz Roberto de Barros Mott, *Escravidão, Homossexualidade e Demonologia* (São Paulo: Icone Editora, 1988).
21. Fernando Torres-Londoño, *A Outra Família: Concubinato, Igreja e Escândalo na Colônia* (São Paulo: Edições Loyola, 1999).
22. The hunting of sexual sinners (fornicators and sodomites in particular) is a whole chapter in the history of Brazilian sexuality, which we unfortunately cannot examine in depth here. It is worth mentioning, however, that while the most punished crime was fornication, sodomites were chased and punished throughout the colonial period. In its very first visit to the colony in 1591, for example, the Portuguese Inquisition judged and condemned to exile in Angola a Portuguese woman named Felipa de Souza, who lived in Bahia and was accused of *sodomia feminarum*. In 1646, after a long debate in the Council of Evora, the same Inquisition concluded that *sodomia feminarum* was not as nefarious a sin as *sodomia masculinarum*. Felipa de Souza is currently the name of the Annual Award given by the International Gay and Lesbian Human Commission to persons whose work makes a difference in the promotion of the human rights of gender and sexual nonconformists.
23. Natalie Reis Itaborahy, "A família colonial e a construção do Brasil: Vida doméstica e identidade nacional em Gilberto Freyre, Sérgio Buarque de Holanda e Nestor Duarte," *Revista Anthropológicas* 16, no. 1 (2005): 171–96.
24. Female orphans under the tutelage of the queen were sent to Brazil to marry colonizers. Incentives were provided to poor or even criminally indicted women to marry men in Brazil, and we can also suppose that many women, in particular prostitutes, may have also escaped to the colony on their own. Later on, ordinances were issued restricting noble young women's entrance into religious orders.
25. Ronaldo Vainfas, *Trópico dos Pecados*, 211–20.
26. Kenneth Maxwell, *Pombal: Paradox of the Enlightenment* (Cambridge: Cambridge University Press, 1995); Mozart Vergetti Menezes and Yamé Galdino de Paiva, "Ilustração, População e Circuitos Mercantis: A Capitania da Paraíba na Virada do Século XVIII," in *Ensaios sobre a América Portuguesa*, ed. Carla Mary S. Oliveira, Mozart Vergetti Menezes, and Regina Célia Gonçalves (João Pessoa: Editora Universitária/UFPB, 2009).
27. Article 91 states that these prescriptions are to be followed so that the indigenous peoples will finally come to understand that "we desire cordially and sincerely to establish with them the reciprocal and cordial union that underlies the happiness of all republics." The Pombaline reforms constitute a fascinating example of how Enlightenment premises and colonial interests intertwined in paradoxical ways with race, ethnicity, sexuality, gender, and procreation. Unfortunately, we do not have enough space here to examine this topic in the depth required.

28. Michel Foucault, *The History of Sexuality,* vol. 1, *An Introduction*, trans. Robert Hurley (New York: Pantheon, 1978).
29. According to Foucault, modernity replaces the power over life and death with "discipline," or biopower—techniques aimed at training and producing individual bodies in particular ways and administered not only or primarily through the state but also through decentralized institutions such as medicine, psychiatry, religion, and penal law. On the other hand, the methods of biopolitics are aimed at regulating whole populations—their size, growth, movements, mortality, and morbidity, and are deployed through state and international agencies as well as medical and religious institutions.
30. Maria José Rosado-Nunes, "O Tema do Aborto na Igreja Católica: Divergências Silenciadas," *Ciência e Cultura* 64, no. 2 (2012): 23–31. The Ordinances recognized the right to life of the fetus when they defined that a pregnant woman condemned to death couldn't be executed before forty days after delivery of her baby. They do not, however, mention the term *abortion*. Rosado cites an opinion of the Congregation of the Universal Inquisition on the baptism of aborted fetus, issued in 1713 (right after the enactment of Brazilian canonical law in 1707), in which the following elaboration is made: "If there is a basis to think that the fetus is animated by a rational soul, it must and should be baptized unconditionally. However, if that certainty does not exist, it should not be baptized under any circumstance."
31. The House became known as "The Wheel" because the platform door in which the newly born were deposited was shaped like a wheel in order to avoid identifying those people who brought babies to the House.
32. Jurandir Freire Costa, *Ordem Médica e Norma Familiar* (Rio de Janeiro: GRAAL, 1999), 165.
33. Maria Luiza Marcilio, "Crescimento Populacional da População Brasileira até 1872," in *XXV Reunião Anual da SBPC* (São Paulo: SBPC, 1973), 14. Although revolts against the Portuguese occurred before 1822 (including the 1789 rebellion known as the *Inconfidencia Mineira* in Brazil's primary gold-mining province), Brazilian independence was not the outcome of a hard-fought anticolonial struggle, as occurred in the neighboring Spanish colonies. Rather, it was the outcome of a successful pact between Brazilian elites and the Portuguese royal family, which kept slavery intact and the Bragança dynasty in power.
34. José Murilo de Carvalho, *Cidadania no Brasil* (Rio de Janeiro: Civilização Brasileira, 2001); Emilia Viotti da Costa, *The Brazilian Empire: Myths and History*, rev. ed. (Chapel Hill: University of North Carolina Press, 2000).
35. As in the past, ecclesiastic authorities fulfilled a state function when performing the sacrament. Canonical norms defined impediments to marriage: age (fourteen for males and twelve for females), consanguinity until the fourth level, a previous undeclared marriage (bigamy or polygamy), double crime of adultery and homicide, vote of chastity, the fact that one of the engaged belonged to a religious order or the secular clergy, "error of the person" (the name of the

situation in which the woman was no longer a virgin), impotency (in some cases), and difference of religion.

36. Brazil was the fifth country in the world and the first south of the Equator to decriminalize the so-called crimes against nature. This criminal reform did not apply, however, to the military—a prescription that remains on the book to today, even after it lost its ability to be enforced in the 1980s.
37. This rule echoed the long-standing concern with concubinage. It is also significant that polygamy was equally criminalized for men and women, as this suggests a rule that would be mainly applied in the case of nonwhite, non-European subjects whose kinship practices may have included polygamy and eventually polyandry.
38. Sonia Corrêa and Maria Lucia Karam, *Brazilian "Sex" Laws: Continuities, Ruptures, and Paradoxes* (forthcoming).
39. Thomas Laqueur, *Making Sex: Body and Gender from the Greeks to Freud* (Cambridge, Mass.: Harvard University Press, 1990).
40. Luis Felipe Alencastro shows that around 43 percent of the four million slaves transported to Brazil arrived between 1801 and 1850, when the traffic was finally abolished. It is to be noted, however, that until 1855 slaves were still smuggled into the country. The epigraph at the beginning of the chapter in fact describes one of the smuggling ports in the northeast of the country. Alencastro, *O Trato dos Viventes*, 69.
41. Lorelai B. Kury, "A Sereia Amazônica dos Agassiz: Zoologia e Racismo na Viagem ao Brasil," *Revista Brasileira de História* 21, no. 41 (2001): 157–72, available at http://www.scielo.br/pdf/rbh/v21n41/a09v2141.pdf; Laura Moutinho, *Razão, "Cor" e Desejo: Uma Análise Comparativa sobre Relacionamentos Afetivo-Sexuais "Inter-Raciais" no Brasil e na África do Sul* (São Paulo: UNESP, 2004), 56–64; Georges Raeder, *O Inimigo Cordial do Brasil: O Conde de Gobineau* (Rio de Janeiro: Paz e Terra, 1988). Both men had direct access to the court and personal contact with Emperor Pedro II, known to be an intellectual knowledgeable in languages, philosophy, and science. Many of these visitors' books and pamphlets on the "problem of race" would circulate widely in nineteenth-century Brazil.
42. Nancy Stepan, *The Hour of Eugenics: Race, Gender, and Nation in Latin America* (Ithaca, N.Y.: Cornell University Press, 1991), 155–67; Thomas E. Skidmore, *Black into White: Race and Nationality in Brazilian Thought* (Durham: Duke University Press, 1993).
43. Wlamyra R. Albuquerque and Walter Fraga Filho, *Uma História do Negro no Brasil* (Salvador: Centro de Estudos Afro-Orientais; Brasília: Fundação Cultural Palmares, 2006), 203–8.
44. Douglas Hume Graham and Sergio Buarque de Holanda Filho, *Migrações Internas no Brasil: 1872–1970* (Brasília: IPE/USP- CNPq, 1984), 36. The first European immigrants coming from Switzerland arrived in the province of Rio de Janeiro in 1818. Before 1850, other small groups established "colonies" in Brazil. But the bulk of European immigration arrived after 1850 and more intensively after 1870.

45. Rosana Baeninger, ed., *Atlas Temático Observatório das Migrações em São Paulo* (Campinas: Nepo/Unicamp, 2013).
46. Thomas E. Skidmore, *Black Into White: Race and Nationality in Brazilian Thought* (Durham: Duke University Press, 1993).
47. Wlamyra R. Albuquerque and Walter Fraga Filho, *Uma História do Negro no Brasil* (Salvador: Centro de Estudos Afro-Orientais and Brasília: Fundação Cultural Palmares, 2006).
48. These figures reflected the effect of partial abolition laws. In September 28, 1871, the Law of the Free Womb granted freedom to all children born after that date. In 1885, a new law freed all slaves older than sixty-five.
49. "Brasil 500 Anos," *Instituto Brasileiro de Geografia e Estatística*, retrieved on January 27, 2014, http://brasil500anos.ibge.gov.br/territorio-brasileiro-e-povoamento/negros/populacao-negra-no-brasil.
50. Robert W. Slenes, *The Demography and Economics of Brazilian Slavery: 1850–1888* (Stanford, Calif.: Stanford University Press, 1976), 697–98.
51. Richard Miskolci, *O Desejo da Nação* (São Paulo: Annablume, 2013).
52. Jorge Tadeu Arantes, "Masculinidade e Branquitude na Construção da República Brasileira," *Agencia FAPESP* (2013): 1, http://agencia.fapesp.br/17292.
53. According to Aristides Lobo, a critic and polemist who closely observed the republican military takeover, the people of Rio de Janeiro watched the events, flabbergasted. Not understanding what was really happening, citizens concluded that they had seen a military parade.
54. José Murilo de Carvalho, *Os Bestializados: O Rio de Janeiro e a República Que Não Foi* (São Paulo: Companhia das Letras, 1999); Carvalho, *Cidadania no Brasil: Edgard Carone, A República Velha* (São Paulo: Difel, 1979). One striking illustration of the classist and antipopular governing logic of the First Republic is provided by the genocide perpetrated by the army in the smashing of the millenarian popular rebellion of Canudos, superbly described in the book *Os Sertões*, written by military engineer Euclides da Cunha and considered to be a twentieth-century literary masterpiece.
55. Clementino Fraga, *Vida e Obra de Osvaldo Cruz* (Rio de Janeiro: Olympio; Brasília: José: Instituto Nacional do Livro, 1972); Nicolau Sevcenko, *A Revolta da Vacina: Mentes Insanas em Corpos Rebeldes* (São Paulo: Scipione, 1993). Although these campaigns were sharply resisted by the urban population in what became known as the Vaccine Revolt (1904), the Brazilian public health establishment was firmly grounded in the state apparatus and rapidly captured the attention of international researchers, campaigners, and donors, as, for example, in the case of international Rockefeller funding initiatives for vaccination and other public health matters in Brazil.
56. Jurandir Freire Costa, *Ordem Médica*; Richard Miskolci, *O Desejo da Nação*.
57. Stepan, *The Hour of Eugenics*, 79. These ideas were brought to Latin America in the first decade of the twentieth century by two Cuban doctors.
58. The term *puericulture,* for example, was in use until the late 1950s and early 1960s.

59. Carolina Moraes Rabelo Silva, "Francisco José Viveiros de Castro: Sexualidade, Criminologia e Cidadania no Fim do Século XIX," Ph.D. diss., Universidade Federal de Rio de Janeiro, 2012. One fascinating character whose writings and juridical decisions illustrate this obsession was the lawyer and prosecutor Francisco José Viveiros Castro, who published an extensive sexual taxonomy of sexual deviations in 1894, comparable to the works of Havelock Ellis and Kraft-Ebbing, which would be re-edited many times until after 1930. Sergio Carrara, *Tributo a Vênus: A Luta Contra a Sífilis no Brasil, da Passagem do Século aos Anos 40* (Rio de Janeiro: Editora FIOCRUZ, 1996); Sonia Corrêa and José Miguel Nieto Olivar, "The Politics of Prostitution in Brazil: Between 'State Neutrality' and 'Feminist Troubles'," in *The Business of Sex*, ed. Laxmi Murthy and Meena Saraswathi Seshu (Delhi: Zubaan, 2013), Cristina Pereira, "Lavar, Passar e Receber Visitas: Debates sobre a Regulamentação da Prostituição e Experiências de Trabalho Sexual em Buenos Aires e no Rio de Janeiro, Fim do Século XIX," *Cadernos Pagu* 25 (2005): 25–54.
60. Despite its stronger disciplinary features, the politicians, lawyers, and doctors influenced by the new criminology were very critical of the 1890 penal code reform. In their view, the new text remained hostage to the "utopia of free will" with regard to criminal offenses, when late nineteenth-century "new sciences" offered effective tools to calibrate the functions that penal law should play in a society as unequal as that of Brazil.
61. The text also included the notion of "error of the person" to cover situations of deception in which either husband or wife was not properly informed about a condition that compromised the union, such as impotency, for example, but also the concealment of loss of virginity on the part of the woman.
62. It is in this same period (1915) that a commission of the Rockefeller Foundation visited Brazil and established funding and collaborative relations with Brazilian public health researchers. Many analysts detect a connection between Rockefeller investments and the blossoming of Brazilian eugenics (Elizabete Mayumy Kobayashi, Lina Faria, and Maria Conceição da Costa, "Eugenia e Fundação Rockefeller no Brasil: A saúde como proposta de regeneração nacional," Universidade Federal do Rio Grande do Sul, August 3, 2009, accessed on February 13, 2014.
63. The list of associates included such names as Juliano Moreira (the "father" of Brazilian psychiatry), Vital Brasil (who extensively researched snake poison antidotes and was an internationally recognized and superb scientist), Afrânio Peixoto (who modernized Brazilian legal medicine), and Belisário Penna (a specialist in sanitation).
64. Laura Moutinho, *Razão, "Cor" e Desejo*, 65–102; Boris Fausto, *O Pensamento Nacionalista Autoritário: 1920–1940* (Rio de Janeiro: Jorge Zahar, 2001), 51–60. The better-known authors are Nina Rodrigues and Oliveira Vianna, whose writings on race, miscegenation, racial impurity, and whitening remained influential until the second half of the twentieth century.

65. Nancy Stepan, *The Hour of Eugenics*; Kobayashi, Faria, and da Costa, "Eugenia e Fundação Rockefeller," 314–51.
66. José Murilo de Carvalho, *Cidadania no Brasil—O Longo Caminho* (Rio de Janeiro: Civilização Brasileira, 2001), 85–125; Carlos Steven Bakota, "Getúlio Vargas and the Estado Novo: An Inquiry into Ideology and Opportunism," *Latin American Research Review* 14, no. 1 (1979): 205–10; Robert M. Levine, *The Vargas Regime: The Critical Years, 1934–1938* (New York: Columbia University Press, 1970); Thomas E. Skidmore, "Politics and Economic Policy Making in Authoritarian Brazil, 1937–71," in *Authoritarian Brazil*, ed. Alfred Stepan (New Haven: Yale University Press, 1973), 3–46.
67. Cristina M. Oliveira Fonseca, *Saúde no Governo Vargas (1930–1945): Dualidade Institucional de um bem Público* (Rio de Janeiro: Editora Fiocruz, 2007) (Coleção História e Saúde). Also published in Luiz Antonio de Castro Santos, Ieda da Costa Barbosa, and Mauro de Lima Gomes, eds., *Caderno de Saúde Pública* 25, no. 9 (2009): 2086–87.
68. The 1937 constitution was inspired by the charter of the dictatorial regime of Josef Pilsudski in Poland and was nicknamed "The Polish." This nickname also evoked, in an overtly sexual tone, the moral degradation of the principles of the 1930 revolution. Polish (in the female delineation) was also how Jewish prostitutes were known. These women who, since the late nineteenth century, have established themselves in large numbers in Rio and São Paulo called themselves Polish to avoid the strong anti-Semitism of Brazilian society. The consolidation of labor laws of 1940 followed closely the Italian Constitucione del Lavoro, and the Department of Press and Propaganda was also copied from a ministry similarly established by Mussolini. The Vargas regime also made large use of the radio as a means to widely disseminate the propaganda of its doings, as also done in Germany and Italy. João Fábio Bertonha, "Divulgando o Duce e o Fascismo em Terra Brasileira: A Propaganda Italiana no Brasil, 1922–1943," *Revista de Historia Regional* 5, no. 2 (2000): 83–112; João Fabio Bertonha, "O Brasil, Os Imigrantes Italianos e a Política Externa Fascista, 1922–1943," *Revista Brasileira Política Internacional* 40, no. 2 (1997): 106–30.
69. Tania Quintaneiro, "A LATI e o Projeto Estadunidense de Controle do Mercado de Aviação no Brasil," *Varia Historia* 23, no. 37 (2007): 223–34; Bertonha, "Divulgando o Duce"; Bertonha, "O Brasil, Os Imigrantes"; Mariteresa Cavalcanti Ellender, *São Paulo—Roma*, 2nd ed. (São Paulo: Gráfica Gordon Limitada, 1940). For example, Brazilian law enforcement agents collaborated with the Gestapo to identify dissidents who fled to Brazil to escape the Nazis. One tragic victim of this long-distance hunt was Olga Benario, the German Jewish partner of Luis Carlos Prestes, the Brazilian Communist Party leader. Though pregnant, she was deported to Germany, where she died in a concentration camp. Cultural connections were also established with the Mussolini fascist regime that subsidized Brazilian writers and journalists to travel to Italy. One of these travelers was Mariteresa Cavalcanti Ellender,

who published a book titled *São Paulo—Roma* in which she appraises the deeds of Mussolini and extensively elaborates on the ideals of perfection and beauty propelled by the fascist regime. The life of Mariteresa is the subject of research being done by Margareth Arilha, one of the authors of this chapter.

70. José Maurício Domingues, "A Dialética da Modernização Conservadora e a Nova História do Brasil," *DADOS—Revista de Ciências Sociais* 45, no. 3 (2002): 459–82. "Conservative modernization" is the frame originally crafted by Barrington Moore (1966) to analyze capitalist development and consolidation of modern nation-states in Germany and Japan in the nineteenth century. That term, however, has been also used subsequently by Marxist authors and critical historians.
71. José Murilo de Carvalho, *Cidadania no Brasil: O longo Caminho*, 3rd ed. (Rio de Janeiro: Civilização Brasileira, 2002), 122.
72. Gilberto Freyre, *The Masters and the Slaves (Casa-grande & senzala): A Study in the Development of Brazilian Civilization*, trans. Samuel Putnam, 2nd ed. (New York: Knopf, 1956).
73. Freyre was a sophisticated thinker who had been trained by Franz Boas in the United States and traveled widely before writing his book. His thesis in fact extended back in time as to track the positive aspects of miscegenation and intermingling in the history of Portugal marked by struggles, but also cultural and sexual and reproductive exchanges with the Moors and Jews. He is not the only thinker of his time to construct a positive narrative on ethnic and racial sexual exchanges and miscegenation. In Mexico, in the 1920s and 1930s, Vasconcelos also launched his vision of the Cosmic Race resulting from these exchanges that was to be seen as superior to the pure races chanted by the eugenic voices. These visions are to be understood as the reaction of Latin American higher-class intellectuals to the long-standing "denigration" and constructions of inferiority and degradation attached to their national cultures by European and North American thinkers.
74. In this context, the alliance between the church and the state to enthrone a black Virgin as the patron of the country is one compelling example of a sharp struggle for cultural hegemony, as it reflects a complex amalgam between Catholic religiosity and the novel ideology of racial democracy enhanced by the work of Gilberto Freyre.
75. Freyre's theories on race and culture, despite their sophistication, have been contested on a wide range of grounds. In addition to the racial discrimination and inequality they conceal, the not-so-subtle celebration of racialized and patriarchal sexual violence and predation and mythologizing of the plantation master household as the only family model in Brazilian society have been subject to systematic criticisms. Mariza Corrêa, "Repensando a Família Patriarcal Brasileira," in *Colcha de Retalhos: Estudos sobre a Família no Brasil*, ed. Antonio Augusto Arantes et al. (Campinas: Editora da Unicamp, 1994); Marcelo Paixão, *Manifesto*

Anti-Racista: Idéias em Prol de uma Utopia Chamada Brasil (Rio de Janeiro: DP&A Editora, 2005).

76. These efforts succeeded, as the church lobby achieved the inclusion of religious teaching in the public school system and the right of priests to vote and hold public office.
77. Carlos Vinícius da Costa Mendonça et al., "Luz, Escuridão e Penumbra: O Governo Vargas e a Igreja Católica," *Dimensões* 26 (2011): 277–91.
78. André Junqueira Caetano, "Fertility Transition and the Diffusion of Female Sterilization in Northeastern Brazil: The Roles of Medicine and Politics," *XXIV General Population Conference* (Paris: IUSSP/UIESP, 2001).
79. In the 1920s in Europe and the United States, developments in the quantitative research field, including demography, and medical technology became increasingly connected with nineteenth-century Malthusian concerns that openly overlapped with the birth control movement, but also with eugenics. These eugenic linkages were blatant in the use of selective vasectomy in the United States, a technique invented by doctor Harry Sharpe, who worked at the Indiana State Reformatory. First he experimented with inmates; when the technique was proved "efficient," crusades to sterilize "mental defectives," mostly black people, began, and state laws were adopted to legally support these interventions. The sterilization programs established by the Nazi regime in Germany were inspired by the American model. Significantly, these were also the years when the International Union for the Scientific Investigation of Population Problems in Europe and the Population Association of America were established. Sonia Corrêa, Rosalind Petchesky, and Richard Parker, *Sexuality, Health and Human Rights* (New York: Routledge, 2008); Sonia Corrêa, Brian R. Davis, and Richard Parker, "Sexuality and Globalities," in *APA Handbook of Sexuality and Psychology*, ed. Deborah L. Tolman et al. (Washington, D.C.: American Psychological Association, 2013).
80. Elisabete Kobaiashy, Lina Faria, Maria Conceição da Cosa, "Eugenia e Fundação Rockefeller no Brasil: a saúde como proposta de regeneração nacional," *Sociologias* 11, no. 22 (2009): 314–51; Ana Maria Canesqui, "Assistência Médica e à Saúde e a Reprodução Humana," *Textos Nepo* 13 (1987): 109–55. Concurrently the eugenic advocates led by Renato Kehl mobilized to advocate for strict immigration provisions to be included in the 1934 constitution.
81. Elza Berquó and Maria Isabel Baltar Rocha, "A ABEP no Contexto Político e no Desenvolvimento da Demografia nas Décadas de 1960 e 1970," *Revista Brasileira de Estudos de População* 22, no. 2 (2005): 233–46. The provision criminalizing the distribution of information on contraceptive methods remained in force until 1979. Definitions concerning substances that induce abortion have been revised by sanitary norms in the 1990s and 2000s, which strictly prohibit the advertisement and sale of misoprostol in Brazil. Margareth Martha Arilha, "Misoprostol: Percursos, Mediações e Redes Sociais para o Acesso ao

Aborto Medicamentoso em Contextos de Ilegalidade no Estado de São Paulo," *Ciência & Saúde Coletiva* 17, no. 7 (2012): 1785–94; Margareth Martha Arilha, "Aborto: Avanços na América Latina e Retrocessos no Brasil?" *Le Monde Diplomatique Brasil* 55 (2012): 10–11; Margareth Martha Arilha, Thaís de Souza Lapa, and Tatiane Crenn Pisaneschi, eds., *Aborto Medicamentoso no Brasil* (São Paulo: Oficina Editorial, 2010).

82. Ana Maria Canesqui, "Assistência Médica e à Saúde e a Reprodução Humana," *Textos Nepo* 13 (1997): 65.
83. In 1946, the International Union for the Scientific Study of the Problem Population dropped the word "problem" from its title, renaming itself as the International Union for the Scientific Study of Population (IUSSP).
84. Margareth Martha Arilha, "O Masculino nas Conferências e Programas das Nações Unidas: Para uma Crítica do Discurso de Gênero," Ph.D. diss., Universidade de São Paulo, 2005.
85. In 1968, while massive numbers of protesters circled the Pentagon shouting "Make love not war," a book entitled *The Population Bomb* by Paul Ehrlich (Newe York: Ballantine, 1968) was published that would become a bestseller in the year to follow. Its Cold War rhetoric triggered fantasies about Third World countries' high fertility rates fueling communist upheavals and provoking a global starvation crisis.
86. Elza Berquó, "Sobre o Sistema Internacional de Pesquisas em Demografia e Saúde Reprodutiva," *Revista Brasileira de Epidemiologia* 11, no. 1 (2008): 73–89; Berquó and Rocha, "A ABEP no Contexto Político"; George Martine, "O Papel dos Organismos Internacionais na Evolução dos Estudos Populacionais no Brasil: Notas Preliminares," *Revista Brasileira de Estudos de População* 22, no. 2 (2005): 257–75.
87. Thomas E. Skidmore, *The Politics of Military Rule in Brazil, 1964–1985* (Oxford: Oxford University Press, 1990).
88. Elio Gaspari, *A Ditadura Envergonhada*, vol. 1 (São Paulo: Companhia das Letras, 2002); Elio Gaspari, *A Ditadura Derrotada*, vol. 3 (São Paulo: Companhia das Letras, 2003). The military regime deployed a systematic discourse regarding its internal enemies: communists; guerrilla groups; "anti-Brazilian voices." It brutally repressed all forms of political dissent.
89. Associação Brasileira para o Bem Estar Familiar—BENFAM (Brazilian Association for the Well-Being of the Family).
90. Maria Isabel Baltar Rocha, "Política de População e Planejamento Familiar: A Proposta do Poder Público e a Atuação das Entidades Privadas," *São Paulo em Perspectiva* 3, no. 3 (1989): 20–23; Berquó and Rocha, "A ABEP no Contexto Político."
91. José Eustáquio Diniz Alves, ´Choque de Civilizações´ *versus* Progressos Civilizatórios, in *Dez Anos do Cairo: Tendências da Fecundidade e Direitos Reprodutivos no Brasil*, ed. André Junqueira Caetano, José Eustáquio Diniz Alves, and Sônia Corrêa (Campinas: ABEP and UNFPA, 2004), 25.

92. José Eustáquio Diniz Alves, "O Planejamento Familiar no Brasil," *Ecodebate*, 2010, http://www.ecodebate.com.br/2010/06/01/o-planejamento-familiar-no-brasil-artigo-de-jose-eustaquio-diniz-alves.
93. Matthews Mathai, "The Global Family Planning Revolution: Three Decades of Population Policies and Programmes," *Bulletin of the World Health Organization* 86, no. 3 (March 2008), http://www.who.int/bulletin/volumes/86/3/07-045658/en/.
94. André Junqueira Caetano, "Fertility Transition and the Diffusion of Female Sterilization in Northeastern Brazil.
95. Vilmar Faria, "Políticas de Governo e Regulação da Fecundidade: Consequências não Antecipadas e Efeitos Perversos," in *Ciências Sociais Hoje*, ed. ANPOCS (São Paulo: ANPOCS, 1989); Potter, Schmertmann, and Cavenaghi, "Fertility and Development." Carvalho has calculated that, under the impact of these factors, fertility rates in Brazil as a whole were reduced by 25 percent between 1970 and 1990. José Alberto Magno de Carvalho, "Demographic Dynamics in Brazil: Recent Trends and Perspectives," *Brazilian Journal of Population Studies* 1 (1997): 5–23.
96. Sonia Corrêa and Maria Betânia Ávila, "Direitos sexuais reprodutivos: Pauta global e percursos brasileiros," in *Sexo & vida: Panorama da saúde reprodutiva no Brasil* (Campinas: Unicamp, 2003), 17–78.
97. José Eustáquio Diniz Alves, "'Choque de Civilizações' *versus* Progressos Civilizatórios," in Caetano, Alves, and Corrêa, *Dez Anos do Cairo*, 27.
98. Elza Berquó, Karen Giffin, and Sarah Hawker Costa, "Ainda a Questão da Esterilização Feminina no Brasil," in *Questões da Saúde Reprodutiva*, ed. Karen Giffin and Sarah Hawker Costa (Rio de Janeiro: Editora FIOCRUZ, 1999).
99. Elza Berquó and Maria Isabel Baltar Rocha, "A ABEP no Contexto Político"; Carmen Barroso, "Direitos Reprodutivos: A Realidade Social e o Debate Político," *Caderno de Pesquisa* 62 (1987): 52–59.
100. Maria Betânia Ávila, "Direitos Sexuais e Reprodutivos: Desafios para as Políticas de Saúde," *Caderno de Saúde Pública* 19, no. 2 (2003): S465–S469.
101. Carmen Barroso, "Direitos Reprodutivos"; Sonia Corrêa, Margareth Martha Arilha, and Sérgio Piola, "Cairo in Action: The Brazil Case" (Washington, D.C.: Population Reference Bureau, 1999); José Eustáquio Diniz Alves and Sonia Corrêa, "Demografia e ideologia: Trajetos históricos e os desafios do Cairo + 10," *Revista Brasileira de Estudos de População* 20, no. 2 (2003): 129–56; José Eustáquio Diniz Alves, "The Context of Family Planning in Brasil," in *Demographic Transformations and Inequalities in Latin America: Historical Trends and Recent patterns*, org. Suzana Cavenaghi (Serie Investigaciones, no. 8) (Rio de Janeiro: ALAP, 2009), http://www.alapop.org/ebooks/sin8/online/index.htm.
102. Margareth Martha Arilha and Elza Berquó, "Cairo+15: Trajetórias Globais e Caminhos Brasileiros em Saúde Reprodutiva e Direitos Reprodutivos," in *Brasil, 15 Anos Após a Conferência do Cairo* (Campinas: ABEP and UNFPA, 2009);

Maria Isabel Baltar Rocha, "População, Reprodução e Saúde: Anotações sobre a Questão de Uma Política Social," *Revista Brasileira de Estudos de População* 5, no. 2 (1988): 21–33; Maria José Oliveira Araújo and Maria Cecília Moraes Simonetti, "Saúde das Mulheres: Questões que se Repetem no Debate sobre Políticas Públicas," *Jornal da Rede Feminista de Saúde* 29 (2011): 18–22; Ana Maria Costa and Estela Leao Aquino, "Saúde da Mulher na Reforma Sanitária Brasileira," in *Saúde, Equidade e Gênero: Um Desafio para as Políticas Públicas,* orgs. Ana María Costa, Edgar Merchan Hamann, and Bébora Tajer (Brasília: UnB, 2000). The state councils on women's rights that have been created since 1982, beginning in São Paulo, as well as the National Council on Women's Rights (CNDM), and the Committee on Human Reproductive Rights (under the Ministry of Health), both established in 1985, supported the new program.

103. Brasil, "Lei n. 9.263, de 12 de janeiro de 1996," *Planejamento Familiar*. Brasília, 1996, http://www.planalto.gov.br/ccivil_03/leis/l9263.htm; Corrêa, Arilha, and Piola, *Cairo in Action*; Arilha and Berquó, "Cairo+15."
104. Jacqueline Pitanguy, "Feminist Politics and Reproductive Rights: The Case of Brazil," *Population and Development Studies* (1994): 101–22. In the same year that the new Brazilian constitution was ratified, the Catholic lobby was victorious in the Philippines and all abortions were defined as unconstitutional, a situation that persists in that country up to today. Similar definitions were adopted across Latin America, either through executive ordinances (as in Chile, 1989), penal code and constitutional reforms (as in El Salvador, 1997—1999), or penal codes reforms (as in Nicaragua, 2007 and the Dominican Republic, 2013). It is also worth noting that while feminists and the progressive sectors of the Catholic Church had been aligned in relation to social justice and democratization, a deep rift between these two sectors was inaugurated with the 1980's Constitutional debates, having abortion rights as its leitmotif.
105. Carmen Barroso and Sônia Corrêa, "Public Servants, Professionals, and Feminists: The Politics of Contraceptive Research in Brazil," *Conceiving the New World Order: The Global Politics of Reproduction* (1995): 292–306.
106. Pitanguy, "Feminist Politics and Reproductive Rights"; Arilha and Berquó, "Cairo+15."
107. Sonia Corrêa, Margareth Arilha, and Sérgio Piola, "Cairo in Action: The Brazil Case" (Washington, D.C.: Population Reference Bureau, 1999).
108. Sueli Carneiro, "Estratégias Legais para Promover a Justiça Social," in *Tirando a Máscara: Ensaios sobre Racismo no Brasil* (São Paulo: Paz e Terra, 2000); Paixão.
109. One main strategy devised and used by the Afro-Brazilian movement to contest the ideology of whitening has been to systematically analyse social and economic data on racial disparities by aggregating the National Census color categories "black" (*preto*) and "brown" (*pardo*) in one sole category under another term to denote black (*negro*). This is how data on racial inequalities offered in the subsequent footnotes are organized. The agenda of racial equality has gained enormous legitimacy over the last thirty years and with even

greater intensity from early 2000s on. In 2003 the National Secretary for the Promotion of Racial Equality was created; since then racial quotas in university admissions and some areas of the public sector were established and in 2010 the Statute of Racial Equality was approved (2010). The agenda of racial equality has gained enormous legitimacy over the last thirty years (and with even greater intensity from early 2000s on, with the creation of the National Secretary for Racial Equality (2004), the establishment of racial quotas in university admissions and some areas of the public sector, and the approval of the Statute of Racial Equality (2010).

110. Brasil Congresso Nacional, *Comissão Parlamentar Mista de Inquérito Destinada a Examinar a Incidência de Esterilização em Massa de Mulheres no Brasil* (Brasília: Presidente: Deputada Benedita da Silva and Relator Senador Carlos Patrocínio, 1993), (Relatório, n. 2); Fernanda Carneiro and Jurema Werneck, *Os Mitos da Esterilização Voluntária* (Rio de Janeiro, 1991) (Texto Apresentado na Sessão Pública de Encerramento da CPI/ALERJ que Investiga a Esterilização em Massa no Estado do Rio de Janeiro).

111. Fernanda Carneiro and Jurema Werneck, "Os mitos da esterilização voluntária," *Texto apresentado na sessão pública de encerramento da CPI/ALERJ que investiga a Esterilização em Massa no Estado do Rio de Janeiro* (Rio de Janeiro, 1991); Berquó, Giffin, and Costa, "Ainda a questão da esterilização feminina."

112. Elza Berquó, "Demografia da Desigualdade: Algumas Considerações sobre os Negros no Brasil," *Novos Estudos CEBRAP* 21 (1988): 74–84; Jurema Werneck, Maisa Mendonça, and Evelyn C. White, *O Livro da Saúde das Mulheres Negras: Nossos Passos Vêm de Longe* (Rio de Janeiro: Pallas, 2000); Estela Maria Garcia Pinto da Cunha, *Recorte Étnico Racial na Saúde* (Campinas: ABEP/NEPO, 2011).

113. For example, in 2010, while 75 percent of white pregnant women had access to more than seven prenatal consultations, the percentage was 55 percent among black women. In 2007, 33 and 59 percent of maternal deaths were of white and black women respectively.

114. The concept of structural violence was crafted by thinkers and researchers informed by the frame of social determinants of health outcomes. It is amply instantiated in Brazilian public health research and analyses of patterns of mortality, but also epidemics such as HIV/AIDS. The concept aims at charting the health and mortality effects of historically constituted political and economic systems, traversed as they are by class, racial, gender constructs and inequalities, patterns of migration, and disparities in the access to structural social policies such as education, health, and social security.

115. Julio J. Waiselfisz, *Mapa da Violência 2013* (Brasília: Presidência da República, Conselho Nacional da Juventude, Secretaria de Promoção da Igualdade Racial, 2013). This differential has sharply accentuated since 2002, when the distribution was of 41 and 58.6 percent for white and black people respectively. The figures are also striking in the case of young people, as between 2002 and 2012

the number of homicides of white young people fell by 39.8 percent, while the number of murders of black youngsters increased by 24.1 percent (Waiselfisz, 88–89).

116. Arilha and Berquó, "Cairo+15"; Elza Berquó Suzana Cavenaghi, "Direitos Reprodutivos de Mulheres e Homens Face à Nova Legislação Brasileira sobre Esterilização Voluntária," *Cadernos de Saúde Pública* 19, no. 2 (2003): S441–S453; Elza Berquó and Suzana Cavenaghi, "Mapeamento Sócio-Econômico e Demográfico dos Regimes de Fecundidade no Brasil e sua Variação entre 1991 e 2000," in *XIV Encontro Nacional de Estudos Populacionais* (Belo Horizonte: ABEP, 2004).
117. The first nationwide income transfer program seen in Latin America was Progresa (1997), later renamed Oportunidad (Opportunity), implemented in Mexico by the Salinas (Partido Revolucionario Institucional) administration. Around the same period, in Brazil the School Grant Program (Programa Bolsa Escola) and another program aimed at eradicating child labor (PETI) began being implemented in specific municipalities. In 2001, Bolsa Escola was nationally expanded, though not yet to all the families living below the poverty threshold. Under Workers' Party administrations (2003 onward) these and other previously existing programs were consolidated in the Family Grant (Bolsa Família), which presently covers all households whose income is below the nationally defined poverty threshold (twelve million families). It is estimated that the program has reduced the number of people living in poverty by roughly 28 percent and inequality levels by 20 percent.
118. Karina Batthyány and Sonia Corrêa, "Health, Gender and Poverty in Latin America," in *Gender Equity in Health: The Shifting Frontiers of Evidence and Action*, ed. Gita Sen and Piroska Östlin (New York: Routledge, 2010), 126–60.
119. José Eustáquio Diniz Alves and Suzana Cavenaghi, "O Programa Bolsa Família, Fecundidade e a Saída da Pobreza," in *Diálogos Transversais em Gênero e Fecundidade: Articulações Contemporâneas*, ed. Margareth Martha Arilha et al. (Campinas: Librum, 2012), 27–47.
120. In August 1997 a major controversy occurred in Congress regarding a bill (PL-20/1991) that sought to guarantee abortion services in the public health system in the two cases permitted by law, which led the minister of health to call for the veto of the provision. Even so, the Cross-Sectorial Commission on Women's Health (CISMU) managed to get the National Health Council to pass a resolution requesting the Ministry of Health to regulate provision of these services. The protocol was finally signed in late 1998. Since then the protocol has become a major target for antiabortion groups.
121. The proposal also extended the time frame to twenty weeks when the pregnancy results from rape, and no limit was defined for abortion in cases of life risk or fetal abnormality incompatible with life. Abortion remained illegal when performed without the woman's consent, and the provision defined that procedures were to be provided freely by the public health system SUS, or else have its costs covered by private health insurance.

122. André Petri, "O Mensalão do Aborto," in *Veja*, August 15, 2005. It is worth quoting an excerpt of the article, as it compellingly describes the episode: "The Lula government was doing well when dealing with social issues, as it sanctioned stem cell research in public universities, distributed emergency contraception in public health clinics, made efforts to reduce racial inequalities, and—most principally—created a special commission to review the outdated abortion legislation. Now that it is stumbling over its feet [because of the corruption crisis], it has started to sell its soul to [the] devil, in relation to social themes. The most recent case is identified in the letter sent by Lula to the Catholic Church hierarchy to salute the opening of the annual General Assembly of the National Conference of Bishops. The most revealing section is found in the sixth paragraph, which reads as follows: 'I want to reaffirm my position in the defense of life in all its aspects and in all its meanings. The debates currently evolving in Brazilian society, in its religious and cultural plurality, are being followed and stimulated by our government, which, however, will not take any measure that may contradict Christian principles.'" http://clubecetico.org/forum/index.php?topic=2661.0 (in Portuguese).
123. Feminists who attended the event when the provision was presented to the House Committee on Social Security and Families portrayed it as an "shameful ceremony" in which key state actors, such as the minister of women's policies, openly showed their discomfort. Personal statement by Angela Freitas on January 20, 2014.
124. Since 2010 this grouping has also tried many times to create a Parliamentarian Inquiry Commission on Abortion. The one proposed in 2013 aimed at investigating international funding for abortion-related activities.
125. Rulian Emmerick, *Religião e Direitos Reprodutivos—O Aborto como Campo de Disputa Política e Religiosa* (Rio de Janeiro: Lúmen Júris Editora, 2013).
126. Corrêa, "Brazil: Abortion at the Frontline."
127. Simone G. Diniz, Ana Flávia Pires, Lucas d'Oliveira, and Sonia Lansky, "Equity and Women's Health Services for Contraception, Abortion and Childbirth in Brazil," *Reproductive Health Matters* 20, no. 40 (2012): 94–101; Simone G. Diniz, "Materno-Infantilism, Feminism and Maternal Health Policy in Brazil," *Reproductive Health Matters* 20, no. 39 (2012): 125–32; Conceição Lemes, "Beatriz Galli: MP 557 is an Absurd Measure; Instead of Protecting Pregnant Women, It Volates Their Human Rights," available at https://www.facebook.com/permalink.php?story_fbid=269355006457789&id=115794808480477.
128. Birthrights Protecting Human Rights in Child Birth, "Obstetric Violence in Brazil," posted on April 4, 2014, http://www.birthrights.org.uk/2014/04/976/.
129. Sexuality Policy Watch, "Forcing a Cesarean Section . . . ," comment posted on the Sexuality Policy Watch Facebook fan page on April 6, 2014, https://www.facebook.com/pages/SPW/115794808480477?ref=hl&sk=timeline.
130. Sonia Corrêa, ed., *Interlinking Policy, Politics and Women's Reproductive Rights: A Study of Health Sector Reform, Maternal Mortality and Abortion in Selected Countries*

of the South (Philippines: Dawn Sexual and Reproductive Health and Rights Program, 2006).

131. Luiz Fernando Dias Duarte et al., eds., *Valores religiosos e legislação no Brasil: A tramitação de projetos de lei sobre temas morais controversos* (Rio de Janeiro: Garamond, 2009).
132. Ricardo Mariano, "Expansão Pentecostal no Brasil: O Caso da Igreja Universal," *Estudos Avançados* 18, no. 52 (2004): 121–38.
133. The PT, it should be noted, emerged from the liberation theology line of activity among workers and has kept connections with the Catholic Church even after its progressive sectors were systematically demolished by the Vatican conservative restoration. Furthermore, during the 1990s it expanded its base among Evangelical sectors. Lula's vice president and two of the five female ministers nominated in 2003 were professed Evangelicals. Furthermore, Lula appointed a conservative practicing Catholic to the post of attorney general.
134. Bernardo Queiroz, Cassio Turra, and Elisenda Perez, "The Opportunities We Cannot Forgo: Economic Consequences of Populations Changes in Brazil," in *XV Encontro Nacional de Estudos Populacionais* (Belo Horizonte: ABEP, 2006).
135. Ana Amélia Camarano, "Perspectivas para Cairo+ 20: Como Avançar na Discussão sobre População e Desenvolvimento," *Revista Brasileira de Estudos de População* 30, no. 2 (2013): 603–8.
136. Paul Amar, "*The Security Archipelago: Human-Security States, Sexuality Politics, and the End of Neoliberalism* (Durham: Duke University Press, 2013).
137. Sonia Corrêa, "Emerging Powers: Can it Be that Sexuality and Human Rights is a 'Lateral Issue'?" in *SUR: Revista Internacional de Direitos Humanos*, vol. 11, no. 20 (São Paulo, June 2014), 171–83.
138. Lilian Abracinskas et al., "The 'Unexpected' Montevideo Consensus," *Global Public Health* (2014): 1-8; Grotz, Fábio, *Loss and Gain in Recent UN Debates on the Family*, August 5, 2015, http://sxpolitics.org/loss-and-gain-in-recent-un-debates-on-the-family/13244.

8

Interpreting Population Policy in Nigeria

ELISHA P. RENNE

What matters is the people's own day-to-day existence and the immediate factor[s] that impinge on it—health, food, shelter, and so forth. Population growth, in other words, is far from their centre of interest. Their concern is with the improvement of the quality of life. And this is the most rational thing from their own view-point. What they need to be told, therefore, is that planning their families is part of the effort to improve their and their children's health and survival as well as their general living conditions. *And the results of this effort must be clearly perceived in order to bring about the desired change in family size.*

—P. O. Olusanya, "Some Aspects of Family Planning Programmes" (my emphasis)

Poverty levels in the country are rising with almost 100 million people living on less than N160 [US$1] a day despite strong economic growth in the country, the National Bureau of Statistics said yesterday. The percentage of Nigerians living in absolute poverty—those who can afford only the bare essentials of food, shelter and clothing—rose to 60.9 per cent in 2010, compared with 54.7 per cent in 2004, the bureau said in Abuja yesterday while announcing the results of a national survey.

—Olayemi R. Ibrahim

The first Nigerian national population policy was introduced in 1988 by President Ibrahim Babangida, who publicized the "Four is Enough" campaign, with the goal that each woman would have only four children. While the 1988 population policy also stressed improvements in health and living conditions as well as the policy's voluntary nature (Federal Republic of Nigeria), it was the "Four is Enough" campaign, initiated to address the prevailing situation whereby women gave birth, on average, to six children, that caught the public's attention. However, the perceived link between population growth and development concerns was not the only reason for the Nigerian government's interest in the 1988 national population policy and associated family-planning programs. Rather, its acceptance was associated with several related factors, which included the appointment of Professor Olikoye Ransome-Kuti as minister of health in 1985, who directed the subsequent implementation of a national primary healthcare program that was launched in August 1987; an agreement for the implementation of an IMF Structural Adjustment Program finalized in 1986; and the concerns of several international nongovernmental organization (NGO) officials who advocated fertility reduction as part of the development process.

The 1988 population policy and the "Four is Enough" program as well as the Structural Adjustment Program and the acceptance of IMF and World Bank loans were widely criticized.[1] While the implementation of the policy led to increased availability of contraceptives that had the potential for improving women's reproductive health, women's groups complained about the policy's focus on women's fertility. Furthermore, religious leaders questioned the role of the state in people's personal, religious lives. There were also suspicions based on ethnic identity. Northern Nigerians—many of whom were Hausa-Fulani Muslims—were suspicious of a policy advocated by Western governments, believing that they sought to reduce the Muslim population.[2] Southern Nigerians, many—but not all—of whom were Christians and monogamously married, saw the policy as favoring northern Muslims who could marry up to four wives. Yet even as Nigerian population and health specialists such as P. O. Olusanya and O. Ransome-Kuti assisted the federal government in developing a population policy that they saw as promoting equitable development as well as better health for mothers and children, its unpopularity and irrelevance in the daily lives of many Nigerians meant that the policy was largely ignored. While the national total fertility rate was reported as 6.0 (meaning that women of reproductive age [fifteen to forty-nine] would have on average six children during their lifetime) when the policy was implemented in 1988,[3] thirteen years later, the Nigeria Demographic Health Survey 2003 reported a total fertility rate of 5.7, a very small decline. Even with the implementation of a revised population policy in 2005 that included a focus on reproductive and population health more generally, the total fertility rate remained the same—5.7 nationally, according to the Nigeria Demographic Health Survey 2008. While the national total fertility rate declined slightly (to 5.5) according the Nigeria Demographic Health Survey 2013 Preliminary report, the 2008 and 2013 contraceptive prevalence rate (the number of women currently using any type of contraception) continued to be low, around 15 percent (table 8.1).[4]

These figures suggest that the population policy has had little impact on many people's reproductive lives in Nigeria, which raises the question of why this is so. Indeed, while Nigeria has had a national population policy for over twenty years, it exists mainly on paper. This situation also raises the question of why, despite its ineffectualness, having a population policy and its associated documents have been so vitally important for Nigerian government and international bilateral, multilateral, and NGO officials. Indeed, Nigerian officials' participation at the London Summit on Family Planning held in July 2012,[5] which supported the distribution of free contraceptives to "the world's poorest girls and women," suggests that little has been learned from past public health interventions and demographic analysis.

In this chapter, I focus on three aspects of population policy in Nigeria. First, I consider why high fertility persists, despite the presence of a national population policy. I suggest that the disconnect between the government population policy and people's concerns about their health and well-being have contributed to continuing high levels of fertility since the original policy implementation in 1988. While some women, mainly those with postsecondary school education, with higher income, and from urban areas in the southern part of the country, have benefited from increased contraceptive use and smaller families (see table 8.2), for many women, particularly those in the northern part of the country, where poverty rates have actually increased,[6] the policy's credibility is undermined by the federal government's failure to improve the conditions of their lives, as the demographer P. O. Olusanya has observed. Without health services that would reduce infant and maternal mortality or government provision of electricity and water that would improve living standards, such a policy remains irrelevant to many women for whom having many children is a means of offsetting the uncertainties of everyday life in Nigeria (table 8.3).

Second, I then consider the most recent population initiative in Nigeria, announced by President Goodluck Jonathan in July 2012. This initiative, which grew out of the 2012 London Summit on Family Planning and its plans to enable "an additional 120 million women in the world's poorest countries to access and use contraception,"[7] has particular gender implications, as its emphasis on contraception suggests a shift away from broader reproductive health issues as outlined in the ICPD (International Conference

Table 8.1. Fertility, Contraceptive Use, Maternal/Infant Mortality, and Population Policy Implementation in Sub-Saharan Africa

Country year	TFR_{urban}	TFR_{rural}	TFR_{all}	$CPR_{modern\ (\%)}$	Maternal	Mortality		Population Policy[a]
						Infant	Under five	
Nigeria, 2013	4.7	6.2	5.5	10	576/100,000	69/1,000	128/1,000	1988
Nigeria, 2008	4.7	6.3	5.7	10	545/100,000	75/1,000	157/1,000	
Nigeria, 2003	4.9	6.1	5.7	8.9		100/1,000	201/1,000	
Nigeria, 1999[b]	4.5	5.44	5.15	8.6		70.8/1,000	133.4/1,000	
Nigeria, 1990	5.3	6.33	6.01	3.8		91.4/1,000	191/1,000	
Benin, 2011–12 prelim	4.3	5.4	4.9	7.9[c]				1996
Cameroun, 2011	4.0	6.4	5.1	16.1	782/100,000	62/1,000	122/1,000	1992
Ghana, 2008	3.1	4.9	4.0	17.0		50/1,000	80/1,000	1969
Ethiopia, 2011			4.8	27		57/1,000	88/1,000	1993
Malawi, 2010	4.0	6.1	5.7	32.6		50/1,000	112/1,000	1994
Rwanda, 2010	4.6	3.4	4.8	25.2		50/1,000	76/1,000	1990
Tanzania, 2010	3.7	6.1	5.4	23.6		51/1,000	81/1,000	1992
Uganda, 2011	3.8	6.8	6.2	20.7		54/1,000	90/1,000	1995

[a] From Sullivan 2006, 30.

[b] These figures are assumed to be low because of underreporting.

[c] This figure represents modern contraceptive use only; the low TFR suggests that other methods—such as withdrawal and abstinence—are being used.

Source: Fertility and mortality figures are from country Demographic Health Surveys, produced in conjunction with ICF Macro, Calverton, Md., with funding from USAID and UNFPA.

Table 8.2. Total Fertility Rate in Nigeria, Based on Background Characteristics, 1999, 2003, 2008

	NDHS 1999[a]	NDHS 2003	NDHS 2008	NDHS 2013	NDHS 2003	NDHS 2008	NDHS 2013
Background characteristics	TFR					Infant / Under five mortality[b]	
Residence							
Urban	4.5	4.9	4.7	4.7	81/153	67/121	60/100
Rural	5.44	6.1	6.3	6.2	121/243	95/191	86/167
Zone							
North Central	—	5.7	5.4	5.3	103/165	77/135	66/100
Northeast	6.79	7.0	7.2	6.3	125/260	126/222	77/160
Northwest	6.45	6.7	7.3	6.7	114/269	91/217	89/185
Southeast	4.64	4.1	4.8	4.7	66/103	95/153	54/131
South-South	—	4.6	4.7	4.3	120/176	84/138	35/91
Southwest	4.49	4.1	4.5	4.6	69/113	59/89	31/90
Education	—						
No education[c]	6.13	6.7	7.3	6.9	124/269	97/209	89/180
Primary	5.55	6.3	6.5	6.1	111/186	89/159	74/128
Secondary	4.91	4.7	4.7	4.6	71/113	70/116	58/91
Postsecondary	2.43[d]	2.8	2.9	3.1	(61)/(80)[d]	48/68	50/62
Wealth quintile							
Lowest	—	6.5	7.1	7.0	133/257	100/219	92/190
Second	—	6.3	7.0	6.7	140/293	103/212	94/187
Middle	—	5.7	5.9	5.7	110/215	86/165	71/127
Fourth	—	5.9	5.0	4.9	87/179	73/129	65/100
Highest	—	4.2	4.0	3.9	29/79	58/87	48/73

[a] The 1999 figures are considered to be low because of interviewer/interviewee underestimation of children; see NDHS 1999, 36.

[b] Infant and under-five mortality figures are rates for the ten-year period preceding the survey per 1,000 live births.

[c] No education means no Western education; it does not include Islamic education, which in northern Nigeria is significant.

[d] These figures are based on a very small sample size, between 250 and 499 women.

Source: Nigeria–Demographic Health Surveys.

on Population and Development) Cairo conference in 1994. However, the London Summit does not ignore health concerns in its program, which "will result in 200,000 fewer women dying in pregnancy and childbirth, more than 110 million fewer unintended pregnancies, over 50 million fewer abortions, and nearly three million fewer babies dying in their first year of life."

Yet its reliance on the distribution of free contraceptives seems out of touch with the situation in rural areas of southern Nigeria and in northern

Table 8.3. Comparison of Women's Socioeconomic, Living Conditions, and Demographic Characteristics, by Selected States, NDHS 2013

State	Education						Water		Electricity			
	None[b]	Some primary	Complete primary	Some secondary	Complete secondary	Postsecondary	Improved	Not improved	Yes	No	TFR	CPR[a]
North Central												
FCT-Abuja	11.4	4.5	11.7	15.8	28.5	30.0	73.3	26.7	77.7	22.0	4.5	20.6
Benue	17.2	20.0	16.8	30.9	9.9	5.2	37.3	62.3	22.1	77.9	5.2	12.1
North East												
Borno	72.4	3.0	5.7	5.3	6.5	7.1	60.4	38.4	33.0	66.5	4.7	1.8
Yobe	85.6	1.4	1.3	4.3	4.7	2.7	45.3	54.7	18.1	81.7	6.6	0.5
North West												
Kaduna	40.5	3.6	11.2	17.8	18.7	8.4	65.8	34.0	53.5	46.2	4.1	18.5
Kano	60.2	4.6	11.2	12.1	9.9	2.0	70.7	28.9	52.1	47.9	6.8	0.5
Sokoto	89.1	1.5	2.4	4.4	2.1	0.6	64.5	35.2	38.9	60.9	7.0	0.7
South East												
Enugu	5.7	6.6	17.4	31.3	28.5	10.6	47.5	52.2	55.4	44.6	4.8	14.3
Imo	0.5	3.0	9.5	32.0	35.7	19.3	83.3	16.6	69.9	30.1	4.8	10.7
South South												
Rivers	3.1	3.9	15.6	23.4	37.3	16.8	71.3	28.5	65.1	34.5	3.8	17.5
Cross	8.7	9.7	18.4	29.5	22.6	11.1	69.6	30.3	57.4	41.4	5.4	1.4
South West												
Ekiti	2.0	2.4	10.3	27.6	32.1	25.5	74.6	25.4	92.7	7.3	4.3	26.6
Lagos	4.4	1.7	11.6	18.0	42.6	21.7	57.2	42.8	99.3	0.5	4.1	26.4

[a] Contraceptive prevalence rate, any modern method used by married women.
[b] Refers to Western education; Islamic education not included.

Nigeria more generally, where primary healthcare clinics are often dysfunctional. Furthermore, the implementation of this sort of top-down program and its working at the national level, as outlined in Summit documents, suggest that women from a range of backgrounds will have little say in its implementation. As the feminist demographers Ruth Dixon-Mueller and Adrienne Germain note,[8] the extent to which women are involved in decision-making about the distribution of these things—contraceptives and information—affects the effectiveness of such programs.

Finally, I address the question of why the Nigerian government continues to promote a population policy when, after so many years, it does not seem to be affecting fertility levels. Indeed, the failure of successive policies to increase contraceptive use and to reduce fertility in Nigeria despite millions of dollars spent on programs to increase contraceptive knowledge and to provide contraception—both through clinics and hospitals and through social marketing—suggests that the policy and its subsequent iterations *are* doing something. This situation suggests that some people are benefiting from the policy and the implementation of its programs. This question also relates to the anthropologist James Ferguson's more general questions about the failure of the intended goals of development projects, which nonetheless are not without consequences.[9]

Before considering these questions, however, I begin with a discussion of the historical background that underlies the particular configuration of population policies in Nigeria.

Linking Population and Development: The Historical Context in Nigeria

Concern with population and fertility has a long history in the area now known as Nigeria. Prior to British colonial rule of Nigeria, which officially began in 1914 with the amalgamation of northern and southern protectorates, women (and men concerned about their wives) went to great lengths to enhance their fertility and to achieve motherhood. This pronatalist cultural preference has a basis in the mainly agrarian and craft societies for which having many children was a benefit, both in terms of forms of kinship organization, which perpetuated family claims to land and political office, and as a source of labor.[10] Nonetheless, social conventions favored long birth intervals supported by two years of breastfeeding and abstinence, effectively limiting the number of children that a woman could have within her reproductive lifetime.[11] During the colonial period, government officials did not pay much attention to population issues except when the spread of infectious diseases such as smallpox affected workers' health.[12] Fertility-related issues and women's reproductive lives were left to maternity hospitals and clinics mainly established by mission groups, such as the Wesley Guild Hospital in Ilesha and the Methodist Maternity Centre, established in 1953 in Ikole-Ekiti.[13] However, with the establishment of major teaching hospitals in the south and north, for example, associated with the University of Ibadan (University College Hospital in 1952) and Ahmadu Bello University (ABU Teaching Hospital in 1968), childbirth and infant and maternal mortality began to be addressed in a more systematic way. In November 1964, the Planned Parenthood Federation of Nigeria was founded. Linked with its home organization, the London-based Planned Parenthood Federation,[14] members sought to encourage married couples to actively plan for the number of children that they wanted and to provide information about contraception.[15] Similarly, in the First National Development Plan (1962–68), government interest in a population policy focused on the idea of voluntary family planning, although no specifics were mentioned.[16] Following the Nigerian Civil War (1967–1970), the Second National Development Plan (1970–74) was formulated, with the specific reference to governmental provision of family-planning facilities within the broader framework of health and social welfare.[17] As the 1970s was a period a great affluence due to high prices for Nigerian crude oil—referred to as the "oil boom" years—government officials viewed a growing population as something that could be absorbed within the larger economic development process. It was only after the oil price crash in the early 1980s and the ensuing financial crises that population and its control were raised as a serious concern in the Fourth National Development Plan (1981–85).[18] With the bloodless coup of December 1983, Muhammadu Buhari took over the democratic government of Shehu Shagari, beginning a period of military rule that was to continue for fifteen years.

The 1988 National Policy on Population for Development, Unity, Progress, and Self-Reliance

General Buhari saw limiting population growth as advantageous for reviving the economy, and he supported the goals outlined in the Fourth National Development Plan, although he did not develop any specific actions. The worsening economy and Buhari's draconian actions of jailing political critics and journalists contributed to another bloodless coup led by General Ibrahim Babangida in August 1985. In order to extricate the country from its debts, Babangida agreed to sign an agreement in 1986 to implement an IMF plan known as a Structural Adjustment Program. While broadly unpopular because it led to the devaluation of the naira (the local currency) and to the reduction of government social welfare and health programs, this agreement released money for future IMF/WB loans, which included funds for a primary healthcare program the following year and for developing the country's first population policy.[19]

General Babangida had long admired Professor Olikoye Ransome-Kuti, whom he appointed as minister of health in 1986. In the same year, Ransome-Kuti used his position to establish a system of Primary Health Care (PHC) centers throughout the country.[20] The PHC program provided basic healthcare, including immunization for the six principal childhood diseases as well as prenatal and antenatal care for mothers in all areas of the country—both urban and rural. In March 1988, the first phase of a national immunization exercise was held at Primary Health Care centers, which included the distribution of free vaccines.

Ransome-Kuti also supported Babangida's development of a National Population Policy. Work on the policy had begun in 1984 and continued through 1988, when it was approved by the Armed Forces Ruling Council in February. Several agencies concerned with maternal/child health and population, particularly the United Nations Population Fund (UNFPA), which provided financial assistance for policy development.[21] Thus, while the 1988 population policy was coordinated by the Federal Ministry of Health, it involved the participation of several ministries, international donor organizations, and family-planning organizations and related programs funded by USAID, the Ford Foundation, Family Planning International, and the Population Council.[22]

Ransome-Kuti wrote the preface for the first population policy document, expressing his understanding that the policy would benefit the health of mothers and children and that the introduction of contraceptives and information about their use would reduce maternal and infant mortality. As he put it, "That Policy was put there for the health of the woman. We told the women, if you don't want to die, don't have more than four children. That was what we were saying. Data shows that after the third child, maternal mortality goes up."[23] While he sought to encourage women to have fewer children, it was not for the purposes of economic development but rather for improving maternal and child health. Other members of the Nigerian educated elite, such as P. O. Olusanya, a demography professor who taught at the University of Ife and later at the University of Lagos, also saw the population policy as beneficial although not simply for economic reasons. For him, it had the potential of expanding opportunities—fewer children, better opportunities for employment for women and for the education of children—and thus leading to a better quality of life.

For Ransome-Kuti, his dream for a functioning national primary healthcare system faded when the responsibility for primary healthcare services was transferred to the local governments as part of the Structural Adjustment Program, which required the federal government to curtail spending on social services in June 1990. In 1991, when federal responsibility for primary healthcare services was transferred to local governments, the availability of vaccines and other medicines drastically declined along with funds for the payment of staff.[24] Furthermore, Babangida's obstruction of the upcoming 1993 national election led Professor Ransome-Kuti to resign his position as minister of health in 1992. By 1996, the primary healthcare program was in shambles and has yet to recover.[25] This situation and the continuing high levels of maternal and child/infant mortality have had implications for family-planning programs and acceptance of contraception in Nigeria (table 8.1).[26]

Why the 1988 Population Policy Has Had Little Impact

There are several reasons why the 1988 population policy had little impact on the total fertility rate and on contraceptive use in Nigeria. From the perspective of ordinary people, it was widely interpreted as promoting the idea of "Four is Enough," limiting family size, and as government's inappropriate interference in people's reproductive lives. As one man, a farmer living in a small Ekiti Yoruba town in southwestern Nigeria in 1997, put it:

> The government of the day is heralding that policy in order to further reduce its responsibilities for people . . . The policy is for government workers who have nothing [other] than staying in the office daily, whose children couldn't identify yam leaves from cocoa leaves. . . . The farmers believe strongly that having many children is helpful, especially on the farm, from which others are given education.[27]

While some townspeople, concerned about the costs of education, thought that the policy did make sense, others were caught in a double bind; they could see the benefits of having fewer children to care for well but also needed children to help them in their old age, for example, to fetch water and for companionship. Smith discusses a similar dynamic among Igbo villagers in southeastern Nigeria, with the importance of having many children related to the continuing salience of patron-client relations in social life. Elsewhere, in the Atyap (a small Christian ethnic group) community in the southern Kaduna State, in northern Nigeria, the sociologist Helen Avong observed that people were receptive to the introduction of contraceptives for use in birth-spacing but opposed the idea of their government deciding the number of children they should have.[28] In the northern part of Kaduna State, however, where the population consists mainly of Hausa-Fulani who are Muslim, the policy was widely rejected, in part because of distrust of Western-sponsored population programs and "concerns about the moral basis of the state's authority over matters concerning human reproduction and about what constitutes progress." Moreover, "The economic calculation of childbearing (represented by family planning programs), [is] viewed as yet another example of Western immorality."[29] As Avong notes in comparing the northern and southern parts of Kaduna State:

> While some Muslims consider the suggestion by government to limit family size to four children for economic reasons to be religiously blasphemous, the Christian Atyap consider its link to national economic recovery to be an unacceptable political gimmick. In spite of their support for smaller family sizes, some respondents strongly argued that a reduction in family size is not the key to [an] improved living standard but a return to God in repentance. They argued that even if Nigerians reduced their family sizes to two children, their economic situation would not improve "unless we change our evil ways."[30]

Thus from the perspective of ordinary people, from many distinctive ethnic backgrounds and with different religious allegiances, particularly those living in rural areas and for many living in northern Nigeria, the 1988 population policy was not acceptable. Nor did many make the link between development—improved living conditions—and fertility decline as depicted by government officials in educational materials (fig. 8.1). Indeed, with the exception of widespread mobile phone service in much of the country, the continuing decline in basic amenities—electricity, water, and healthcare—also reinforces the idea that having many children is necessary to provide services and to ensure that one will have some surviving descendants.

The 1988 population policy was also affected by interdepartmental and federal-state competition for funds and authority over programs. While the initial policy was formulated under the authority of the Federal Ministry

Figure 8.1. Poster and printed material from the 1996 Ekiti State Population Day activities, depicting the good and bad choices that those accepting family planning can make (Ekiti State, National Population Commission).

of Health, the federal government established a Department of Population Activities within the Federal Ministry of Health in 1987. The demographer Olukunle Adegbola explains the complicated system of funding that contributed to interdepartmental and agency competition:

> To demonstrate its financial commitment to the implementation of the policy, the Federal Government of Nigeria established a fund, the Population Activities Fund (PAF) to be managed by the Population Activities Fund Agency (PAFA), which was established in 1992 as a parastatal of the Federal Ministry of Health and backed by law in 1994. Both Department of Population Activities and the Population Activities Fund Agency were to work closely for the achievement of the goals and objectives of the policy. The vehicle through which both institutions were to operate was the NPP [National Population Project].[31]

Indeed, as Adegbola notes, there were several reasons that explain the policy's failure to affect the national population growth rate: (1) "the emphasis on process rather than on immediate outcome"—namely a focus on building institutional capacity and a family-planning bureaucratic infrastructure; (2) the inability of the government to implement population programs that were culturally relevant to different sections of the country, particularly for northern Nigeria, where "the political, economic and cultural landscape in the

North still encourages high fertility and thus makes nonsense of government policy"; and (3) interagency conflict, specifically, "the unhealthy bureaucratic struggles among the various Federal Government agencies vying for the heart of the population policy implementation."[32] Ebigbola has made a similar assessment and also argued that the 1988 population policy was mainly implemented to assuage foreign concerns with overpopulation:

> Government's political will to enforce population control measures is rather weak. It appears that the formulation of the policy was more of a response to external pressure from bilateral and multinational organizations who provided the seed money that enabled policy implementation to take off.[33]

Additionally, the political situation in Nigeria when the 1988 population policy undermined the policy's popularity and effectiveness. In the seventeen-year period from the time when the policy was first implemented until its replacement with a revised population policy in 2005, Nigerians had five different political leaders. This situation helps to explain why the policy's implementation was "rather weak"; political leaders had other concerns on their minds.

The 2005 National Policy on Population for Sustainable Development

With the election of Olusegun Obasanjo and the return to democratic rule in 1999, government officials once again began to consider the issue of population. The 2005 population policy revisions were devised to bring the national policy up to date with more recent population-related concerns, associated with the Dakar/Ngor Parliamentary Declaration,[34] the UN Conference on Environment and Development ("the Rio Declaration"),[35] and the International Conference on Population and Development held at Cairo, which stressed women's reproductive health and women's education (see fig. 8.2).[36] The revised population policy, published in January 2004 and adopted by the federal government in February 2005, was renamed the National Policy on Population for Sustainable Development. New issues were included, particularly HIV-AIDS and gender equity, although the new policy continued to stress "respect for the rights of couples and individuals."[37] Unlike the 1988 policy cover, which consisted of a Nigerian flag, the cover of the 2005 document's strategic plan, published in 2008, depicts an outline of

Figure 8.2. After the Cairo ICPD Conference held in September 1994, women's reproductive health, education, and income became an increasing focus of population programs in Nigeria, as this 1996 issue of the journal *Nigeria's Population* suggests.

the map of Nigeria filled with people, suggesting the diversity of Nigerians as well as the urgency of reducing population size. In 2004, President Obasanjo put the National Population Commission in charge of implementing the new policy, and in 2007, government officials, NGO representatives, and members of research institutions and universities met in Kaduna to finalize a strategic plan.[38] In the document that emerged from this meeting, each subsection—health concerns, education, adolescent and young people, and so on (table 8.4)—is followed by a matrix that lists "specific strategies, activities, targets, objectively verifiable indicators, means of verification, responsible agencies, resources required, and time frame."[39]

For some subsections, the strategies, activities, resources, and time frame are quite specific. For example, in the subsector "Sexual and Reproductive Health," the development and distribution of reproductive health advocacy

Table 8.4. Strategic Plan 2008: Components of Subsectors

Subsector 1: Health
1A. Sexual and Reproductive Health
1B. Family Planning and Fertility Management
1C. Women's Health and Safe Motherhood
1D. Child Health and Child Survival
1E. HIV/AIDS
1F. Male Reproductive Health

Subsector 2: Adolescents and Young People
2A. Adolescents and Young People

Subsector 3: Education
3A. Population and Family Life Education

Subsector 4: Communication
4A. Behavioral Change Communication
4B. Advocacy and Leadership Commitment

Subsector 5: Population Dynamics
5A. Population Distribution, Urbanization, and Migration
5B. Population Groups with Special Needs
5B.I. Nomads
5B.II. The Elderly
5B.III. Persons with Disabilities
5B.IV. Refugees and Displaced Persons

Subsector 6: Environment
6A. Population, Development, and Environmental Interrelationships

Subsector 7: Social-Cultural Barriers and Legal Support

Subsector 8: Gender

Subsector 9: [Population and Development]
9A. Population Variables Integrated into Development Planning
9B. Sectorally Integrated Reproductive Health Concerns

Subsector 10: Population Statistics
10A. Reliable and Timely Generated Population and Health Data
10B. Monitoring, Evaluation, and Research

Subsector 11: Inter-Agency Collaboration
11. Inter-Agency Coordination

kits are described, to be carried out by the Federal Ministry of Health within the period from the first quarter of 2007 through December 2010, with five million naira set to be spent on development/distribution and ten million naira spent on review. Similarly, a plan to "rehabilitate and re-equip all existing primary health care facilities to provide quality RH services"—for the period from January 2008 to December 2015, with twenty billion naira required to be spent for the period—is to involve personnel from the National Population Commission, the Federal Ministry of Health, and the Federal Ministry of Information and National Orientation.[40] While these goals are admirable, it is unclear how much has actually been accomplished, what funds have been released by the government for these projects, and furthermore what their impact on population well-being has been. For example, in November 2011, in 'Yanhamar village in Kumbutso Local Government Area, Kano State, reporters found that the primary healthcare clinic had not been rehabilitated:

> The only dispensary at the village has been under lock and key for years, with no medical personnel attending to the health needs of the community. The building itself is dilapidated, while bats have taken over its roofs, emitting [a] foul stench. All attempts to get local or state government to put the structure to use for the benefit of the community have proved abortive, residents said. Consequently, people in the village always go to another dispensary located far away in another village for medical attention.[41]

It is difficult to know precisely how much of the matrices presented in the 2008 Strategic Plan were actually addressed by 2012. Yet the anthropologist Daniel Smith's work with a project funded by UNFPA suggests that while funds may be distributed for population-related work, many of the benefits accrue to "institution-building" for those within particular social networks:

> For example, the Project Coordinator was able to select personnel from the ministry who served as trainers and facilitators for project training activities, and thus pay out sizable honorariums and per diems. Opportunities to travel to and participate in training workshops are significant perks controlled and allocated by project officers. . . . In addition, people from the Project Coordinator's natal community and her husband's community frequently visited the project office in hopes of employment or the awarding of a contract to refurbish a building, print data collection forms, or provide maintenance for equipment such as photocopy machines and air conditioners.[42]

Similarly, project funds are spent on myriad workshops that transmit project information and enable participants to expand their networks.[43] In both cases, direct work with ordinary people outside these clientage networks may be minimal. As Ebigbola has noted regarding the Nigerian population policy programs:

> [While they] appear rosy on paper, their implementation was half-hearted at best. The usual procedure for designing and implementing these programmes has been the top-down approach, which means that the services provided by the planners were not those required by the targeted population.[44]

However, since the time frame for several of the goals enumerated on the 2008 Strategic Plan for the National Population Policy for Sustainable Development is projected to be carried out through 2015, it is impossible to say how much officials will have accomplished. The current situation is particularly acute in northern Nigeria, where poverty, insecurity, and high levels of fertility make implementing family-planning programs a daunting task. Indeed, the 2005 policy goal of achieving "a reduction in total fertility rate of at least 0.6 children every five years" may not be met.[45]

A Recent Population Initiative in Nigeria: The 2012 London Summit on Family Planning

In the section "Women's Health" in the 2005 population policy document, the proposed target of an increase in the contraceptive prevalence rate by 2 percent per year until 2015 requires the availability of contraception. While not specifically referring to modern contraceptive use, such contraception is considered more reliable; in Nigeria, the main modern contraceptives women report preferring are injectables, pills, male condoms, and IUDs.[46]

On July 11, 2012, the London Summit on Family Planning was convened to "mobilize global policy, financing, commodity, and service delivery commitments to support the rights of an additional 120 million women and girls in the world's poorest countries to use contraceptive information, services and supplies, without coercion or discrimination, by 2020."[47] Nigeria, along with many other countries, sent delegates to the summit, and President Goodluck Jonathan announced his intention to spend N33.4 million on family-planning contraceptives that would be made available free of charge to Nigerian women, thereby raising "Nigeria's contraceptive prevalence rate (CPR) . . . [to] 36%."[48] The two main sponsors of the summit—the UK government (specifically, the Department of International Development [DFID]) and the Bill and Melinda Gates Foundation—along with UNFPA and other international donors, have made considerable financial commitments to the project, which has three main objectives:

1. Revitalize global commitments to family planning and access to contraceptives as a cost-effective and transformational development priority
2. Improve the access and distribution of contraceptive supplies
3. Remove and reduce barriers to family planning[49]

The 2012 London Summit on Family Planning is a global public health project, not a population policy per se. But with its focus on contraception and women, it counters the aims of the 1994 Cairo Conference, which expanded the agenda of population policies that were based on the idea of limiting fertility (and thereby improving development) to policies that include women's reproductive health.[50] Summit documents do make reference to women's health and note that provision of contraceptives will reduce the number of dangerous aborted pregnancies. Nonetheless, the focus of this project is free contraceptive distribution to poor women.

In Nigeria, President Jonathan's announcement has had mixed responses. Leaders of the two largest religious groups in Nigeria—the sultan of Sokoto, Muhammad Sa'ad Abubakar III, the head of the National Council for Islamic Affairs, and Pastor Ayo Oritsejafor, president of the Christian Association of Nigeria—asked for more information about the program but did not rule out the acceptance of contraception, particularly with respect to maternal mortality and planning for raising children. Similarly, local NGOs raised questions about the program but were in favor of increased availability of free contraceptives.[51]

However, the inability of the Nigerian government to provide basic services for its citizens was a common theme of those who were critical of the new family-planning initiative. For example, Sanusi Abubukar, an editorial writer, wrote in the northern Nigerian newspaper *Daily Trust*:

> Since when has Government bother [ed] about those wretched souls [the poor]? It is when you provide schools, hospitals, water, electricity, housing and social security that you earn the right to tell people anything about their family size. So *wetin* [what] concern [does] Government [have] with how many people are born when it has abdicated its responsibilities to "market forces"?[52]

One letter writer, Beenzu Nwosu, who wrote to the editor of the southern Nigerian newspaper *The Guardian*, questioned the wisdom of the focus on family planning, coming from the instigation of outsiders:

> How long will draconian policies be forced on us without a vote from the people who own their lives? How many human rights are being trampled upon under the guise of modernity and forward-thinking? If the government won't think for us, then the onus is on us to look out for ourselves. . . . Let us think slowly and deeply about this.
>
> I have a few questions for the [Bill and] Melinda Gates Foundation: Would you help fund our decayed primary health care system? We have no needles, no cotton wool, there are torn mosquito nets in the wards, no running water, no

> medicines, no ambulance services for the poor, no . . . And the list could go on and on. Would the [Bill and] Melinda Gates Foundation assist in training birth attendants to handle emergencies more efficiently in remote and isolated areas with little or no access to primary healthcare centres?[53]

Aminu Magashi, the health writer for the *Daily Trust*, also questioned the government's sincerity in making unrealistic claims regarding fertility decline:

> We have also pledged to spend N33.4 million on family planning commodities and in doing that to raise Nigeria's contraceptive prevalence rate (CPR) of 36%. . . . Achieving CPR of 36% by 2018 isn't achievable and not realistic when one analyses the trend of CPR over the last 15 years. Achieving the 36% CPR will require establishing a clear framework to ensure availability of the commodities all over the nation and to also track and report progress.[54]

Furthermore, Magashi raised three questions concerning how free contraceptives would be interpreted by recipients:

1. What will be the implication in terms of family planning implementation, accessibility, availability, perception of users and distribution, when it is free?
2. Is there a possibility that making it free may decrease utilization?
3. Can we learn from other commodities in Nigeria that we are providing free and gauge public perception and impact of such intervention in the longer term?

He is referring to the long-standing rumors about various Western commodities and the oral polio vaccine, distributed free of charge, which were believed to be contaminated with "family planning substances."[55] That these rumors about the polio vaccine circulated mainly in northern Nigeria—the very area with the highest fertility rates and lowest contraceptive use—does not bode well for the London Summit Family Planning initiative, which, like the Global Polio Eradication Initiative, also entails significant Gates Foundation funding.[56]

Adegbola correctly identifies poverty as a factor explaining high fertility rates in the north, observing "that one-third of Nigeria's poor are concentrated in the three northwest states of Kaduna, Kano and Sokoto."[57] Yet his conclusion, "It is thus obvious that in the northern parts of the country where fertility rates are highest and where the need for contraceptive use is most urgent some incentives including subsidized price of contraceptives is desirable," may not be correct. Rather, as several writers in Nigeria (e.g., P. O. Olusanya) and in the population and development literature, such as the economist Lant Pritchett, suggest:

> Reducing fertility is best seen as a broad problem of improving economic and social conditions, especially for women: raising their levels of education, their economic position, their (and their children's) health, and their role and status in society. That is a task altogether more difficult, but with more promise, than manipulating contraceptive supply.[58]

Gender Implications of London Summit on the Family-Planning Program

The importance of women's education and economic status has been noted as a critical factor in supporting fertility decline.[59] However, the shifts from the initial focus on fertility and development to reproductive and maternal/child health and back again to family planning and fertility reflected in Nigerian population policies and the more recent acceptance of the London Summit on Family Planning initiative underscore the peripheral position of women in the constitution and implementation of these programs. For example, while the 1988 population policy was written after several years of consultation among various groups, according to the National Council of Women's Societies (the first women's organization in Nigeria, founded in 1959), this organization was not involved in the process. Not surprisingly, they objected to the "Four is Enough" program's focus on women, which was seen as discriminatory since men's fertility was not at issue.[60] They also objected to the policy's statement that "the patriarchal family system in the country shall be recognized for stability of the home," implying that women were not equal partners of family decision-making but were subordinate to men.[61] While the 2005 population policy included three sections that included the specific needs of women—health, education, and gender concerns, its implementation of specific goals in these areas remains to be seen. However, in some parts of the country, the link between lower levels of fertility and higher levels of education may clearly be seen (tables 8.2, 8.3,).[62] A more recent study of 2008 DHS data from Ghana suggests a similar pattern.[63] Although the authors of this study focus on sexual empowerment—"women's perception of their right to sexual and reproductive health and equity"—in relation to contraceptive use, how this sexual empowerment is constituted relates to educational (formal education), economic (increasing income), social (unmarried), and religious (Christian) factors in Ghana (see table 8.1 for a comparison of fertility rates and completion of secondary school in ten African countries).

The figures on contraceptive use from the 2008 Nigerian DHS suggest that this pattern of differential use of contraceptives is also the case in Nigeria; in the North West, North Central, and North East zones of Nigeria, contraceptive use is considerable lower and fertility is higher than in the southern parts of the country (tables 8.2, 8.3).[64] While the Muslim women's organization FOMWAN (Federation of Muslim Women Associations of Nigeria) has been involved in women's reproductive health initiatives in northern Nigeria, it appears that greater involvement of women at all levels of society in northern Nigeria in discussions about maternal/child health, family size, and sexual empowerment (although the latter two topics may not be considered socially appropriate for public debate) would be critically important for ascertaining appropriate means for the provision of family-planning methods there. As Dixon-Mueller and Germain have noted more generally:

> Policy decisions relating to childbearing and the delivery of family planning and health services have the potential to affect the lives of women of all social classes in fundamental ways. Whether policies have a positive or negative impact may depend on the integration of women from diverse backgrounds into the decision-making process. Whether or not women are recognized—and recognize themselves—as a primary constituency in population and family planning decisions is, therefore, a key public policy issue.[65]

Population Policy "Misconceptions" in Nigeria

Following the Nigerian population policies of 1988 and 2005, the recent focus of the London Summit program of contraception provision suggests that the sponsors of such an approach have come back to the initial position of some demographers, social scientists, international aid workers, and government officials—that provision of contraceptives will lower fertility and solve development problems.[66] Almost twenty years ago, Lant Pritchett argued that "because fertility is principally determined by the desires for children, contraceptive access (or cost) or family planning effort more generally is not a dominant, or typically even a major, factor in determining fertility differences."[67] A return to a strategy that did not work in the past and is unlikely to work in northern Nigeria (precisely where the poorest women with the highest fertility reside) raises the question of why the 2012 London Summit on Family Planning was supported by many European and Asian donor countries, international foundations, and recipient countries such as Nigeria.[68]

A consideration of James Ferguson's analysis of development projects is useful for thinking about this recent population initiative and Nigerian population policy documents. As he observes:

> "Development" institutions generate their own forms of discourse and this discourse simultaneously constructs Lesotho [or one could substitute *population* here] as a particular kind of object of knowledge and creates a structure of knowledge around that object. Interventions are then organized on the basis of this structure of knowledge, which, while "failing" on their own terms, nonetheless have regular effects, which include the expansion and entrenchment of bureaucratic state power.[69]

Thus while levels of fertility and maternal/child mortality rates are high and contraceptive use rates are low in Nigeria, the National Population Commission of Nigeria has a board of directors, an informational website with documents and publication, and an office and staff in Abuja (as do the UNFPA, WHO, the World Bank, the UK DFID, and the Gates Foundation).

Aside from establishing their institutional bureaucratic framework, the National Population Commission was also responsible for developing a strategic plan for the implementation of programs relating to the 2005 population policy. The strategic plan is divided into subsections addressing different population issues (table 8.4), with gridded pages with headings listing "Expected result by components of sub-sectors," Specific Strategies," "Activities," "OVI [objectively verifiable indicators]," "MOV [means of verification]," Responsible Agency," "Resources Required," and "Time Frame." The authors of the strategic plan note that its purpose "is to ensure the full implementation of the [Population] Policy and to achieve its goal" of improving the lives of Nigerian citizens.[70] The resemblance of the 2012 London Summit's plan to establish FP2020 Task Team and Working Groups—which will also have its own plan of action "to support the design and implementation of global and national accountability and M&E [monitoring and evaluation] arrangements"—to the Nigerian 2008 strategic plan suggests that developing and producing documents "to support data collection and reporting, and accountability frameworks" and writing reports based on program evaluations are a primary function of these projects, rather than effecting socioeconomic changes that might actually achieve the goals of these policies and programs. Aside from their authors' affection for acronyms, these documents reflect a particular discourse and structure of knowledge about population that, as Ferguson explains, supports these interventions and strengthens bureaucratic state and, in this case, nongovernmental organization power in Nigeria.

The importance of nongovernmental organizations in population policies and programs raises another point made by Ferguson, namely the role that politics plays in development interventions, even if any mention of politics is muted. While population policies have supported the expansion of Nigerian federal and state bureaucracies, these policies and the family-planning programs associated with them, have been underwritten by bilateral, international, and nongovernmental organizations. The demographer Rachel Robinson, in her study of the population policy adoption in Nigeria, discusses the roles of donors such as World Bank- and USAID-supported organizations such as the Futures Group and Family Health International in its initial policy formulation. She also raises the possibility that the 1988 population policy was implemented by Babangida as a political strategy for placating donors, thus receiving considerable funds for family-planning programs.[71]

Nonetheless, as the sociologist Marcel Mauss observed, "All gifts beg a return," and in this case, the acceptance of funds for developing a population policy and implementing population programs undermines the power of the state by introducing policies and programs determined by outsiders, as the letter writer to the *Guardian* cited earlier suggests. The historian Matthew Connelly, in his book *Fatal Misconception*, has described this situation as "Empire Lite," whereby "international and nongovernmental organizations exercise stewardship on behalf of the 'international community,' . . . albeit with the best of intentions."[72] The nongovernmental organizations' focus on population and family-planning programs in Nigeria, accepted by government officials without a national conversation about these issues, is reminiscent of colonialism and indirect rule. Despite the fact these policies and programs such as the 2012 London Summit on Family Planning are questioned by many ordinary Nigerians, international organizations such as DFID, the Gates Foundation, and UNFPA, which purport to speak for the global community, are able "to make rules for other people without having to answer for them," which the Nigerian government must, at times, have to do.[73] While Nigerian government officials may ignore the three questions raised by the Nigerian journalist Aminu Magashi about the implications of distributing free contraception, people's rejection of this program and their refusal to cooperate in other "global" population-related initiatives, particularly in northern Nigeria, without a significant improvement in health, education, and employment opportunities, are likely to perpetuate high levels of fertility and maternal/child mortality. As Connelly notes, "The great tragedy of population control, the fatal misconception, was to think that one could know other people's interests better than they knew it [*sic*] themselves."[74]

Conclusion

> A senior colleague, during a meeting in Abuja on ICPD + 20 (International Conference on Population and Development) mentioned jokingly that no one could fault Nigeria in making good policies, strategies, and declarations of commitment on any issue related to health. We are only at fault in implementation.[75]

After twenty-five years with a population policy in place and after millions of dollars spent on family-planning programs in Nigeria, one might ask why women, on average, in Nigeria as of 2008 were projected to have almost six children within their lifetimes. Or to be more specific, why, when indicators associate higher levels of women's education and income with lower fertility, particularly in the federal capital territory of Abuja, and in Lagos State (see table 8.3), has there not been a countrywide push to improve this situation? Similarly, if high levels of infant and under-five mortality led families to have large families as insurance against future deaths, why hasn't the primary healthcare system been renovated and reimplemented? And why haven't potable water and electricity been made available to all rural Nigerian citizens, as is the case of Ghana and other African countries (table 8.3)? Some progress may be seen in southwestern Nigeria, where the economy, particularly in Lagos State, is doing relatively well, where 62.3 percent of women graduate from secondary school, where infant mortality is the lowest in the country, and many Yoruba Christians (and some Yoruba Muslims) accept Western education and values. There couples are having smaller families (tables 8.2 and 8.3).[76] For these women, population policy messages may make sense and the provision of free contraceptives may help them to space their children and possibly reduce the size of their families. However, in many parts of northeastern Nigeria, where many live in impoverished circumstances, where economic growth is hampered by a lack of infrastructure, government planning, and political insecurity,[77] where infant and child mortality rates are the highest in the country, and where the percentage of women with secondary education is half that among southwestern Nigerian women, the population policy in and of itself makes little sense. Furthermore, religious beliefs about fertility and the moral basis of life as well as suspicions held by Muslim Hausa northerners about the motivations for Western-sponsored public health, and specifically population interventions, mean that a free contraceptive program would not be readily accepted. As Pritchett and others have observed, "since many couples in developing countries currently perceive they are better off with large families, the best (and perhaps the only palatable) way to reduce fertility is to change the economic and social conditions that make large families desirable."[78] Indeed, under the present economic and political circumstances, many Nigerians have their own ideas about appropriate family size and interpretations of population policy.

Notes

1. "Editorial: Structural Adjustment and Health in Africa," *Lancet* 335 (1990): 885–86; Elisha P. Renne, *Population and Progress in a Yoruba Town* (Ann Arbor: University of Michigan Press, 2003), 12–14.
2. Elisha P. Renne, "Population Policy, Development, and Family Planning Programs in Northern Nigeria," *Studies in Family Planning* 27 (1996): 107–14.
3. Federal Office of Statistics, Nigeria, *Nigeria Demographic and Health Survey 1990* (Columbia, Md.: IRD Macro International, 1992).
4. The modern contraceptive use rate was estimated at 10 percent. Modern contraceptives include: the pill, injectable contraceptives, IUDs, condoms, implants, and diaphragms. Other contraceptive methods include withdrawal, the rhythm method, and abstinence. Postcoital contraceptives such as Postinor are not listed in the Nigerian demographic and health surveys. Elisha P. Renne, "Postinor Use Among Young Women in Southwestern Nigeria: A Research Note," *Reproductive Health Matters* 6 (1998): 107–14.
5. UK Department for International Development (UK DFID) and the Bill and Melinda Gates Foundation. London Summit on Family Planning—July 2012, http://www.londonfamilyplanningsummit.co.uk/, accessed December 25, 2012.
6. Olayemi Ibrahim, "100m Nigerians in Absolute Poverty, Bureau Says," *Daily Trust*, February 14, 2012, www.dailytrust.com, accessed February 14, 2012.
7. UK DFID and the Gates Foundation, "London Summit."

8. Ruth Dixon-Mueller and Adrienne Germain, "Population Policy and Feminist Political Action in Three Developing Countries," *Population and Development Review, Supplement* 20 (1994): 197–219.
9. James Ferguson, *The Anti-Politics Machine: "Development," Depoliticization, and Bureaucratic Power in Lesotho* (New York: Cambridge University Press, 1990).
10. J. C. Caldwell, I. O. Orubuloye, and P. Caldwell, "Fertility Decline in Africa: A New Type of Transition?" *Population and Development Review* 18 (1992): 211–42; G. O. Ehusani, *The Politics of Population Control* (Zaria, Nigeria: Ahmadu Bello University Press, 1994); Renne, *Population and Progress.*
11. Indeed, abstinence is considered to be a contraceptive technique in recent Nigerian Demographic and Health Surveys.
12. Colonial officials generated numerous reports documenting health initiatives and formulating ordinances such as the Vital Statistics Birth and Death Ordinance announced in the *Annual Gazette*, which were largely unenforced and unenforceable.
13. Renne, *Population and Progress*, 62–64.
14. The IPPF was founded in London in 1952, with Margaret Sanger as its first president.
15. For example, in 1970, the PPFN and IPPF-London sponsored the making of the film *My Brother's Children*, about the head of a small urban Nigerian family who sought to convince his rural brother to have fewer children in order to "raise them better." His arguments had little effect on the brother or on rural viewers to whom the film was shown. See F. O. Okejiji and W. Ogionwo, "Experiment in Population Education and Attitude Change: An Evaluation of the Film 'My Brother's Children'," in *Two Rural Nigerian Communities* (London and Ibadan: African Regional Council of the International Planned Parenthood Federation and the Family Planning Council of Nigeria, 1973).
16. J. A. Ebigbola, "National Population Policy: A Viable Option to Human Development," in *Population and Development Issues: Ideas and Debates*, ed. P. O. Olusanya, J. A. Ebigbola, and E. P. Renne (Ibadan: African BookBuilders, 2000), 10–11.
17. Ebigbola, "National Population Policy," 11.
18. Ebigbola, "National Population Policy," 13.
19. According to Olukunle Adegbola, the Nigerian government approached the World Bank for the provision of a credit to finance the development of the National Population Policy. Olukunle Adegbola, "Population Policy Implementation in Nigeria, 1988–2003," *Population Review* 47 (2008): 62.
20. Oluwole Olatimehin, "Some Aspects of Family Planning Programmes and Fertility in Selected ECA Member States," Working Paper, *African Population Studies Series, No. 9* (Addis Adaba: UNECA, 1985). Professor Ransome-Kuti also supported the revision of the abortion laws in Nigeria, although public response against the legalization of some forms of abortion led to Babangida abandoning the proposal in 1992. Elisha Renne, "Abortion as Illegal Conduct and Its Sequelae," *Curare: Studies in Ethnomedicine* 29 (2006): 81–95.

21. In June 1980, at its twenty-seventh session, the Governing Council of the United Nations Development Program (UNDP) approved UNFPA assistance in the amount of $1.2 million over a five-year period, to support a population policy formulation and development planning component of its 1981–86 assistance of $17.3 million to Nigeria . . . UNFPA-funded program costing $17.3 million being executed over a five-year period (1981–86). About half of this sum ($8.3 million) was earmarked for maternal and child health and family planning (MCH/FP) while population information, education, and communication accounted for $2.15 million. See Adegbola, "Population Policy," 61; see also Fred T. Sai and Lauren A. Chester, "The Role of the World Bank in Shaping Third World Population Policy," in *Population Policy: Contemporary Issues,* ed. Godfrey Roberts (New York: Praeger, 1990), 189.
22. Adegbola, "Population Policy," 61.
23. Ransome-Kuti, as cited by Rachel Sullivan Robinson, "Negotiating Development Prescriptions: The Case of Population Policy in Nigeria," *Population Research Policy Review* 31 (2012): 284.
24. Michael Reid, "Nigeria Still Searching for Right Formula," *Bulletin of the World Health Organization* 86 (2008): 657–736; Abubakar Umar, "No Free EPI Vaccines to States From '90," *New Nigerian*, October 27, 1989.
25. Aliyu Machika, Halima Musa, Yusha'u A. Ibrahim, and Lawal Ibrahim, "Primary Health Care Centres in Shambles," *Daily Trust*, September 21, 2008, www.dailytrust.com, accessed September 21, 2008.
26. See also Ebere Ameh, "Contraceptives Do Not Stop Child and Maternal Death, Good Governance Does," *The Guardian*, November 17, 2012, www.guardiannewsng.com, accessed December 15, 2012; Aminu Magashi, "Mr. President and Maternal Mortality in Nigeria," *Daily Trust*, December 20, 2011, www.dailytrust.com, accessed December 20, 2011.
27. Renne, *Population and Progress*, 12–13.
28. Helen Nene Avong, "Perception of, and Attitudes Toward, the Nigerian Federal Population Policy, Family Planning Program and Family Planning in Kaduna State Nigeria," *African Journal of Reproductive Health* 4 (2000): 66–76.
29. Renne, "Population Policy," 131.
30. Avong, "Perception of, and Attitudes Toward, the Nigerian Federal Population Policy," 73.
31. Adegbola, "Population Policy," 61. Later known as the National Commission on Population, a parastatal department (under the authority of the Office of the Presidency), "the Commission was reconstituted in 2001 with a Chairman and 37 members representing each state of the federation and the Federal Capital Territory," National Population Commission of Nigeria.
32. Adegbola, "Population Policy," 101–2.
33. Ebigbola, "National Population Policy," 17.
34. See United Nations Population Fund, Nakar-Ngor Parliamentary Declaration, *Global Population Policy Update* 28, June 11, 2004, http:www.unfpa.org/public/

cache/bypass/parliamentarians/pid/3615;jsessionid=F8E20729780244127A926 82076D2954F?newsLId=7221, accessed December 29, 2012.

35. See United Nations Environmental Program (UNEP), Rio Declaration on Environment and Development, 1992, http://www.unep.org/documents .multilingual/default.asp?documentid=78&articleid=1163, accessed December 29, 2012.
36. C. Alison McIntosh and Jason L. Finkle, "The Cairo Conference on Population and Development: A New Paradigm?" *Population and Development Review* 21 (1995): 223–60.
37. Federal Government of Nigeria, "National Policy on Population for Sustainable Development" (Abuja: Federal Government of Nigeria, 2004), x.
38. National Population Commission (NPC) [Nigeria] and ICF Macro, *Nigeria Demographic and Health Survey 2008* (Abuja, Nigeria: National Population Commission and ICF Macro, 2009); see also Oladele Arowolo, "Designing a National Programme for Population Policy Implementation," in *Population and Development Issues: Ideas and Debates*, ed. J. A. Ebigbola and E. P. Renne (Ibadan: African BookBuilders, 2000), 25–47.
39. National Population Commission (NPC) [Nigeria] and ICF Macro, vii.
40. National Population Commission (NPC) [Nigeria] and ICF Macro.
41. Lawan D. Adamu, "Polio Returns with Menace in Kano," *Weekly Trust*, November 5, 2011, www.dailytrust.com, accessed November 5, 2011. As a consequence of the condition of their village clinic, people refused to allow visiting immunization teams for the Polio Eradication Initiative to vaccinate their children. (See also Ruby Leo and Judd-Leonard Okafor, "Weighty Effects of Birth Control on Polio Eradication," *Daily Trust*, July 10, 2012, 51.) One health worker told me that she knew of three villages in northern Nigeria where local clinics were renovated in exchange for parental permission for polio vaccination.
42. Daniel Smith, "Patronage, Per Diems and the 'Workshop Mentality': The Practice of Family Planning Programs in Southeastern Nigeria," *World Development* 31 (2003): 710.
43. Smith, "Patronage, Per Diems and the 'Workshop Mentality'," 712–13.
44. Ebigbola, "National Population Policy," 20.
45. According to the *Nigerian Demographic Health Survey 2008*, the total fertility rate (TFR) for Nigeria was 5.7, the same TFR as was reported in the *Nigerian Demographic Health Survey 2003* (see table 8.1). The national TFR for the three years prior to 2013 would need to be 5.1 to satisfy this reduction. According to preliminary results of the *Nigerian Demographic Health Survey 2013*, the countrywide TFR is 5.5.
46. National Population Commission (NPC) [Nigeria] and ICF Macro; see also Judd-Leonard Okafor, "Muslim Women Opt for Hormonal Contraception," *Sunday Trust*, December 9, 2012, www.dailytrust.com, accessed December 12, 2012. The percentages of women reporting preferred methods is much higher

than the number of women currently using any method, although the four methods mentioned and used are the same.

47. UK DFID and the Gates Foundation, "London Summit."
48. Aminu Magashi, "2nd National Family Planning Conference; Matters Arising," *Daily Trust*, December 11, 2012, www.dailytrust.com, accessed December 12, 2012.
49. UK DFID and the Gates Foundation, "London Summit."
50. At the time, the Cairo conference statements were highly contested, both by religious leaders who were opposed to various forms of abortion and contraceptives and by some NGOs involved in family planning who saw the move to reproductive health as weakening the focus of their program of fertility reduction. See McIntosh and Finkle, "The Cairo Conference."
51. Judd-Leonard Okafor, "Nigeria's Christian, Muslim Leaders Back Population Control," *Daily Trust*, November 28, 2012, www.dailytrust.com, accessed December 12, 2012. This acceptance was greeted with skepticism by one reader of this *Daily Trust* news report, who wrote, "I am disgusted. What is growing beyond sustainable level is corruption and not population."
52. Sanusi Abubukar, "Jonathan and His Proposed Population Control Law," *Daily Trust*, July 3, 2012, 56.
53. Beenzu Nwosu, letter to the editor, "Melissa Gates and Africa's Population," *The Guardian*, August 29, 2012, www.guardiannews.com, accessed December 28, 2012.
54. Magashi, "2nd Family Planning Conference."
55. Renne, "Population Policy"; Elisha P. Renne, *The Politics of Polio in Northern Nigeria* (Bloomington: Indiana University Press, 2010). Indeed a news story reported immediately after President Jonathan's free family-planning announcement discussed its impact on the polio vaccination initiative that distributes polio vaccine and other health incentives free of charge. See Leo and Okafor, "Weighty Effects."
56. Renne, *Politics of Polio*, 14.
57. Adegbola, "Population Policy," 104 n. 10.
58. Lant H. Pritchett, "Desired Fertility and the Impact of Population Policies," *Population and Development Review* 20 (1994): 42.
59. Teresa Castro Martín, "Women's Education and Fertility: Results from 26 Demographic and Health Surveys," *Studies in Family Planning* 26 (1995): 187–202.
60. Dixon-Mueller and Germain, "Population Policy," 204.
61. Dixon-Mueller and Germain, "Population Policy," 204.
62. Martín, "Women's Education and Fertility."
63. Halley P. Crissman, Richard M. Adanu, and Siobán D. Harlow, "Women's Sexual Empowerment and Contraceptive Use in Ghana," *Studies in Family Planning* 43 (2012): 201.
64. In southwestern Nigeria, the population is dominated by groups claiming a Yoruba ethnic identity; approximately half are Christian and half are Muslim.
65. Dixon-Mueller and Germain, "Population Policy," 197.

66. Paul Demeny, "Social Science and Population Policy," *Population and Development Review* 14 (1988): 451–79; Dennis Hodgson, "Demography as Social Science and Policy Science," *Population and Development Review* 9 (1983): 1–34.
67. Pritchett, "Desired Fertility and the Impact of Population Policies," 39.
68. UK DFID and the Gates Foundation, "London Summit on Family Planning"—Summary of Commitments—December 2012. http://www.londonfamilyplanningsummit.co.uk/, accessed December 25, 2012.
69. Ferguson, *The Anti-Politics Machine*, xiv.
70. National Population Commission (NPC) [Nigeria] and ICF Macro, vii.
71. Robinson, "Negotiating Development Prescriptions," 276, 288. "Nigeria did receive large amounts of funding for population activities following adoption of the policy. The World Bank issued Nigeria a credit of $78.5 million for the National Population Project, to be administered by the Population Activities Fund Agency, an organization created specifically for that task. . . . The World Bank–funded National Population Project was approved in 1991 and in addition to provision of family planning, emphasized institutional restructuring. . . . USAID also gave $67 million, making Nigeria the number-one recipient of population aid from the agency at the time" (Robinson, "Negotiating Development Prescriptions," 289).
72. Matthew Connelly, *Fatal Misconception: The Struggle to Control World Population* (Cambridge, Mass.: Belknap Press of Harvard University Press, 2008), 379.
73. The nationwide strike against fuel price increases in January 2012 is just such an example of citizens effectively forcing their government to back down on an unpopular program. See Amina Alhassan, Mulkat Mukaila, Imaobong Esu, Hamisu Mohammed, Francis Okeke, Ismail Mudashir, Rukaiya Aliyu, Halima Musa, and Rakiya Mohammed, "Why 'Occupy Nigeria' Protests are Spreading," *Weekly Trust*, January 7, 2012, www.dailytrust.com, accessed January 7, 2012. Furthermore, the Nigerian government does to not always carry through on its commitment to international partners. As of January 2014, the 2013 allocation for reproductive health services promised during the 2012 London Summit on Family planning had not been released.
74. Connelly, *Fatal Misconception*, 378.
75. Aminu Magashi, "Another Health Commitment by Nigeria." *Daily Trust*, October 30, 2012, www.dailytrust.com, accessed December 14, 2012.
76. See also Smith, "Patronage, Per Diems and the 'Workshop Mentality'."
77. The Islamic group Jama'atu Ahlus-Sunnah Lidda'Awati Wal Jihad (JASLWJ), popularly known as Boko Haram (literally, "Western education is forbidden") is said to be responsible for over seven hundred deaths in 2012, although military police have been accused of violence as well (Agence France-Presse, "Attacks Tied to Islamic Sect Kill at Least 30 in Nigeria," *New York Times*, October 21, 2012, A18.). In the first three months of 2014, Amnesty International reported fifteen hundred deaths in northeastern Nigeria attributed to Boko Haram and to the Nigerian military police. The resulting sense of insecurity has been felt in many parts of northern Nigeria.
78. Pritchett, "Desired Fertility and the Impact of Population Policies," 41.

9

Liberation without Contraception?

The Rise of the Abortion Empire and Pronatalism in Socialist and Postsocialist Russia

MIE NAKACHI

In the beginning of the twentieth century, the Soviet Union introduced some of the world's most progressive policies to advance women's positions in both the public and private spheres. After the 1917 revolution, legal equality between men and women was guaranteed. In 1920, the Soviet Union became the first country in the world to legalize abortion on demand. Young women enjoyed legal guarantees for equal educational opportunities with young men, and a large number of Soviet women entered universities in the 1930s. After the revolution, women took up professions traditionally considered men's, such as aviation, tractor operation, engineering, science, and medicine. Already by 1940 women represented approximately 40 percent of the labor force, and between 1970 and the end of the socialist regime, this percentage was consistently over 50 percent. In the field of national politics women's achievements were more modest, but at local levels female deputies were quite visible before World War II. These were significant achievements, even in comparison with North America and western Europe, where feminist calls for women's advancement crystallized as a movement only in the 1960s. Along many vectors, the USSR was the pioneer of women's liberation.

Despite benefiting from progressive policies that elevated women in society and the family, one area where Russian women lagged behind was the contraceptive revolution. The "contraceptive revolution" refers to the introduction and spread of modern contraception, first, the diaphragm and spermicides, and later birth control such as the pill, intrauterine devices, and safe sterilization. In North America and western Europe, the introduction of modern contraception was extremely important in expanding women's roles outside the home, allowing women to effectively avoid, delay, and generally plan the timing of pregnancy. The availability of modern contraception also had a role in dramatically reducing fertility, in particular, the number of unwanted pregnancies. This was all the more remarkable since the sexual revolution of the 1960s in the West, which promoted the idea of women's sexual freedom, could have resulted in a higher rate of unwanted pregnancies. The contraceptive revolution contributed to the sexual revolution by separating women's sexuality from their childbearing functions.[1]

Soviet scholars have generally argued that there was no sexual revolution in Russia. Likewise Soviet citizens considered themselves sexually conservative, as in the famous pronouncement of the Soviet Everywoman: "We don't have sex."[2] In contrast to the abundance of sexual depictions in the entertainment industry, popular literature, and advertisements of the capitalist West, indeed, Soviet official culture looked rather prudish. However, by the 1970s, under the veneer of this official conservatism, women, especially, began to ignore taboos against nonconjugal and premarital sex as well as other injunctions mandating conservative sexual values. Indeed, the divorce rate in the Soviet Union was one of the highest in the world. I have argued elsewhere that Soviet-era fears about population decline and the resulting official pronatalist policy after World War II were decisive in encouraging the separation of sex and marriage in the Soviet Union. This unexpectedly led to a kind of state-led postwar sexual revolution in Russia.[3]

Not surprisingly, the experience of an early twentieth-century regime of legal abortion, together with a midcentury sexual revolution without modern contraception, created an abortion empire, where according to the existing official abortion statistics, women had, on average, four abortions.[4] Experts have estimated that the "true" level of abortions was higher by something between 10 and 50 percent.[5] Why did abortion become the primary method of fertility control? Why was modern contraception never widely introduced in the Soviet Union? This chapter attempts to answer these questions.

The fall of the Soviet Union in 1991 was a major historical turning point, ending the bipolar world of Cold War military, political, economic, and cultural conflicts. The Communist Party (CPSU) control over politics, economics, society, and culture ended, and private ownership, the market economy, and democratic multiparty elections were introduced. The end of communism also meant the end of the Soviet socialist welfare system, and most important, free education and medical care. However, despite radical changes in many areas, the end of the Communist regime in Russia has not brought an end to the abortion empire. My analysis will therefore link reproductive policies of socialist and postsocialist Russia in a long twentieth century that continues until today.

The Soviet case shows how interactions among ideological promises, a centrally planned modernization scheme, and subsequent demographic changes together shaped reproductive policies in a socialist country. What we see here is not only ideology shaping reproductive politics, but also reproductive practice and demography shaping politics.[6] As an ideology of development, socialism could support a wide range of reproductive policies, from legal to criminalized abortion, or from pronatalist to antinatalist policies. The Soviet Union's broad influence took this model beyond Russian borders to the whole socialist world, as illustrated in the conclusion.

This chapter discusses three themes that affected the development of reproductive policies in Soviet and postsocialist Russia. First, I discuss the socialist ideology of population, women, and reproduction. Socialism had a distinct vision of demographic development and the role of women. This vision influenced Soviet demographic and reproductive policies, as well as the justification for introducing these policies. Abortion and contraception policies were also informed by socialist ideology.

Second, I analyze the development of abortion, contraception, and family policies. One of the characteristics of socialist ideology was that it rejected neither abortion nor contraception, even if they were not considered essential for socialist reproduction. After revolutionary ideology dictated the 1920 legalization of abortion, abortion and contraception policies were influenced by pronatalism, first emphasizing quantity, and then quality. This shift corresponded to criminalization in 1936, and then to relegalization in 1955. I analyze these changes and identify key causes in the postwar period that led to relegalization. Similarly, contraceptive policy paralleled abortion policy—available while abortion was legal, and prohibited when criminalized. However, a major departure occurred in the early 1970s, when the development of modern contraception was decisively halted, apparently by a demographic policy decision at the highest levels.

Third, I discuss demographic policy and the development of demography as a discipline in the Soviet Union. The shift in the modern state's population thinking from quantity to quality is often associated with the Malthusian theory of "overpopulation" and the subsequent development of statistical techniques and demographic studies. As Soviet population policy was based on anti-Malthusianism, it did not fit neatly into this model. Insisting on quantity, Stalin disregarded statistics and demographic studies to the point that demography became a disgraced field between the late 1930s and late 1950s. When a new approach to population policy became possible after the death of Stalin in 1953, women demanded that the state legalize abortion in order to improve their reproductive experiences. But concerns about quality and future economic development then took on an ethnonationalistic dimension, as demographers made a comeback in the 1960s and attempted to convince the policymakers of the usefulness of their science in the 1970s. This development of a new demographic debate in the 1970s decisively terminated Russia's opportunity to end the abortion empire.

Socialist Ideology of Population and Reproduction

There is no single text that outlines socialist population ideology. Rather, some key texts defined socialist views on population, reproduction, abortion, and contraception. The core of Soviet population ideology is characterized as anti-Malthusian and anti-neo-Malthusian. Malthusian population theories posited that there was an optimal level of population for a state, depending on the level of resources and food production. Malthus's proposition was significant because it challenged the conventional view of the eighteenth century that the greater the population, the stronger and more prosperous a state could become. Malthus argued that "overpopulation," or excessive population, could actually make a state weaker and poorer. Without sufficient resources, the excess population would become impoverished, creating economic, social, political, and public health problems. The underlying argument was that some countries, such as England, were already approaching this optimal level, creating widespread misery in that country and elsewhere.[7]

Malthus's theory questioned the efficacy of the English Poor Law, originally enacted in 1601 to provide the poor with minimum support at the level of subsistence. He argued that such a law actually increased poverty by raising wages, increasing unemployment, and encouraging indulgent practices, in particular, early marriage, childbearing, and drinking. In his view, the poorest should be left alone; then they would practice late marriage and childbirth, reducing the birth rate. Without the Poor Law, the population would not grow beyond what the available supply of food could support, and poverty would not spread further.[8] Drawing on his beliefs as an Anglican priest, Malthus promoted late childbirth not through use of contraception, but through moral strength and abstinence.[9]

In their central works, Marx and Engels rejected Malthusian theory as a bourgeois ideology, masking the main evil of our times, namely, unequal class relations under capitalism. Engels published his first attack on Malthus in 1844 in *Outlines of a Critique of Political Economy*:

> Now the consequence of this [Malthus's] theory is that since it is precisely the poor who constitute this surplus population, nothing ought to be done for them, except to make it as easy as possible for them to starve to death; to convince them that this state of affairs cannot be altered and that there is no salvation for their entire class other than that they should propagate as little as possible. . . . We shall destroy the contradiction simply by resolving it . . . there will disappear the antithesis between surplus population in one place and surplus wealth in another, and also the wonderful phenomenon—more wonderful than all the wonders of all the religions put together—that a nation must starve to death from sheer wealth and abundance; and there will disappear too the crazy assertion that the earth does not possess the power to free mankind.[10]

In the fourth volume of *Capital*, Marx goes further insisting that for Malthus a "deep baseness of thought is typical, the kind of baseness that only a priest could allow himself, [the kind that] sees poverty as punishment for sin."[11]

Malthusianism simply assumed that affluent people would have access to resources and wealth, hindering both efficient development of production and fair distribution of goods and food to the rest of the population. Under communism, Marx argued, the means of production would be nationalized, assuring efficient and sufficient production of food and other goods, which would then be distributed fairly to the population, each according to her or his needs, enabling the state to support a much larger population than Malthus had suggested.

In this way, the dialogue with Malthus defined the socialist view of anti-overpopulation: *socialist* society could sustain a growing population. But would there ever be a limit to the growth? Marx himself was not particularly concerned about whether or not "ultimately" there would be a limit to the optimal population size a state could support, given limited resources even in the ideal world of communism. It probably seemed likely to him that if there would be a limit, it was still far away. Engels too did not think "the question [of overpopulation] to be at all a burning one." However, he did express his thoughts about the "abstract possibility" of overpopulation, arguing logically, if hypothetically, that if there could be overpopulation in the future, realization of the socialist system would be even more urgent, because only "enlightened" workers under socialism would have the "moral restraint upon the instinct for reproduction which Malthus himself puts forward as the easiest and most effective countermeasure against overpopulation." Elaborating on this vision of socialism in a letter to Karl Kautsky, the German Marxist leader, on February 1, 1881, Engels wrote,

> But if at some stage communist society finds itself obliged to regulate the production of human beings, just as it has already come to regulate the production of things, it will be precisely this society, and this society alone, which can carry this out without difficulty. It does not seem to me that it would be at all difficult in such a society to achieve by planning a result which has already been produced spontaneously, without planning, in France and Lower Austria. At any rate, it is for the people in the communist society themselves to decide whether, when, and how this is to be done, and what means they wish to employ for the purpose. I do not feel called upon to make proposals or give them [professorial socialists who ask for answers on the issue of overpopulation] advice about it.[12]

As shown below, this letter became crucial for the development of China's one-child policy almost a hundred years later.

More urgent and important for Marx and Engels was to critique Western capitalist thinking, which justified large families for the rich, if they chose, but pressed the poor to keep their families small. As a poor family man himself, Marx would have understood these pressures well. Marx and Engels consistently strove to uncover and condemn the "subtext" of Malthusian overpopulation, which actually encouraged and justified villainous actions of the upper against the lower classes.

August Bebel, one of the grand theorists of women's liberation under socialism (together with Engels), had a clear vision about the issue of overpopulation that he expressed in his seminal text, *Woman in the Past, Present, and Future*.[13] "Overpopulation" is the last major theme discussed in the third part of the book, "Woman in the Future." Here Bebel clarifies Engels on the tie between population and women's liberation by claiming that overpopulation under socialism is impossible because liberated women, who engage in economic, political, social, and cultural activities, will themselves want to regulate the number of children:

> We must finally take into account that woman will occupy a totally different position in the society of the future, and will have no inclination to bring a large number of children, as "gifts of God," into the world; that she will desire to enjoy her freedom and independence, and not to spend half or three quarters of the best years of her life in a state of pregnancy, or with a child at her breast. Certainly there are few women who do not wish to have a child, but still fewer who wish to have more than a limited number. All these things will work together in regulating the numbers of human beings, without there being any need for our Malthusians to rack their brains at present. The question will be solved at last, without any injurious abstinence or any repellent preventive measures.[14]

Under socialism, according to Bebel, women would understand their interests and exert their will to slow population growth, even without contraception.

This discussion of overpopulation and women's liberation reveals, of course, certain unresolved theoretical tensions. Regarding population growth, Marxism argues that in the world of socialism, workers' improved living conditions would support many children, leading to population growth. From the perspective of women's liberation, however, Bebel argues that women under socialism will want to have fewer children, implying a declining birth rate and forestalling overpopulation. Another unresolved issue was contraception. Clearly, Marxists were against the promotion of contraception or abstinence even under socialism but did not offer any practicable alternative to the use of contraception. How were liberated women supposed to limit the number of births? These inconsistencies left room for a range of interpretations and rationales when the issue of fertility became a matter of policy in the Soviet Union. In particular, since abortion was not explicitly condemned, it could be interpreted either as an acceptable or unacceptable method of fertility control from the theoretical point of view. Contraception was also not entirely rejected. However, abortion and contraception were not treated exactly the same way, either. Abortion was understood as a common practice of fertility control among peasants and working women. On the other hand, contraception was often frowned upon as a tool for bourgeois indulgence in sexual pleasure.

Not surprising, Lenin's views on Malthus followed Marx's closely. In his only known article on the subject, published in *Pravda* on June 16, 1913

(O.S.) above the initials "V. I." and entitled "The Working Class and Neo-Malthusianism," Lenin considered the adoption by a congress of doctors of a resolution against criminal punishment for women who underwent abortion. Dr. N. A. Vigdorchik, who had been active among Kiev Social Democrats in the 1890s and was an early visionary of the potential of motherhood under socialism, had spoken out to "welcome contraceptive measures" at the Congress.[15] Lenin explained to the readers of *Pravda* that the "stormy applause" did not surprise him since the "listeners were bourgeois, both middle and petty" applauding the "full mediocrity (*ubozhestvo*) of 'social neo-Malthusianism.'" Workers, on the other hand, wanted children. Lenin then nuanced his position by adding that Social Democrats would continue to demand the removal of all laws making abortion illegal or circumscribing the distribution of literature explaining contraception.[16]

This episode indicates Lenin's skepticism regarding legal abortion and the spread of contraception. He believed that only the bourgeoisie was enthusiastic about limiting childbirth, but not workers, who would rather be able to have more children. Lenin did, however, accept legalization and birth control education as a temporary measure because he recognized that under the tsarist government, workers, though reluctantly, regularly controlled fertility through dangerous underground abortion. Indeed, once Lenin took power, he legalized abortion as a temporary measure and tolerated contraception, although products were of poor quality and supplies limited. Lenin was willing to compromise with reality until such time as the workers would have a better life under communism, and neither legal abortion nor contraception would be necessary. Stalin would speak to this issue in 1936.

Soviet population ideology would follow the anti-Malthusian line sketched by the founding fathers of Marxism-Leninism. By extension, high fertility among workers under communism came to be considered a sign of happiness among workers and a legitimization of the communist regime. Marxian anti-Malthusianism in the Soviet Union also led to the view that "true" women workers naturally wanted to give birth and would do so, given material support. If a woman worker decided not to become a mother, this could only reflect an impoverished economic and social environment. In the very distant future, under fully developed communism, women might legitimately want to limit the number of children or decide not to have a child.[17] In short, socialist population ideology was basically pronatalist, in the sense of its commitment to population growth and its expressed commitment to improving the lives of the laboring masses.

Another key feature of the socialist view of population was its ideological commitment to equality among all nationalities. Marxists criticized the oppression of the poor, which included different categories of people, such as women and ethnic minorities. Lenin was an anti-imperialist, and, reflecting this position, the Soviet Union became an "affirmative action empire" where ethnic minorities were given priority in higher education and job placement, especially in their "home" republics. Officially, all forms of racism, including anti-Semitism, were condemned. This was in stark contrast to many population policies developing in Europe. On the one hand, western European countries feared shrinking population and adopted pronatalist policies.[18] On the other hand, following Malthus, there was also a sense of contempt toward countries and societies with high fertility, particularly in colonies, where high fertility was regarded as a marker of the "less civilized parts of the world."[19] In this application, neo-Malthusian theory nurtured a powerful justification for promoting birth control among the poor and in poor countries.[20] The Soviet Union, by rejecting the Malthusian concept, claimed considerable moral high ground from which to challenge this European double standard. Where Marx saw Malthus as an aid to capitalists, the editorial footnote on neo-Malthusianism published in Lenin's 1961 *Complete Works* a century later notes that this theory "is widely used by contemporary ideologists of imperialism to justify the politics of colonialism and war preparations."[21]

Thus, the socialist ideology of reproduction and population can be characterized as anti-Malthusian and anti-neo-Malthusian, essentially pronatalist, anticontraception, and antiracist. It encouraged women's increased role in economy, politics, and society, but at the same time generally assumed that all right-minded women workers under socialism would become mothers and give birth to several children, supporting a necessary level of population growth under socialism. In the distant future women might want to limit their reproduction, but methods for achieving this goal were not explored further. Abortion was one of the most obvious possibilities, as it was prevalent among all classes of women, including workers and peasants, in spite of its criminality in many European and Christian nations. Socialists were wary of contraception because of its association with bourgeois practice, but nevertheless Lenin rather grudgingly accepted the need to spread contraceptive knowledge in order to distinguish socialism from the preceding Imperial Orthodox regime. Importantly in these writings by the founding fathers, the distinctiveness of socialist reproduction was mostly framed in terms of the relationship between working women and the state. There was little to no discussion of the new role and practice of working men in socialist reproduction.

Abortion without Contraception: The Making of an Abortion Empire

The theoretical discussions of population and reproduction shaped revolutionary policies governing abortion and contraception. However, after reality began to diverge from the theoretical predictions, demographic politics began to affect Soviet policies. There were three stages in the development of an abortion empire in Russia. First is the period between 1920 and 1936, when legalization was provided as one of the tools to differentiate the revolutionary regime from imperial Russia. Second is the period between 1936 and 1955, when abortion was criminalized as a part of an explicit pronatalist policy. This change was initiated by Stalin, who saw that, contrary to socialist prediction, population was not growing steadily in the 1930s. Then the demographic crisis caused by World War II encouraged the Soviet leadership to take further action to increase the birth rate. However, the extreme pronatalism of the 1944 Family Law with its implicit encouragement of out-of-wedlock births also drove up demand for illegal abortions. Mariia D. Kovrigina, who became the all-Union minister of health in 1954, the first woman to occupy this post, exercised strong initiative to change the existing abortion and contraception policies. Her greatest success, the legalization of abortion in 1955, forms the baseline for the third period, although the development and dissemination of modern contraception continued to be blocked by pronatalist concerns.

Revolutionary Legalization

After the 1917 October Revolution, the Bolshevik government introduced revolutionary policies to free society from religious influences and class and gender-based discrimination developed under the Romanov monarchy. The Family Law of 1918 proclaimed that only mutual consent of a man and a woman could be the basis for marriage, and that only civil marriage was legal. Authority over marriage registration was instantly transferred from religious authorities to the Soviet state. Revolutionary family law also eliminated legal distinctions between legitimate and illegitimate children so that all children would be equal before the law.[22] In 1920, abortion, illegal before the revolution, became legal. The Soviet Union became the first country in the world where any woman could receive a clinical abortion on demand. The Russian Orthodox Church's moral influence on women's reproductive decisions never completely diminished, but over time its impact on abortion became negligible throughout the Soviet period.[23]

This policy was the result of a socialist ideological position that aimed to alleviate hardship among poor women; progressive medical discourse supported this position. Medical professionals believed that illegal abortions were often damaging women's health probably because many illegal procedures were self-induced or performed by unskilled practitioners, *babki*, and at the time, there were no antibiotics to prevent the infections likely to occur when operations were performed in secret and less-than-sanitary settings.[24] Consistent with its modernizing mission, the Soviet regime provided women with clinical abortion, just one of the many public health services the Bolshevik regime would provide until the socialist government could transform Russia into a true socialist state where women could happily raise as many children as they wanted. Contraception, promoted as a better alternative than abortion, was being developed in the 1920s, but was always in short supply, and often ineffective.[25] Yet, because Russia was going through a series of destabilizing wars and revolutions that devastated its economy, ever larger numbers of women sought free clinical abortions, and the registered number of abortions soared in the 1920s.

Criminalization

As abortion was not recognized as a right of women, but as a revolutionary gift, the policy could change when the demands of the revolution changed. After Stalin began rapid industrialization in the late 1920s, young women went into factories on an unprecedented scale. Accordingly, the percentage of female labor in the overall labor force increased from 24 percent in 1928 to 39 percent in 1940.[26] The average number of children an adult woman gave birth to plummeted significantly, from 6.8 to 3.7 between the mid-1920s and mid-1930s.[27] To halt the declining birth rate, the Family Law of 1936 criminalized abortion, arguing that women, now educated and cultured under communism, and now presumably enjoying equality with men, were receiving everything necessary to raise children. This was in line with Stalin's 1935 proclamation, "Life has become better, life has become more cheerful."

Apparently during the public debate on the draft law, most women expressed negative views on the recriminalization, a position ignored by the law.[28]

The same Family Law that criminalized abortion granted mothers who had seven or more children large government subsidies for several years. This policy promoted the ideal of a large family and gave incentives to mothers with several children to have additional children. Almost certainly, this was an attempt to restore high fertility in rural areas, while the ban on abortion was aimed primarily at urban areas. This effort to glorify and reward highly fertile citizens developed variously, but remained in place until the end of the Soviet Union and reappeared in postsocialist Russia. Additionally, the law stated that the network of childcare institutions would be expanded, created more complex requirements for divorce registration, increased oversight for paternal child support, and introduced harsher punishments for those who failed to pay.[29]

Thus, this first pronatalist policy aimed to increase fertility by requiring Soviet working women to keep pregnancy to term and by increasing men's responsibility for reproduction. The important implication was that the new family law defined reproductive and productive roles of women in terms of state goals. With this law, reproduction and production became the most important obligations of Soviet women in their relationship to the state, while the state promised women that their male partners would share the responsibility of raising children materially (but not necessarily physically). The state also promised to provide a dependable social, legal, and economic environment for childrearing.

This pronatalist policy change did not, in fact, reduce abortions or increase fertility over time. In 1937 the birth rate increased and the registered number of abortions dropped dramatically from 1,932,118 (1935) to 570,926 (1937).[30] But reverse tendencies quickly began to appear as desperate women focused on new ways and means. Beginning in 1938, the number of nonclinical abortion cases rose steadily. The number of deaths from incomplete abortions that ended up in a medical institution also began to rise.[31] Prevalence of abortion was primarily due to the increasing numbers of women in the labor force throughout the 1930s and uncertainties regarding the future, due to the Great Terror purge and impending war.

Making matters worse for women, various services promised for working mothers were still inadequate in quantity and quality. In urban areas, the expansion of maternal healthcare and childcare facilities continued: the total number of permanent crèches increased to 62,000 in 1928 and then leaped to 600,900 in 1932.[32] Kindergartens, which accommodated children between the ages of three and six, expanded greatly during the First Five-Year Plan, and the total number went from 2,155 in 1927 to 19,611 in 1932 and 23,999 in 1940.[33] But doubts remained about the quality of care. There is much evidence to suggest that public childcare facilities were scarce and often not desirable places to send children because of inadequate supervision, unsanitary conditions, and unhealthy food. In the 1920s and 1930s babushkas (grandmothers or grandmother-like figures) seem to have been the primary childcare providers, and nannies were also available to a few privileged urban families.[34] Finally, housing for young couples was often unavailable, causing many husbands and wives to live separated from each other in factory dorms long after marrying or even to live in their parents' room until they could be allocated a separate room in an apartment, which often took years, especially before the 1960s.

Whatever the challenges for individuals, population growth became policy and Stalin's prognoses became law. When the 1937 census ran afoul of Stalin's personal statistics, the demographers were purged, making demography powerless and irrelevant as a field of research and policy formulation for a generation. These scholars were among the first victims of pronatalism. Promotion of high fertility probably had immediate positive effects only for a limited number of already fertile mothers who had more than six children. According to the law, for the seventh child, a mother would receive two thousand rubles per year for five years, which would have been a meaningful cash sum, especially in rural areas where most income was paid in kind.[35] In Moscow oblast, more than four thousand applications were said to have been submitted in the first month after the law was issued.[36] But clearly, 1 percent of fertile mothers could not have a significant impact on overall fertility, especially given the increasingly urban female population.[37]

One important implication of this policy in the long run was its effects in Central Asia, where fertility was particularly high. Culturally, this new aid for fertile mothers had the unintended consequence of promoting traditional Muslim values after a period of persecution in the 1920s.[38] Under pronatalism, fertile mothers in Central Asian villages, who had only recently been portrayed as "backward," became model Soviet mothers.[39] The celebration of fertile Central Asian mothers continued into the postwar period.

The full potential effect of the 1936 Family Law will never be known, as the Soviet Union's entrance into World War II began with the Winter War against Finland in 1939, only three years after the law was implemented. Before this war, the country had already experienced demographic crises associated with World War I, revolutions, civil war, collectivization, the 1932–33 famine, and the Great Purges of the late 1930s. However, World War II produced a devastation on an even greater scale. The USSR lost twenty-seven million soldiers and civilians, and the sex ratio imbalance deteriorated enormously. In this period, in some rural areas, the average ratio of men to women of reproductive age was as low as 19:100. Furthermore, a large percentage of the Soviet population was dislocated by repeated mass mobilization, evacuation, deportation, and occupation. As a result, many families broke up. The general reproductive health of men and women also deteriorated due to widespread venereal and gynecological disease after the war. Malnutrition and fatigue were also rampant.

Predictably, the birth rate plummeted and abortion shot up during the war, and the question of how to increase postwar population became a major concern of the Soviet leadership. In 1944, Nikita Khrushchev, then the leader of the Ukraine, the most demographically devastated part of the Soviet Union, and later Stalin's successor as the leader of the Soviet Union, designed the most comprehensive and extreme pronatalist policy among a group of proposals submitted to Moscow. Departing from the prewar approach that tried to increase fertility by increasing support for mothers and making men more responsible fathers, Khrushchev proposed to increase incentives for men to impregnate women as a form of pronatalism, a policy I call "conception first." He also proposed to introduce much severer punishment for women who sought abortion and those who aided them. Given that there were not enough men for women to marry in the postwar period, Khrushchev proposed complete elimination of paternal responsibility for childrearing, thereby encouraging out-of-wedlock births and creating the category of *illegitimacy*, a status that betrayed a key principle of socialism, equality among all children. The proposal also included new government support for single mothers and a more elaborate version of rewards, awards, and medals for mothers with multiple children, refining further the reproductive hierarchy of citizens in their relationship with the state. Another aspect of this proposal was to stabilize "legitimate" families by making divorce even harder to get than before. Now a divorce procedure involved two layers of court systems and expensive fees.

Khrushchev's proposal was quickly modified and codified as the 1944 Family Law entitled "On increasing government support for pregnant women, mothers with many children, single mothers, and the reinforcement of the protection of motherhood and childhood; on the establishment of the honorary title 'Mother Heroine,' the foundation of the order 'Motherhood Glory,' and the medal 'Motherhood Medal.'" As this name suggests, the policy was publicly framed as increased postwar support for mothers and children, as well as their personal glorification, while obscuring the government's aim to increase postwar population, a move suggesting that the government leaders considered promoting out-of-wedlock births and creating the legal category of illegitimacy problematic. The actual extent of World War II losses was also kept secret, so the urgency of pronatalism had to be soft-pedaled. Khrushchev's proposal to increase punishment for illegal abortions was not included in the final law. This excision reflected medical and legal advice and sheds light on the future path of reform efforts.

In the new postwar pronatalist framework, Soviet women, regardless of their marital status, were expected to give birth to more than two children; otherwise, they would have to pay a small family tax. In return, the state promised to increase material assistance to women. However, in contrast to the provisions of the 1936 Family Law, the task of raising children was to be shared only in the case of a legally married mother and father. An unmarried father would have no legal, economic, or moral responsibility for offspring. Reproduction became increasingly an affair between women and the state.

Relegalization

Because statistics became a state secret and censuses were prohibited in this period, there was no contemporary analysis of the effects of pronatalism. But nuanced evaluation of the 1944 Family Law can be made by examining the discussions among legal and medical professionals and women activists. Postwar legal specialists pointed out the growing distress among women giving birth to "illegitimate" children, who by law had no father's name on the birth certificate. Even biological fathers who wanted to recognize paternity could not be registered as the legal father. Many unmarried mothers expressed deep concerns for the fact that their children would be considered "fatherless" and would face discrimination. Legal specialists argued that these conditions constituted a problem of inequality among children.

Medical professionals focused on harmful repercussions for female and juvenile health and well-being. Their studies of underground abortions in the late 1940s demonstrated that the two most important reasons that postwar women were having abortions were unstable relationships with the partner/

husband and/or material difficulties. These studies showed clearly that both married and unmarried women had abortions as a way to avoid raising children alone. The deputy minister of health, Mariia D. Kovrigina, argued that fathers should be held equally responsible for childrearing with the mothers. Women activists investigated working single mothers and reported a typical, gendered narrative: in the postwar era, women wishing to marry and start a family were regularly impregnated and abandoned by men who had promised to marry them.

Medical professionals saw an opportunity to advance a reform agenda. Using abortion statistics and results of research conducted by the Ministry of Health regarding the reasons for postwar abortions in the late 1940s and early 1950s, they concluded that the criminalization of abortion had been ineffective, as women regularly sought underground abortions. Criminalization was also unfair to women because the reasons that drove women to get abortions were gender relations and poverty. Many Soviet women wrote letters to Soviet leaders, asking for permission for a clinical abortion, arguing that although they wanted to become mothers, the timing was not good. Many of those letters were forwarded to the Ministry of Health and may have had an impact. Discussions for reform began in the late 1940s, but after Stalin's death in 1953, reversal of the dictator's policies seemed possible. Soviet ob-gyns argued that abortion rates would necessarily decline if effective contraceptive devices became available. But, of course, there were no prospects of providing women with effective contraception any time soon. In the event, driven by the personal initiative of Kovrigina, the USSR minister of health since 1954, abortion was relegalized in the Soviet Union in 1955. Significantly, the preamble of this law recognized a woman's right to decide the *timing* of motherhood, reflecting Kovrigina's argument to medical professionals. However, this right was never extended in Russia to include women's right to decide whether or not to become a mother.

As in the 1920 legalization, the relegalization of abortion did not intend to encourage women to get abortions. In fact, antiabortion propaganda campaigns were launched simultaneously with legalization.[40] Women still had to go through an abortion committee to obtain approval, and the committee generally encouraged women to reconsider. Also, because of this formal procedure, unmarried women generally avoided legal abortion and arranged underground abortion. Nevertheless, married women were generally happy about having the option of clinical abortion and received time off from work for the operation. Notably, with relegalization came the revival of abortion statistics and research, facilitating the study of the sexual and reproductive behaviors of Soviet citizens.

Modern Contraception

The development of Soviet contraception moved forward in the late 1950s and 1960s under the influence of Kovrigina's argument that the medical profession should develop effective and easy-to-use contraception. Since most abortions previously performed underground had now become clinical abortions, relegalization had little immediate impact on fertility.[41] Nevertheless, the successful implementation of the 1955 legalization led to a new reform consensus in the medical profession, one promoting contraception to make abortion less frequent and improve the health of Soviet women.[42]

There were significant institutional developments for contraceptive research in the late 1950s and 1960s. Soon after the 1955 legalization of abortion, on October 23, 1956, an all-Union conference was organized. At this meeting, Kovrigina emphasized the importance of teaching the population that abortion harmed women's health, spreading knowledge about contraceptive methods and devices, and training medical personal regarding the reasons for abortions, including nonclinical abortion, even under a legalized abortion regime.[43] At an Academy of Medical Science (AMS) conference in April 1957, the leaders of the health administration criticized (*pred'iavliat' ser'eznyi schet*) Soviet scholars for not having done anything to advance methods for preventing pregnancies for over twenty years.[44]

The late 1950s and 1960s were the golden age for contraception research. In 1958, a new Scientific Research Institute for Physiology and Pathology of Women was founded in Tbilisi, Georgia, in order to study abortions and infertility. Around this time, under AMS, a special laboratory for research and approval of new contraceptive methods was created. In 1958–59, the health administration of the Russian Federation conducted a survey of abortion, involving 25,902 women. In 1959, a "special expanded meeting" at the Institute for Obstetrics and Gynecology of AMS SSSR was organized to discuss contraceptive means (*protivozachatochnye sredstva*) and infertility. In 1960–64 an experimental study on contraceptive devices was conducted in a Moscow woman's clinic by the Institute for Obstetrics and Gynecology of the Ministry of Health SSSR. Media covered these issues, in effect conducting a tutorial on the subject for the broader medical profession. *Medical Worker* (*Meditsinskii rabotnik*), the main medical newspaper, and several medical journals published several articles on contraception and abortion in the late 1950s and early 1960s. The problem of criminal abortion was taken up in *Izvestiia*, a major all-Union newspaper, on September 1, 1962.[45] The Soviet medical community was determined to develop contraception in order to decrease the incidence of abortions, which threateningly and seemingly inexorably increased every year from 1955 until 1965, the first decade after legalization.

Several contraceptive devices were available with very limited distribution in the Soviet Union in the late 1950s and 1960s. These included condoms, cervical caps, and spermicide. The development of new products was undertaken. For example, the All-Union Scientific and Research Institute for Chemistry and Pharmacy had introduced gramicidin, an antibiotic element to be used for contraceptive purposes.[46] According to a study conducted by N. I. Sorokina, all of the three methods listed above were considered equally effective.[47] But in general, barrier methods seemed more effective and reliable than chemical contraception.

Soviet research on oral contraception was far behind that of the West, but, recognizing its significance, researchers tried to catch up, purchasing various modern contraceptive products from Western countries.[48] In the 1960s Soviet medical doctors eagerly conducted research on hormonal pills. They followed the Western medical literature and conducted experiments. In the 1970s, a major symposium on hormonal contraception was conducted at the All-Union Scientific Research Institute for Obstetrics and Gynecology.[49] Soviet ob-gyns' enthusiasm for advancing reproductive medicine was reflected in the foundation in Moscow in 1972 of one of the four international research centers for the World Health Organization's (WHO) Human Reproduction Project. In 1974, the WHO program in Moscow expanded research on hormonal pills even further.[50] The USSR's top doctors were well informed of the latest international developments in oral contraception.

In the 1970s, however, contraceptive research and development faced several political obstacles in the Soviet Union. As I discuss below, after the 1970 census showed declining fertility, especially among Slavic populations, demographic decline was again considered a major problem. Soviet leaders had many objections to contraception. It caused fertility decline, chiefly among Slavic women, and certainly not Central Asian women. They also believed it encouraged promiscuous behaviors associated with the sexual revolution in the West. Moreover, the earliest reports on high-dose hormonal pills suggested serious side effects, so the medical profession considered oral pills unsafe. Furthermore, due to its anti-neo-Malthusian position, the Soviet leadership was essentially against the use of modern contraception in the Western-led family-planning projects in Asia and Africa. All of these issues made for a hostile environment toward modern contraception.

Clearly, Soviet leaders decided to halt further development of modern contraception and severely limit the production level. The most symbolic event occurred in 1974, when oral contraception was practically banned by a Ministry of Health instruction that listed thirty contraindications to its use. As a result, 80–90 percent of Soviet women became ineligible for the pill.[51] Moreover, the Ministry of Health made condoms and IUDs available at less than 20 percent of the estimated demand.[52] While politics could not have decided the fate of the production and development of contraception in a capitalist country, in the Soviet planned economy, politics was decisive because research and production of contraception were not possible unless resources were allocated centrally.

Instead of contraception, easier and safer abortion became available. In the early 1980s, in addition to curettage, the practice of vacuum aspirations, known as miniabortions (*mini-abort*), became widespread in large cities as an out-patient procedure. Because this procedure was classified as "menstrual regulation" rather than abortion, most were performed before the twelfth week of pregnancy at nonstate clinics and were not even included in official abortion statistics.[53] By 1987, clinical abortion was approved up to the twenty-eighth week of gestation.[54]

In this way, the goal of providing contraception as a way of reducing unwanted pregnancies was abandoned. As A. A. Popov has argued, the Soviet medical profession's negative evaluation of the first generation of oral contraception in an environment where other forms were minimally available meant the end of the whole plan to promote modern contraception. As contraceptive development became impossible because of demographic politics, the medical profession focused on improving and expanding abortion. After all, the introduction of modern contraception required too many levels of political and economic decisions, whereas new methods of abortion relied primarily on medical skills and inexpensive technologies. Out of the pioneering position as the first country in the world to offer abortion on demand, the pronatalist imperative had created the world's first abortion empire. Other socialist countries would also follow this path.

Demography and New Demographic Politics

As I discussed earlier, the socialist vision of population was pronatalist from the nineteenth century on. In line with their ideological preconceptions Soviet leaders and demographers believed that population would grow and continue to grow under socialism, because working mothers would be fully supported, removing any need to limit the number of children. During the 1920s, no questions arose on this point, because the size of population and birth rate still remained relatively high compared to major European countries. The 1926 census, which was conducted in preparation for the First Five-Year Plan showed Soviet women giving birth to an average of 5.37 children. There seemed to be little reason for alarm.[55]

The situation in terms of both fertility and population changed in the 1930s. The significant decline in fertility was due to mass mobilization of women into industry during Stalin's industrialization and upheaval in the villages due to collectivization and attendant social violence, which prompted mass migration. Obviously, the 1932–33 famine also negatively affected fertility as well as the level of population. A large migration of women into urban areas would result in much larger numbers of abortions and other attempts to control fertility.[56] For all these reasons limiting fertility, population also declined.[57]

Soviet leaders, including Stalin, did not associate the declining birth rate with their ideological and strategically driven economic and social policies. Like France, Germany, and Italy, in the 1930s the Soviet government considered depopulation a blow against labor and military force, the very measures of national power.[58] But for the Soviet Union, depopulation represented an inconsistency in an ideology that posited that under socialism, as living conditions improved, workers would have many children, increasing population. When Soviet leaders came to accept the relationship between their policies and declining population, they decided to suppress demographic data and analysis, instead of either admitting their responsibility or proposing a new interpretation of Marxian population ideology.

At the Seventeenth Party Congress in 1934, Stalin announced that the Soviet population had already reached 168 million and was increasing by 3 million per year. Stalin presented these numbers in his opening speech on the evening of January 26, 1934, and the world learned of the claim from the front page of *Pravda* on January 28.[59] A month later on February 25,

N. Osinskii (Obolenskii), director of the Statistics Administration, obtained an appointment and came to ask where the announced number came from. Stalin responded that he himself knew what numbers to indicate.[60] Osinskii was soon demoted, but Stalin would not forget him. The USSR Academy of Sciences Demographic Institute, opened in Leningrad in 1930, closed in 1934.[61]

The preliminary tabulation of the 1937 census, reported to Stalin and Molotov in March 1937, made it clear that the population was six million short of Stalin's 1934 estimate.[62] For Stalin, this could only mean that "wreckers" and "spies" had infiltrated the census process. The census results were immediately sealed. The Central Statistical Administration (TsSU) took the brunt of Stalin's anger, accused of sabotage on behalf of the Germans. M. V. Kurman, whose work on the regional tables of the 1937 census was about to make it clear that Ukrainians and Kazakhs had died en masse and the Volga region had lost millions, was scooped up from his apartment in a nighttime raid. He would spend the next eighteen years in exile, first in Kolyma, then in Kazakhstan. His boss, the director of the census, O. A. Kvitkin, was arrested and shot. I. A. Kraval, the TsSU director, had two audiences with Stalin in April, but then was quickly sentenced to "the highest measure [of punishment] (*k vysshei mere*)" and shot. The previous director, Osinskii, was also arrested and shot.

A new director, I. D. Vermenichev, was brought in to conduct the purge, but only lasted six months before being arrested and shot as well. Dozens of others were arrested or fired. By the following year, there was a 75 percent turnover in TsSU personnel.[63] In 1938, the USSR's last institute of demography, in Kiev under the Ukrainian Academy of Sciences, was eliminated.[64] What this meant was that the socialist state, which claimed to plan its economy and society scientifically based on statistics, would deny, punish, and murder those who provided accurate data. The field of demography would not recover its independence as a profession for two decades, and the 1937 census results disappeared from view for over half a century. On March 10, 1939, at the Eighteenth Party Congress, Stalin announced that the Soviet population had reached 170 million and made it clear that he envisioned further demographic and economic growth:

> The population of the Soviet Union is 170 million, and the population of England is no more than 46 million. The economic capacity of industry appears not in the volume of industrial products as a whole, regardless of the country's population, but in the size of the demand for this product per capita (*na dushu*

> *naseleniia*) . . . the more population there is in a country, the more there is demand for goods, which means (*stalo byt'*) the more volume there should be for industrial production in such a country.[65]

In the postwar period, several demographers who miraculously survived both the Great Terror of the 1930s and World War II proposed to begin preparations for a new census in order to accurately understand the devastation of war and the contemporary demographic situation. However, this proposal was rejected and demographers were advised to study foreign demography or earlier periods. Moreover, in 1948 statistics was classified as a state secret. Demography was effectively removed from the population-planning process for three decades.

After the death of Stalin in 1953, as the total population reached two hundred million in the late 1950s, Nikita Khrushchev allowed preparations for the first postwar census to be taken in 1959. Demographers began campaigning for a reinstatement of demographic studies as a discipline. No demographic institute was organized, but the renewal of demographic studies was reflected in several scientific institutions. The first examples were the 1962 formation of the section on population within the Scientific-Technical Council of the USSR Ministry of Higher and Middle Specialized Education and the 1963 organization of the Department of Demography in the Scientific-Research Institute of TsSU USSR. The late 1960s saw the reappearance of articles on Soviet demography in the professional journal *Vestnik statistiki* and the development of the Center for the Study of Population in the Economics Department of Moscow State University.[66]

One key analysis of the newly available census data showed declining birth rates among Slavic women and the widening gap in fertility between the Slavic and Central Asian mothers. Some demographers, notably B. Ts. Urlanis, began to argue that the Soviet government should develop demographic policy informed by social scientific data, as this gap would only expand without political intervention. This argument challenged one of the fundamental tenets of the socialist vision of population, that is, nondifferentiation among nationalities, a particular problem for the Soviet leadership, as throughout the 1960s it was criticizing the West's family-planning programs in Asia and Africa as a form of neo-Malthusian colonialism. Only after the Soviet leadership recognized the usefulness of demographic studies for policymaking in 1967 did the Soviet position begin to change.[67] At the World Population Conference in Bucharest in 1974, the Soviet Union accepted the usefulness of family planning in some countries with high birth rates.[68] But the Soviet government was not willing to accept the need for modern contraception for its own highly fertile population.

At home, the 1970 census raised further alarm. When compared with the 1959 census results, it showed that in this era of rapid urbanization, the population was growing too slowly, and the growing percentage of working women was the chief correlate. Urban population in the Soviet Union stood at 48 percent in the 1959 census, but grew to 56 percent by 1970.[69] The female employment rate had reached an all-time high of 56 percent in 1945, declined to 46 percent in 1955, and grew again, to 51 percent by 1970.[70] The Soviet government organized a campaign to mobilize housewives to join the labor force in the late 1950s and the 1960s, a movement that successfully achieved near universal employment of women by the end of the 1960s.[71] This "success" in mobilizing women into the labor force would reduce the size of the labor force in the future unless measures were taken to help working mothers to balance work and family life.

Indeed, between 1965 and 1970, the total fertility rate (TFR, the average number of children a woman gives birth to throughout her reproductive life) fell below replacement level (2.1 per woman). Women were now giving birth to only one or two children on average, a development that preceded similar declines in Germany and Sweden, which experienced this phenomenon in the 1970–75 period.[72] In 1976, the Twenty-Fifth Party Congress for the first time called for effective demographic policy to support economic development in the Soviet Union.[73]

It is important to emphasize that those Soviet experts, including Urlanis, who were concerned about fertility differentials among different nationalities did not view this development as a threat to the Slavic identity of the Soviet Union. Rather, demographers and economists focused on the imbalance in labor allocations throughout the Soviet Union because industrial centers, mostly located in Slavic areas, were experiencing a labor shortage. The fact was that this problem could have been solved if Central Asian workers had migrated to the industrial centers of the Soviet Union. However, specialists argued that Central Asian workers were generally not very mobile, and they could not be easily trained as industrial workers because of their low level of education and poor knowledge of Russian.

This new discourse of ethnonationalism and economic development, together with the revival of demographic and sociological studies, produced heated debates about how to deal with the disproportionally high fertility of certain nationalities. Demographers in the Central Asian republics and their supporters generally perceived this analysis as racist, while Slavic demographers and policymakers presented these perspectives as part of an attempt to resolve a labor allocation issue. In contrast, the idea that additional pronatalist measures were necessary to raise fertility among Slavic women, who generally gave birth to only one or two children, was not controversial. In the 1970s and 1980s, the traditional glorification of highly fertile mothers, rural or Central Asian, was significantly toned down, and the new direction of pronatalism slowly focused on helping mothers of one or two children regardless of their marital status and on providing more aid to unmarried mothers than before. A 1970 government decree instituted lump-sum payments upon the birth of the first, second, and third child.[74] At the same time, government aid to unmarried single mothers was raised to 20 rubles per child per month rather than 5 rubles for the first child, 7.5 rubles for two children, and 10 rubles for three children, and the cutoff age for aid was extended from twelve to sixteen.[75]

A 1974 all-Union edict provided low-income families with twelve rubles monthly support for each child up to age eight, more than the ten rubles that a mother with the order of "Motherhood Glory" would receive monthly for her seventh or eighth child.[76] In 1980 "honorary" (*pochetnoe*) was omitted from the words "honorary title" (*pochetnoe zvanie*) referring to the awards of Mother Heroine, Motherhood Glory, and Motherhood Medal.[77] The new policies clearly shifted the focus of support from large families to small families and increased support for low-income working mothers and single mothers with only one or two children. Not surprisingly, when the new pronatalism focused on supporting fertility among Slavic mothers, the government, still hoping for more Slavic babies, decided not to promote modern contraception because the users would have been primarily Slavic.

In the late 1970s and 1980s, contemporary sociological and demographic studies demonstrated that most Soviet women wanted to be mothers and have at least one child. However, a new gender discourse emerged linking low fertility among Slavic women to issues of femininity. This discourse attacked both socialist promotion of equality between the sexes and women's economic advancement. The Soviet press featured discussions among educators and sociologists about the "loss of femininity" among women and "loss of masculinity" among men, as a cause of the high rate of divorce and low birth rate. Men suffered from demoralization as, under attack by the state and women, they lost their previous roles as family head. Women were characterized as failing to understand the differences between the sexes. Women were accused of seeking public roles instead of taking care of the family and the household. Although Russian families were predominantly two-child families at that time, writers claimed that any woman with fewer than three children was not feminine. Moreover, women who expected their husbands to help with household work or childrearing were in error. Men did not properly possess the skills for that work, and those men who did were hopelessly feminized.[78]

This discourse on femininity and masculinity apparently had an impact on policymakers and resulted in the adoption of sexual socialization education in 1984 in the European, but not Central Asian, parts of the Soviet Union. The school course Ethics and Psychology of Family Life was offered for two hours per week for students in the ninth and tenth grades. Boys were taught to be honest, responsible, intelligent, brave, decisive, and noble, whereas the curriculum for girls taught them to be kind, affable, tender, sincere, natural, trusting, and good housekeepers. Marriage and family were presented as the model for happiness, and motherhood and children were the most essential parts, not only because socialism brought perfect conditions to women, as in the 1930s, but because of women's innate natures. The course also taught children the harmfulness of the one-child family, which was, at the time, an expanding demographic phenomenon.[79]

Importantly, this education did not insist that women should stay at home. Since the war, women had become too crucial a component of the Soviet labor market for politicians, economists, demographers, sociologists, educators, or anyone else to discourage women from working. Instead, social scientists and educational specialists argued for the legitimization of gender specific roles for Soviet women and men, where women were expected to hold down a full-time job, manage household chores, and take responsibility for rearing multiple children. Men were enjoined to focus on their public work. A contemporary time-budget study, which analyzed the number of hours men and women spent on average on the job, shopping, household work, taking care of children, and leisure, confirms that practice closely followed this gender ideology.[80] Just when Western feminists were vociferously challenging these mandates, the Soviet government practically decreed that the "double burden" was "natural" to women, a position even endorsed by M. S. Gorbachev, the last CPSU general secretary, in some not-so-new thinking. In his 1987 book *Perestroika: New Thinking for Our Country and the World*, he argued,

> Over the years of our difficult and heroic history, we failed to pay attention to women's specific rights and needs arising from their role as mother and home-maker, and their indispensable educational function as regards children. . . . That is why we are now holding heated debates in the press, in public organizations, at work and at home, about the question of what we should do to make it possible for women to *return to their purely womanly mission*.[81]

In this way, as the Soviet Union moved toward demise, the national problem of low fertility was expressed by authorities pointing fingers at insufficiently "feminine" Soviet women. Authorities did not raise the real problems that women faced, such as fertility control, husbands who did not contribute to domestic labor, inadequate housing, and the general difficulties of a triple burden—balancing employment, household management, and childrearing. Children were taught that the notion of equality between the sexes was false and harmful. They were instructed in the contours and qualities of a fully gendered world and were encouraged to form families with at least two children.

After 1991

New Russia began with a rapidly declining birth rate due to the generally declining trend in births combined with the demographic echo of the decimated wartime generation, which produced fewer women of reproductive ages. On top of this, in the 1990s, uncertainties about the future, unstable incomes, rising mortality rates among adult men, and the collapse of the socialized healthcare system were all factors convincing many women to defer or abandon the idea of having a first or additional child. The result was a declining birth rate.[82] With the independence of the former Central Asian republics, the only parts of the USSR with strong population growth had been lost, making the situation even worse. The 1989 Soviet census, the last to be conducted in the Soviet Union, counted 286 million Soviet citizens, but by the 2002 Russian census, now within contracted borders, the number had shrunk to 145 million Russians.[83]

In the 1990s, some reform-minded public health specialists tried to introduce modern contraception to Russian citizens, for example, by making more contraceptive devices available, and by reducing the reliance on abortion. In the early 1990s, under Russia's first president, Boris Yeltsin, family-planning programs became a part of the presidential program called Russia's Children (*Deti Rossii*). The Health Ministry organized family-planning centers that included specialists who designed sexual education programs for youth.[84] Since then, the number of abortions has been steadily declining, and the use of contraception has been increasing.[85] By the end of the 1990s, however, the government defined the growing trend of population decline due to lower fertility and higher mortality as a national crisis. To address the crisis, federal funding for family planning ended in 1998, and many sexual education programs implemented in the early 1990s were canceled. Public health educators who were trying to continue sex education began to focus on strengthening the family and the morality of reproduction rather than on the dissemination of contraceptive knowledge, in order to protect themselves from the growing attacks of conservative forces.[86]

Instead of the Communist Party, in post-Soviet Russia, the impressive revival of religious organizations, especially the Orthodox Church, led to a campaign against widespread abortion. After Vladimir Putin became the second president of Russia, state-regulated medicine acted in parallel with the church. A series of measures to restrict women's access to abortion was introduced: in 2003, the list of nonmedical criteria for abortion shrunk to a third of its previous length; in 2007 the list of medical criteria for abortion was reduced by two-thirds; also in 2007, an official order was issued requiring all women having abortions to be informed about possible complications and side effects of the operation; and in 2009, a federal law put limitations on the advertisement of abortion services.[87] In 2011, a federal law was issued to require that advertisements of abortion services use at least 10 percent of their space to describe the dire consequences of abortion and never indicate that termination of pregnancies could be done safely.[88] In 2013, the lower house of the Russian parliament discussed the bill on the exclusion of abortion from national medical insurance coverage.[89]

Other recent measures also recall postwar, pronatalist policies such as increased material help to mothers, discourses defining the government's generous commitment to mothers and children, and the glorification of large families. In 2006, Vladimir Putin announced an initiative to improve Russia's rate of population growth and introduced a law on "motherhood (family) capital (*materinskii (semeinyi) kapital*)," which grants 250,000 rubles for a child born or adopted after January 1, 2007, as the second or additional child.[90] Putin celebrated 2007 as the Year of Children and 2008 as the Year of Family. Dmitrii Medvedev, who worked on demographic policy as the first vice premier (*pervyi vitse-prem'er*) under Putin, became the next president and continued the same line of policy together with Putin as prime minister until 2012, when Putin was re-elected president. Similarly to the 1944 Family Law's introduction of the "Mother Heroine," in 2008 Medvedev instituted the order "Parental Glory" (*Roditelskaia slava*) to promote long-lasting marriage and large families, and presented awards to eight families with four or more children at a January 2009 Kremlin ceremony. Pronatalist policies such as provision of significant state aid and glorification of large families are clearly inspired by Soviet mandates and by the continuing preoccupation with the nation's need to stimulate population growth. Today, however, awards are presented to both parents, rather than mothers only.

Conclusions

Despite its pronatalist orientations, the Soviet regime created a system that produced the highest abortion rates and one of the most rapidly declining birth rates in the world. This legacy is alive and well today.[91] The impact of the abortion empire went beyond the borders of the Soviet Union. Postwar Soviet pronatalist measures, with roots in Marxism, were exported to many countries after World War II, almost automatically as part of the Sovietization package. In most European countries abortion had been illegal in the prewar period. Exceptions, such as Romania, made abortion illegal in 1948, the same year the Communists took power. In East Germany, a brief period of wider access to abortion under Soviet occupation ended in 1950.[92] Following Moscow's 1955 legalization, abortion became easier to obtain in Bulgaria, Czechoslovakia, Hungary, Poland, and Romania. The reason for the change followed the Soviet logic, emphasizing the harm of underground abortion to women's reproductive health.[93]

As in the Soviet Union, the results of wider access to abortion without promotion of contraception were very high rates of abortion and rapidly declining birth rates in eastern European countries in the 1960s. Hungary and Romania particularly had very high abortion rates. In the mid-1960s, socialist countries had some of the lowest birth and natural population growth rates in the world.[94] This rapid fertility decline was "unforeseen," and many countries tried to reverse the trend by reversing liberalized abortion policy, since it was believed that availability of abortion was the cause of the decline. Czechoslovakia, Hungary, Bulgaria, and Romania enacted restrictive measures between the late 1960s and early 1970s.[95] The most serious consequences were in Romania, where Nicolae Ceauş ʻescu introduced an extreme pronatalist regime in the 1970s, producing millions of abandoned children and illegal abortions until his demise in 1989.[96]

The ability of socialism to bring about a rapid decline in the birth rate was further proven in China. The Soviet origins of Chinese pronatalism are clear. After the founding of the People's Republic of China in 1949, China followed key features of the Soviet postwar system, and adopted the 1944 Soviet Family Law and celebrated "Mother Heroines."[97] Mao insisted that population was an advantage for China. Certainly, this was the prevailing attitude in the Chinese countryside with which Mao identified.[98] In the mid-1950s, China liberalized restrictions on abortion and contraception. This gave an opportunity for criticism of runaway population growth, most famously by the president of Beijing University, Ma Yingchu, in 1957. Ma soon became a victim of the Hundred Flowers cum antirightist campaign. In announcing the Great Leap Forward in 1958, Chairman Mao proclaimed that a population of a billion would not be "cause for alarm."[99] In contrast to the problem of low fertility in the Soviet Union and eastern Europe, China's demographic debate in the 1960s and 1970s was about its high population growth rate. But the official recognition of China's need for fertility decline was delayed until socialist theoreticians could overcome the identification of fertility reduction as Malthusian. This happened in 1974, when officials discovered the aforementioned letter from Engels to Kautsky in 1881, which discussed the possibility of fertility control among socialist women in the distant future.[100] Thus, the one-child policy did not represent a diversion from socialist population ideology. Instead, it answered Engels's statement: "It is for the people in the communist society themselves to decide whether, when, and how this [regulating the production of human beings] is to be done, and what means they wish to employ for the purpose." From then on, the Chinese state set demographic targets, and women's reproduction became a part of socialist production planning, which provided citizens with methods of modern contraception and clinical abortion.

To conclude, this history has demonstrated that in spite of overwhelming similarities in terms of ideology and political, economic, and social systems, socialist regimes produced varieties of reproductive policies, ranging from the Soviet Union's abortion empire; to Nicolae Ceauş 'escu's extreme pronatalism in Romania, where medical institutions recorded menstruation cycles; to the one-child policy in China, where local committees also kept the record of women's menstruation patterns, but for antinatalist purposes.

What all these had in common was the socialist state's ability to create a nationwide network of reproductive surveillance leading to the rampant practice of abortion.

Notes

1. Linda Atkinson, Richard Lincoln, and Jacqueline Darroch Forrest, "The Next Contraceptive Revolution," *Family Planning Perspectives* 18, no. 1 (January–February 1986): 19–20.
2. L. N. Ivanova, a participant in a televised discussion between Soviet and American citizens on July 17, 1986, commented in Russian, "Well, we don't have sex. We are categorically against this." See entry entitled "U nas seksa net" in *Entsyklopedicheskii slovar' krylatykh slov i vyrazhenii* (Moscow: Lokid-Press, 2003).
3. Mie Nakachi, "A Postwar Sexual Liberation? The Gendered Experience of the Soviet Union's Great Patriotic War," *Cahiers du monde russe* 51 (2011–12): 423–40.
4. A. G. Vishnevskii, ed., *Demograficheskaia modernizatsiia Rossii, 1900–2000* (Moscow: Novoe izdatel'stvo, 2006), 216.
5. A. A. Popov, "Induced Abortions in the USSR at the End of the 1980s: The Basis for the National Model of Family Planning," a conference paper prepared for the 1992 Annual Meeting for Population Association of America in Denver, Colorado, April 30–May 2, 1992, 4.
6. Susan Gal and Gail Kligman, "Reproduction as Politics," *The Politics of Gender after Socialism* (Princeton, N.J.: Princeton University Press, 2000), 15–36.
7. Thomas Robert Malthus, *An Essay on the Principle of Population* first appeared as an anonymous pamphlet in 1797. Various modified and expanded editions were published after 1803. T. R. Malthus, *An Essay on the Principle of Population; or A View of Its Past and Present Effects on Human Happiness; With an Inquiry into Our Prospects Respecting the Future Removal or Mitigation of the Evils which It Occasions*, selected and introduced by Donald Winch (Cambridge: Cambridge University Press, 1992).
8. See, in particular, "Of the English Poor Laws," in Malthus, *An Essay on Population*, 89–123.
9. Malthus, *An Essay on Population*, 23–24, 368–69.
10. Ronald Meek, ed., *Marx and Engels on Malthus* (London: Lawrence and Wishart, 1953), 59–62. This is an excellent, but not exhaustive, compendium.
11. Karl Marks and Friedrich Engel, *Sochineniia*, vol. 26, part 2, 2nd ed. (Moscow, 1963), 122. In this thirty-nine-volume collection, "Malthusianism" is a long index entry, divided into twenty subcategories. Some of their titles suggest the ways in which the orthodox Communist keepers of the Marxian legacy continued the anti-Malthusian heritage in Soviet times. I list a few: "As the expression of conservative and anti-popular tendencies of the aristocrats in bourgeois society . . . a reactionary population theory . . . its plagiarized character . . . defense

of the interests of parasitical layers of society . . . justifying the poverty of the working classes . . . its vulgar explanation of profit." See Institut Marksizma-Leninizma pri TsK KPSS, *Predmetnyi ukazatel' ko vtoromu izdaniiu Sochinenii K. Marksa i F. Engel'sa*, part I (A–M) (Moscow, 1978), 405.

12. "Population and Communism," in Engels's letter to Kautsky of February 1, 1881, in *Marx and Engels on Malthus*, 108–9.
13. This was an earlier version of his more commonly known text, *Die Frau und der Sozialismus* (Women and Socialism) published in 1879.
14. August Bebel, *Woman in the Past, Present, and Future*, trans. H. B. Adams Walther (London: William Reeves, 1893), 255.
15. In the 1930s Vigdorchik was arrested. Stalin supposedly was outraged at his December 1930 suggestion to conduct a study on "The Role of Socialist Competition and Shockwork in Increasing Morbidity." Lewis Siegelbaum, "Okhrana Truda: Industrial Hygiene, Psychotechnics, and Industrialization in the USSR," in *Health and Society in Revolutionary Russia*, ed. Susan Solomon and John Hutchinson (Bloomington: Indiana University Press, 1990), 235.
16. The full text can be found in V. I. Lenin, *Polnoe sobranie sochinenii*, vol. 23 (Moscow, 1961), 255–57, 488, 530.
17. The logic of the 1920 legalization of abortion was that providing medical abortion widely was important because the material and cultural level of women, who grew up in tsarist Russia, was low. This meant that there was an assumption that once material well-being and a higher cultural life were ensured by communism, women would not need medical abortion in order to limit pregnancy, because they would always be happy and socially supported in their decision to have children.
18. On England, see Richard Soloway, *Demography and Degeneration: Eugenics and the Declining Birthrate in Twentieth-Century Britain* (Chapel Hill: University of North Carolina Press, 1990). On France, Theodore Zeldin, *France, 1848–1945: Anxiety and Hypocrisy* (Oxford: Oxford University Press, 1981), 184, states that "the French worried obsessively and increasingly about the slow rate at which their population increased." Joshua Cole, *The Power of Large Numbers: Population, Politics, and Gender in Nineteenth-Century France* (Ithaca, N.Y.: Cornell University Press, 2000). On pronatalism in Germany, see Annette Timm, *The Politics of Fertility in Twentieth-Century Berlin* (New York: Cambridge University Press, 2010); and Michelle Mouton, *From Nurturing the Nation to Purifying the Volk: Weimar and Nazi Family Policy, 1918–1945* (Cambridge: Cambridge University Press, 2007).
19. This phrase is a part of the title of Book I of Malthus's *Essay* and was used by Malthus to refer to the world as operated by the law of nature, in which species multiply when food is sufficiently available, but have little possibility of significantly increasing production of food at a rate faster than the increasing rate of birth. Specifically, he refers to the people of Africa and Asia, and sometimes North America. Only people in Europe, he argues, have the chance to escape from the law of nature. Malthus, *An Essay on Population*, 13–20.

20. By the early 1820s in England and the early 1830s in the United States, books recommending artificial birth control as a solution were published by advocates of Malthus. In the early 1860s, Charles Bradlaugh founded the Malthusian League, and from the late 1870s contraception was often described as neo-Malthusian by the Dutch and English. In India, Malthusian views had a great influence on the way the British saw local developments. John Caldwell argues that India's first-in-the-world family-planning program in 1952 had a strong neo-Malthusian heritage. John C. Caldwell, "Malthus and the Less Developed World: The Pivotal Role of India," *Population and Development Review* 24, no. 4 (December 1998): 679–96.
21. Lenin, *Polnoe sobranie sochinenii* 23, 488.
22. From "The Code of Laws concerning the Civil Registration of Deaths, Births, and Marriages, of October 17, 1918," in *The Family in the USSR*, ed. Rudolf Schlesinger (London: Routledge and Kegan Paul, 1949), 33–37. The dominant Russian Orthodox Church had its property nationalized and its top clergy purged in 1922. Already by 1919 the Eighth Party Congress had called for a scientific antireligion campaign. By the 1930s, the Orthodox Church had lost much of its earlier influence on family. David Ransel describes both the persecution of religion and the persistence into the 1920s of the belief that baptism was essential. David Ransel, *Village Mothers: Three Generations of Change in Russia and Tataria* (Bloomington: Indiana University Press, 2000), 166–69.
23. The generation of Orthodox women in the villages born between 1914 and 1928 tended to consider abortion a great sin, but because of the economic hardship caused by collectivization and famine, they considered it a necessity. Most women (but not all) born after the late 1920s tended to show no moral compunction about abortion on religious grounds. Ransel, *Village Mothers*, 102–19.
24. Wendy Goldman, *Women, the State and Revolution: Soviet Family Policy and Social Life, 1917–1936* (Cambridge: Cambridge University Press, 1993), 254–57.
25. Even physicians who considered contraception harmful, generally agreed that abortion was worse. Frances Bernstein, *The Dictatorship of Sex: Lifestyle Advice for the Soviet Masses* (DeKalb: Northern Illinois University Press, 2007), 167.
26. Gail W. Lapidus, *Women in Soviet Society: Equality, Development, and Social Change* (Berkeley: University of California Press, 1978), 166.
27. Sergei Zakharov, "Russian Federation: From the First to Second Demographic Transition," *Demographic Research* 19, no. 24 (July 2008), 910.
28. Sheila Fitzpatrick, *Everyday Stalinism: Ordinary Life in Extraordinary Times: Soviet Russia in the 1930s* (New York: Oxford University Press, 1999), 152–56.
29. I use "child support" rather than alimony for the translation of the Russian word *alimenty*, which includes various types of family support. For details of the 1936 law, see "O zapreshchenii abortov, uvelichenii material'noi pomoshchi rozhenitsam, ustanovlenii gosudarstvennoi pomoshchi mnogosemeinym, rashirenii seti rodil'nykh domov, detskikh iaslei i detskikh sadov, usilenii ugolovnogo nakazaniia za neplatezh alimentov i o nekotorykh izmeneniiakh v zakonodatel'stve

o razvodakh," *Sobranie zakonov i rasporiazhenii SSSR* 34 (1936): 509–16. For a detailed discussion of the development of the 1936 Family Law, see Goldman.

30. GARF f. 8009, op. 1, d. 119, ll. 1–6, 47; TsMAMLS f. 218, op. 1, d. 187, l. 46.
31. Report to Stalin and Molotov in RGASPI f. 82, op. 2, d. 538, l. 19.
32. Nicholas DeWitt, *Education and Professional Employment in the USSR* (Washington D.C.: National Science Foundation, 1961), 74.
33. DeWitt, *Education and Professional Employment*, 75.
34. Various memoirs mention either grandmothers or domestic servants who helped with childcare. For example, see Galina Vladimirovna Shtange, "Remembrances," in *Intimacy and Terror: Soviet Diaries of the 1930s*, ed. Veronique Garros, Natalia Korenevskaya, and Thomas Lahusen (New York: New Press, 1995), 167–218; Inna Shikheeva-Gaister, *Semeinaia khronika vremen kul'ta lichnosti 1925–1953, Pamiati nashikh roditelei i mladshei sestrenki posviashchaetsia* (Moscow, 1998), 7; Valentina Bogdan, *Mimikriia v SSSR, Vospominaniia inzhenera, 1935–1942 gody* (Frankfurt am Main: Polyglott-Druck, 1981), 18, 47, 59; Vladimir Kabo recalls that in the 1920s and 1930s, every family in the building where he lived had a domestic servant. Vladimir Kabo, *The Road to Australia: Memoirs* (Canberra: Aboriginal Studies Press, 1998), 42–43; Kent Geiger's study discusses Harvard Interview Project responses regarding grandmother and domestic servant as primary household worker and caretaker of children. Kent Geiger, *The Family in Soviet Russia* (Cambridge, Mass.: Harvard University Press, 1968), 201–2; Gijs Kessler shows that after the civil war, urban areas saw the formation of three-generational households, consisting of an elderly woman, a younger couple, and a child/children. This was a common arrangement due to the remarrying of older men with younger women and the shortage of housing in the twenties. Such households made up 20 percent of all urban households in 1926. By the end of the 1930s this number declined to 14–16 percent. Gijs Kessler, "A Population Under Pressure: Household Responses to Demographic and Economic Shock in the Interwar Soviet Union," in *The Dream Deferred: New Studies in Russian and Soviet Labour History*, ed. Donald Filtzer, Wendy Goldman, Gijs Kessler, and Simon Pirani (Berne, Switzerland: Peter Lang, 2008), 337.
35. For the eleventh and additional child, a mother received 5,000 rubles as one-time payment in the year of the birth, and 3,000 rubles for the next four years. "O zapreshchenii abortov, uvelichenii material'noi pomoshchi rozhentsam, ustanovlenii gosudarstvennoi pomoshchi mnogosemeinym, rasshirenii seti rodi'nykh domov, detskikh iaslei i detskikh sadov, usilenii ugolovnogo nakazaniia za neplatezh alimentov i o nekotorykh izmeneniiakh v zakonodatel'stve o razvodakh," *Pravda*, June 28, 1936.
36. *Moskovskaia krest'ianskaia gazeta*, September 9, 1936, 2, as cited in Fitzpatrick, *Everyday Stalinism*, 155.
37. In May 1944, of the estimated 37,486,000 adult women, 253,000 were estimated to have seven or eight children, 36,000, nine children, 10,000, ten children, and 2,000, more than eleven children by V. N Starovskii, the head of the Central

Statistical Administration. RGASPI, f. 82, op. 2 d. 387, l. 93. It is most likely that his estimates were based on the corresponding percentages in 1940.

38. Paula Michaels, "Motherhood, Patriotism, and Ethnicity: Soviet Kazakhstan and the 1936 Abortion Ban," *Feminist Studies* 27, no. 2 (Summer 2001): 322. On the shifting strategies of Soviet power toward women and their liberation in Central Asia, see Gregory Massell, *The Surrogate Proletariat: Moslem Women and Revolutionary Strategies in Soviet Central Asia, 1919–1929* (Princeton, N.J.: Princeton University Press, 1974). More recently on an archival base, Douglas Northrop, *Veiled Empire: Gender and Power in Stalinist Central Asia* (Ithaca, N.Y.: Cornell University Press, 2004).
39. Michaels, "Motherhood, Patriotism, and Ethnicity," 327.
40. Amy Randall, "'Abortion Will Deprive You of Happiness!' Soviet Reproductive Politics in the Post-Stalin Era," *Journal of Women's History* 23, no. 3 (2011): 13–38.
41. The major visible improvement was that approximately four thousand women per year recorded between 1949 and 1954 (TsMAMLS f. 218, op. 1, d. 187, l. 48) as lost to incomplete abortions, were no longer exposed to this risk. The production of penicillin began in the Soviet Union after World War II, but it was most likely not widely available, as medicine in general was extremely scarce in the Soviet Union.
42. E. A. Sadvokasova, *Sotsial'no-gigienicheskie aspekty regulirovaniia razmerov sem'i* (Moscow: Izdatel'stvo , 1969), 6.
43. M. D. Kovrigina, "O merakh po dal'neishemu uluchsheniiu meditsinskogo obsluzhivaniia naseleniia" (1956) cited in Sadvokasova, *Sotsial'no-gigienicheskie aspekty*, 125.
44. Sadvokasova, *Sotsial'no-gigienicheskie aspekty*, 125.
45. Sadvokasova, *Sotsial'no-gigienicheskie aspekty*, 6, 125–28.
46. O. K. Nikonchik, "Problema kontraktseptsii i organizatsiia bor'by s abortami v SSSR," *Akusherstvo i ginekologiia* 6 (1959): 5. Other substances whose contraceptive properties were studied around this time were polyphenol and galascorbine. For example, see R. P. Tel'nova, "Kontraktseptivnye svoistva nekotorykh polifenolov," *Akusherstvo i ginekologiia* 6 (1959): 11–13; and L. Ia. Gorpinenko, "Mikroflora vlagalishcha i sheiki matki u zhenshchin pri mestnom primenenii galaskorbina kak protivozachatochnogo sredstva," *Akusherstvo i ginekologiia* 6 (1959): 13–15.
47. Sadvokasova, *Sotsial'no-gigienicheskie aspekty*, 135.
48. National Archives and Records Administration, State Department Files, MMD 959000, "Soviet Family Planning, Visit of Miss Laura Olson," dated on December 21, 1965, 2.
49. A USSR Ministry of Health report on this symposium was cited in Andrej Popov, Adriaan Visser, and Evert Ketting, "Contraceptive Knowledge, Attitudes, and Practice in Russia during the 1980s," *Studies in Family Planning* 24, no. 4 (July–August 1993): 235.

50. L. S. Persianinov and I. A. Manuikova, "O rasshirennoi programme VOZ [WHO] po reproduktsii cheloveka," *Akusherstvo i ginekologiia* 6 (June 1975): 1–3; and Persianinov and Manuikova, "Sostoianie i perspektivy nauchnykh issledovanii v Moskovskom nauchno-metodicheskom tsentre VOZ po reproduktsii cheloveka," *Akusherstvo i ginekologiia* 6 (June 1975): 3–7.
51. *O pobochnom deistvii i oslozhneniiakh pri primenenii oral'nykh kontratseptivov: informatsionnoe pis'mo*, compiled by E. A. Babaian, A. S. Lopatin, and I. G. Lavretskii (Moscow: USSR Ministry of Public Health, 1974) as cited in Popov, Visser, and Ketting, "Contraceptive Knowledge," 232.
52. Popov, "Induced Abortions," 20.
53. Popov, "Induced Abortions," 12–13.
54. Popov, "Induced Abortions," 33–34.
55. On birth rate, see *Naselenie Rossii v XX veke 1900–1939*, vol. 1 (Moscow, 2000), 204.
56. For a comprehensive discussion of urbanization, industrialization, collectivization, famine, political repression, and deportation as causes of falling birth rate in the 1930s, see *Naselenie Rossii*.
57. Because the number of births in rural areas was much higher than that of urban births, fertility patterns in the villages affected population more significantly than fertility change in urban areas. In 1936, in Russian Soviet Federated Socialist Republic (RSFSR), rural women gave birth to three times (2.7 million) as many children as urban women did (0.9 million). *Naselenie Rossii*, 205. For example, the number of births in the rural area per 1,000 population in the European part of the Soviet Union dropped in the villages from 45.6 in 1926 to 32.2 in 1935. *Naselenie Rossii*, 223.
58. David Hoffmann, "Mothers in the Motherland: Stalinist Pronatalism in Its Pan-European Context," *Journal of Social History* 34, no. 1 (Autumn 2000): 35–38.
59. In his 1930 book built on 1927 data, economist S. G. Strumilin estimated annual population increases between three and four million, arriving at 162.7 million for 1932, the final year of his projection. This may well have been the source of Stalin's politically authoritative approximation. S. G. Strumilin, *Ocherki sovetskoi ekonomiki: Resursy i perspektivy* (Moscow: Gosudarstvennoe izdatel'stvo, 1930), 398.
60. Stalin's famous comment that he knew what number to quote (*sam znaet, kakuiu tsifru emu nazyvat'*) is quoted in A. G. Vishnevskii, "Sud'ba odnogo demografa: Portret na fone epokhi," *Cahiers du monde russe et sovietique* 34, no. 4 (1993): 600. Osinskii, who entered the Communist Party in 1907, was a revolutionary nickname. V. I. Ivkin, *Gosudarstvennaia vlast' SSSR: Istoriko-biograficheskii spravochnik* (Moscow, 1999), 446–47. His visit to Stalin is dated from the logbook of Stalin's Kremlin office in *Istoricheskii arkhiv* 4 (1998): 136.
61. *Sovetskaia demografiia za 70 let* (Moscow, 1987), 9.
62. Iu. A. Poliakov et al., "A Half Century of Silence: The 1937 Census," *Russian Studies in History* 31, no. 1 (Summer 1992): 3, 17–27.
63. On the purge, see Alain Blum and Martine Mespoulet, *L'Anarchie bureaucratique: Pouvoir et statistique sous Staline* (Paris: Découverte, 2003), 138–40.

64. *Naselenie Rossii*, 223. Since its 1919 founding it had been run by the internationally recognized Ukrainian demographer, M. V. Ptukha. For the next twenty years, he focused his research on the history of Russian statistics until the nineteenth century. A list of his publications can be found in M. V. Ptukha, *Ocherki po statistike naseleniia* (Moscow, 1960), 454–56.
65. I. V. Stalin, *Sochineniia*, vol. 1 [XIV] *1934–1940*, ed. Robert H. McNeal (Stanford, Calif.: Hoover Institution on War, Revolution, and Peace, 1967), 350.
66. T.V. Riabushkin et al., eds., *Sovetskaia demografiia za 70 let: Iz istorii nauki* (Moscow: Nauka, 1987), 9–10. See also Alexandre Avdeev, "Avenir de la demographie en Russie," in *Les contours de la demographie au seuil du XXIe siecle*, ed. Jean-Claude Chasteland and Louis Roussel (Paris: Colloque International, 1995), 369–96.
67. The 1967 Party decree on the social sciences acknowledged possible usefulness of demography for the first time in thirty years. Murray Feshbach, "The Soviet Population Policy Debate: Actors and Issues," Rand Corporation, December 1986, v.
68. Matthew Connelly, *Fatal Misconception: The Struggle to Control World Population* (Cambridge, Mass.: Belknap Press of Harvard University Press, 2008), 313.
69. Ellen Mickiewicz, ed., *Handbook of Soviet Social Science Data* (New York: Free Press, 1973), 54.
70. There was a huge variation between the most "European" parts of Russia and Muslim regions. Lapidus, *Women in Soviet Society*, 166.
71. Andrei Markevich, "Soviet Urban Households and the Road to Universal Employment, from the End of the 1930s to the End of the 1960s," *Continuity and Change* 20, 3 (2005): 449.
72. Philip Morgan and Miles Taylor, "Low Fertility at the Turn of the Twenty-First Century," *Annual Review of Sociology* 32 (2006): 377.
73. Feshbach, "Soviet Population Policy Debate," 5.
74. Working and student mothers received fifty rubles for the first child, one hundred rubles for the second and third child. Nonworking mothers received thirty rubles for the first, second, and third child. "Ob utverzhdenii polozheniia o poriadke naznacheniia i vyplati posobii beremennym zhenshchinam, mnogodetnym i odinokim materiam," August 12, 1970, *Svod zakonov SSSR*, vol. 2 (Moscow: Izvestiia, 1984), 725.
75. If the child was in school, the aid was extended up to age eighteen. "Ob utverzhdenii polozheniia," 720.
76. Ukaz Prezidiuma Verkhovnogo Soveta SSSR, "O vvedenii posobii na deti maloobespechennym sem'iam," in *Svod zakonov SSSR*, vol. 2 (Moscow: Izvestiia, 1984), 728–29.
77. Ukaz Prezidiuma Verkhovnogo Soveta SSSR, "O vnesenii izmenenii v nekotorye zakonodatel'nye akty SSSR," July 18, 1980, *Vedomosti Verkhovnogo Soveta Soiuza Sovetskikh sotsialisticheskikh respublik* 30 (July 1980): 633–35.
78. Lynne Attwood, *The New Soviet Man and Woman: Sex-Role Socialization in the USSR* (London: Macmillan, 1990), 165–82.

79. Attwood, *New Soviet Man*, 184–91. In 1983, K. K. Bazdyrev published a popularizing book called *Only Child*, with a print run of fifty thousand going to "a broad group of readers, demographers, sociologists, and economists" to caution against the phenomenon. K. K. Bazdyrev, *Edinstvennyi rebenok* (Moscow, 1983).
80. Markevich, "Soviet Urban Households," 466.
81. Emphasis is mine. Mikhail Gorbachev, *Perestroika: New Thinking for Our Country and the World* (New York: Harper and Row, 1987), 116–18.
82. Statistical indicators can be found at http://www.ined.fr/en/pop_figures/developed_countries/developed_countries_database/. Last accessed on August 10, 2015.
83. V. I. Iakunin et al., *Gosudarstvennaia politika vyvoda Rossii iz demograficheskogo krizisa* (Moscow: Ekonomika, 2007), 33. This particular estimate comes from a nine-hundred-page team analysis led by a close supporter of President Putin, Vladimir Iakovlevich Iakunin. He has also been associated with government projects involving the Russian Orthodox Church. In its historical section, the book reviews such "successful" pronatalist projects as Nazi Germany in the 1930s and Romania in the 1960s, both for their positive and negative measures (222–25).
84. According to Rosstat data, the absolute number of abortions went down from 4,103.4 thousand (1990) to 2,138.8 thousand (2000), and the number of abortions per 1,000 women aged between fifteen and forty-nine declined from 113.9 (1990) to 54.2 (2000). This analysis and data is provided in a very informative article by Viktoriia Sakevich and Boris Denisov, "Pereidet li Rossiia ot aborta k planirovaniiu sem'i?" in *Demoskop Weekly*, nos. 465–66 (May 2–22 2011). The influence of religion on the use of contraception seems negligible. According to the Rosstat survey on contraceptive practice among women between fifteen and forty-four years old conducted in May 2013, only 0.1 percent responded that religious belief was the reason for not practicing contraception. "Vsemirnyi Den' kontratseptsii—2013," *Demoskop Weekly*, nos. 569–70 (September 30–October 13, 2013).
85. According to a survey conducted by Rosstat in 2013, more than 80 percent of women over twenty years old responded that they have sometimes used modern contraception. However, reflecting the Ministry of Health's data that show that modern contraception is introduced after the first birth or abortion, less than 30 percent of women under twenty have used modern contraception. "Vsemirnyi Den' kontratseptsii—2013," *Demoskop Weekly*, nos. 569–70 (September 30—October 13, 2013).
86. Michele Rivkin-Fish, *Women's Health in Post-Soviet Russia: The Politics of Intervention* (Bloomington: Indiana University Press, 2005), 5, 100–102.
87. Sakevich and Denisov, "Pereidet li Rossiia."
88. "V Rossii uzhestochaiutsia trebovaniia k reklame abortov," *Rossiiskaia gazeta*, July 14, 2011.

89. "Zakonoproekt no. 381372-6, O vnesenii izmeneniia v stat'iu 35 Federal'nogo zakona 'Ob obiazatel'nom meditsinskom strakhovanii v Rossiiskoi Federatsii'," cited in "Obshchestvennaia diskussiia legitimnosti aborta v Rossii prodolzhaetsia," *Demoskop Weekly*, nos. 577–78 (December 2–25, 2013).
90. This was approximately US$10,000 in 2007. However, this is not given as cash, but as a certificate. The amount is indexed to inflation, and could be used for designated purposes: the child's education, toward housing, or toward the mother's pension savings. Men who adopt two or more children were also eligible after January 1, 2007. *Materinskii kapital* will continue until December 31, 2016. "Federal'nyi zakon Rossiiskoi Federatsii ot 29 dekabria 2006 g. N256-FZ O dopolnitel'nykh merakh gosudarstvennoi podderzhki semei, imeiushchikh detei," in *Rossiiskaia Gazeta*, December 31, 2006.
91. Here only countries that keep abortion statistics are considered. United Nations Statistics Division's abortion rate is available at http://data.un.org/Data.aspx?d=GenderStat&f=inID%3A12. Last accessed on August 10, 2015. In fact, among sixty-one countries where abortion data were collected, as of 2007 the top ten were all former or current communist countries: Russian Federation, Vietnam, Kazakhstan, Estonia, Belarus, Romania, Ukraine, Latvia, Cuba, and China. Russia's number one status has not changed as of 2009, according to Sakevich and Denisov, "Pereidet li Rossiia."
92. In East Germany, millions of rapes perpetrated by the Red Army led to hundreds of thousands of abortions, making it hard to argue for a strict ban. Donna Harsch, "Society, the State, and Abortion in East Germany, 1950–1972," *American Historical Review* 120, no. 1 (February 1997): 57.
93. Interestingly in Poland, wider access to abortion was partially justified by the claim that the church had supported criminalization. The first and only communist family-planning association was formed in 1957 with a claim that Polish fertility was too high. John Besemeres, *Socialist Population Politics: The Political Implications of Demographic Trends in the USSR and Eastern Europe* (New York: M.E. Sharpe, 1980), 123.
94. Besemeres, *Socialist Population Politics*, 32–33.
95. Thomas Frejka, "Induced Abortion and Fertility: A Quarter Century of Experience in Eastern Europe," *Population and Development Review* 9, no. 3 (September 1983): 495. An interesting exception is Poland. In the Polish case, although the movement to ban abortion found a steady supporter in the Catholic Church, restrictions on abortion were reintroduced only in 1990. Andrzej Kulczycki "Abortion Policy in Postcommunist Europe: The Conflict in Poland," *Population and Development Review* 21, no. 3 (September 1995): 474.
96. On this, see Gail Kligman, *The Politics of Duplicity: Controlling Reproduction in Ceausescu's Romania* (Berkeley: University of California Press, 1998).
97. Tyrene White, *China's Longest Campaign: Birth Planning in the People's Republic, 1949–2005* (Ithaca, N.Y.: Cornell University Press, 2006), 20.

98. Other than Mao, there is much evidence that leaders of Communist China actually advocated measures for lower fertility, especially on the ground that women who would be active participants in revolutionizing China needed birth control. Deng Yingchao (the wife of Zhou Enlai), Deng Xiaoping, and Liu Shaoqi all supported making birth control widely available in the early 1950s. Susan Greenhalgh and Edwin Winckler, *Governing China's Population: From Leninist to Neoliberal Biopolitics* (Palo Alto, Calif.: Stanford University Press, 2005), 64–67.
99. Greenhalgh and Winckler, *Governing China's Population*, 55–74.
100. Susan Greenhalgh, *Just One Child: Science and Policy in Deng's China* (Berkeley: University of California Press, 2008), 70.

10

China's Population Policy in Historical Context

TYRENE WHITE

For nearly forty years, China's birth limitation program has been the definitive example of state intrusion into the realm of reproduction. Although the notorious one-child policy did not begin officially until 1979, the state's claims to a legitimate role in the regulation of childbearing originated in the 1950s and the enforcement of birth limits in the early 1970s. What was new about the one-child policy was not the state's claim of authority over the realm of human reproduction; that claim had been staked long before. What was new was the one-child-per-family birth limit, and the strengthened commitment of Chinese Communist Party (CCP) leaders to enforce this limit.

The formal retirement of the one-child birth limit in 2014—the result of a long-debated decision to allow all childbearing-age couples to have a second child if either the mother or father were only children, will no doubt invite many retrospective assessments of its impact on China's development process, on women and families, and on Chinese society. Some will emphasize the hubris of the Chinese government, its audacity in supposing it had the right to impose strict birth limits and make all adults ask and receive official state permission to conceive and give birth. Others will look at it from an entirely different perspective, one that emphasizes the contribution of China to what they perceive as the problem of global overpopulation. Still others will use economic analysis to determine how much of China's post-1979 economic growth can be attributed to the reduced rates of population growth and fertility that resulted from the policy. A fourth category might emphasize the gendered dynamics of the Chinese program.[1]

Each of these perspectives has its virtues, but one limitation will be the tendency to see the one-child policy as a starting point—as the beginning of China's great social experiment of the late twentieth century, rather than the culmination of a political and policy process that had been unfolding in China since 1949, and a global process of social change as the ideas and instruments of population control evolved and spread during the nineteenth and twentieth centuries. To understand the meaning and significance of the one-child policy, however, it must be examined against the backdrop of these global and domestic forces. Domestically, Marxist theory and Soviet practice combined with China's post-1949 revolutionary politics and Maoist doctrine to produce a unique language for population policy and carve out a set of institutions and practices that laid the foundation for strict state regulation of childbirth. Globally, the debate over the relationship between population and development, which could be traced to its Malthusian origins, had been mixed with the ideas of social Darwinism and the institutions of colonial rule to produce growing anxiety over the rapid growth of the nonwhite population and the potential threat it posed to the established hierarchy of power relations and to the quality of the human species.[2]

These dynamics provided the social and political matrix within which China's population policy evolved, and at the broadest level, explain how China came to embrace the one-child policy. In similar fashion, it was the evolution of these same domestic and global forces that led to its decline and retirement.

Before turning to a brief history of the evolution of China's population policy, a note about the meaning of the so-called one-child policy. It is important to keep in mind that "one-child policy" is a useful and descriptive label for the birth limitation program that China adopted in 1979, but it does not capture the complexity or variability of the policy as implemented over time and space and ethnic group. Although all of China's childbearing-age population was urged to have only one child, China's minority groups (approximately 10 percent of the population) were never required to limit births to one child, nor were many farm households who inhabited relatively poor and sparsely populated regions of the country. Parents of children born with serious physical or mental limitations were also permitted to have another child. And beginning in 1984, five years after the policy's inception, rural resistance and widespread reports of female infanticide, combined with central-level conflict over the direction of reform, led the regime to relax the policy for rural residents whose first child was a girl. Under this revised policy, labeled a "one-son or two-child policy," rural couples whose first child was female were given official permission to have a second child after a waiting period of three to five years. There were also periods when Beijing ceded to local authorities more room to adapt policy to local conditions, as long as they did not exceed their birth and population growth targets for the year. At other times, however, they exercised more centralized control. In addition, regulations permitted couples comprised of two only children to have a second child. As large numbers of the one-child generation entered their marriage and childbearing-age years after 2000, therefore, the numbers eligible to have a second child grew rapidly. In short, the "one-child policy" is a label that accurately describes the policy goal, and generally describes the policy in effect for most urban households through 2013, but it obscures the reality of a much more complex pattern of regulation and enforcement that varied over time and space.

Additionally, undue focus on the one-child policy years obscures the significance of what came before 1979. Yet without the steps taken during this earlier period, state capacity to limit couples to one child would have been lacking. With that in mind, I will look closely at developments prior to 1979 that help illuminate the connections between China and the wider world.

Chinese Politics and Population Policy: An Overview

The history of China's population policy between 1949 and 1979 echoes the overall history of the People's Republic over that same period. After the defeat of Japan in 1945, the CCP fought a civil war against the US-backed Nationalist Party. After the Communist victory in 1949, the CCP took several years to consolidate its authority and begin the transition to socialist government (1949–52). This was followed by the First Five-Year Plan period from 1953 to 1957, which saw the collectivization of agriculture and the socialist transformation of the industrial economy. Divisions within the leadership over such issues as the pace of collectivization, the role of material incentives, and the virtues of mass mobilization over bureaucratic governance were temporarily but forcefully reined in by Mao Zedong, who launched the Great Leap Forward in 1958. This frenzied campaign was grounded in the Maoist belief in *voluntarism*, or the capacity of human action, if properly led and motivated, to override the limits of the material conditions through massive and sustained human effort.[3] In the case of the Great Leap Forward, the goal was to overtake the Soviet Union in level of development through one great burst of mobilization. Rather than achieve that goal, by 1961 the campaign had resulted in around fifty million excess deaths due to starvation and related factors, the near-collapse of collective agriculture, and overall economic stagnation.[4] While other political leaders (including Deng Xiaoping) worked to restore order and revive the economy from 1962 to 1965, Mao retreated to focus his attention on the international socialist movement. What he saw happening in the USSR discouraged him, and led him to believe that it was possible for the revolution to be undermined by "revisionists" who courted the capitalist West and preferred negotiation to revolutionary warfare. Concluding that the Bolshevik Party in Moscow had been corrupted in this way, he began to build momentum for a great purge of the CCP. Rather than follow the standard practice of rectifying the party through an internal process controlled by the party this purge was to be conducted by the masses, who were encouraged to root out capitalist-roaders within the party and purge society of all aspects of traditional or bourgeois culture. As Red Guards began to follow Mao's call in 1966, the Great Proletarian Cultural Revolution began, and government, police, and security operations came to a halt. Red Guards meted out harsh justice to anyone believed to have deviated from the Maoist path, and not content with those battles, they began to fight among themselves over who should be considered the true followers of Chairman Mao. When the political devastation and social disruption grew too severe, Mao chose to rein in the Red Guards, but the political and policy changes that began during this period (1966–69) continued through 1976.[5]

Despite the continuation of radical Maoist policies, Premier Zhou Enlai led a revival of the normal operations of state governance, and the first order of business was to draft a Fourth Five-Year Plan (1971–75). In 1975, this was followed by a call for "modernization by the year 2000," an ambitious goal that was intended to prevent China from falling farther behind its rapidly developing neighbors. Before any significant momentum could be built toward that goal, however, both Mao and Zhou died in 1976. The leadership struggle that followed was not resolved until 1978, when Deng Xiaoping and his allies relaunched the campaign for "modernization by the year 2000" and took the first steps toward reform. This new path of reform allowed China to meet and exceed the development goals it had set for the year 2000.[6]

It was against this backdrop of political volatility that China's approach to population policy evolved, and like many other policies, it became a pawn in leadership struggles and was subject to changing political winds. During the first two decades of the Maoist era, however, the proper approach to demographic issues was hotly debated and contested. Initially, the CCP and its leader, Mao Zedong, resisted any suggestion that a large population constituted a problem. They rejected the claim that China was overpopulated, arguing instead that the appearance of overpopulation was actually the result of the exploitative system of capitalism, and would disappear as capitalism was replaced by socialism.

It did not take long, however, for top officials in the CCP to begin to worry quietly about the pressures created by a large and rapidly growing population. When the results of China's first national census were tallied in 1954, the leadership began to understand the dimensions of the problems China faced, and some began to worry that the CCP could never meet its promises to the peasantry to end the hunger and want that had characterized their lives before the revolution. Some began to speak in more practical ways about the burden of population growth, and to recommend that China amend its population policy to provide more support for family-planning education and allow the import of condoms and other contraceptive supplies.[7]

Before these first steps could yield any meaningful results, however, the radicalization of domestic politics interrupted the effort, and advocates of family planning were branded as "rightists," or enemies of the revolution. At the same time, however, the middle and late 1950s was a period of intensified state planning. All institutions and bureaucracies were mobilized to put into place annual five-year performance plans that would help China achieve its goal of becoming an advanced socialist economy and society. In this context, it was Mao who suggested in 1957 that China should attempt to plan reproduction in the same way it aspired to plan material production. The focus on planning made it more difficult for critics to undermine birth control efforts, since it was the logic of socialist planning, and not Malthusian pessimism, that prompted it. Planning could be associated with either pronatalism or antinatalism.

At the time, birth planning (*jihua shengyu*), that is, the attempt to regulate population growth so as to keep it in balance with levels of economic production and growth, was only a goal to be reached at some more advanced stage of socialist development. As China's population continued to grow rapidly in the 1960s, however, key leaders such as Premier Zhou Enlai came to believe that birth planning could no longer be postponed. In 1965, Zhou proposed the first national population control target—reducing the annual rate of population growth to 1 percent by the end of the century, and by 1972 he had authorized the creation of an extensive family-planning bureaucracy to oversee implementation of population policy, provide free access to contraceptives, abortions, and sterilizations, and monitor the enforcement of local birth targets. Socialist planning thus came to embrace human reproduction in much the same way that it embraced agricultural and industrial production. Local officials who were responsible for meeting grain and steel production quotas now began to receive quotas for babies.[8]

In the early and mid-1970s, the policy focus was "later, longer, fewer," that is, promoting later marriage, longer spacing between births (three to five years), and fewer births (a two-child ideal and a three-child limit). By mid-decade, the childbearing norm began to tighten; the new slogan was "One is not too few, two is enough, three is too many." In the cities, young couples began to feel pressure to have only one child. In the countryside, they were urged to have no more than two. In 1979, a group of China's top scientists announced that if China was to achieve its economic goals by the year 2000—a goal that the new Deng regime had expressed as achieving a per capita gross national product of $1,000 by the year 2000 (subsequently reduced to $800 per capita), population had to be contained within 1.2 billion. In turn, this meant that the official birth limit had to be lowered to one child per couple (with some exceptions for special circumstances). The scientists, whose computer models and calculations were based on faulty and inadequate data, succeeded in persuading Deng Xiaoping of the absolute necessity of the one-child policy, and it soon became official policy.[9]

In an extraordinary "Open Letter" to CCP members that was published in all newspapers in September 1980, China's leaders defended the new policy and made it clear to the CCP membership the high level of priority they attached to it. They argued that the two-decade delay after 1949 was a fateful mistake. By the time the state began to encourage fertility control, a huge new generation of young people had already been born who were approaching their childbearing years. As a result, even with declining fertility levels (i.e., the average number of children born to a woman during her reproductive years), demographic momentum meant continued growth of total population size. That growth threatened to reach 1.5 billion by century's end if no action was taken, the letter argued, a number that would doom China to poverty and backwardness through another generation if urgent action was not taken by this generation.[10]

Implementing the One-Child Policy

The one-child policy was inaugurated just as the Deng regime was about to embark on a far-reaching reform program that gradually transformed China's economy, polity, and society. The collective economy was gradually decollectivized and marketized; politics was deradicalized and political institutions revived; society was granted relief from the all-intrusive party-state that had permeated every aspect of public and private life. Change came in fits and stops, with periods of dramatic change often followed by a partial retreat to safer political ground. This pattern gave Chinese politics a cyclic or wave pattern, not unlike the high tides and low tides of the mass campaigns of the Mao era. Through all of these changes and fluctuations in political atmosphere, the insistence on strict birth control never faltered. It was a constant in an otherwise volatile situation.

In the early years of the program (1979–83), as the Deng regime fought against the lingering influences of the Cultural Revolution, it was possible to use the tools and institutions of the Maoist era to press for strict enforcement of birth quotas that were handed down to each city, county, neighborhood, and village. Thirty years of Maoism had taught Chinese citizens to be wary of voicing opposition to the latest campaign, taught officials that they could intimidate and coerce anyone who dared to defy them, and taught party leaders at all levels that the failure to meet campaign quotas was one of the seven deadly sins of Chinese politics. A poor campaign performance could spell the end of a promising career.

The tasks local officials faced were formidable. All childbearing-age couples, urban and rural, had to receive official birth permits from the state in order to give birth legally. In addition, provinces and local governments drafted regulations offering economic incentives to encourage policy compliance and imposing stiff sanctions on policy violators. All childbearing-age women were required to undergo periodic gynecological exams to ensure they were not carrying an "unplanned" pregnancy, and if they were, they were pressed to undergo an abortion immediately. The new regulations often came with a three-month window before enforcement began; women who were already pregnant, but did not have an official birth permit, were thus duly warned, and faced the difficult choice between abortion or family ruin.[11]

In China's cities and towns, the total fertility rate had declined from 3.3 in 1970 to about 1.5 by 1978, a remarkably low level for a developing country. Determined to push it even lower, however, state monitoring intensified in workplaces and neighborhoods. Monthly or quarterly gynecological examinations for childbearing-age women, plus a system of marriage and birth permits provided by the collective work unit or the neighborhood committee, made it hard for anyone to escape the tight surveillance net. Those who did faced severe penalties if caught, including fines and loss of employment, perhaps even one's coveted urban household registration.[12]

Rural China posed a far greater challenge. Agricultural work requires household labor, and even very young children can be put to work in service of the family income. Moreover, children were the only guarantee of old-age support, and the most destitute villagers were inevitably those who were alone and childless. Only a son could assure a couple that they would be spared such a fate. Daughters usually married out of the village, and upon marriage a daughter's first obligation transferred to her husband's family. In addition to these practical considerations, the traditional emphasis on bearing sons to carry on the ancestral line remained deeply entrenched in the countryside. As a result, although rural fertility levels were cut in half between 1971 and 1979 (declining from approximately 6.0 to 3.0), much of rural China remained hostile to a two- or one-child limit, including the village officials who would have to enforce the policy. When the rural reforms implemented after 1978 began to relax the state's administrative grip on the peasantry just as the one-child policy was launched, therefore, it set the stage for an intense struggle over the control of childbearing.[13]

The struggle took a variety of forms. In some villages, women who refused to abort an unplanned birth were subjected to endless meetings where they were berated, intimidated, and threatened into cooperation. In others, medical teams and party cadres swooped in unexpectedly, in an effort to catch women who were eluding them. At worst, women were forced onto trucks and taken directly to the township headquarters, where medical personnel would perform abortions and sterilizations and insert intrauterine devices. The use of some form of birth control after the first or second child became mandatory, and in the countryside the preferred method was the IUD, since it was always in place and not easily removed. The insertion of an IUD immediately after childbirth became standard practice.

Villagers resisted in a variety of ways, including leaving the village until the campaign was over and the baby was born, using bribery to get a birth permit, attacking or killing family-planning officials, resorting to female infanticide, or, more common after the mid-1980s, sex-selective abortion. Absent the one-child policy, it was common in the countryside to consider the birth of a daughter a "small happiness" and a son a "big happiness." When this pattern of son preference was reinforced by a one-child birth limit, some were driven to use any means possible to guarantee they would have a son.[14]

Rather than retreat in the face of resistance, the state intensified its efforts. In late 1982, a massive sterilization campaign was launched, with the goal of eliminating all third and higher births. The result of this massive campaign was a fourfold increase in the number of tubal ligations performed in 1983, as compared with the previous years, and large increases across every category of birth control procedures. So severe were the local pressures to meet sterilization targets that many women who had long since completed their intended childbearing, and had been effectively utilizing some form of birth control, were forced to undergo sterilization.[15]

As the campaign began to play itself out and elite politics took a more "liberal" turn, inplementation moved into a second phase (1984–89). A decision was made to modify the one-child policy to allow for more exceptions. Fearful of a breakdown of authority in the countryside and widespread anger over the one-child limit and the often brutal tactics used to enforce it, leaders in Beijing decided to simply concede the need for a son in the countryside. Henceforth, the rural policy became a one-son or two-child policy.[16] Village couples whose first child was a daughter would be allowed to have a second child, allowed to try again for a son. This concession was made in the hopes of pacifying restless villagers, improving enforcement, and reducing the upsurge in female infanticide and female infant abandonment, but over a period of several years, the net effect of this and other rural reforms was to encourage local governments to unduly relax their enforcement efforts. Village officials who themselves were subject to the birth control policies often colluded with their neighbors to avoid enforcement efforts undertaken by outside teams. As the agricultural reforms destroyed the instruments of control and power that officials had enjoyed in the past, they found it difficult to enforce birth limits, and found it easier to report false numbers than fight with neighbors and kin.[17]

The net effect of this policy "slippage" was to weaken central control over the levers of enforcement, and provide support for experts and birth-planning officials who argued that the policy should be more flexible across different regions of China, allowing those in the most impoverished areas with difficult, hilly terrain to have two children, allowing those in average circumstances to have one son or two children, and limiting those in more prosperous areas to only one child. They believed that the same results could be achieved, with less effort and more willing compliance, than if the policy did not respond to the nuances of family need and economic circumstance.

This more differentiated policy was put into place in the latter half of the 1980s, only to be upset by the events of May–June 1989, which ended in a military crackdown on Tiananmen protesters and their supporters in Beijing and around the country. The martial atmosphere that returned to Chinese politics for the next two to three years made it possible to once again tighten local enforcement, ushering in a third phase of policy enforcement (1989–95). As in 1982–83, fears about a poor performance justified the revival of campaign methods. Cadres who had been warned off those methods in the mid-1980s were now instructed to use "crack troops" and "shock attacks" to break through resistance and meet the new goals of the 1991–95 plan period. They were also chastised over the failure to meet the goals of the five-year plan ending in 1990. China's population control targets for that year had been exceeded by a very substantial margin, giving fuel to those who believed that it was acceptable to use coercion in service of the higher goal of achieving the per capita economic goals that had been set for the year 2000. It was also justified by the preliminary results of the 1990 census, which indicated that China's population had grown more quickly than planned or expected.[18]

These numbers prompted the conservative leadership to tighten enforcement, returning to a strict formula that limited all urban couples to only one child, and all rural couples to one son or two children. Exceptions were granted only to some of China's smaller minority nationalities, and to parents whose first child was mentally or physically handicapped to such a degree that they were unable to function as a healthy, working adult. Local officials were put on notice that they were liable for strict enforcement, and that failure to achieve their performance targets for birth planning would result in economic penalties, administrative sanctions, and even demotions. They were to assume that meeting population targets was just as important to their future career success as meeting key economic goals.[19]

This success came at a price, however. Evidence of intimidation and coercion was widespread, particularly in areas that had done poorly prior to 1990. Rural cadres who sided with their fellow villagers did what was necessary to give the appearance of compliance, but also behaved as they had in the past when the work was hard and the campaign targets too ambitious—by lying, exaggerating, or finding other ways to manipulate the system. Because of these practices and others, many Chinese demographers expressed great skepticism when survey data suggested in 1995 that China's fertility level had dropped to 1.4.[20]

The reversion to a more radical political atmosphere began to fade after several years, ushering in yet another phase of policy evolution and implementation (1995–2013). Responding to the new challenges, the post-Tiananmen politics of conservatism gave way to a new wave of reform and opening that rapidly transformed the political, economic, and social landscape.

It was in this context that many of China's population specialists began again to challenge the wisdom of the administrative and punitive approach to population control that had been relied on since the 1970s. Leading figures in China's new generation of highly trained demographers and sociologists criticized the assumption that "fewer births is everything," arguing that it led to "short-sighted actions (such as surprise raids on big-bellied women)." Frankly acknowledging that China's fertility decline had been induced through the widespread use of coercion, the authors insisted on the need for a broader and more complex view of population dynamics and a population policy better suited to an overall strategy of "sustainable development." Writing that "the curtain is gradually closing on the era of monolithic population control," the authors went on to discuss the disturbing consequences of that approach (including sex ratio imbalances and a rapidly aging population) and the necessity of shifting to a developmental approach that emphasized improvements and investments in the quality of the population.[21] In short, they argued that development was the best route to fertility decline, rejecting in the process the sort of "population determinism" (fewer births is everything) that was so deeply embedded in China's population control strategy.

Domestically, the problem of rural unrest and instability was again preoccupying the leadership, and buttressed the position of advocates of reform. One of the major complaints of villagers was the use of coercive birth control tactics to collect taxes and fees owed to the local government. Not only did new documents on rural taxation explicitly forbid the use of those measures, a family-planning document issued in 1995 codified them as seven types of prohibited behaviors: (1) illegally detaining, beating, or humiliating an offender or a relative; (2) destroying property, crops, or houses; (3) raising mortgages without legal authorization; (4) imposing "unreasonable" fines or confiscating goods; (5) implicating relatives or neighbors of offenders, or retaliating against those who report cadre misbehavior; (6) prohibiting childbirths permitted by the local plan in order to fulfill population targets; (7) organizing pregnancy checkups for unmarried women.[22] This itemization of unacceptable behaviors underscored the extent to which the increasingly professional family-planning bureaucracy sought to distance itself from the coercive methods of enforcement that had remained prevalent in the countryside.

Meanwhile, changes in the international discourse on population and development also encouraged advocates of policy reform. When China began to implement its one-child policy in 1979, the discourse on population issues was still dominated by a "population control" paradigm that saw population growth as an impediment to national advancement and a threat to global survival. By the mid-1990s, another school of thought had emerged and displaced the old paradigm. This alternative approach focused on women's reproductive health and rights, and emphasized the organic relationship between the elevation of the status of women (especially through increased education and employment outside the home), the elimination of poverty, and declining fertility levels.[23]

Convinced that change was already overdue, many demographers and family-planning officials embraced this new discourse, and called for the reform of China's policy. Change came slowly, however, despite the unsavory consequences of the policy, including a distorted sex ratio and a rapidly aging population. After some internal debate, the Chinese government officially reavowed its one-child policy in 2000 and in 2001 passed a long-debated Population and Family Planning Law that upheld the existing policy and gave compliance the force of law.[24] Although the law included provisions that called for an "informed choice of safe, effective, and appropriate contraceptive methods," and one prohibiting officials from infringing on "personal rights, property rights, or other legitimate rights and interests," it reaffirmed China's basic approach to population control. Subsequently, however, as the one-child generation matured and married in growing numbers, the state reiterated the right of two single children to have a second child if desired.

Despite the political reluctance to abandon the one-child policy, policy developments in other areas began to shift the focus away from raw population numbers. The decade was dominated by growing concerns over the lack of a social insurance system and retirement support for an aging society, rapidly rising healthcare costs associated with both aging and environmental degradation, and sustainability and climate change. Taken together, these issues formed a development trifecta that revealed the need for a more flexible and supple population policy. As a result, pressures for reform grew. By 2012, those pressures led to the publication of a pro-reform report by the China Development Research Foundation, a top-tier think tank that is supported by, and advises, the State Council on policy issues.[25] The report, which urged that the one-child policy be phased out by 2015, paved the way for decisions announced subsequently during the Eighteenth Party Congress and National People's Congress in 2013.

China's Population Control Program in Global Perspective

In 1989, when the Deng regime crushed the prodemocracy movement, China still inhabited a world defined by the contours of the Cold War. By 1992, that world had disappeared, and the CCP now faced the problem of how to survive in a post-Leninist, postsocialist world. The answer, in part, was to lift the conservative strictures that had been imposed after June 4, 1989, and return to the path of economic reform. As was the case in 1979, however, strictures on childbearing remained firmly in place. Justifications of the one-child policy in 1980 were based on the argument that socialist modernization could not be achieved without it, and the CCP was obliged to take all steps necessary to achieve that goal. By 1995, with the end of the Cold War and collapse of the Soviet Union, the language of socialism was more muted. Modernization was everything, and even as China's economy steamed toward levels of economic development that had only been dreamed of in 1979, the leadership refused to revisit the one-child policy in any serious way. Annual reports and speeches attributed China's great economic success to correct economic policies and directives. Population control, which in 1980 was argued to be the crucial factor on which all development goals rested, was given little credit by the late 1990s. And yet the "numbers are everything" approach, long abandoned in other parts of the economy, remained the rigid foundation on which China's population policy was premised.

China's move in 1979 to limit childbearing-age couples to only one child was a unique and unprecedented state intervention into the realm of reproduction, a confirmation, if you will, of Michel Foucault's vision of all-encompassing state hegemony.[26] Taking that step took audacity, authority, institutional capacity, and a degree of leadership commitment that is rare in any regime. If there were distinctive qualities of the Chinese context that made the conception and enforcement of a one-child policy possible, however, there were also other ways in which Chinese experience ran parallel to that of many other developing world countries, especially in Asia. For all of its unique elements, the Chinese case was also part of a broader global history and was significantly influenced by it.

Turning first to the distinctive aspects of the Chinese experience, China succeeded in intensifying its population control policy and reducing the birth limit to one child by relying on a number of unique ideas and institutions, and by wedding population control to the regime's highest priority of all—rapid modernization. The idea of *jihua shengyu* or "birth planning," a concept central to the Chinese program, allowed advocates of birth control to elide the internal struggle between leftist and rightist forces, a development that helped to insulate the government's increasingly bold antinatalist stance from the radical politics and policies of the Cultural Revolution decade (1966–76). This development was crucial, allowing advocates of birth control and regulated childbirth to block charges from the left of neo-Malthusianism, and charges from cultural conservatives within the party who objected to the expansion of family-planning education and access on moral grounds. In the early attempts to advocate family planning, supporters had used the liberal language of the West, translating "family planning" literally as *jiating jihua*, population control as *renkou jiezhi*, and birth control as *shengyu jiezhi*. The shift to *jihua shengyu*, or *birth planning*, was purposeful, placing the entire project within the politically unassailable context of socialist economic planning. From the time of the second birth control campaign in the mid-1960s, therefore, birth planning defined China's policy, and *jiating shengyu* (family planning) was used only to distinguish China's approach from the liberal, bourgeois model of the West.

In addition to this unique language, China benefited from unique institutions. The CCP was the key institution, since it penetrated all levels and all organizations of Chinese society. Its pervasive presence in every town and village, and the regime's insistence after the revolution that there be no independent sources of influence or authority, meant that leaders in Beijing had a reliable instrument of enforcement. Whatever the limitations and weaknesses in Beijing's ability to compel a disciplined response from party officials down the line—and there were many—those limitations paled in comparison with the challenges faced by other developing world regimes. Although the reform era made it increasingly difficult to maintain that discipline, Beijing adapted as necessary. In the early 1990s, for example, lax enforcement of birth limits led Beijing to introduce the "one-ballot veto system" for assessing the work of local officials. This system was intended to make birth control targets as important as economic targets by making their achievement critical to annual assessments of cadre performance. Under this system, fulfilling or even exceeding all economic targets was insufficient to gain a positive assessment and receive bonuses and other perks. Cadres also had to meet their birth control goals. If not, this one failure would taint their evaluation, and perhaps their career.[27]

A second unique institution that Beijing could draw on was the mobilization campaign, which embodied a Maoist approach to policy implementation. Mass mobilization campaigns were an endemic part of the political and policy process in China, and were used extensively to galvanize the party to swift action, mobilize the masses to participate in the campaign, and push toward the fulfillment of the campaign's goals. During the Maoist era, these campaigns followed a predictable pattern. First came the call to mobilize, then came the campaign to carry out the program, which led to frenzied efforts on the part of local authorities that often provoked a backlash and resistance from the targets of the campaign. This reaction to the overreach by local enforcers led to a moderation of the program, which sometimes was followed by a second hard push for enforcement. Party officials at all levels were highly motivated to meet the targets or goals they had been assigned, since failure to do so could result in a major career setback or, even worse, a political attack on officials' revolutionary commitment.[28]

Frequent repetitions of this pattern during the Maoist era had the effect of turning it into China's primary institution for policy implementation, and it was this instrument that the new Deng regime turned to when it launched the one-child policy. And here we stumble upon a great historical irony. At the very moment when the Deng regime was setting out to undo much of the Maoist legacy, liberate Chinese politics and society from the disruptive consequences of repeated political campaigns, and routinize Chinese governance, the new leaders put their full weight behind a massive campaign to implement the one-child policy and turned a blind eye to the waves of coercion that swept through many parts of China over the next few years as local officials were pressed to meet exacting and difficult population targets.

Although the one-child policy and campaign was launched in 1979, it was the "Open Letter" to all CCP members, published in the flagship newspaper on September 20, 1980, that stands as the most potent marker of the campaign, and once again sets China apart. Not only did China's leaders expect party members to carry out the campaign, they expected them to abide by it. Younger party members were called on to take the lead in signing a certificate pledging to have only one child, and undergoing sterilization after the birth of their first child. Older party members in positions of leadership were urged to support their childbearing-age children in taking the one-child pledge. By making this call public, party leaders brought pressure to bear on reluctant local-level officials who shared the view of their neighbors that one child was not enough, and that failing to produce a son to carry on the ancestral line would bring a worse fate than defying the one-child limit. Ultimately, many did defy that limit by using influence, bribes, or falsely acquired medical certificates to get around it. Comparatively speaking, however, what is remarkable is the extent to which the CCP organization was able to discipline its members at all levels. The unprecedented "Open Letter" was a clear signal to all local officials that the one-child policy was a top priority of the Politburo, and had to be treated as such.

Another set of institutions assured a high level of compliance among the urban population. In the early years of reform, China's system of collectivized work units remained in place, allowing for close supervision of childbearing-age couples. While compliance with the one-child limit brought tangible benefits such as free healthcare and priority status for school admissions, failure to comply could mean being fired, denied housing, and denied access to the many other collective benefits that came with being part of a work unit. Rather than risk these consequences, most acquiesced in the program, which for childbearing-age women meant subjection to gynecological exams monthly or quarterly to be sure they had not become pregnant without the necessary state-issued birth permit. This step was only one of many ways in which women's bodies became the site for policy implementation. The massive 1983–84 sterilization campaign, for example, forced many compliant women to abandon the birth control method they had been using reliably and undergo sterilization instead. They were pressured to do so by local officials who had to meet their quotas and targets for sterilization procedures within a certain period of time, and could not do so without sterilizing women who were no risk to the birth limits.[29]

Rural institutions were disrupted by the new reforms more quickly than urban ones, placing rural officials in a more precarious position in attempting to carry out birth control work. With their monopoly of economic power beginning to dissolve and with their own desire to have more than one child, rural officials were often caught in a difficult position that only a campaign launched from higher levels could alleviate. As a result, poorly performing counties or districts were often called upon to launch a localized campaign, assisted by medical personnel drafted from county hospitals to speed the rate at which birth control procedures—abortions, IUD insertions, sterilizations, and vasectomies—could be carried out. Large numbers of personnel would descend on a particular locality with the goal of ending all "unplanned" pregnancies (that is, pregnancies that were not authorized by the requisite state-issued birth permit) and sterilizing those who had already violated the one-child birth limit. If resistance was encountered, as it often was, officials used whatever means necessary to coerce compliance. Popular methods included destroying new homes or other personal property of farmers, holding one or more of the offender's parents or grandparents in custody until they relented, or subjecting the pregnant women to isolation and harangue until they gave in. All of these methods were officially outlawed in the mid-1990s, but they were used extensively before that time and continued to be used more sporadically over the next twenty years. The campaigns became routinized to coincide with Spring Festival (Chinese New Year), when families gathered, marriages occurred, and spouses living in different places were reunited, or the summer harvest (August or September), when farmers got a respite from their ongoing labor.[30]

It is important to note that the effectiveness of the campaign approach was progressively eroded by the success of China's economic reforms, which brought economic development, social change, and a shift to more routine forms of bureaucratic governance. These changes led to increased reliance on legal and administrative measures and a decline in tolerance for the more blunt and coercive tactics associated with campaign-style enforcement. This shift did not prevent, however, the episodic recurrence of campaigns in scattered localities by local officials determined to make quick progress on lowering fertility levels. Those enforcement practices, in turn, fomented the popular anger that became more pronounced over time.

If the institutions and practices described above were distinctive to China, in other respects the Chinese program, its motives, and its evolution were the product of the same global forces that influenced demographic policies elsewhere. Whether responding to, or reacting against, international influences, China's policy has been shaped far more by external sources than is generally acknowledged.

The influence of international forces on the evolution of China's population policy can be seen in several ways. First is the influence of the early twentieth-century Euro-American movements supporting birth control and eugenics. While the Chinese revolution unfolded in the early and mid-twentieth century, anxieties among Western elites about the growth and quality of global population—anxieties fueled by Malthusian and social Darwinian ideas—helped to galvanize the international family-planning movement and shape their views of China. Margaret Sanger, who sat at the intersection of the family-planning and eugenics movements, traveled to China, Japan, and Korea in 1922 to lecture on the subjects and received an enthusiastic reception from local supporters, who began to organize a local birth control league.[31] Many Chinese feminists and supporters of the New Culture Movement supported her call for birth control, and female physicians began to open clinics devoted to the needs of women and children, including birth control education and services. Due to the political turbulence of the 1920s and 1930s, however, these developments were limited in their scope and impact, and nationalist elites proffered a range of views.[32]

The Chinese Communist Party, by contrast, took a more unified view of the matter, dismissing limited measures such as access to birth control as bourgeois and calling for socialist revolution to truly liberate Chinese women. Their official party policy in the 1930s and 1940s was pronatalist; high birth rates among the peasantry were seen as the only means to compensate for losses due to war, disease, and high infant mortality. At the same time, the demand for access to birth control by urban women joining the revolution led to an official policy advocating delaying marriage until the end of the war with Japan. For married couples, birth control was sanctioned as a means to delay childbirth.[33]

This policy did not go unchallenged, however. Opponents writing in the newspaper *Liberation Daily* (*Jiefang ribao*) argued that birth control surgery was dangerous and bad for women's health. Others opposed birth control on moral grounds, arguing that giving birth was a natural human phenomenon that should not be artificially regulated.[34] In the face of this opposition, restrictions were placed on access to abortion and sterilization, but birth control after marriage was officially sanctioned.

At liberation, this birth control policy remained in force, despite the adoption of a pronatalist line. With the party leadership absorbed with more pressing issues, decision-making on birth control devolved to the newly created Ministry of Public Health. Dominated by Western-trained medical professionals who were inclined by tradition and training to be conservative on the issue of contraception, the ministry drew up regulations that imposed severe restrictions on access to contraception, abortion, and sterilization. In April 1950, regulations were issued governing access to abortion by female cadres in party, government, and military posts in the Beijing District. The regulations were designed to severely limit access, and those who met the strict conditions were required to obtain a series of written approvals before the procedure could take place.[35] By May 1952, national regulations had been drafted; they were approved at the end of the year and disseminated on a trial basis.[36] The regulations outlawed sterilization or abortion except in cases of severe illness or threat to the woman. In addition, no woman was eligible for sterilization unless she was thirty-five years old, had six or more children, and had one child aged ten or above.[37] Reinforcing this strict line, the Ministry of Health also moved to limit access to contraceptives. In January 1953, only days after the regulations were approved, the ministry notified customs officials that they should stop the import of contraceptives.[38] This ban, combined with the restrictive policy that discouraged the production of contraceptives domestically, meant that even the rudimentary and unreliable contraceptive supplies available at that time would continue to be extremely scarce. Supporters of family planning thus faced formidable opposition, and that argument unfolded in the mid-1950s in the form of the rise and quick fall of China's first family-planning campaign. Access to contraceptives and education on family planning, then, were no less contested in revolutionary China than they were in the West, and despite the socialist doctrine that framed the debate, the issues were precisely the same.

A second external influence on the CCP's early position on population and family planning was the emerging Cold War. In 1949, the US government, seeking to explain the defeat of its allies, the Nationalists, despite massive aid and military support, prepared an extensive official history of US policy in China, explaining why it had ultimately withdrawn support from the Nationalists, why the CCP was winning, but also why the Communist regime was bound to fail. The analysis argued that the CCP would not be able to meet its obligation to feed its population because of the unchecked population growth. In other words, it argued that the Malthusian dilemma would defeat them.[39] Mao Zedong's response was to condemn this "pessimistic view" emanating from the capitalist West as reactionary, Malthusian, and "utterly groundless," and to insist instead that China's large population was a great asset.[40] This rejection of what he saw as Malthusian logic was justified by Marxist ideology, which saw "overpopulation" as a byproduct of capitalism that would be eliminated by the revolution. It was also consistent with the party's pre-1949 pronatalist policy, as well as the Soviet Union's pronatalist policy after World War II. Nevertheless, this exchange of verbal hostilities elevated an ongoing and complex internal process of sorting out party policy on population issues to the status of international insult, creating even greater resistance within the CCP to family planning.

A third external factor that influenced China was the successful implementation of family-planning and birth control programs in its neighboring countries. In the 1950s and 1960s, Japan, South Korea, and Taiwan all developed birth control programs, and in the case of Japan, it was also very apparent by the mid-1960s that the Japanese economy was recovering rapidly from its destruction in World War II. Chinese premier Zhou Enlai was especially taken with these developments, particularly given the toll of the Great Leap Forward on China's economy. Between 1963 and 1966, Zhou spoke frequently and forcefully on the issue of birth control, arguing that it was a "shortcoming" (*duanchu*) of the socialist system that it did not have a "population plan." Zhou explained this by noting that neither Marx nor Lenin had confronted the problem; their writings therefore offered no guidance or solutions. Foreshadowing later developments, he also remarked: "In my opinion, after having two children, it is best to undergo sterilization."[41]

In July 1963, in a speech to high school graduates, Zhou defended the birth control policy against charges that it was Malthusian. Noting that Malthus relied on war and pestilence to solve the population problem, Zhou said:

> We can't rely on war to solve the population problem, and we can't rely on pestilence, and we certainly can't rely on overseas developments. . . . [Instead] we must study advanced experience.[42]

He went on to use the example of Japan as a country whose achievements in reducing birth rates deserved China's attention. He advocated sending experts to Japan to study their methods, or inviting Japanese experts to China. Zhou apparently was struck by the fact that Japan's population growth rate had dropped to about 10 per 1,000 by the mid-1960s, so much so that in the fall of 1965 he urged in several speeches that China strive to achieve the same low growth rate by the end of the century.[43] His repeated references to the Japanese example are remarkable given the recent history of Japan's invasion and occupation of China between 1937 and 1945, and it is indicative of the urgency Zhou felt about China's rapid population growth. Unfortunately, the radical politics of the Cultural Revolution prevented any further action, but as soon as the most radical phase was over, Zhou began to restore normal government work, develop a new five-year plan, and press for a bigger investment in birth control.

Yet a fourth influence on China was the evolving global discourse on population control. Whereas an international conference held in 1964 was dominated by those who voiced unbridled enthusiasm for population control, the 1974 UN conference on population and development, held in Budapest, was divided between a pro-population control coalition of mostly developed world states, and delegations from the global South who took a neo-Marxist view that saw population and poverty as a by-product of long-standing exploitation by the capitalist North. To redress this inequity, they called for debt forgiveness and economic restructuring to bring about a redistribution of wealth.[44] China, which had long positioned itself in foreign affairs as an advocate of nonaligned Third World regimes, publicly supported this view, while continuing to push aggressively at home to lower fertility rates.[45]

When the reform era began a few years later and China's commitment to population control became more transparent, the UN Fund for Population Activities, along with many NGOs, academic centers, and scholars, provided enthusiastic support to Chinese authorities who were anxious to improve their facilities and expertise on demographic issues. They helped train a new cohort of Chinese demographers and offered technical assistance as China prepared to carry out a population census in 1982. Since that time, China has participated in a vast number of international meetings and conferences, collaborated with UN organizations and NGOs on research and applied projects, and become an important source of expertise to countries who wish to draw on China's impressive demographic resources and experience.

The profoundly important role of international actors and ideas on China's program is best illustrated by two examples. The first is the role of Song Jian, a prominent scientist, in leading China toward a one-child policy. Attending his first international conference in Sweden in 1978, Song became interested in the scientific modeling techniques that had been used to develop the Club of Rome report called *The Limits to Growth* in 1972, and *Mankind at the*

Turning Point in 1974.[46] Though his expertise was in cybernetics, and though the techniques and the predictions they produced had been widely criticized and dismissed in the West, he returned to China and used similar modeling techniques to convince Deng Xiaoping that China's only hope for modernization was with a one-child birth limit.[47]

The second example comes in the 1990s, when internal criticism of China's one-child policy and its consequences began spilling out into academic journals and professional conferences. This criticism was provoked in part by the new campaign that had gotten underway in the early 1990s to crack down on violators of the birth limit, giving rise to a new round of coercion in many areas of the countryside. It was also provoked by the now very wide divide that existed between the highly professionalized scholars and bureaucrats who advised and manned the top ranks of the family-planning bureaucracy, and the old guard political leadership that resisted all calls for policy reform. In this context, two high-profile international conferences gave support and momentum to the reformers.

The first was the 1994 UN Conference on Population and Development that was held in Cairo, and the second was the UN Conference on Women that was held in Beijing in 1995. For many feminists, the Cairo conference was the culmination of a decade or more of work to shift the discourse on population and development from one focused on reducing population numbers to one focused on reproductive rights and women's status. Despite continued differences among representatives over language pertaining to abortion, in particular, the conference report embraced the new language and emphasized the organic relationship between the elevation of the status of women (especially through increased education and employment outside the home), the elimination of poverty, and declining fertility levels.[48]

The substance of the conference was reported in some detail in the Chinese media and in population journals, and shortly thereafter, the influence of the new international language on Chinese policy became clear. In China's "Outline Plan for Family Planning Work in 1995–2000," for example, stress was placed on the impact of the socialist market economy on population control, and on the necessity of linking population control to economic development. In addition, the plan placed special emphasis on the role of education, and urged aggressive efforts to increase women's educational level in order to promote lower fertility. This emphasis dovetailed with the Millennial Development Goals adopted by most UN member states in 2000, specifying a set of goals to be reached by 2015. China took an active role in supporting this agenda, which included a focus on women's empowerment and education, along with gender equality.[49]

A second UN conference, the UN's Fourth World Conference on Women, held in Beijing in 1995, strongly reinforced the Cairo message, provoking a new wave of feminist thinking and action, and further encouraging SFPC officials to consider a more client-centered approach that gave greater consideration to women's needs and their reproductive health. This conference was also important in stimulating the growth of nongovernmental organizations in China, with greater focus on issues related to women and gender, and it encouraged established organizations like the Women's Federation to become stronger advocates for women.[50]

Still another way in which global forces influenced the evolution of China's population policy was the revolution in telecommunications that made it increasingly difficult to deflect and bury reports that contradicted claims that birth limits were enforced by routine administrative means, and not through the use of coercion. During the 1980s and 1990s, Chinese citizens with complaints against local officials often turned to domestic or foreign journalists when their complaints fell on deaf government ears. By the later 1990s, however, the arrival of social media platforms, along with a more prosperous and tech-savvy population that had easy access to them, made containment impossible. In 2012, for example, the family of a woman who was forced to abort her seven-month old fetus used social media to publicize her story. Supported by gruesome photographs of the aborted fetus, the story drew enormous attention and public outcry, revealing through posted comments the depth and breadth of the hatred of the one-child policy and the hostility toward those who enforce it.[51] Repeated episodes of this sort were an embarrassment to a regime moving to the forefront of global affairs, and the public hostility they revealed tapped into anxieties about regime stability. Taking incremental steps toward retiring the policy was a way to deal with those concerns and dampen popular resentment.[52]

Ultimately, of course, the decision to retire the one-child policy was an economic and social one. With a rapidly aging population, the policy no longer paid the substantial economic dividends that it had in previous decades. On the contrary, it was setting China up for economic difficulties in the future. Socially, the pressure to abandon the policy was rising, especially as those born under the one-child policy were now eligible to have two children if both parents were only children. Skewed sex ratios, recognized as one of the worst social consequences of the one-child limit, remained a major problem, one that would constrain marriage options of millions of young men for decades to come. Just as important, corruption and wealth had allowed many to buy their way to a second, or even third child, by simply paying the required fines. In a social climate where there was great resentment of official corruption and economic inequality, retaining a policy that was being enforced so unevenly was an increasingly dangerous proposition.

Consequences and Legacy of China's One-Child Policy

The one-child policy was adopted just as the reform era began in 1979. This poses two problems for assessing its impact. First, the consequences of the one-child program are deeply intertwined with the consequences and results of economic and political reform, so much so that it can be difficult to distinguish the effects of birth planning from other effects of reform. And where those effects are clearly entangled, it is even harder to weigh the relative influence of one versus the other. Second, looking at the consequences of the one-child policy from today's vantage point, it is easy to forget that the consequences have been unfolding and evolving since 1979. They are not static or categorical. This fluidity means that there can be no definitive assessment that takes into account the unfolding story of the policy and China's socioeconomic transformation.

Despite these two important caveats, it is still clear that the implementation of China's one-child policy has had an enormous impact on Chinese society, though not always the impact that has been claimed by the state. On the one hand, there can be no doubt that the size and composition of China's population at the beginning of the reform era—young, educated, and underemployed—aided in China's rapid economic development, or that maintaining lower levels of fertility freed up more resources than would otherwise have been available to invest in human capital. Eager to justify two decades of state control, however, at the end of the century Chinese authorities declared that China's population policy had prevented four hundred million births since 1970. At the time, this assertion went unchallenged in public forums, with the result that it became a widely known figure and was republished as fact in many media reports. In fact, the calculations that led to this estimate were as faulty as the ones that led to the adoption of the one-child limit, exaggerating greatly the impact of the one-child policy and China's overall birth-planning program.[53]

That this number was designed to aid state propaganda efforts is made clear by the choice of 1970 as the starting point for measurement. In 1970, China's fertility level remained high. The years 1970–79 did see a gradual increase in pressures to have fewer children, but the most important developments of those years were the depoliticization of arguments for population control, the creation of a family-planning system to provide education and support for family planning, and most important, the provision of free contraceptives to encourage and hasten adoption of some form of birth control. These efforts had a profound effect on China's urban and rural fertility levels, all before the one-child policy got underway. This suggests that while state action was crucial in hastening fertility decline, these policy developments coincided with increased demand for access to contraceptives and increased desire of childbearing-age couples to manage their childbearing and limit their number of children. As theorists of fertility decline have noted, a population must be "ready, willing, and able" to limit childbearing before sustained fertility decline can begin. China provided the tools that enabled young men and women to act on their fertility preferences, encouraged them with propaganda and education, and created political and economic incentives to comply.

Choosing the 1970 fertility level as the starting point for calculating the impact of China's population policy, therefore, obscured the impact of the one-child policy while allowing the state to offer further justification for it. It ignored the widespread patterns in fertility decline seen elsewhere in the world, particularly the impact of development on childbearing preferences in the absence of heavy-handed state intervention. Nor did the calculation offer any way to compare the impact on population size of the one-child policy, as opposed to a universal two-child policy that focused on the spacing of children, or an approach premised entirely on guaranteed and substantial rewards for compliance, or even one that maintained the de facto late-marriage policy that had been in place during the Cultural Revolution.[54]

If it is difficult to calculate the number of births that were prevented exclusively by the one-child policy, it is easy to observe other effects of the policy. First, it meant that an entire generation of childbearing-age couples was subjected to state control over the number of children they were permitted to have, and *when* they were permitted to have them. It is important to separate these two impacts to understand their full implications. The one-child birth limit meant that childbearing-age couples were not permitted to have more than one child (or two for couples who met specific conditions), and women were subjected to constant monitoring by the state and its local agents to ensure that couples who were compliant at the age of twenty remained compliant at the age of thirty. Less well understood, however, is that in the early years of the campaign, many women who became pregnant with their *first* child, but without official permission, were required to have an abortion. And in more recent years, as the numbers permitted to have a second child grew, failure to comply with regulations requiring couples to wait three or four years to have a second child could also result in pressure to abort.

Women were also the subjects on which most medical procedures were carried out. Their bodies bore the physical weight of enforcement, and the state used the birth of a first child or the abortion of a subsequent pregnancy as an opportunity to insert an IUD or carry out a tubal ligation. This was particularly true in the countryside, where resistance to the one-child limit was widespread and campaign-style roundups of pregnant women were frequent events. Despite recognition in the 1980s that vasectomy was a cheaper and safer medical alternative to tubal ligation, only a very small proportion of men underwent the procedure, and no major educational campaigns were carried out to encourage male sterilization. When asked about this issue in the early 1990s, both male and female officials in the countryside felt that attempts to increase the rate of male sterilization were futile. They claimed that women preferred to take the risk of undergoing sterilization, fearing that male sterilization would reduce permanently the strength and virility of their husbands. When asked why those attitudes could not be changed with the same investment of state resources that had been devoted to implementing the one-child policy, it was clear they had never considered that possibility.[55]

While men were exhorted to support the one-child policy, the female reproductive system, one of the few areas that had not been completely subsumed by the radical politics of the Mao era, was explicitly redefined as a public domain. In addition to the policies and regulations passed at each level of government that brought reproduction under state authority, an even more visible symbol of state intrusion was the widespread practice in rural China of publicly documenting the menstrual cycle and birth control method of each childbearing-age woman in the village. Public exposure contributed to other pressures to conform and underscored the power of local authorities to engineer family size, composition, and change.

In addition to its direct impact on reproductive age women, the one-child policy influenced the Chinese family and society in a variety of ways. The most direct impact on Chinese society was to create a two-track society and a two-track generation: children who were born in urban areas were overwhelmingly likely to be single children (singletons), and children who had one or more siblings were most likely rural-born. By 2010, about 63 percent of all Chinese families had a single child, but in cities the percentage was much higher. Children were reared, then, in an atmosphere where they were uniformly surrounded by other singletons, a revolutionary change from the recent past, and one that raised deep concerns in China about the temperament, values, and psychological well-being of this generation. Development and commercialization meant that these singletons experienced a degree of wealth and disposable income that was inconceivable to their parents and grandparents when they were young. Indulged by grandparents and parents, they became important consumers in the new economy, altering the balance of power within the family.[56]

With no competition from other siblings, singletons were the sole beneficiary of their parents' resources and attention. This contributed to parents' ability to invest in their child's education and devote themselves to their socioeconomic advancement, an important dividend of the one-child policy.[57] It also increased pressure on the child to succeed in school, career, and marriage, sometimes to the detriment of their psychological health. Meanwhile, the decline and collapse of the aversion to divorce that had been characteristic of the Maoist era, combined with a simplified process for legal divorce, meant that growing numbers of singletons were the children of divorce, living with a single parent or with a parent and stepparent.[58] These changes, of course, are consistent with social changes that have occurred in other developing societies, and are not the direct byproduct of the one-child policy. The role of the one-child policy was to remove the cushion from these events sometimes provided by siblings, who can support one another as they move through wrenching family changes.

Another important consequence of the one-child policy was to create a family structure composed of an inverted triangle: four grandparents, two parents, and one child (the so-called 4-2-1 phenomenon). Given the traditional Chinese emphasis on care for the elderly, the weight of obligation to be carried by singletons was a source of concern, both on the micro and macro levels. At each level, the issue was the same. In micro form, the question was how a singleton could pay for the care and well-being of seven family members, or two married singletons care for fifteen people, including their single child. In macro form, the question translated into the problem every society faces with population ageing: how can the working adults in a society care for very large numbers of elderly and youth, and simultaneously maintain the levels of economic productivity necessary to sustain economic growth?

As China moved through an exceptionally rapid fertility decline in the last decades of the twentieth century, it did so having already achieved an increase in life span and a decline in mortality that was exceptional in the developing world. As a result, its younger generation is smaller than the one that came before it, and its older generation will have an average life span consistent with that of advanced industrialized countries. This dependency ratio (most commonly defined as the total number of elderly and youth as a percentage of the number of working-age adults) has worsened in many countries in the industrialized world that have very low fertility (e.g., Italy and Japan). China is unique, however, in the degree to which the dependency factor has grown prior to reaching income levels equivalent to those of advanced industrialized countries. In 2012, China experienced its first ever natural absolute decrease in its labor force, with 3.45 million fewer workers than the previous year and a projected decline of about 29 million by the end of the decade. Put more starkly, in 2009 there were thirteen working-age adults for each elderly person; by 2050, there will be only two. Persons aged sixty or older comprised 8.8 percent of China's population in 1990, reached 10 percent by the end of the century, and was at 13.7 percent in 2013. Though this figure did not yet place China among those countries with the highest percentages of elderly population, the raw numbers show the scope of what China faces. By the year 2013, the elderly population numbered approximately 185 million, on its way up to an estimated 284 million by 2025, and 440 million by 2050.[59] This trend will place tremendous pressure on the working adult population, as their labor will be expected to generate much of the national wealth needed to care for their elders and their children.

Another way in which the one-child policy has impacted society is through its contribution to migration and to the creation of a class of children collectively known as *heiren*, that is, "black" or illegal persons. This term, which emerged in the 1980s, is used to describe individuals born without state permission, and who therefore do not officially exist. As children, *heiren* are denied access to any services or benefits that come from being registered officially as part of a household or locale, including access to healthcare and schooling. Faced with pressures to abort or pay exorbitant fines for "unplanned" or illegal births, some parents choose to run, becoming part of the enormous migrant population that has spread over China during the reform era. This buys them time to give birth to the child, but it does not solve the problem of registration. Recent efforts to reform the household registration (*hukou*) system, and to permit migrants to register for school in the location where the family lives, may slowly improve the situation, but in the short run, those unable to pay the fines for giving birth outside the plan will continue to be caught in bureaucratic limbo.[60]

One of the most disturbing effects of the one-child policy is its contribution to a marked sex ratio imbalance in those born after 1979. Over time and across many different human populations, sex ratios at birth—that is, the number of males born during a given time period compared to the number of females—hover around 105 boys for every 100 girls. On occasion, for a limited period of time, this ratio may vary naturally, with a few more or a few less boys for each 100 girls. Data from China's 2000 census, however, revealed that the sex ratio at birth was approximately 119 boys for every 100 girls, and the 2010 census gave similar results. If that were not serious enough, the national figures mask much more severe distortions, with some provinces and regions recording sex ratios of 125 or more males for each 100 females.[61]

From the beginning of the one-child policy, there was concern that the traditional preference for sons that was deeply embedded in Chinese culture might result in an imbalanced sex ratio at birth. In the September 1980 "Open Letter" on the one-child policy, for example, several of the most common objections to the policy were aired, including fears that it would lead to female infanticide and abandonment and, consequently, to an imbalance in the sex ratio. These fears were initially discounted, but they proved to be warranted. In the early 1980s senior officials became alarmed about the many reports of female infanticide and female abandonment on the part of couples desperate to have a son. The infanticide reports produced a firestorm of controversy at home and abroad, leading the regime to respond in two contradictory ways. First, it denied that there was a widespread problem; census and survey data were used to show that China's sex ratio at birth was well within what was considered to be the normal range and in keeping with China's own population history. Though conceding that incidents of infanticide and abandonment did occur, it was insisted that such cases were rare, and that they occurred only in the most backward regions of the countryside, where the "feudal mentality" remained entrenched. The solution proposed was an education campaign to uproot such backward ideas, but education alone was of little use, given the social and economic realities that privileged male offspring.

By 1984, as reports of female infanticide multiplied and the All-China Women's Federation (ACWF) began to insist that the problem be faced and addressed, the state changed tack. Rather than address the underlying causes of gender bias, however, it made concessions to rural sensibilities and adjusted the one-child policy to allow single-daughter households to try again—for a son. In the countryside, the state conceded, women were considered socially inferior and worth less economically. Sonless couples were disadvantaged economically and socially, the potential prey of stronger families and kin groups. Single-daughter households should therefore be given special consideration, just as minority groups and the parents of invalids were given special consideration. Although the intent of the 1984 policy change was to legitimize what was already happening in the countryside, it had the effect of reinforcing existing prejudices against females. A woman with a single daughter and no sons might be applauded by local officials, but in the real world of the village she was likely subject to a lifetime of pity, social ridicule, and blame, much of it heaped upon her by other rural women who had themselves endured such pressures.

Faced with intense demands from the state, on the one hand, and their peers and elders, on the other, some took the desperate course of female infanticide to preserve the chance to have a son. As the 1980s progressed, however, two alternative strategies emerged. The first was infant abandonment, which increased substantially in the late 1980s and 1990s in response to a tightening of the birth control policies. Although some infants were placed with relatives or rural families without children, in keeping with long-standing custom in China during times of political upheaval and economic crisis, many were left to be discovered by strangers who turned them over to public security officials. From there, they were sent to local orphanages, where new procedures were slowly developed to create avenues for adoption. Fearful that domestic adoption by young couples would undermine the one-child policy, however, the adoption law passed in 1991 only allowed couples over the age of thirty-five and childless to adopt a child. This restriction, in turn, led to an upturn in international adoption, as couples and singles from the prosperous regions of North America, Europe, and Asia arranged for adoptions.[62]

The second strategy for guaranteeing a son was the use of ultrasound technology and sex-selective abortion. By the early 1990s, most state-run hospitals and clinics had acquired ultrasound equipment capable of fetal sex determination. And as private clinics proliferated in the 1990s, they too were equipped with ultrasound technology, providing easy access for a fee. Despite repeated condemnations of sex-selective abortion and attempts to outlaw the use of ultrasound technology for fetal sex identification, easy access to the technology, combined with the lure of lucrative bribes and consultation fees, made ultrasound use very popular. Contrary to official statements blaming rural backwardness for the problem, it quickly became clear that the sex ratio distortions were widespread. In 1981, the Chinese sex ratio at birth, 108.5 males for every 100 females, had already been slightly in excess of the norm. Over the next twenty years, the sex ratio in favor of males at birth rose dramatically, to approximately 111 in 1985, 116 in 1992, and 119 by 2000. A decade later, the 2010 census showed sex ratios at birth were still hovering around 119 males per 100 females.[63]

In the early 1990s, Chinese experts attributed most of the skew in the sex ratio to underreporting of female births, particularly illegal births, implying that the actual sex ratio at birth remained within, or close to, acceptable norms. Provoked by Amartya Sen's provocative 1990 essay on the "100 million women" missing in India and China, however, scholarly research and writing on the issue increased dramatically, as did research on the situation in China.[64] By the late 1990s, candid assessments by Chinese scholars concluded that sex-selective abortion was widespread and was the main cause of the distorted sex ratio. Moreover, accumulating data indicated that the phenomenon was not just a rural problem, nor was it concentrated in the least-educated segment of the population. Instead, the combined effect of the one-child birth limit, traditional son preference, and easy access to a technology that allowed couples to make sure they had a son was to tempt people from a wide variety of socioeconomic backgrounds to choose sons over daughters. Just as the state had justified its attempts to engineer national population growth, couples justified the use of sex-selective abortion to engineer the sex of their only child.

The resulting skew in the sex ratio has raised alarms over the "army of bachelors," or as they are referred to in Chinese, "bare branches" (*guang gun-er*), who are now, or will be in the future, unable to find wives as adults. Although this problem has already begun to appear among those born after 1980, it will get much worse before it gets better. Census data for 2000 revealed about 8.5 million missing girls, but by 2010 the number had risen to more than 20 million.[65] In 2012, there were an estimated 18 million more boys than girls under the age of 15, and by 2020, estimates suggest there may be anywhere from 30 to 40 million males in marriage-age cohorts who will be unable to find wives. Even if the sex ratio imbalance returns to balance by 2020, that number will grow, and the impact of these deficits will be felt late into the twenty-first century.[66]

This deficit of females has already begun to have an impact on marriage markets in China. Rural men of marriage age compete for a limited number of wives from the local area, and as the number of "leftover" men continues to grow, the higher the costs of marriage become. Men whose families are unable to raise enough money are unable to marry, and frequently resort to marriage brokers to help them find brides from other provinces.[67] Despite these and other efforts, however, the number of unmarried men in their late twenties is rising rapidly. While the shortage of women has allowed some brides to marry into a higher economic or social status, others have become more vulnerable to human trafficking, or to abuse in their new homes, where they are far removed from their family support system. Conversely, disadvantaged men are vulnerable to being cheated by marriage brokers, or by the bride and her family. There have been many reports of brides disappearing days after their marriage, once the bride's family had received the compensation they had demanded for their daughter.[68]

Conclusion

In his astute essay on the collapse of the Soviet regimes in eastern Europe in 1989, Daniel Chirot pointed to the great irony of attempting to build the socialism of the future on forms of industrial organization that were rapidly growing obsolete. Massive concentrations of industrial plants and workers was a late nineteenth- and early twentieth-century approach that helped Russia overcome its slow start on the road to industrialization, but it was an inadequate response to the mid-twentieth-century conditions that increasingly privileged innovation, speed, adaptability, and global reach. Post-World War II socialist economies, therefore, were built on structures that were rapidly becoming an anachronism.[69]

The same irony pervades the history of China's population policy, especially the one-child policy. By the time China embraced the one-child policy, nearly everything that inspired it was on the cusp of becoming obsolete. The intellectual hubris of the population control movement that peaked between the mid-1960s and 1980 would shortly thereafter begin to flounder under the combined challenges of the Green Revolution, revisionist demographic theories that challenged the orthodox view that population growth impeded development, and feminist and conservative challenges. Indeed, in retrospect one might argue that the 1984 UN conference on population held in Mexico City marked the beginning of the end for orthodox demographic theories that assumed population control was essential for successful economic development. At that conference, the Reagan administration sent a conservative delegation to challenge family planning on revisionist and moral grounds, while developing countries like Mexico, who were still deeply suspicious of neo-Malthusian arguments in 1974, embraced the orthodox view on the necessity of population control, and NGOs representing feminist views embraced a reproductive rights approach that would win the day in Cairo a decade later.[70]

In the midst of this ferment, China moved to embrace precisely the "numbers is everything" approach that was the core belief of the population controllers, wrapping it in a language of socialist modernization that was uniquely Chinese. Once in place, and with the full weight of the new reform leaders behind it, the legitimacy of the project and the validity of the method were difficult to challenge. The party had declared that the achievement of "modernization by the year 2000" depended on the successful implementation of the one-child birth limit. Even when it became clear that China would exceed all expectations for economic growth by the year 2000, even when it became clear that the social consequences of the policy were severe, even when "population control" had become a discredited approach to demographic challenges, the policy remained in place. It recedes now as an anachronism, but its social and political consequences will be felt for decades to come.

Beyond the consequences discussed above, there is the rage left behind in many Chinese over the state's unwillingness to adopt a two-child policy many years earlier, and its reliance on an enforcement system that privileges the rich, allowing them to effectively purchase a second child by paying a large "social compensation fee," while avoiding the pressure, harassment, or outright coercion experienced by ordinary Chinese whose pregnancy is deemed illegal. As Chinese writer Ma Jian noted in a 2013 op-ed in the *New York Times*, however, venting popular anger against wealthy and famous individuals like film director Zhang Yimou (accused of fathering seven children with four different women) "plays into the party's hands" by deflecting public outrage away from "the government's barbaric policy."[71] However one judges the one-child policy—as an economic and social necessity, a barbaric violation of human rights and dignity, or a dual-edged sword—it is important to keep in mind that although the one-child birth limit will disappear, the state has not conceded its authority to plan China's population growth. The birth limit is changing, but the logic that led to a one-child policy remains in place. Changing demographics, rising popular protest, and global influences have certainly moderated China's approach to implementation of birth limits, as well as the language used to describe the program, but the Chinese approach to population policy remains grounded in the principle of state sovereignty over reproduction. This enduring claim, and its policy consequences, will continue to set the Chinese case apart for many years to come.

Notes

1. See, for example, Feng Wang, Yong Cai, and Baochang Gu, "Population, Policy, and Politics: How Will History Judge China's One-Child Policy?" *Population and Development Review* 38, no. 1 (2013): 115–29; Jing-bao Nie, "China's One-Child Policy, A Policy without a Future," *Cambridge Quarterly of Healthcare Ethics* 23 (2014): 1–16; Michael Gross, "Where Next for China's Population Policy?" *Current Biology* 24, no. 3 (2014): R97–R100; Karen Eggleston et al., "Will Demographic Change Slow China's Rise?" *Journal of Asian Studies* 72, no. 3 (2013): 505–18; Zhigang Guo, "End to the One Child Policy?" *World of Chinese* 4, no. 1 (2014): 74–75.
2. For a broad view of the history of these ideas, see Matthew Connelly, *Fatal Misconception: The Struggle to Control World Population* (Cambridge, Mass.: Belknap Press of Harvard University Press, 2009); and also by Connelly, "To Inherit the Earth: Imagining World Population, from the Yellow Peril to the Population Bomb," *Journal of Global History* 1, no. 3 (2006): 299–319; Frank Dikötter, "Race Culture: Recent Perspectives on the History of Eugenics," *American Historical Review* 103 (1998): 467–78; Alison Bashford, "Nation, Empire, Globe: The Spaces of Population Debate in the Interwar Years," *Comparative Studies in Society and History* 49, no. 1 (2007): 170–201; Kenneth L. Garver and Bettylee Garver, "Eugenics: Past, Present, and the Future," *American Journal of Human Genetics* 49, no. 5 (1991): 1109.
3. On Maoist ideology and practice, see Maurice Meisner, *Mao's China and After: A History of the People's Republic* (New York: Simon and Schuster, 1999); Nick Knight, *Rethinking Mao: Explorations in Mao Zedong's Thought* (Lanham, Md.: Lexington Books, 2007). On the mass campaign, see Elizabeth

J. Perry, "Moving the Masses: Emotion Work in the Chinese Revolution," *Mobilization: An International Quarterly* 7, no. 2 (2002): 111–28. For a classic study of how mass campaigns worked in the early years of the People's Republic, see Ezra Vogel, *Canton under Communism: Programs and Politics in a Provincial Capital, 1949–1968* (Cambridge, Mass.: Harvard University Press, 1969).

4. Yang Jisheng, *Tombstone: The Great Chinese Famine, 1958–1962* (New York: Macmillan, 2012); Frank Dikötter, *Mao's Great Famine: The History of China's Most Devastating Catastrophe, 1958–1962* (New York: Bloomsbury, 2010); Dali L. Yang, *Calamity and Reform in China: State, Rural Society, and Institutional Change since the Great Leap Famine* (Stanford, Calif.: Stanford University Press, 1996); David Bachman, *Bureaucracy, Economy, and Leadership in China: The Institutional Origins of the Great Leap Forward* (New York: Cambridge University Press, 2006); Wei Li and Dennis Tao Yang, "The Great Leap Forward: Anatomy of a Central Planning Disaster," *Journal of Political Economy* 113, no. 4 (2005): 840–77; Ralph Thaxton, *Catastrophe and Contention in Rural China: Mao's Great Leap Forward Famine and the Origins of Righteous Resistance in Da Fo Village* (New York: Cambridge University Press, 2008); Jasper Becker, *Hungry Ghosts: China's Secret Famine* (London: John Murray, 1996).

5. For a comprehensive and detailed history of this period, see Roderick MacFarquhar, ed., *The Politics of China: The Eras of Mao and Deng* (New York: Cambridge University Press, 1997).

6. MacFarquhar, *The Politics of China*, chap. 4.

7. On the first family-planning campaign, see H. Yuan Tian, *China's Population Struggle: Demographic Decisions of the People's Republic of China, 1949–1969* (Columbus: Ohio State University Press, 1973); Leo A. Orleans, *Every Fifth Child: The Population of China* (London: Eyre Methuen, 1972); Pi-Chau Chen, *Population and Health Policy in the People's Republic of China* (Washington, D.C.: Smithsonian Institution Press, 1976).

8. Tyrene White, *China's Longest Campaign: Birth Planning in the People's Republic, 1949–2005* (Ithaca, N.Y.: Cornell University Press, 2006).

9. For a detailed account of these events, see Susan Greenhalgh, "Science, Modernity, and the Making of China's One-Child Policy," *Population and Development Review* 29 (June 2003): 163–96; and also by Greenhalgh, *Just One Child: Science and Policy in Deng's China* (Berkeley: University of California Press, 2008).

10. For an English-language translation of the "Open Letter," which was published in *People's Daily* on September 25, 1980, see Tyrene White, ed., "Family Planning in China," *Chinese Sociology and Anthropology* 24, no. 3 (Spring 1992).

11. For an example of local regulations that were to be implemented three months after their publication, see the Birth Planning regulations for Wuhan, Hubei Province, June 1979.

12. On the range of penalties outlined in regulations, see White, *China's Longest Campaign*, chaps. 3–4.

13. On the struggle to implement the one-child policy in the countryside and rural resistance, see White, *China's Longest Campaign*, chaps. 5–6; also by White, "Domination, Resistance, and Accommodation in China's One-Child Campaign," in *Chinese Society: Change, Conflict, and Resistance*, ed. Elizabeth Perry and Mark Selden, 3rd ed. (New York: Routledge, 2010), 171–96; Jeffrey Wasserstrom, "Resistance to the One-Child Family," *Modern China* 10 (July 1984): 345–74; Susan Greenhalgh, "Controlling Births and Bodies in Village China," *American Ethnologist* 21, no. 1 (1994): 3–30.
14. For a classic and powerfully moving documentary that explores gender issues in rural China, see the film by Carma Hinton, *Small Happiness* (1982). On the challenges faced by rural women as they struggled with this problem, see Chu Junhong, "Pre-natal Sex Determination and Sex Selective Abortion in Rural Central China," *Population and Development Review* 27, no. 2 (2001): 259–81.
15. On the 1983 sterilization campaign, see White, *China's Longest Campaign*, chap. 5.
16. For an English translation of Central Document #7 (1984), which established the "one-son or two-child" policy, see Tyrene White, ed., "Family Planning in China," special issue of *Chinese Sociology and Anthropology* 24, no. 3 (Spring 1992).
17. Tyrene White, "Birth Planning between Plan and Market: The Impact of Reform on China's One-Child Policy," in *China's Economic Dilemmas in the 1990s: The Problems of Reform, Modernization, and Interdependence. Study Papers Submitted to the Joint Economic Committee, Congress of the United States* (Washington, D.C.: U.S. Government Printing Office, 1991), 1:252–69.
18. On the failure to meet population targets for 1990 and preparations for the census, see White, *China's Longest Campaign*, chap. 8, "Campaign Revivalism and Its Limits."
19. For one example of how the "one-ballot veto" system worked, see Document #7, issued by the Hubei provincial government in 1994, entitled, "Guanyu shixing jihua shengyu 'yipiao foujue quan' de guiding" (Decision on implementing the 'one-ballot veto system' for birth planning) in Hubei sheng jihua shenghy weiyuanhui, *Jihua shengyu zhengce fagui ziliao xuanpian, 1983–1997* (Compilation of laws and regulations pertaining to birth-planning policy, 1983–1997) (Wuhan, 1997), 596–97.
20. On skepticism over the reported low fertility levels by the mid-1990s, see Chinese demographer Zeng Yi's influential article, "Wo guo 1991–92 nian shengyu lu shifou dada diyu daiti shuiping?" (Has our country's 1991–92 fertility rate dropped far below replacement level?), in *Renkou yanjiu* (Population research) 19, no. 3 (1995): 7–14.
21. Gu Baochang and Mu Guangzong, "A New Understanding of China's Population Problem," *Renkou yanjiu* 5 (1994): 2–10.
22. The text of Document 138, issued by the Policy and Legislation Department of the SFPC on July 1, 1995, may be found on the UNESCAP website, www.unescap.org/pop/database/law_china.

23. For one example of the argument in favor of a reproductive rights approach, prepared in anticipation of the Cairo conference, see International Women's Health Coalition, "Women's Voices, '94: Women's Declaration on Population Policies" (1993); on the conference itself, see C. Alison McIntosh and Jason L. Finkle, "The Cairo Conference on Population and Development: A New Paradigm?" *Population and Development Review* 21, no. 2 (June 1995): 223–60.
24. For the full text of China's Population and Family Planning Law, see *Population and Development Review* 28, no. 3 (September 2002): 579–85.
25. China Development Research Foundation, *China Development Report: Changes in Population Trends and Adjustment in Population Policies* (Beijing: China Development Press, 2012).
26. See, for example, Michel Foucault, *Security, Territory, Population: Lectures at the College de France, 1977–1978* (New York: Picador, 2009); and also his *The Birth of Biopolitics: Lectures at the College de France, 1977–1978* (New York: Picador, 2010).
27. See note 19.
28. The classic work on the mass campaign in China is Gordon Bennett, *Yundong: Mass Campaigns in Chinese Communist Leadership*, China Research Monograph, No. 12 (Berkeley: Institute of East Asian Studies, University of California, 1976). See also Perry, "Moving the Masses"; Vogel, *Canton under Communism*; White, *China's Longest Campaign*; and Sebastian Heilmann and Elizabeth Perry, *Mao's Invisible Hand: The Political Foundations of Adaptive Governance in China* (Cambridge, Mass.: Harvard University Press, 2011).
29. White, *China's Longest Campaign*, chap. 6.
30. White, *China's Longest Campaign*, chaps. 6 and 7.
31. Sanger discussed her experience in China, as well as Japan, in a speech delivered at Carnegie Hall on October 31, 1922, titled "Birth Control in China and Japan." The text can be found online at http://www.nyu.edu/projects/sanger/webedition/app/documents/show.php?sangerDoc=101865.xml (accessed July 8, 2014). These and other documents have been made available online as part of the Margaret Sanger Papers Project of the History Department of New York University. The project's online site can be found at http://www.nyu.edu/projects/sanger/.
32. For a brief look at developments in China after Sanger's visit, see the blog post by Cathy Moran Hajo, "What Happened Next: A Look at Birth Control Organizing in China Following Margaret Sanger's 1922 Visit," January 9, 2014, online at https://sangerpapers.wordpress.com/2014/01/09/what-happened-next-a-look-at-birth-control-organizing-in-china-following-margaret-sangers-1922-visit/.
33. Shi, *Zhongguo jihua shengyu huodong shi*, 52–53. See also Liu Shaoqi, "Tichang jieyu" (Promote Birth Control), in Zhongguo shehui kexueyuan renkou yanjiu zhongxin (Population Research Center of the Chinese Academy of Social Sciences), *Zhongguo renkou nianjian, 1985* (Population Yearbook of

China, 1985) (Beijing: Chinese Academy of Social Sciences Publishing House, 1985), 4–5.
34. Shi, *Zhongguo jihua shengyu huodong shi*, 50–51.
35. First, the woman's husband had to authorize the abortion in writing. Second, the head of the department or organ where the woman worked had to authorize the procedure. And third, the attending physician had to approve the decision. Failure to obtain all the necessary approvals would result in administrative punishment. Shi, *Zhongguo jihua shengyu huodong shi*, 111.
36. The regulations were entitled "Provisional Method for Limiting Birth Control Surgery and Abortion" (Xianzhi jieyu ji rengong liuchan zanxing banfa). Shi, *Zhongguo jihua shengyu huodong shi*, 113.
37. Deng Lichun and Ma Hong, eds., *Dangdai zhongguode weisheng shiye, xia* (Health Work in Contemporary China, vol. 2) (Beijing: Chinese Academy of Social Sciences Publishing House, 1986), 231.
38. Shi, *Zhongguo jihua shengyu huodong shi*, 115.
39. This position was set forth by Secretary of State Dean Acheson in the China White Paper, the official US State Department document on China that was issued in 1949. See US Department of State, *The China White Paper, August 1949* (reissued) (Stanford, Calif.: Stanford University Press, 1967).
40. Mao Tse-tung, "The Bankruptcy of the Idealist Conception of History," in *Selected Works of Mao Tsetung*, vol. 4 (Beijing: Foreign Languages Press, 1961).
41. Mao, "Bankruptcy," 145–46.
42. Mao, "Bankruptcy," 146.
43. For a brief overview of Japan's family-planning program between 1945 and 1965, see Minoru Muramatsu, "Japan," in *Family Planning and Population Programs: A Review of World Developments*, ed. Bernard Berelson, Richmond K. Anderson, Oscar Harkavy, John Maier, W. Parker Mauldin, and Sheldon J. Segal (Proceedings of the 1966 International Conference on Family Planning Programs) (Chicago: University of Chicago Press, 1967), 7–20; *Zhou Enlai Xuanji, II* (Beijing: People's Press, 1980), vol. 2, 445; Shi, *Zhongguo jihua shengyu huodong shi*, 151–52.
44. Jason L. Finkle and Barbara B. Crane, "The Politics of Bucharest: Population, Development, and the New International Economic Order," *Population and Development Review* 1 (1975): 87–114.
45. Finkle and Crane, "The Politics of Bucharest."
46. Donella H. Meadows, Edward I. Goldsmith, and Paul Meadow, *The Limits to Growth: A Report for the Club of Rome's Project on the Predicament of Mankind* (London: Earth Island, 1972); Mihajlo Mesarović and Eduard Pestel, *Mankind at the Turning Point: The Second Report to the Club of Rome* (New York: Dutton, 1974).
47. Susan Greenhalgh, "Missile Science, Population Science: The Origins of China's One-Child Policy," *China Quarterly* 182 (2005): 253–76.
48. C. Alison McIntosh and Jason L. Finkle, "The Cairo Conference on Population and Development: A New Paradigm?" *Population and Development Review* 21

(1995): 223–60; Amy J. Higer, "International Women's Activism and the 1994 Cairo Population Conference," in *Gender Politics in Global Governance*, ed. Mary K. Meyer and Elisabeth Prügl (Boulder, CO: Roman and Littlefield, 1999), 122–41.

49. On the UN Millennium Development Goals, see the UN website, http://www.un.org/millenniumgoals.
50. Elizabeth L. Larson, "United Nations Fourth World Conference on Women: Action for Equality, Development, and Peace (Beijing, China: September 1995)," *Emory International Law Review* 10 (1996): 695–739; Jude Howell, "Women's Organizations and Civil Society in China Making a Difference," *International Feminist Journal of Politics* 5, no. 2 (2003): 191–215; Sally McIntosh and Jason L. Finkle, "Who Needs [Sex] When You Can Have [Gender]? Conflicting Discourses on Gender at Beijing," *Feminist Review* 56 (1997): 3–25.
51. For a sample of the Chinese netizen reaction to this story, see "Netizen Rage over China's Unborn (Updated)," posted by Anne Henochowicz, June 14, 2012, on the blog *China Digital Times*. Online at http://chinadigitaltimes.net/2012/06/netizen-rage-over-chinas-unborn/.
52. See Wang Feng, "Bringing an End to a Senseless Policy," op-ed, *New York Times*, November 19, 2013.
53. For a full analysis of the claim, see Wang, Cai, and Gu, "Population, Policy, and Politics."
54. For an early effort to demonstrate that alternatives could work, see John Bongaarts and Susan Greenhalgh, "An Alternative to the One-Child Policy in China," *Population and Development Review* 11 (1985): 585–617.
55. Tyrene White, Interview Files, 1983.
56. For analysis of singleton families, see Barbara H. Settles, Xuewen Sheng, Yuan Zang, and Jia Zhao, "The One-Child Policy and Its Impact on Chinese Families," in *International Handbook of Chinese Families*, ed. Chan Kwok-bun (New York: Springer, 2013), 627–46.
57. On parental investments in their child's education, see Guangyu Tan, "The One-Child Policy and Privatization of Education in China," *International Education* 42, no. 1 (2012): 43–53.
58. Settles et al., "One-Child Policy."
59. Mark W. Frazier, "No Country for Old Age," *New York Times*, February 18, 2013, http://www.nytimes.com/2013/02/19/opinion/no-country-for-old-age.html; "China's Population: The Most Surprising Demographic Crisis," *The Economist*, May 5, 2011; "Young Chinese Couples Face Pressure from '4-2-1' Family Structure," *People's Daily*, August 25, 2010, http://english.people.com.cn/90001/90782/7117246.html; "China's Predicament: 'Getting Old before Getting Rich,'" *The Economist*, June 25, 2009.
60. The burdens faced by unregistered children and their families are discussed in Celia Hatton, "Children Denied an Identity under China's One-Child

Policy," BBC News, January 17, 2014, online at http://www.bbc.com/news/world-asia-china-25772401.

61. For a visual view of sex ratios across provinces, see figure 1.1 of UNICEF's Atlas on Children of China, online at http://www.unicef.cn/en/index.php?m=content&c=index&a=show&catid=196&id=778.
62. On infant abandonment and China's 1991 adoption law, see Kay Johnson, "Politics of International and Domestic Adoption in China," *Law and Society Review* 36, no. 2 (2002): 379–96. For the text of the revised adoption law enacted in 1998, see http://english.gov.cn/2005-08/31/content_26770.htm. On the broader issue of infant abandonment in China, see Kay Johnson, *Wanting a Daughter, Needing a Son: Abandonment, Adoption, and Orphanage Care in China* (St. Paul, Minn.: Yeong and Yeong, 2004). For data on international adoptions from China into the United States, see the Intercountry Adoption data provided by the US Department of State, online at http://adoption.state.gov/about_us/statistics.php.
63. "China's Total Population and Structural Changes in 2011," National Bureau of Statistics of China, January 20, 2012; Wei Xingzhu, Li Hu, and Theresa Hesketh, "China's Excess Males, Sex Selective Abortion, and One Child Policy: Analysis of Data from 2005 National Intercensus Survey," *BMJ (British Medical Journal)* 2009, 338: b1211, April 9, 2009, http://www.bmj.com/content/338/bmj.b1211. For a superb analysis based on the results of the 2010 census, see Yong Cai, "China's New Demographic Reality: Learning from the 2010 Census," *Population and Development Review*, September 2013.
64. Amartya Sen, "More Than 100 Million Women Are Missing," *New York Review of Books*, December 20, 1990, http://www.nybooks.com/articles/34081.
65. Cai, "China's New Demographic Reality."
66. Cai, "China's New Demographic Reality."
67. Lige Liu, Xiaoyi Jin, Melissa J. Brown, and Marcus W. Feldman, "Male Marriage Squeeze and Inter-provincial Marriage in Central China: Evidence from Anhui," *Journal of Contemporary China* 23, no. 86 (2014): 351–71.
68. Liu et al., "Male Marriage Squeeze."
69. Daniel Chirot, "What Happened in Eastern Europe in 1989?" in *The Crisis of Leninism and the Decline of the Left: The Revolutions of 1989*, ed. Daniel Chirot (Seattle: University of Washington Press, 1991).
70. On the politics of the Mexico City conference, see Jason L. Finkle and Barbara B. Crane, "Ideology and Politics at Mexico City: The United States at the 1984 International Conference on Population," *Population and Development Review* 11 (1985): 1–28.
71. Ma Jian, "China's Brutal One-Child Policy," *New York Times*, May 21, 2013.

Index